Introduction to

THE
HEBREW
PROPHETS

JAMES D. NOGALSKI

Introduction to

THE HEBREW PROPHETS

Abingdon Press

Nashville

INTRODUCTION TO THE HEBREW PROPHETS

This book is printed on acid-free paper.

Library of Congress Cataloging-in-Publication Data has been requested.

ISBN: 978-1-4267-4228-6

18 19 20 21 22 23 24 25 26 27—10 9 8 7 6 5 4 3 2 1
MANUFACTURED IN THE UNITED STATES OF AMERICA

Contents

Contents

Contents

Contents

Contents

Contents

List of Abbreviations

AB	Anchor Bible
ATD	Das Alte Testament Deutsch
BBET	Beiträge zur biblischen Exegese und Theologie
BCE	Before Common Era
BEATAJ	Beiträge zur Erforschung des Alten Testaments und des antiken Judentum
BETL	Biblicotheca Ephemeridum Theologicarum Lovaniensium
BN	Biblische Notizen
BZAW	Beihefte zur Zeitschrift für die alttestamentliche Wissenschaft
CE	Common Era
CEB	Common English Bible
ch/chs	Chapter/chapters
cp	common plural
cs	common singular
FAT	Forschungen zum Alten Testament
FB	Forschung zur Bibel
FRLANT	Forschungen zur Religion und Literatur des Alten und Neuen Testaments
fs	feminine singular
Heb.	Hebrew
HeBAI	Hebrew Bible and Ancient Israel
HSM	Harvard Semitic Monographs
HThKAT	Herders Theologischer Kommentar zum Alten Testament

HUCA	Hebrew Union College Annual
IECOT	International Exegetical Commentary on the Old Testament
JBL	Journal of Biblical Literature
JSOT	Journal for the Study of the Old Testament
JSOTSup	Journal for the Study of the Old Testament Supplement Series
KAT	Kommentar zum Alten Testament
KJV	King James Version
LHBOTS	The Library of Hebrew Bible/OTS
LXX	Septuagint
mp	masculine plural
ms	masculine singular
MT	Masoretic Text
NAS	New American Standard Bible
NET	New English Translation
NICOT	New International Commentary on the Old Testament
NIV	New International Version
NRSV	New Revised Standard Version
OAN	Oracles against the nations
OT	Old Testament
OTL	Old Testament Library
OTS	Old Testament Studies
PRS	Perspectives in Religious Studies
SBLDS	SBL Dissertation Series
SBLMS	SBL Monograph Series
SHBC	Smyth and Helwys Bible Commentary
v./vv.	Verse/verses
VT	Vetus Testamentum
VTSup	Supplements to Vetus Testamentum
WMANT	Wissenschaftliche Monographien zum Alten und Neuen Testament
ZAW	Zeitschrift für die alttestamentliche Wissenschaft

Acknowledgments

No book is ever the work of a single person, and this book is no exception. I have benefitted from conversations with numerous colleagues through the years concerning the prophetic scrolls. I have learned much from many. I am grateful for all of the opportunities I have had through the years to speak about prophetic literature with others at conferences and meetings. I am grateful, as well, to have great colleagues at Baylor University who have asked about this book on numerous occasions and encouraged me in its completion. Thanks also to Baylor University for the gift of a research leave to complete this volume. The time away from administrative duties allowed me the time to finish it. To name all of those to whom I am indebted would take yet another volume, but I would be remiss if I did not mention three people by name. First, I want to thank David Teel and his editorial team at Abingdon. David has encouraged me in numerous ways as we talked about how to put thoughts on paper that others would be willing to read. We spoke frequently, sometimes at length and sometimes just to touch base. His encouragement helped keep me accountable and keep me on target.

Second, I want to express my appreciation to Will Briggs, my graduate assistant. He provided careful reads of the chapters, tracked bibliographic details, and created the glossary of key terms that is at the back of this volume. His willingness to help is only exceeded by the abilities he brought to these tasks.

Finally, I owe immeasurable gratitude to my wife and partner, Melanie. She has patiently listened to ideas that were half-baked and prodded me with questions until things became clear. Her encouragement never wavered. Her engagement in the questions of this book has been ongoing for most of our adult lives, and I am fortunate indeed to have her as a collaborator in life. She enriches my life and my work beyond measure.

Preface

The Prophets and the Canon

The order of the books in the English Bible does not reflect the earliest orders of those books. The Hebrew canon is called the Tanach, which represents a Hebrew anagram for its three parts: T for Torah, N for Nebi'im, and K for Ketubim. *Torah* has the basic meaning of "instruction," but is often translated as Law, somewhat misleadingly, since only portions of the Torah contain legal material. *Nebi'im* means Prophets, and *Ketubim* means Writings. The last label includes a wide array of poetic, wisdom, and narrative materials that came to be recognized as canonical but were not part of the Torah or the Prophets. Students of the English Bible will notice that there is no section called "Historical Books," as Joshua–Kings are frequently called. Instead, the Hebrew canon originally consisted of eight scrolls that are collectively called the Nebi'im. Four of these scrolls (Joshua, Judges, Samuel, and Kings) tell the story of Israel and Judah from the time of Israelite entry into the land until shortly after Jerusalem's destruction. Rather than being called Historical Books, these four scrolls constitute the four Former Prophets, while four additional scrolls constitute the Latter Prophets: Isaiah, Jeremiah, Ezekiel, and the Twelve. Daniel was not included among the Nebi'im, and the Twelve represents twelve prophetic collections that were written on a single scroll and counted as one book, not twelve books. The Nebi'im thus consisted of four Former Prophets and four Latter Prophets.

The current volume will focus on the four scrolls known as the Latter Prophets. These collections have been treated differently through time. Throughout much of the history of biblical interpretation, these books were considered the writings of great prophetic minds from the time of the monarchy into the Persian period. Critical scholarship began to question this idea from the medieval period onward, and by the beginning of the twentieth century, most biblical scholars drew a sharp distinction between the speeches delivered by the prophets and the books in which they appeared. The latter, it was recognized, contained considerable material from the hands of editors who collected, shaped, and arranged the speeches and narratives about the prophets within the books. Scholars realized that the material within each scroll represented the work of many hands.

Throughout this time, the focus remained on the individual speeches or on the impossible task of trying to uncover the original words of these prophets. In the last quarter of the twentieth century, however, scholars began to turn their attention to the literary qualities of the books. Why were they arranged as they are? Given that material in one scroll can come from hundreds of years after the lifetime of the prophet for whom the book was named, why was new material added? Also, scholars began to see patterns and cross-references within these scrolls that were not always evident at first glance and that suggested that meaning might be gained by reading these collections as composite works with distinct literary and theological agendas. The task of learning how to read these collections is not, however, easy to accomplish without guidance, so this volume will attempt to offer some suggestions on how scholars have begun sorting out the literary and theological goals of the collections. The scrolls, however, represent the words of generations of composers including ancient prophets, close associates who transmitted the memories of those prophets, and later prophetic scribes who faithfully copied them and kept their message updated. In a real sense, then, these prophetic scrolls represent the works of communities, not individuals, who were committed to preserving these traditions.

This Introduction and Groups Behind the Prophetic Scrolls

We have no narrative description of how the four prophetic scrolls came to be. We are left to infer some broad outlines. The four scrolls represent a collection, or perhaps better, a small library that ultimately functions as a kind of curriculum of instruction regarding what went wrong for Israel, Judah, and Jerusalem. The Latter Prophets supplement the largely narrative accounts of the Former Prophets (Joshua, Judges, Samuel, and Kings). Seen from a sociological and historical level, each of the four scrolls has roots in and served the interests of various groups who preserved and transmitted the tradition, but the diverse interests of these groups sometimes peek through. The scrolls both testify to areas of theological conflict and show signs they have been blended together. They allow us to speculate about theological developments of temple scribes in the Persian period who shaped the scrolls into their final forms.

The order in which these collections appear (Isaiah, Jeremiah, Ezekiel, and the Twelve) has a long history, and it is not the only order that existed. Nevertheless, the order of the four collections emphasizes their role as a group that seeks to explain and correct the longstanding problems that led to Jerusalem's destruction. Isaiah and the Twelve begin in the eighth century BCE and continue into the Persian period (539–332 BCE). Jeremiah and Ezekiel deal with events surrounding Jerusalem's destruction.

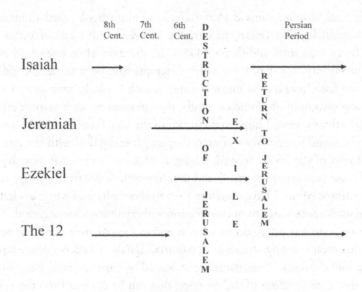

The Chronological Scope of the Prophetic Corpus

The discussion of the scrolls in the following work will thus follow this traditional order. One chapter will be devoted to each of the Major Prophets: Isaiah, Jeremiah, and Ezekiel. For pragmatic reasons, the Book of the Twelve will be presented in three chapters. This decision reflects my sense of the general outlines of how the books came to be gathered together into a single corpus. One chapter will deal with the core collections of Hosea, Amos, Micah, and Zephaniah, which were edited together beginning in the sixth century BCE. A second chapter deals with Haggai, Zechariah, and Malachi because a large contingent of Old Testament scholars think that Haggai and Zechariah 1–8 were published together in the aftermath of the reconstruction of the temple. Simultaneously, debate exists about when Zechariah 9–14 and Malachi were added, but most of the relevant information for this debate concerns their relationship to Haggai and Zechariah 1–8. Finally, the last chapter of this book deals with five prophetic compositions whose locations in the larger scroll of the Twelve relate to thematic considerations more than chronology. These five (Nahum, Habakkuk, Obadiah, Joel, and Jonah) also show an increased sophistication in the art of scribal prophecy, where the composition of these five books has likely been influenced by their location in the Book of the Twelve (though some argue that the completed compositions were placed in their locations because the thematic connections were already present).

This book also functions as a particular kind of textbook called an introduction. Traditionally, Old Testament introductions deal with issues of authorship, dating, unity, structure, and themes. Gone are the days when one could expect to find unanimity on any of these issues. Attempts have been made, therefore, to explain the fault lines on the major debates in each book. In most cases I weigh in with my own opinion. Fundamentally, my opinions on such matters attempt to do three things. First, I hope to do justice to the final form of the text. For this reason, the lengthiest portions of each chapter generally deal with the structure and contents of the book. Second, I long ago became convinced that the final form of these four prophetic scrolls did not, however, derive from a single author or even a single editor. I have therefore tried to show why and where evidence of editorial work (both in terms of compilation and expansion) has occurred. Third, I have sought to pay attention to what it means to read these scrolls as scrolls. Often, this means paying attention to editorial signals as well as various types of allusions and citations. These issues are informed by current discussions, and my hope is that consideration of the meaning that can be derived from the reading of the scrolls, not merely short sayings or isolated verses, helps shed light on these collections. In particular, attention has been given (especially in Isaiah and the Twelve) to the ways in which assumptions about and interpretations of historical events have been woven into these prophetic collections.

Isaiah blends a deep knowledge of the Zion tradition with the text of an exilic prophet (40–55) interested in inspiring a return from Babylon. The theology of Isaiah 40–55 thus shares some common themes with Ezekiel (particularly the rejection of idolatry as a threat to the community's identity). At the same time, this prophetic tradition differs dramatically from Ezekiel. Theological claims in Isaiah 56–66 suggest that difficult debates took place once both groups returned to the land. Nowhere is this difference more pronounced than in Isaiah 56, which uses language from Ezekiel and Deuteronomy to argue against Ezekiel's antagonism toward foreigners.

Jeremiah represents the Deuteronomistic traditions of those who remained in the land, though the Deuteronomistic perspective of Jeremiah has its own unique flavor. Its narrative elements recount events from inside the land, leading the reader up to and beyond Jerusalem's destruction. In the book, Jeremiah suffers because his prophetic role puts him in danger from kings whose policies he must confront. His life is even threatened by his own family.

The language of Ezekiel is imbued with priestly formulations and ideas. Studies detail how both priestly traditions in the Holiness Code and the Priestly Torah leave their marks in the book. In many respects, the theological perspective of the book of Ezekiel aligns closely with the theological agenda of Ezra and Nehemiah. In contrast to the other three scrolls, Ezekiel never mentions Zion by name. The book rejects the indigenous leadership of Jerusalem and privileges the interests of one particular group of exiles. In contrast to the portrait of Jeremiah, the elders of Judah seek out Ezekiel for consultation on more than one occasion, and YHWH warns the prophet about his countrymen trying to flatter him. Hence, these three scrolls have dominant paradigms from which they recount God's prophetic message: the Zion tradition, Deuternomistic tradition, and priestly tradition. Yet each scroll presents the character of the prophet differently and filters the paradigmatic traditions through a wide range of social locations and experience.

The Book of the Twelve exhibits tradition elements from each of the three other scrolls. The Zion tradition plays a major role in Joel, Obadiah, Micah, and Zephaniah. Portions of Hosea, Amos, Micah, and Zephaniah share certain elements of the Deuteronomistic tradition, and Obadiah and Zechariah quote Jeremiah in highly significant ways. Haggai, Zechariah, and Malachi have often been noted for their hierocratic (i.e., priestly) orientation. And yet the Twelve stands at odds with much of what one finds in Ezekiel, while it shares much with Isaiah in terms of its scope and its theological emphases. The Book of the Four Prophets that began the collection was structured geographically, thematically, and chronologically to explain the fall of Jerusalem. The collection blames Jerusalem for not learning the lesson of Samaria's destruction. In this sense, these four books take up the rejection of the Northern Kingdom reflected in 2 Kings 17–23. Nahum and Habakkuk deal with the rise and fall of Assyria and Babylon, drawing from concepts in Exodus and Isaiah. Haggai and Zechariah 1–8 focus upon the reconstruction of the temple and reconstitution of its leadership, but from a vantage point of those in the land, which contrasts with the visions of Ezekiel in a number of ways. Key texts in Zechariah (1:12; 7:5) draw upon the tradition of a seventy-year punishment as it appears in Jeremiah.

Later texts in the Twelve continue their interest in how the temple functions properly. Joel provides certain parallels to Ezekiel in its concern for the role of the priests and other cult personnel, but at the same time Joel orients its message to those in the land. Its hopes include the removal of armies, a renewal of the land's fertility, and YHWH's judgment of the nations who have perpetuated violence on Judah. Malachi deals with priestly conflict that threatens the covenant of Levi, but its openness to YHWH worshipers among the nations differs markedly from the exclusive theology of Ezekiel. Recurring fertility imagery in Hosea, Joel, Amos, Haggai, Zechariah, and Malachi emphasizes the wine, vine, grain, and oil. These elements represent the offerings that would have been brought to the temple from which Levites and priests benefitted. The recurring message of the coming days of YHWH adds an eschatological emphasis to the Twelve that looks similar to the expectations in the later stages of Isaiah.

Zechariah 9–14, in several respects, challenges the message of Ezekiel. Most notably, Zechariah 11:4-17 completely reverses the parable of the sticks in Ezekiel 37:15-28. Whereas Ezekiel hopes to reunify Judah and Israel under a Davidic king, Zechariah 11 and 13 abandon such hopes entirely.

Jeremiah and Ezekiel have a more limited chronological focus upon the decades following Josiah's death leading to the destruction of Jerusalem and its aftermath. By contrast, Isaiah and the Twelve largely skip this time period by jumping from Hezekiah's reign in the eighth century (Isaiah) or Josiah's reign in the seventh century (the Twelve) to the Persian period in order to recount YHWH's prophetic message to Judah.

Taken together, the four prophetic scrolls present something like a symphony.[1] Judgment mixes with deliverance. Despair blends with hope. These scrolls testify to YHWH's engagement with Judah and Israel during the monarchy. Whether one looks at the long view of history in Isaiah and the Twelve or the more narrow, chronological focus of Jeremiah and Ezekiel, the Latter Prophets articulate YHWH's power, the longevity of the sin of the people and their leaders, and a powerful sense of hope for YHWH's presence in the future.

Discussion Questions

1. Why do we talk about four prophetic scrolls in the Hebrew Bible, and what is the relationship of the four prophetic scrolls to the Nebi'im?

2. Describe the curricular function of the four prophetic scrolls.

Chapter 1

Isaiah

Isaiah of Jerusalem:
The Prophet and the Book

Most Isaiah scholars acknowledge that we know very little about the person for whom the book is named. Presumably, the name of his father, Amoz, reflects a genuine tradition about the prophet. Most scholars would also assume that Isaiah either comes from Jerusalem or lived there most of his adult life. He appears to have had ready access to King Hezekiah and refers to events surrounding the siege of the Assyrian king Sennacherib in 701 BCE. At least portions of the material in chapters 7–9 bear witness to the inner workings of the monarchy at the time of the Syro-Ephraimite War (734–732 BCE). Isaiah 6 is often interpreted as the prophet's call experience, and the vision is set in 742 BCE, "the year that King Uzziah died." Some scholars give historical credence to some of the descriptions of the actions of the prophet, such as Isaiah walking around naked for three years as a symbolic act condemning Egypt and Ethiopia (20:1-6). Quite a number of scholars reckon with the earliest material comprising the so-called Isaiah memoir (portions of chapters 6–8) along with portions of chapters 28–31.[1]

For all of this information that points to an eighth-century prophet named Isaiah, little more can be said, except that the entire tenor of the book of Isaiah, throughout its many historical settings, exhibits a strong interest in the fate of Judah and Jerusalem. This consistent emphasis does not mean, however, that all the material comes from the prophet himself. Critical scholars universally recognize that chapters 40–66 stem from no earlier than 539 BCE. Recent models concerning the composition of the book conclude that significant portions of

1

chapters 1–39 refer to events of the eighth century, but do so with knowledge of the destruction of Jerusalem or the postexilic community. Where the voice of the prophet appears, it generally functions as part of a literary context that has been shaped to a considerable degree by tradents—persons passing down the tradition—living well after the time of the prophet. Consequently, while this introduction will have much to say regarding the role of the prophet in the book, it will not attempt to offer insights into the historical Isaiah.[2]

Historical Backdrops

A Developing Corpus Covering the Eighth Century BCE to the Persian Period

Isaiah and the Book of the Twelve share a common chronological framework that runs from the middle of the eighth century BCE into the Persian period (539–332 BCE). Both prophetic collections begin with superscriptions (Hos 1:1; Isa 1:1) naming four Judean kings: Uzziah (786–746), Jotham (756–741, serving as co-regent with Uzziah for ten years), Ahaz (742–725), and Hezekiah (725–696). The Book of the Twelve links Hosea's chronological notes to superscriptions in Amos, Micah, and Zephaniah. In Isaiah, scholars have long recognized that major sections stem from anonymous prophets reflecting contexts from the Babylonian exile (chapters 40–55) and the Second Temple period (chapters 56–66). Consequently, the Book of the Twelve and the book of Isaiah serve a similar function: to document YHWH's prophetic word to the people of Judah and Israel from the Assyrian to the Persian period when Judah increasingly lost territory and political control to regional superpowers (before exiled groups returned to rebuild the temple, the city walls, and the political and cultic structure in the Persian period). While the Book of the Twelve covers this time span with the names of twelve different prophetic voices, the book of Isaiah mentions only the eighth-century prophet by name.

Assyrian expansion and international intrigue form the backdrop for much of the early material in Isaiah. A series of Assyrian kings made a concerted effort to create an empire that reached from Assyria (modern-day Iraq) to the Mediterranean and from there into Egypt. The Assyrian Empire reached its zenith in 663 BCE, when it captured the Egyptian capital Thebes. They also controlled Syria, Phoenicia, Philistia, Israel, Judah, Ammon, Moab, and Edom. In the book of Isaiah, chapters 7–9 reflect upon events surrounding the Syro-Ephraimite War (734–732 BCE), and chapters 36–39 focus upon the Judean account of the siege of Sennacherib (701 BCE). These events had a major impact upon Judah and Israel. Israel lost its status as an independent state following 732, and a series of revolts led the Assyrians to remove Israel's king from power in 722. Judah's relationship to Assyria was more complicated, since for much of his reign Hezekiah allied himself with Assyria and benefited territorially from that alliance. In the end, however, Hezekiah rebelled, and Sennacherib laid siege to Jerusalem. Hezekiah apparently arranged to pay the Assyrians, and thereafter Judah's king controlled very little territory.

After chapter 39, however, the historical setting of the book jumps to the Persian period. Chapter 40 begins with an address to a group about to embark upon a return to Judah from Babylon (where it had been exiled after Jerusalem's destruction in 587 BCE). Chapters 44 and 45 specifically mention Cyrus (king of Persia from 539–529 BCE) as the monarch allowing the group to return (see 44:28; 45:1). Cyrus defeated Babylon in 539 BCE, more than 160 years after the siege of Sennacherib. The material in chapters 40–66 shows awareness of these events, both before (most of 40–48) and after (most of 49–55) the group returns to Jerusalem. It also includes material from a time after the temple has been rebuilt (chapters 56–66). This material presumes changes that take Judah into the Persian period if not the Hellenistic period. These changing chronological backdrops have to be taken into account when reading the final form of Isaiah.

Updating the Corpus in the Reign of Josiah?

A significant group of scholars at the end of the twentieth century argued persuasively that the development of Isaiah 1–33 resulted from a major shaping of the tradition in the time of Josiah (639–608 BCE).[3] Despite widespread agreement that the Isaiah collection was updated during this time, debate continues concerning precisely which parts of the texts this shaping affected.[4]

Updating the Corpus through the Persian Period

Isaiah 40–66 reflects settings from the early, middle, and late Persian period (or, for some passages, the Hellenistic period). First, the core of Isaiah 40–55 represents an early Persian-period prophetic collection. Portions of 40–48 constitute the earliest materials, since rhetorically they focus upon convincing the addressees to return to Jerusalem from Babylon. Chapters 49–55 likely come from a slightly later setting because they reflect upon the journey from the perspective of Jerusalem. Most of these chapters still have the optimistic outlook of 40–48 and do not presuppose the existence of the temple.

3

By contrast, chapters 56–66 generally presuppose a functioning temple in Jerusalem (i.e., after 515 BCE) and testify to an increasing hostility directed toward the tradents of the book by other groups associated with the temple. Three text blocks suggest that this conflict grew over time. The earliest core (chapters 60–62) maintains the generally optimistic outlook of 40–55, but the descriptions of hope are decidedly less utopian and reflect a sense of delay in the grand promises of 40–55. The language of these chapters, however, remains deeply imbued with the imagery of 40–55 and anticipates a bright future for Zion.

In a second stage, consisting primarily of chapters 56–59, the delay in fulfilling the promises for Zion is largely based upon the need for changes in behavior. Language of repentance and social justice permeate these chapters as requirements before salvation can be implemented. One finds affirmations of YHWH's power to save if and when changes are made: "Look! The Lord does not lack the power to save, nor are his ears too dull to hear, but your misdeeds have separated you from your God. Your sins have hidden his face from you so that you aren't heard" (Isa 59:1-2 CEB).

The final stage, chapters 63–66 and 56:1-8, demonstrates a further deterioration of relationships with other groups in the temple, specifically over the question of the inclusion of foreigners supported in these chapters as well as the condemnation of certain cultic practices. Relatedly, by the end of the book, YHWH's impending judgment against the wicked presumes a distinction within Judah and Jerusalem between those who will survive YHWH's judgment and those who will not. Likewise, the wicked among the nations will be punished, but some among the nations who recognize YHWH will be saved.

Important Dates for Isaiah

Death of Uzziah (742 BCE)

Isaiah 7–9: Syro-Ephraimite War (734–732 BCE)

Death of Ahaz/Tiglathpilesar III (727 BCE)

Isaiah 13–23 (OAN early core, 727–701 BCE)

Fall of Samaria (722 BCE)

Ashdod Rebellion (713–711 BCE)

Isaiah 36–39: Siege of Sennacherib (701 BCE)

Josiah's Reforms (622 BCE)

Josiah's Death (609 BCE)

Nineveh/Assyria's destruction (612 BCE)

Exile of 597 BCE

Destruction of Jerusalem (587 BCE)

Isaiah 13–23 (OAN anti-Babylon update, after 539–482 BCE)

Cyrus takes Babylon and the Persian Period (539 BCE)

Persian Period (539–333 BCE)

Isaiah 40–55 (539–521 BCE)

Completion of temple (515 BCE)

Isaiah 60–62 (500–450 BCE)

Ezra comes to Jerusalem (458 BCE)

Wall rebuilt by Nehemiah (445 BCE)

Isaiah 56–59 (450–400 BCE)

Isaiah 63–66 and 24–27 (400–300 BCE)

Alexander the Great and the Battle of Issus (333 BCE)

Death of Alexander (323 BCE)

One further characteristic of the Isaiah corpus bears mentioning. Later materials increasingly draw upon the phrasing, concepts, and themes within the developing book. Nearly all the compositional models of Isaiah incorporate this tendency. Hugh Williamson argues that this process begins already with the author of chapters 40–55.[5] Odil Hannes Steck argues that Isaiah 34–35 serves as a bridge text connecting the early collection of Isaiah with 40–66. Steck makes the case in part by paying attention to the links between the judgment against Edom anticipated in chapter 34 and the victory hymn of 63:1-6, which assumes that this judgment has just taken place.[6] Similarly, scholars now recognize thematic and lexical *inclusios* (literary bracketing devices framing and focusing the content for readers) linking chapters 65–66 with chapters 1–2 and 11. The beginning of the scroll has also been modified to anticipate the themes of the book as a whole. The creation of such links suggests that the scribes working on Isaiah recognized the developing corpus as a cohesive document in its own right. These links between older and newer material represent more than just artistic decoration. They reflect a conviction that the older material had relevance in new settings. The updates to the collection thus reflect ongoing theological engagements with their tradition by these prophetic tradents.

The Structure and Contents in Isaiah

Isaiah 1–12: Introductions to the Book and to Early Traditions

Isaiah 1: The Book's Thematic Introduction

Scholars now recognize that Isaiah 1 has either been compiled or composed as an introduction to the entire book (chapters 1–66). At least portions of this chapter contain passages that are best understood as a framing *inclusio* with chapter 66. As such, both the themes and the perspective of Isaiah 1 orient themselves to the postexilic community, at least in their final form, not to an audience in the lifetime of the prophet Isaiah who lived in the eighth century BCE.

Isaiah 1 and 2:2-4 participate in a deliberate *inclusio* with the book's latest passages. These *inclusios* frame Isaiah's message to the remnant that survives Jerusalem's destruction. Recent studies call attention to four framing motifs in these chapters:

- the role of heaven and earth as witnesses

- reforming the sinful cult

- restoring the remnant of Zion

- foreign nations worshiping YHWH in Zion[7]

These links condemn improper sacrifices (1:11; 66:3) in the temple courts (1:12; 56:5) or in gardens (1:29; 65:3; 66:17). They anticipate the punishment of the rebellious (1:20; 66:24), the rejection and restoration of the sabbath (1:13; 56:2, 4; 66:23), and the inclusion of foreigners as temple functionaries (2:3; 66:22-23). The image of the nations worshiping YHWH in Jerusalem that appears in 2:2-4 also functions as part of the thematic *inclusio* that reappears at the end of the book (66:18-23). In short, virtually every motif appearing in the accusatory rhetoric of Isaiah 1 returns at the end of the book as part of promises for the remnant who will survive YHWH's coming judgment.

The idea that the people do not understand (1:2-3, 5-6) also represents a *leitmotif* that runs through the corpus in various ways.[8] The sinful nation is condemned for the wrongdoings of the community against YHWH, who has consequently punished it severely (1:4-6). This call to attention (1:2-3) and brief woe oracle (1:4-6) function as an accusatory summary about three problems: rebellion (1:2, 5), sin (1:4), and guilt (1:4). The oracle accuses the entire people and its descendants of abandoning YHWH, making them responsible for the coming punishment.

Isaiah 2–4: Removing Idols and Injustice

Isaiah 2–4 starts with a second superscription (2:1) that marks the beginning of a new unit. Most of these three chapters contain oracles that focus upon two themes: the elimination of idols and idolaters (2:6-22) and the problem of social injustice in Judah and Jerusalem (3:1–4:1). They provide concrete examples of the sins mentioned in Isaiah 1. The first passage also anticipates judgment on the day of YHWH (2:11, 12, 17, 20).[9]

The elimination of idols and idolaters in 2:6-22 presupposes a polemic that condemns false worship by focusing upon foreign influence in the cult/worshiping community, by emphasizing idols as human creations, and by exposing the inability of idols to protect those who turn to them. The removal of social injustice from Judah and Jerusalem represents the prominent common denominator of the punishment pronounced in Isaiah 3:1–4:1. These verses describe divine punishment for oppression and unethical behavior when neighbors turn against one another (3:5). Consequently, as indicated throughout the chapter, YHWH abandons them to a current and future time of punishment (3:1-4, 9, 12; 3:24–4:1). The depiction of this punishment moves from social chaos to military defeat.

The final thematic unit in Isaiah 1–4 addresses the remnant who survive Jerusalem's destruction (4:2-6). This passage presupposes that the punishment anticipated in chapter 3 has been executed in that it speaks of the devastation to Jerusalem because of its bloodshed and the disgrace of its women, thus summarizing the two dominant charges of violence and pride that appeared in the accusations of chapter 3. The fact that this passage addresses those in the aftermath of Jerusalem's devastation has led a number of scholars to treat the text as a later reflection upon the consequences of Jerusalem's destruction that also anticipates a time when YHWH's glory will return to Jerusalem (4:5-6).[10]

Isaiah 5:1–10:4: Judgment on the South and the North

Chapters 5–10 reflect a deliberate shaping, based upon a chiastic combination of motifs, genres, and sources, as frequently noted by scholars.[11] Following the parable of the vineyard (5:1-7), these chapters consist of a frame of seven woe oracles (5:8-24; 10:1-4) that surround the so-called Isaiah memoir (6:1–8:18) and a series of poetic oracles concerning the Northern Kingdom (9:1-21).

The parable of the vineyard (5:1-7). This passage explores an analogy, comparing a landowner's care for a vineyard with the relationship between YHWH and YHWH's people. When the vineyard produces rotten fruit, the gardener chooses to destroy it. This parable purposively concludes with an application to both Judah and Israel (5:7), since the fate of both plays a major role in chapters 5–10. These chapters presume knowledge of the events leading to the Syro-Ephraimite War (which pitted Judah against Israel and Syria and opened the door wide for Assyrian incursion into the region).

Seven woe oracles (5:8-24; 10:1-4). Even though these woe oracles are separated by four chapters, scholars have long treated the material as an originally integrated unit or an artistically created frame around the Isaiah memoir. The dominant theory avers that redactors moved the seventh and final woe oracle of this collection (10:1-4) from its original location after 5:24 in order to frame the Isaiah memoir (6:1–8:18) and the judgment sayings against northern territories (9:1-21), and to anticipate the anti-Assyrian polemic of 10:5-34.[12] Concurrently, 5:25-30 originally began the judgment oracles against Israel (9:1-21), but it was placed after the sixth woe oracle. In so doing, pieces of two source blocks were separated from their original positions to form a frame around a third source block, the Isaiah memoir.

The Isaiah Memoir (6:1–8:18). The Isaiah memoir contains what many consider to be an early collection about the prophet, though how early remains debated.[13] Four prophetic narratives alongside various commentaries on these narratives constitute this memoir: Isaiah's call narrative and the commission of the prophet to a futile task (6:1-13), the confrontation of Ahaz by Isaiah and his son Shear-jashub (7:1-9), the birth of Immanuel and its portents for the future (7:10-23), and the birth narrative of Maher-shalal-hash-baz alongside commentary on the fate of Judah and Israel relative to Assyria (8:1-18). The three birth narratives involve children with symbolic names as signs about the events surrounding the Syro-Ephraimite War (734–732 BCE).

Isaiah 6 begins with a vision report (6:1-8) that has long been known as the prophet's call narrative. This first-person account, set in the year that King Uzziah died (circa 742 BCE), describes the throne room of the heavenly temple and the seraphim who serve as attendants proclaiming YHWH's holiness (6:1-3). The prophet describes the presence of YHWH as terrifying (6:4-5) since the prophet considers his own lips unclean. In response, one of the seraphim brings a live coal from the fire and touches it to the prophet's lips, thus cleansing him of his guilt and symbolically sanctifying his speech (6:6-7). The vision report closes with the prophet's commission. YHWH calls for a volunteer and the prophet famously responds: "Here am I; send me!" (6:8). Following this dramatic scene of purification and commission, the narrative continues describing the prophet's task as that of a messenger doomed to experience the futility of trying to change a stubborn people (6:9-13). The prophet questions YHWH: "How long, oh Lord?" YHWH's response offers little reprieve, since YHWH tells the prophet that the result will be the devastation of the land and the exile of its people, so that only a small remnant shall remain.

Chapter 7 contains two narrative reports (7:1-9, 10-17) intended to be read in tandem, followed by a series of four "on that day" sayings (7:18-25) regarding future attacks from Egypt and Assyria. The first narrative relays a command to the prophet and his son Shear-jashub (a name that means "a remnant shall return") to confront King Ahaz (742–725 BCE) of Judah. Ahaz has learned that the kings of Syria and Israel plan to attack Judah, and this knowledge causes Ahaz and the people to "shake like the trees of the forest before the wind" (7:2). The prophet admonishes Ahaz not to fear because both Syria and Israel will fail (7:4, 7-9).

The second narrative (7:10-17) recounts a danger from the king of Assyria that supersedes the danger posed by the kings of Syria and Israel. This narrative has a more ambiguous message than the previous narrative since it combines a sense of foreboding with a subtle message of endurance. The prophet points to a sign: "See the young woman is pregnant and she will bear a son" (7:14). The prophet seemingly continues with a word of encouragement because the young woman will name the child "Immanuel," a name that, as every Hebrew reader of this text would recognize, means "God is with us." The elaboration of the sign, however, focuses not upon the hope of God's presence, but upon the imminent danger that the country will soon experience before the child knows how to distinguish evil from goodness (7:16). Thus, the same verse that announces YHWH will punish Syria and Israel ("the land whose two kings you fear," v. 16) also announces that the king of Assyria will create a crisis not seen since Judah and Israel split after the death of Solomon (7:17).

The remainder of chapter 7 contains a series of four pronouncements, each beginning with "on that day" (7:18, 20, 21, 23) and each describing the future as a time of desperation. The first of these sayings warns of danger from both Egypt and Assyria (7:18-19), while the second portrays the king of Assyria as a dangerous man who intends to slash those who stand in his way with a razor (7:20). The third and the fourth "on that day" sayings (7:21-22, 23-25) focus upon the agricultural devastation of the land.

Like 7:1-9, Isaiah 8 involves the birth of a son, this time to the prophet. Like 7:10-17, the son has a symbolic name that serves as a sign (8:1-4). The prophet conceives a son by "the prophetess" and names him Maher-shalal-hash-baz, a name that means "swift the booty, speedy the prey." The name implies an imminent military defeat for Syria and Israel (8:4). The remainder of the Isaiah memoir

9

consists of a series of short prophetic pronouncements warning Syria, Israel, and Judah against attempting to withstand the onslaught of Assyria (8:5-18).

The oracles of 9:1-21 (probably along with the transitional unit, 8:19-22) represent a thematic grouping that points in several directions. The major theme focuses on the impending loss of territory associated with the Northern Kingdom.[14] Isaiah 9 begins, however, with a message of hope for a restored kingdom after a time of punishment (9:1-7) that contrasts with the preceding signs of the Isaiah memoir and with the loss of territory in the north anticipated in 9:8-21. Isaiah 9:1-7 anticipates the theme of chapter 10 (the destruction of Assyria) and 11 (a renewal of David's line). The message is one of hope for Israel and comes with a political twist: although Israel will be punished, a Judean monarch from the "throne of David" (9:7) will reunite the kingdom.[15]

Isaiah 10:5–12:6: Punishment of Assyria and Restoration of King and People

Isaiah 10:5–11:16 anticipates the downfall of Assyria's king (after YHWH uses him to punish YHWH's people), the renewal of the Davidic king (11:1-9), and the restoration of peace for YHWH's people (11:9-16). Thereafter, 12:1-6 marks the end of the first major section of the book with a cultic song of thanksgiving that sounds more like a psalm than a prophetic oracle. The collections that follow in 13–27 focus on judgment against foreign nations.

Isaiah 10:5-34 contains a series of anti-Assyrian oracles climaxing with the downfall of the Assyrian king. Thematically, this passage juxtaposes judgment and restoration against the backdrop of the Assyrian period. The content includes both divine judgment against Judah by the king of Assyria and announces that the Assyrian king will be punished for his insolence. It declares both punishment against the king of Judah and the future restoration of Davidic rule.

Isaiah 11 provides a series of eschatological poems regarding the enduring nature of the Davidic dynasty. As such, it forms a thematic counterpart to 10:5-34. Whereas 10:5-34 announces YHWH's punishment of Judah by using the king of Assyria before punishing the king of Assyria, chapter 11 focuses upon the survival of the Davidic line of Judah and the return of Judah and Ephraim. Both of these chapters likely reflect a complex redactional history, but together they affirm YHWH's decision that Judah will survive while Assyria will not.

Isaiah 12 ends the first major block of Isaiah with a song of thanksgiving and praise. These genre elements play a significant role as both a response to the promises of chapter 11 and an anticipation of the oracles against the nations in chapters 13–27. The placement of this song suggests awareness of the literary context at several points.[16]

The thematic overlap across the various compositional blocks of chapters 1–12 creates a sense of movement for the reader of the book as a whole. Chapters 1–12 introduce the major themes of the entire collection (especially 1–4, 5), and they offer theological reflections on the significance of the Assyrian period (6–11). Narratives, poems, and oracles demonstrate that internal struggles between Judah and Israel, the lack of social justice, and the refusal to return to YHWH radically limited YHWH's options. YHWH chose to use Assyria to punish Judah and Israel. Still, the block ends with a strong word of hope for the future when a peaceable kingdom will be established and the people will rejoice for what YHWH has done.

Isaiah 13–27: Judging the Nations and the World

Isaiah 13–27 consists of two thematic blocks: oracles against the nations in 13–23 and a universalizing conclusion in 24–27. Recent studies understand 13–23 as an early collection of oracles that was expanded several times. Critical scholars generally date 24–27 later than the bulk of 13–23 and associate 24–27 with the latest redactional layers of Isaiah during the late Persian or Hellenistic period. Increasingly, scholars treat 24–27 as a composite text designed to conclude and to universalize the message directed against particular nations in 13–23.[17] Consequently, the contours of Isaiah 13–27 make the most sense if one treats them as a developing block that includes (1) a core group of texts warning of the consequences for resisting Assyria, (2) a Babylonian expansion, (3) a second expansion focusing on the restoration of Zion, and (4) texts that reflect a late eschatological perspective anticipating a universal judgment separating the righteous from the wicked, not by ethnicity but by theological commitments.

Isaiah 13–23: Judgment against Foreign Nations

The Early Core of Isaiah 13–23

In the last three decades, scholars have clarified the characteristics that define the early core of the oracles in chapters 13–23 (14:28-32; 17:1-3; most of 18–20 and 22). These texts counsel against political or military resistance to Assyria. This judgment against anti-Assyrian activity lines up well with the attitudes displayed in the core narratives within chapters 1–10 and 28–33. In other words, the oracles against these nations do not castigate them for being foreign nations, but for their failure to recognize and to submit to YHWH's use of Assyria to reset the political realities in the region and for their failure to recognize Egypt as a false ally.

The death notice of King Ahaz (who died in 727 BCE, in the same year that Tiglath-pileser III of Assyria also died) in 14:28 would have fit well after chapter 10 prior to the additions of the eschatological material in chapter 11 and the thanksgiving song in chapter 12. These additions now round off 1–12 as an editorial block of the book. This death notice introduces the oracle against the Philistines (14:28-32) that essentially warns the Philistines not to attempt to take advantage of the power vacuum.[18] This oracle presages the Ashdod rebellion (713–711 BCE) when that Philistine city rebelled against the Assyrians, a setting that dominates the early core of 18–22.

Isaiah 17:1-3 denounces Syria in the aftermath of the Syro-Ephraimite War (734–732 BCE).[19] The sayings against Ethiopia (chapter 18) and Egypt (chapter 19) offer political counsel to Hezekiah: do not trust those who support rebellion against Assyria.[20] The narrative of 20:1-6 reflects the prophet's warning against those in his own country who see Egypt and Ethiopia as powerful allies against Assyria.[21] Isaiah 22:1-14 also reflects the prophet's condemnation of foreign nations and those within Judah who counseled resistance against the Assyrians and who paid a price for their support of Ashdod. The narrative at the end of the chapter (22:15-25) recounts the replacement of the king's steward, Shebnah, in the buildup to the siege of Sennacherib in 701 BCE.

Thus, the early core of chapters 13–23 essentially takes the reader from the death of Ahaz in 727 BCE through the Ashdod rebellion (713–711 BCE) as it warns Hezekiah against joining forces with those who attempt to resist Assyria. This early material takes the reader to, but not beyond, the siege of Sennacherib in 701 BCE, an event that becomes the focus of the core material beginning in chapter 28. This early material displays a consistent message: those who antagonize Assyria will pay dearly. In contrast to these early passages, the second stage in the development of chapters 13–23 changes the focus dramatically by turning its attention to the role of Babylon in the plans of YHWH.

The Babylonian Expansion

According to a developing consensus, an editor, or several editors, expanded the early core of chapters 13–23 significantly, updating the existing material with a series of oracles condemning Babylon (13–14; 21:1-10; 23).[22] While a majority of commentators recognize this process has occurred, no consensus yet exists regarding the sequence or the dates of this process.[23]

The nature of these debates involves complex and difficult issues, and a clear path forward at this point seems unlikely in terms of a date for the Babylonian expansion.[24] Nevertheless, while the *when* remains debated, a clearer consensus regarding the *how* has taken shape. An early core of oracles was updated to include perspectives articulated for the community well after the destruction of Jerusalem in 587 in order to emphasize that Babylon—like Assyria before it—would face destruction when God chose to act.

A Zion Expansion in 13–23

In addition to the early core and the anti-Babylonian expansion, several texts within Isaiah 13–27 stand out for their positive assumptions regarding the relationship of foreign nations to Zion. This Zion emphasis appears prominently in chapters 24–27 but also shows up in those passages within chapters 13–23 that stand out thematically from the judgment against foreign nations. These Zion texts do not focus upon judgment against foreign nations. They do, however, exhibit similar characteristics to some of the Zion material in chapters 1–12 (most notably, Isa 2:1-4), where the righteous in Israel and the righteous among the nations will make a pilgrimage to Zion.[25]

While it remains unclear whether all these passages come from the same hand, they do share striking hermeneutical similarities, including the assumption that Zion's current fate will change for the better—based, in part, upon the support of foreign nations who will recognize YHWH's rule. They anticipate a future when YHWH rules from Zion after Jerusalem has endured punishment and a future when the nations will contribute to Zion's renewed prominence. This hope for Zion reflects one of the recurring themes connecting most of the major sections of Isaiah, and these themes likely stem from the Persian period.

Isaiah 24–27: A Shift to Universal Judgment

Isaiah 24–27 constitutes a late compositional block that houses much of the fourth theological focus in 13–27: universal judgment. Chapters 24–27 have been increasingly recognized for their awareness of a wide range of texts coming from both within Isaiah and beyond it (especially creation and flood language). Chapters 24–27 take up the perspectives of judgment against Babylon and restoration of the righteous in Zion and universalize them so that they are "elevated to the world plane."[26] These chapters do not mention Babylon specifically, but depict impending judgment against "the earth" and an unnamed "city of chaos," whose anonymity makes it possible for this city to serve as a cipher for virtually any political entity that opposes YHWH.[27] This judgment presupposes Judah's own punishment from which a remnant survived, but it also anticipates a restoration in Zion that is aided by the righteous among the nations. The general outline running through these chapters, while not recounted in narrative form, can nevertheless be seen. YHWH has judged the earth (24:1-6), so YHWH reigns in Zion, where the nations rejoice with Israel (25:1-5) and YHWH presents a festival banquet (25:6-10). Isaiah 26:1-6 contrasts the fate of the city that has been restored (i.e., Zion) with the fate of the city that has been brought low. The remainder of the chapter (26:7-19) contrasts the fate of the righteous with that of the wicked, before returning to the topic of cosmic judgment with the destruction of the chaos monster Leviathan (26:20–27:1). Chapter 27 offers two restoration texts concerning the establishment of a new vineyard (27:2-6, playing off the song of the vineyard in Isa 5) and a return of the diaspora (27:12-13). These texts frame a passage (27:7-11) that affirms YHWH's judgment as expiation for the sins of Jacob.

Universal Judgment for the Righteous and the Wicked

The poems in 13–23 reflect judgment against particular nations, but this focus gives way to images in 24–27 that presuppose YHWH will judge all the wicked, both inside and outside Judah. The separate fates of the righteous and the wicked play a prominent role in chapter 26. This chapter expresses ideas of universal judgment against the wicked (26:10) who do not learn from their punishment (in contrast to the "inhabitants of the world" who "learn righteousness" in 26:9). This openness to (some among) the nations has a close thematic similarity to the promises given to some among the nations in 13–23 who will aid Zion (e.g., 19:18-21).

Nevertheless, chapters 24–27 do not define the wicked merely as foreigners. From the very beginning of 24–27, inescapable judgment will come against all the earth and will include all humanity (24:1-5), from which only a remnant will survive (24:6). The guilt of Jacob is often presumed and occasionally stated explicitly (27:8-9, 11b). The conclusion of 24–27, however, anticipates the restoration of Jacob (27:1-6) and the return of exiles from Assyria and Egypt (27:12-13). Thus, the beginning and end of 24–27 express judgment against YHWH's people as well as foreign nations. This universal judgment results in the return of a remnant to Zion.

A Thematic Hinge between 13–23 and Beyond

The appearance of typical Isaianic themes and vocabulary in chapters 24–27, as is frequently cited in recent literature, has led a number of scholars to see this section as a rounding off and a universalizing of the oracles in 13–23. Yet more needs to be said regarding the function of chapters 24–27 in the book of Isaiah. On the one hand, 24–27 certainly provides a hermeneutical lens by

14

which to understand the judgment against foreign nations in 13–23, and that recognition is a significant step forward in Isaiah studies. On the other hand, this understanding does not adequately explain the totality of 13–27 for three reasons. First, it fails to explain the role of Zion in 13–23 or 24–27. Second, it does not adequately account for the words of judgment against YHWH's own people in 13–27. Third, it does not adequately explain this universalizing tendency within the rest of the book. Many treatments of 24–27 do not contemplate the question, why here? Why do 13–23 and 24–27 interrupt the Assyrian context that dominates 1–11 and 28–32? Too often, the treatment of 24–27 still subtly suffers from the remnants of earlier models that treated these chapters as a late appendage haphazardly placed at the end of 13–23. While the use of Isaianic themes, vocabulary, and theology have led many to abandon this older idea in theory, few pause to consider the placement of these chapters within the book as a whole. Chapters 13–27 function literarily as an extended parenthetical discourse that anchors YHWH's prophetic warnings to the nations as part of a larger plan. Contextually, the voice of the prophet speaks these words in the midst of the Assyrian threat facing Judah at the end of the eighth century BCE. Yet, these prophetic pronouncements foreshadow events from the perspective of a Persian-period audience, thereby allowing the prophet to anticipate judgment against Judah and Israel that leads to exile, as well as the ultimate downfall of Assyria, Babylon, and their respective allies. All of these themes reappear in 28–66.

Isaiah 28–35: An Early Core and Persian-Period Updates

Recent commentators argue that Isaiah 28–35 consists of an early core in 28–31 and a *series* of insertions and continuations (*Fortschreibungen*) in 32–35 from the Persian period. These recent treatments share at least three commonalities even though they differ in certain details. First, they see chapters 32–35 as a series of updates, not a unified composition. Each of the four chapters builds upon something in the preceding text, but introduces new elements, some of which are best classified as corrections of previous material. Second, these recent treatments offer a number of arguments for categorizing the perspectives within 32–35 as bridge texts. They pick up ideas and wording from the book preceding chapter 32, and they anticipate texts in 40–66. Third, the literary anticipations within 32–35 have diachronic implications. Some links include only texts from 40–55, while others involve 56–66, thus suggesting that the growth in the middle of the book manifests a deepening reflection upon the second half of Isaiah.

Isaiah 28–31: Calls for Change

As in Isaiah 7–10, chapters 28–31 contain an early core of material that confronts those in the king's retinue who argue for action against Assyria, and they contain material updated for a Persian-period audience.[28] Chapters 28–31 include various groups (Ephraim, leaders in Jerusalem, the personified city of Jerusalem, and the people) and alternate confrontational rhetoric with words of hope. Additionally, these materials warn against trusting Egypt and antici-pate renewal for regions in the Northern Kingdom that had been lost to Assyria (Lebanon and Carmel). The core message of the confrontational sections seeks to convince leaders in Jerusalem to change course, while the Persian-period updates imagine a restoration and subtly imply hope for reunifying the family of Jacob (i.e., the north and south), thereby restoring the promise of Abraham.

Isaiah 28 begins with a woe oracle (28:1-4) against the leaders of Ephraim, the name of the central territory of the Northern Kingdom where its capital Samaria was located. A word of encouragement for the future follows the woe oracle addressed to "the remnant of his people" who trust in YHWH's "spirit of justice" (28:5-6). One could understand these distinct messages as concern for the remnant of Ephraim, but 28:14-29 makes clear that the pronouncements about Ephraim function as a lesson to the leaders of Jerusalem: Samaria's fate could befall Jerusalem (28:14).[29] Thus, the rhetorical logic of the chapter assumes the events of 722 BCE have occurred. Isaiah 28:7-13 continues the thought of verses 1-4, expanding the judgment from the "drunkards of Ephraim" (28:1) to the priests and prophets (28:7), whose drunken behavior invites disdain and makes them unreliable messengers of instruction (28:9). Isaiah 28:13 announces their doom. Beginning in 28:14, the text addresses those ruling in Jerusalem who have made a "covenant with death" (28:14, 18). Destruction from YHWH will affect the entire land (28:22). This covenant relates to the anti-Assyrian policies of Hezekiah, which the early core of Isaiah consistently opposes.

Isaiah 29 contains six sections of thematic variations (1-8, 9-10, 11-14, 15-16, 17-21, 22-24). As with chapter 28, chapter 29 opens with a woe oracle (29:1-8), but this time it addresses personified Jerusalem, here called Ariel (which means the City of God). Ariel is the city where David camped before he took it (29:1), but now YHWH will encamp against it (29:3) to lead a host of nations against it (29:7). Despite this warning, the people will pay no attention (29:9-10). Further, 29:15 signals a second woe oracle (29:15-16) that condemns leaders who think they operate in secret but whose secrets are not hidden from YHWH (29:15-16). The end of the chapter anticipates deliverance, however, and pro-claims that the house of Jacob and his children will be redeemed just as Abraham was redeemed (29:22-24).

16

Isaiah 30 continues the same juxtaposition of words of judgment (30:1-17) with words of hope (30:18-33). It begins with a fourth woe oracle against those seeking help from Egypt without seeking counsel from YHWH (30:1-5) and those offering financial incentives to Egypt (30:6-7).[30] The meaning is clear: God does not approve of their plans, and the prophetic speaker commands that the words be recorded in a book as a witness for the future (30:8). Here, one finds a mixture of Isaianic and Jeremianic images used to condemn the people who would not listen to the prophets (30:9-14). The chapter ends with hope that YHWH will deliver Zion (30:18) from Assyria (30:31). In the process, the people of Zion will take instruction from YHWH and destroy their idols (30:20-22).

Isaiah 31 also begins with a woe oracle (the fifth in Isa 28–31) that warns against placing hope in Egypt (31:1-3). Instead, the chapter contends, YHWH will deliver Zion (31:4-5) from the Assyrians (31:8) if the people will turn from their idols (31:7).

Most recent studies identify occasional comments in 28–31 as updates from the Persian period that link to topics in chapters 32–35.[31] In contrast to 28–31, Isaiah 32–35 shows more interest in events following Jerusalem's destruction, though some of the material also evokes images that could refer to the siege of Sennacherib.

Isaiah 32–35: Literary Bridges

Chapters 32–35 largely function as a hinge that anticipates a future beyond the eighth century BCE, a future that presupposes life after Jerusalem's destruction. Isaiah 32 focuses thematically upon the return of the king to Jerusalem.[32] The chapter frames its message to those who have experienced dramatic upheaval by offering hope for a new set of rulers who seek peace and justice and who will make Zion a place of rest. The return of peace and righteousness begins and ends the chapter (32:1-2, 15-20) while 32:3-8 and 32:9-14 explain the coming punishment from different perspectives. Verses 3-8 formulate the purpose of the punishment: to remove the leaders (labeled as fools and villains) who plot iniquity and practice wickedness against the poor. To get there, however, means that punishment will come to Jerusalem, so 32:9-14 describes this coming punishment in graphic terms: the land will not produce, the city will be depopulated, and animals will take over.

Isaiah 33 constitutes a pastiche of rhetorical pieces forcing the reader's attention in different directions while serving a larger aim. Collectively, these pieces describe life after Jerusalem's destruction and offer comfort that Jerusalem will ultimately be restored. The chapter begins with a sixth woe oracle, this time directed against the foreign destroyer.[33] The rhetorical thought breaks down thematically into two sections (33:1-13, 14-24), each with its own complex logic that scholars suggest did not result from a single hand.[34] The first portion focuses upon YHWH's action against the enemy.[35] The second portion describes YHWH's return to Zion as king and addresses the population of Zion from inside and outside the land.[36]

Isaiah 34–35 constitutes a second bridge text that more overtly connects the themes and motifs from chapters 1–33 with those of 40–66, but these chapters likely do not constitute a text that arose from one author or one time. Recent redactional models show a strong tendency to treat most of Isaiah 34 with the incorporation of (at least portions of) 40–55. By contrast, Isaiah 35 contains numerous links to the wording and concepts not only of early portions of chapter 40 but also some of the later portions of 63–66, thereby suggesting a later stage of development.[37]

Isaiah 36–39: An Adapted Narrative

Isaiah 36–39 brings the reader back to events in the eighth century through a series of prophetic narratives concerning Isaiah and Hezekiah. Significant portions of these texts represent parallel narratives to 2 Kings 18–20 and 2 Chronicles 29–32. Scholars have long concluded that the Isaiah version typically derives from the Kings account, though the nature of the borrowing is complex.[38] The Isaiah and Kings accounts were written prior to the composition of Chronicles. Lengthy stretches of these chapters parallel each other verbatim, and both accounts narrate the story of Hezekiah and Isaiah in three vignettes that likely originated as independent traditions brought together in 2 Kings: the Assyrian threat and Jerusalem's miraculous deliverance (2 Kgs 18–19; Isa 36–37); the miraculous healing of Hezekiah (2 Kgs 20:1-11; Isa 38:1-8); and Hezekiah's visit from the Babylonian delegation (2 Kgs 20:12-19; Isa 39). The thanksgiving song in Isaiah 38:9-20 appears only in Isaiah and is almost universally recognized as the insertion of the Isaiah redactor who added chapters 36–39. Recently, it has become more common to recognize that the redactor who incorporated 36–39 also modified the tradition to embed it in Isaiah.

A number of authors in the last two decades have mounted challenges to the primacy of the Kings version.[39] The challenges have not succeeded, by and large, in displacing the theory that the Kings account came first, but they have succeeded in demonstrating that the author of the Kings account knew and was influenced by the Isaiah collection that was available at the time. The Isaiah redactor also drew upon the vocabulary and the concepts of the Isaiah scroll to adapt the Kings account into Isaiah.[40] Perhaps the most enduring significance related to this ongoing scholarly discussion has been twofold: explaining the diverging portraits of Hezekiah and the literary function of Isaiah 36–39 in the scroll of Isaiah.

Most scholarly treatments (including both synchronic and diachronic treatments) now recognize that the portrait of the relationship between Isaiah and Hezekiah derived from Isaiah 36–39 differs markedly from the messages that confront Judah's royal policies as found in the early core of the Isaiah speeches in chapters 7–10 and especially 28–31. The early material boldly challenges Hezekiah's policies that were putting Judah on a path to war with Assyria. By contrast, the later accounts have a much more positive take on Hezekiah, and this positive spin plays a pivotal role in the book of Kings, where Hezekiah functions as the good king in between the bad kings Ahaz and Manasseh.[41]

Debate remains on whether Isaiah 36–39 functioned as part of a deliberate linking of some portion of 1–35 with some form of 40–66 or whether chapters 36–39 were first added as an appendix to some form of 1–35.[42] The fact that chapters 36–39 largely contain preexisting material complicates this question. Nevertheless, the redactor's decision to incorporate virtually unchanged (39:1-8) the vignette describing the visit of the Babylonian delegation speaks in favor of the bridging function of these chapters. This passage exposes a subtle threat, specifically Hezekiah's failure to see Babylon's desire to take Jerusalem's wealth. In response, the prophet Isaiah announces the obvious: Babylon will take away this wealth and will exile Hezekiah's descendants to Babylon (39:7-8). For his part, Hezekiah seems willfully oblivious to the implications of this pronouncement because it will not happen in his own lifetime (39:8). This sense of foreboding pushes the reader forward in time since the reader knows that Babylon ultimately destroys Jerusalem. This threat contrasts dramatically with the very next verses in Isaiah 40 that announce the end of the exile in Babylon for Jerusalem.[43]

Isaiah 40–55: Returning from Exile

Chapters 40–55 have long been recognized as a composition that presumes knowledge of the Persian period. Since at least the time of Bernhard Duhm, the vast majority of critical scholars recognize Isaiah 40–55 as a literary block that cannot have come from the lifetime of the eighth-century prophet Isaiah.[44] Rather, scholars showed that this block of texts came from the sixth century at the earliest and reflects events surrounding the defeat of Babylon in 539 BCE by Cyrus the Great, king of Persia, who is mentioned by name in Isaiah 44:28; 45:1, 13. In the last two decades, a significant number of scholars have put forward new theories regarding chapters 40–55 on at least two fronts: the shifting perspectival changes from Babylon to Jerusalem and the question of authorial unity. Relatedly, scholars have paid more careful attention to the thematic shifts within these chapters and thus are more likely to subdivide 40–55 into two sections, distinguishing 40–48 from 49–55. Chapters 40–48 address their message to and speak about Jacob/Israel. Thematically, they largely focus on the release from exile as YHWH's new initiative, the impending journey out of Babylon, and polemics against idolatry. Chapters 49–55 focus on the restoration of Zion in ways that extend chapters 40–48, but 49–55 frequently presume a different setting.

Isaiah 40–48: Leaving Babylon

Evidence for distinguishing chapters 40–48 from 49–55 derives from four topics and terms that are exclusive to 40–48. Relatedly, chapters 49–55 deviate from 40–48 regarding the role of the servant and the conceptualization of restoration. Together, these exclusive and changing messages distinguish the two parts from each other.

Topics Distinctive to 40–48

Isaiah 40–48 contains four significant topics and terms that play little or no role in 49–55: a formal emphasis upon Jacob/Israel, barbed statements against the worship of idols, explicit mention of Cyrus and Babylon, and a contrast between former things and new things.

Preference for Jacob/Israel. Isaiah 40–48 demonstrates a clear preference for the terms *Jacob* and *Israel* when speaking of the community of exiles. Jacob appears nineteen times in 40–48 and fifteen times in 1–39, but then only five times (58:1, 14; 58:14; 60:16; 65:9) after Isaiah 49, and none of those appear in 50–55. The fact that Jacob appears three times in Isaiah 49 (49:5, 6, 29) suggests Isaiah 49 could be a composition of the disciples of Deutero-Isaiah reflecting the change to the Zion-oriented material in 49–55.[45]

Similarly, Israel appears thirty-three times in 40–48 but only three times in 50–55 and five times in 56–66 (56:8; 60:9, 14; 63:7, 16). By way of contrast, Zion is mentioned explicitly three times in 40–48 (40:9; 41:27; 46:13), but eight times in 49–55 (49:14; 51: 3, 11, 16; 52:1, 2, 7, 8) and eight times in 56–66 (59:20; 60:14; 61:3; 62:11; 64:10; 66:8). One of these texts also introduces a speech of Zion quoted by YHWH (49:14). Less obvious in English, several passages in 49–55 use feminine singular referents in 49–55 to address Lady Zion directly (e.g., 49:15-26; 51:12b; 51:17-21; 52:1-8; 54:1-16) or to speak to the people about her (as in the reference to "your mother" in 50:1 or the description of "her" comfort in 51:3).

Condemnation of Idols. In addition to these forms of address, chapters 40–48 contain several texts that satirically mock the impotency and absurdity of idol worship. While the condemnation of the worship of images is not absent from other parts of Isaiah, it does not appear in 49–55.[46] Also, chapters 40–48 mock the making of idols with a vehemence not found elsewhere and exhibit a particular focus on Babylonian deities.

This polemical tone leaves no room for misunderstanding. These passages make no attempt to understand the religious function played by the physical representations of the deities among the adherents of the worship practices of the Babylonians. Rather, by ridiculing the idols as human creations, these texts portray the impotence of these icons as nothing more than an artisan's handiwork. Consider the poignant polemical rant in 44:9-20. It begins with a thematic introduction highlighting the human design and craftsmanship of the idols and the ineffectual consequences both for those worshiping them and for the artisans who created them (44:9-11). Next, this passage emphasizes the human artistry that goes into making the idols. By stressing the skills of the ironsmith (44:12) and the carpenter (44:13), these verses convey considerable knowledge of the process involved in forging and carving idols. The purpose, in both instances, turns quickly to the human needs of these artisans who must eat to survive. The ironsmith works so hard hammering that he becomes weak and seeks nourishment. The carpenter becomes the focus of an extended parable (44:13-17) that culminates by gleefully mocking the fact that the artisan uses half the tree to cook his dinner (44:15, 16) and the other half to make an idol to which he prays for deliverance (44:17). Following this dramatic story, 44:18-20 admonishes the listeners not to be like those who worship the idols in ignorance because they should see the idol for the fraud it is.

While 44:9–20 serves as the explanatory anchor to the animosity toward idol worship, the motif of the impotence of idols representing Babylonian deities appears elsewhere in 40–48. A series of texts preceding 44:9-20 highlights the impotence of idol worship in contrast to the power of YHWH (40:18-20; 41:7; 42:17). After Isaiah 44:9-20, the worship of idols functions as one of the reasons for Babylon's demise (46:1-7), and relatedly as a means of proclaiming YHWH's omnipotent power in 48:5. In 46:1-7, the prophet warns those depending upon images of Bel and Nebo that these idols have no power to deliver them.

The condemnation of idols thus mentions particular deities (46:1-7) and plays a role in the motifs of YHWH's incomparable power and the forthcoming journey during which YHWH's people will be led by YHWH. The specific reference to Babylonian deities who will soon fall fits well with other explicit historical entities mentioned in 40–48, namely Cyrus, king of Persia, and Babylon, the city and the empire defeated by Cyrus.

Cyrus and Babylon in 40–48. In the middle of Isaiah 40–48, one finds explicit references to Cyrus (44:28; 45:1, 13), the Persian king who defeated Babylon in 539 BCE, and to Babylon or the Chaldeans (43:14; 47:1, 5; 48:14, 20). The mention of Cyrus played a large role in recognizing that Isaiah 40–55 came from a different time period than the lifetime of the prophet Isaiah for whom the book is named. The material within the book that is associated with Isaiah the prophet covers a period of over thirty years at the end of the eighth century, including interpretations of events from the Syro-Ephraimite War (734–732 BCE) to the siege of Sennacherib (701 BCE). The prophet, therefore, completed his public ministry over 160 years before Cyrus took Babylon in 539 BCE.[47] These Cyrus texts, moreover, function integrally within the immediate and larger contexts. These texts assume that YHWH will use Cyrus, king of Persia, to accomplish two tasks: (1) to punish the nations who have oppressed YHWH's people (45:1-4), and (2) to liberate YHWH's people and make it possible for them to return to their homeland in Judah (45:13). A number of recent commentators also consider Cyrus to be the figure addressed in 48:14-16, even though he is not mentioned explicitly by name.[48] This optimistic attitude toward Cyrus disappears entirely in 49–55.

Contrast of Former Things and New Things. A fourth topic that functions prominently in Isaiah 40–48 (but not 49–55) is the contrast between the new things that YHWH is about to undertake and the former things. The former things generally refer to the status of the Judeans in exile or the behavior of their ancestors that led to YHWH's decision to punish them.

Isaiah 42:9 announces that the former things have come to pass (referring to judgment upon YHWH's people) and that YHWH is about to declare a new thing, subsequently identified in 42:15-16 as a journey where the blind will be led to safety while those worshiping idols will be shamed. Similarly, in Isaiah 43:18-19, YHWH admonishes the people not to remember the old things because YHWH is about to do something new: YHWH is about to lead them on a journey through the wilderness from Babylon to Judah. Hence, the "new thing" is the return from exile.

The contrast between the "former things" and the "new things" that YHWH is about to do represents a central part of the message in 48:1-6, in which 48:3 refers to YHWH's punishment that he announced in advance (48:3, 5), punishment that he also enacted against the people because of their obstinance (48:4). In this passage, the term "new things" refers to the content of the prophet's message that is not a message of judgment (48:6-7). While the "new things" about which YHWH speaks, according to this passage, do not *explicitly* relate to an impending journey, the context treats them as the cessation of YHWH's anger (48:9-10).

Other passages somehow relate the "former things" to the impotence of idols or the power of YHWH. Isaiah 41:21-24 offers a disputation concerning idols by asking the people who worship them to present the idols so the idols can tell of the former things and what is about to happen. The passage contrasts YHWH's power with the absurdity of idol worship, a critique that permeates 40–48. Isaiah 43:9 refers only to the "former things" known by YHWH that neither the people (43:8) nor the nations (43:9) could have known, thus emphasizing the incomparable power of YHWH as the only God (43:10). With 46:9, the "former things of old" (as with 43:9) also relates to the motif of YHWH's power.

In contrast to 43:18-19 (which says not to remember the things of old), Isaiah 46:8-9 commands the people to "remember the things of old" in referring to 46:1-7 and the uselessness of idols when facing YHWH. Hence, the "former things" refer both to the knowledge of YHWH's superiority handed down from long ago (43:9; 46:9) and to the punishment the people have endured in more recent times (43:18). The contrast with "new things" does not appear when the "former things" refers to the knowledge of YHWH's incomparable power, but does appear when anticipating the impending journey to Jerusalem.

Topics Shared but Distinct in 40–48 and 49–55

The Servant Songs. In addition to the four distinctive elements of 40–48 that do not appear in 49–55, one should briefly mention two recurring motifs that cross 40–48 and 49–55: the servant of YHWH and the restoration. These motifs, however, have a different focus in the two sections. Four poems appear in Isaiah 40–55 that have long been designated as the Servant Songs: 42:1-4; 49:1-6; 50:4-11; and 52:13–53:12. Since Bernhard Duhm's commentary at the end of the nineteenth century, which treated these poems as preexisting literary entities that was incorporated into chapters 40–55 in the fifth century BCE, scholars have attempted to explain the complex role of the Servant Songs in 40–55. Twentieth-century interpretations of these poems spent a great deal of time and effort hypothesizing about the original identity of the servant. They often (but not always) assumed the songs had a prehistory as a collection in their own right. A number of proposals argued that the servant was an individual (either Cyrus or the prophet who authored chapters 40–55) or represented an anthropomorphized collective entity (either Jacob/Israel as a whole or some select portion thereof). More recently, trends have shifted to pay more attention to the differences among these songs, to the multiple identities (even in the original setting), to their function within their respective contexts, and to the way in which the Servant Songs interact with larger structural shifts.

In this context, the first Servant Song (42:1-4) has a decidedly more optimistic tone than the other three poems, all of which attest to some level of resistance or violence toward the servant. This growing hostility appears to come both from within the Judean community and from foreigners. Only the first Servant Song appears in chapters 40–48, but a number of other passages refer to Jacob/Israel as servant (44:1, 2, 21, 26; 45:4). Even though a plausible case can be made for understanding Cyrus as the original servant in the first Servant Song, the larger literary context of 40–48 conveys the strong impression that YHWH's people in exile function as the referent of the servant within 40–48.[49] In 49–55, the servant speaks clearly as an individual and suffers increasing levels of violence.

Conceptualizing Restoration in 40–48. By and large, the material in 40–48 frames its message to the community in Babylon who will soon be departing to return. After chapter 48, the perspective changes. Speeches address Lady Zion directly, and refer to her waiting and watching for the arrival of her children to come to her and rebuild her structures. No longer does the action reflect the perspective of those leaving, but the reader sees things from her vantage point as she waits for them to arrive.

For example, Isaiah 40 opens with a call for comfort to the people and to Jerusalem, and the comfort comes in the form of an announcement of the end of punishment (40:1-2). The end of punishment leads to the announcement of an imminent journey through the wilderness that will reveal the glory of YHWH (40:3-5). This comfort to Zion and the people plays a significant role in the commands in the rest of the chapter since both Zion (40:9) and the people (40:18) are commanded to respond. Chapter 48 concludes (48:20-22) with a reference back to the journey through the wilderness with which chapter 40 began. The thematic *inclusio* marks the end of this major section, but it also specifies this journey outward as a journey out of Babylon: "Go forth from Babylon, flee from Chaldea" (48:20 RSV).[50] This command to flee Babylon also represents the last explicit mention of the place of the exile in Isaiah.

The polemic against idolatry becomes its most concrete when it mentions the Babylonian gods Bel and Nebo by name in Isaiah 46:1. Bel is the name often used for the Royal God Marduk, and Nebo is the Hebrew spelling of the deity Nabû, the Babylonian deity affiliated with wisdom and writing. More to the point, Isaiah 46:1-7 alludes to a procession in which these deities are carried. This procession of gods took place regularly in Babylon to demonstrate that the deities were returning to their places in order to symbolize the renewal of the fertility of the land. These references to the carrying of the gods in 46:1-2, 7, however, convey a message of judgment by describing the impotence of Bel and Nebo to save themselves (and by implication their people). The deities will be abased and sent into captivity (46:2), unable to move or provide deliverance (46:7). By contrast, 46:3-6 describes YHWH's incomparable power and salvific ability. Consequently, this message has often been interpreted as reflecting a Babylonian

24

setting, near the time of Babylon's overthrow in 539 BCE, that anticipates the fall of Babylon and the salvation of the exiles of Judah.

Isaiah 40–48 contains a number of texts anticipating YHWH's new action that will contrast with what has been the norm. Consider Isaiah 42:9: "See, the former things have come to pass, and new things I now declare; before they spring forth, I tell you of them." This new activity involves YHWH going forth as king and warrior (42:13) who defeats the enemies and who will then lead his people on a journey on paths they do not know (42:15-16; see also the repetition of these motifs in 43:18-19). YHWH's pronouncement that he is about to do something new appears for the last time in 48:6.[51] These perspectival commonalities that address the community in Babylon and anticipate a return to the land of Judah call the reader to identify with the community in Babylon. By contrast, the material in chapters 49–55 calls for a reorientation of the reader's perspective as the reader sees the scene from Lady Zion's (= Jerusalem) perspective as she looks out from her place while waiting for the people to return.

Isaiah 49–55: Coming to Jerusalem

While the perspective of the addressees and the recurring themes that dominate chapters 40–48 focus upon the imminent departure of Israel/Jacob from Babylon, those characteristics change in 49–55. The perspective of the addressees shifts noticeably to Jerusalem's waiting for the arrival of her people, while the recurring themes change to topics associated with the social and religious practices of the community in Jerusalem.

The change in perspective begins in the first sections of chapter 49 (49:1-7, 8-13), the first of which contains the speech of the servant of YHWH who speaks to the nations (49:1a), recounts his selection as YHWH's servant (49:1b-3), and acknowledges that his strength comes from YHWH (49:4). From there, the servant recounts that YHWH has expanded the servant's task from restoring the survivors of Israel to being a light to the nations (49:6).

This speech of the servant also explicitly identifies the servant as none other than Israel itself by quoting YHWH's direct address to the servant: "You are my servant, Israel, in whom I will show my glory" (49:3). The second servant of YHWH speech in 49:1-7 expands upon the servant's role, broadening that role from leading Jacob/Israel to return as testimony to the nations of YHWH's power (see especially 42:5-9) to a role which the servant will play as a "light to the nations" to bring salvation to the entire earth (49:6; cf. 42:6). In the first Servant Song and its commentary (42:1-4, 5-9), the servant's task centers upon the redemption of those in exile described as the blind and as prisoners (42:7). In that song, the "former things" referred to the punishment that Jacob/Israel was experiencing, and the "new thing" referred to the anticipated departure (42:9). In the first Servant Song, as with the second, the servant is called a light to the nations (42:6; 49:6). In the first song, however, that light is to reflect YHWH's power to redeem YHWH's people, while the task of the servant in the second song is to be a light to the nations to bring salvation to the ends of the earth.

The second section of Isaiah 49 (49:8-13) issues a charge to the returned community while continuing to draw references to the form of the servant of YHWH. This community, unlike the one in 42:1-4, 5-7, is portrayed as having experienced YHWH's deliverance: "On a day of salvation, I helped you. I have guarded you, and given you as a covenant to the people" (49:8 CEB). The perspective in these verses changes in comparison to chapters 40–48. Rather than anticipating a journey *going forth to* Jerusalem *from* Babylon, this passage anticipates the *arrival* of a group from multiple directions *coming* to join the servant in Jerusalem.

The third section (49:14-21) addresses Lady Zion directly, using feminine singular forms of address in the remainder of the chapter (49:14-21, 22-26). Moreover, 49:14-21 addresses Lady Zion while appropriating language from chapter 40 and lament songs.[52] The appropriation of this terminology for Lady Zion serves several purposes rhetorically, but arguably the most significant would be the reversal of the lament language and the transfer from a corporate Jacob/Israel/servant in 49:1-13 to Lady Zion in 49:14-22.

The return of the community from Babylon assumed in 49–55 also means that most of the texts assume that YHWH has also returned to Jerusalem. For example, in 49:22 the imagery presupposes that YHWH is in Jerusalem when it depicts YHWH raising his hand as a signal to the nations to return Zion's children to her. Isaiah 51:3 assumes that YHWH will offer comfort in the devastated places of Zion, while 51:4 inverts the picture so that YHWH's instruction will go forth from Jerusalem. YHWH asks in 52:5, "Now, therefore, what am I doing *here?*" (NRSV). This locative adverb refers to Jerusalem. Explicitly, 52:8 describes YHWH's victorious return as seen by Jerusalem's sentinels, while 52:9-10 commands the people to break forth in joyful song because of YHWH's victory.

Those in exile, often called the *golah* group, have returned to the land and see themselves as the servant of YHWH, but they encounter resistance from those still in the land, a situation evident in portions of 50–53. For example, the children of Zion are confronted regarding their own sin for which their mother—a reference to Lady Zion—was put away (50:1). The servant has been attacked, but will be vindicated (50:6-7). Texts speak of the reproach of others, presumably other Judeans, but affirm that faith in YHWH will lead to long-lasting deliverance in contrast to the death that will face those who revile the righteous (51:7-8, 12).

26

This change in perspective has been interpreted variously in recent years. For some, chapters 49–55 represent a new composition(s) that reflects life back in the land.[53] For others, the changes still reflect the work of the prophet in Babylon who projects what life in the land will be like.[54] The latter appears less likely since these changes generally have to do with presuppositions embedded in the text, not explicit statements that indicate to the reader that these shifts represent a change in location.

The significance of the perspectival changes should not overshadow the prominence of Zion personified in 49–55. As already noted, Lady Zion plays a crucial role in these chapters, but the rhetorical changes that occur across these chapters relative to her character create a dynamic portrait as well. YHWH frequently speaks directly to Lady Zion, as indicated by second feminine singular verbs and pronouns (49:14-26; 51:17-23; 52:1-8; 54:1-14). These texts assume that punishment has ended and encourage Zion to recognize the change that has occurred. YHWH has returned and will restore Zion's stature and splendor as queen (49:23; 54:12-13), will punish those who torment her (51:22-23), and will call for the return of her children (49:19-26; 54:1-3).

Isaiah 56–66: Contention and Debate in the Second Temple Period

Consensus, Fractures, Models

Dramatic differences in content and setting in Isaiah 56–66 create the need for additional explanations. Since the time of Bernhard Duhm at the end of the nineteenth century, Isaiah 56–66 has been widely recognized as a series of texts that reflect later settings than those of 40–55. Despite this consensus, debate continues regarding the absolute dating of these texts and the process by which they came together. For much of the twentieth century, these chapters were often treated as the speeches of a single anonymous prophet, a figure who was given the name Trito-Isaiah. In the last thirty years, however, the center has shifted dramatically so that a smaller percentage of scholars attribute these chapters to a single prophetic figure. Instead, scholars have increasingly subdivided 56–66 into compositional blocks added sequentially so that it is no longer adequate to refer to these chapters as "Trito-Isaiah" without adding significant qualifiers to this term to avoid the impression that the texts come from a single hand.

Today, scholars draw upon a multitude of compositional models that presume rather diverse settings. A significant part of the problem for finding agreement on the time of compositions results from the lack of concrete historical references within these chapters. Recently, scholars have noted at least eight models that span a spectrum of hypotheses from unified to fragmentary to supplemental.[55]

For our purposes, these models can be understood in three categories, each of which exhibits significant variations. They approach Isaiah 56–66 as the work of a single author or compiler, as a series of core compositions updated by subsequent commentators, or as sources for socio-historical studies. Some overlap of these categories is unavoidable.

Work of a Single Author/Compiler. This first model treats chapters 56–66 largely as a single composition (either 1–66 or 40–66 or 56–66). Nevertheless, the reasons for this unified approach take at least five different forms. First, on one end of the spectrum, a few staunchly conservative scholars stress that only one named prophet appears in the book.[56] This group privileges the prophet named in Isaiah 1:1. A second group treating 56–66 as part of a larger, single composition of the book operates from a systematic skepticism about historical reconstruction.[57] These scholars prefer to downplay signs of heterogeneous material in favor of unifying themes or editorial techniques, which they claim get lost in the focus upon the diverse (and debated) origins of individual passages.

A third version of the single author category assumes that a unified 56–66 derives from the author of 40–55. In this approach, Deutero-Isaiah's hopes became more subdued over time as he met resistance when he returned to Jerusalem.[58] This group recognizes that 56–66 exhibits a distinct theological agenda when compared to chapters 40–55, but they assume a model of individual authorship can account for the less optimistic theology as a consequence of hostility faced by the anonymous exilic prophet, Deutero-Isaiah, upon his return to Jerusalem.

A fourth group attributes chapters 56–66 to a disciple of Deutero-Isaiah during the time of the rebuilding of the temple. This model also seeks to come to terms with the material in 56–66 that differs from the theological agenda of chapters 40–55, while at the same time recognizing a significant number of places that allude to or make use of chapters 1–55.[59] Critiques against this model focus upon the questionable term "disciple" because the term implies someone who studied at the feet of the master. These critics contend that 56–66 presupposes too lengthy a time span and too broad a spectrum of theological diversity to assume that these chapters were taught by a single prophet from the middle of the sixth century. Rather the tradents responsible for the latest material in these chapters almost certainly lived a century or more after Cyrus, king of Persia, who defeated Babylon in 539 BCE. Consequently, the term "disciple" could not refer to a follower who had direct contact with the teachings of the exilic prophet.

A fifth version of the single author approach recognizes literary dependence of passages in 56–66 not only on texts in Isaiah 40–55, but also on Malachi, Ezra-Nehemiah, and some postexilic psalms. Because of the recognized dates of these other texts, this group consequently dates Isaiah 56–66 to the fifth or fourth century.[60] Contrary to the single author approach, the majority of scholars dealing with compositional issues in Isaiah 56–66 today reject arguments for a single author because they fail to account for the numerous places in Isaiah where the plain sense of the text reflects settings from significantly divergent time periods with different theological agendas.

Redactional Compilations with Actualizations. The second category treats 56–66 as the work of multiple contributors. One group of these scholars denies an orderly design can be found within 56–66. They argue for a fragmentary collection that lacks a single editorial agenda.[61] This group has not won many adherents because, despite its complexity, most scholars find some kind of organizational cohesion even if that develops in stages.

A second group articulates redaction-critical hypotheses that build upon a core of Trito-Isaiah texts that are expanded with *Fortschreibungen*, a term that refers to redactional updates that comment upon an existing text, usually for the purpose of making texts relevant for a later time. Westermann attributes a foundational core to Trito-Isaiah (57:14-20; 60–62; 65:16b-25), to which a number of supplemental texts were added.[62] Vermeylen argues for six redactional stages stemming from the fifth into the third century BCE.[63] Koenen, Sekine, and Lau also suggest a Trito-Isaiah core, essentially located in 60–62, expanded by anywhere from two to six layers of editorial expansions.

A third group is similar to the second, but their redaction-critical proposals argue that the core texts do not reliably go back to a single author. Rather, they attribute these texts to the work of scribes who were interested in knitting together preexisting compositions in order to contribute to the developing book of Isaiah. Steck is perhaps the major proponent of this model.[64] This model allows scholars to deal with a diversity of texts that have their own independent structural propensities and theological agendas alongside texts that reflect an awareness of the immediate and larger contexts of the book.

Socio-historical Approaches. A number of recent works have focused upon sociological presuppositions of texts in 56–66, thereby seeking to avoid source-critical debates. Like the redaction-historical models, this model's proponents treat 56–66 as anonymous compositions but find the underlying unity in the communal setting and the tradition streams in which they were composed and collected. For Plöger and Hanson, the common setting reflects the conflicts of the early Persian period which pitted two groups against one another: the righteous and the wicked.[65] The righteous represent the eschatological visionaries whose roots went back to Deutero-Isaiah, but whose agendas were generally ignored and whose people persecuted. The wicked represent the hierocratic (i.e., priestly) power structures supported by the temple bureaucracy and personnel who increasingly push the visionaries to the margins of the religious establishment. Hanson identifies the visionaries as a group who had remained in the land, while the priestly group reflects the agendas of the returning exiles to reestablish the temple with the support of resources provided by the Persians.

A number of scholars have criticized Plöger and Hanson for creating a binary system of conflict that is too simplistically arranged in an either/or cast of heroes and villains. Schramm, in particular, questions how the visionaries could have produced the most influential of the prophetic books if they had been as marginalized as Hanson suggests.[66] Instead, Schramm notes that Isaiah scholarship has demonstrated the numerous ways that Isaiah 56–66 depends on a deep knowledge of 40–55, which, by most accounts, stems from a *golah* group. Such familiarity contradicts Hanson's claim that Isaiah 56–66 reflects the interests of an indigenous group that remained in the land.[67] Schramm argues that the group responsible for 56–66 had more in common with the Zadokites than Hanson realized and that the polemical words of Isaiah 56–66 would have been directed against those practicing "traditional preexilic Israelite religion."[68]

Beuken focuses upon the continuity between the servant of 40–55 and the servants in 56–66 as indicative of a continuing tradent group which saw themselves as heirs to the suffering servant.[69] He also recognizes that chapters 65–66 constitute a well-composed unit that wraps up thematic explorations of Trito-Isaiah (chapters 56–64), Deutero-Isaiah, and the book of Isaiah.[70] Beuken carefully analyzes the manner in which the servants are present in 56–66 on the basis of interrelated vocabulary even when they are not mentioned explicitly. Beuken understands these servants to be Zion's children. He recognizes that the servants stand over against another group in the text, but he does not speculate about specific identities in a concrete historical setting beyond these general acknowledgments.

Albertz reiterates that the identification of transmission groups is not merely a question of documenting literary techniques, but of recognizing that such groups coalesce around shared political or religious ideologies.[71] Albertz treats eschatological prophecy in the early Persian period as the result of official religion's complex response to the failed promises of Deutero-Isaiah that were not realized with the building of the temple.[72] Where exilic compromise had resulted in a revision of the Torah, the failure of prophetic promises to usher in a new age of prosperity led to three responses in prophetic literature of the early Persian period: (1) toning down the prophetic expectations with very general statements, (2) social marginalization of prophetic groups which did not acquiesce to hierarchical structures as the cult developed, and (3) an increasing level of eschatological expectations.[73]

In Isaiah 60–62, one finds evidence for all three responses. Albertz cites an example of the change in the concrete expectation of royalty compared to kingship language in Haggai (2:20-23). Instead, Isaiah 62:3 portrays Zion personified as a royal figure. Social marginalization is reflected in the loss of priestly status. Rather referring only to the priesthood, this text portrays the people as a whole in priestly terms (61:6; 62:12), and the people serve as priests for the nations, who come with many gifts. Increasing eschatological expectations also appear. Promises of economic prosperity still appear (60:5-9; 61:4-5), but their unrealized grandiosity pushes those promises further in the future.

The Compositional Blocks

Despite the wide variety of models used to explore Isaiah 56–66 noted above, significant points of agreement have begun to emerge. Primarily, when looking at Isaiah 56–66, it is best to divide these chapters into three or four larger units. In terms of relative chronologies, these compositional blocks include chapters 60–62; 56–59; and 63–66 (which is sometimes subdivided into 63–64 and 65–66).

Isaiah 60–62: Conversations with Lady Zion and the Servant

Largely considered the oldest block of material in 56–66, chapters 60–62 share the optimistic outlook for Zion that appears in 40–55, but the setting assumed in 60–62 has a later perspective. These chapters draw extensively upon imagery in Isaiah 40–55, and they cross-reference other parts of 60–62.[74]

Chapters 60 and 62 address Lady Zion directly (second feminine singular pronouns and verbs) while 61 addresses the people as a group. The speaker in these chapters frequently changes speech forms from speaking about YHWH in the third person (e.g., 62:2-3, 5-7, 9, 11-12) to YHWH speaking in the first person (62:1, 8). The majority of scholars date the core of these chapters to the first half of the fifth century before some of the issues became as contentious as they appear to be in Ezra and Nehemiah.

Isaiah 60 draws heavily from 49 and 51, while Isaiah 61 takes language from the Servant Songs of 42 and 49. The speaker in 61:1-3 claims the characteristics of the servant of YHWH with specific allusions to 42:1, 3, 6-7 and 49:8-9, along with a smattering of phrases that also appear in chapters 40–55. Rhetorically, the speaker in 61:1-3 claims the mantle of YHWH's servant to reiterate the goal of restoration in 61:4-6: to rebuild the land (61:4) so that foreigners will serve YHWH's people (62:5), who will in turn serve as priests to YHWH (62:6). In so doing, Isaiah 61 largely transfers the task of the servant to the people.

Isaiah 62 draws upon phrasing in chapters 40, 48, 49, 51, and 52, but adapts the language for a new situation. For example, Isaiah 62:4-5 alludes to 54:1-6 with its references to Zion as the woman who is the "abandoned one" (54:6; 62:4; 60:15), the "desolate one" (54:1; 62:4; 61:4), and the "married one" (62:4, which uses the feminine participle of *b'l* to refer to Zion as the spouse while 54:5 uses the masculine participle of *b'l* to refer to YHWH). By contrast, Zion's status has changed in 62:4-5 since she is no longer abandoned or desolate, and her husband takes delight in her. For the reader of chapter 62, then, these formulations once again provide both continuity and a sense that time has elapsed. Something has changed even though many of the promises have not been fulfilled.

Reference to the walls of Zion having sentinels and people going through her gates appear by the end of the block (62:6-10), though the block begins (60:10) with expectations that the walls and the gates will soon be built. Consequently, one sees some level of movement, spatial and chronological, in the arrangement of the three chapters. Notice should also be taken of the task of the sentinels. The text presumes that the sentinels' primary job is to petition YHWH to make good on his promises of Zion's glory (62:6b-7). The hope expressed in Isaiah 62 does not look for walls of silver and gold, as in Isaiah 60:2, 6, 9. Rather, it articulates promises of Zion glorified for its righteousness and beauty like a queen (62:2-3). It longs for the normal rhythms of life. The verses speak of a hope that the food raised will not be taken by foreigners, but will provide sustenance for those who raised it (62:8). It hopes that Zion's gates will be opened to a holy and redeemed people.

Isaiah 56:9–59:21: Blaming the People and Awaiting a Change

By the middle of the fifth century, despite the return to Judah and the rebuilding of the temple, all could see that these events did not result in the promised restoration of Zion as anticipated in the earlier portions of chapters 40–55 (+ 60–62). The people had returned, the temple had been rebuilt, but still Zion's economic status failed to live up to the utopian expectations pronounced in the preceding chapters.

The failure of those promises necessitated a revision of the message. In response, Isaiah 56–59 lays the blame on the people and ultimately claims that only those who turn away from the sins of Jacob will benefit from the arrival of the redeemer (*gōēl*) to restore justice and righteousness (see 59:15b-21). By placing these arguments before 60–62, those who composed 56:9–59:21 added accusations of wrongdoing and calls to repent to clarify that fulfillment of the restoration promises would happen only for those who turned their back on the sins of Jacob.

The sins of Jacob thus prevent the restoration from becoming fully realized. The sins articulated in these chapters represent a combination of the failure of cultic and ethical practices. The cultic practices condemned include the worship of idols as well as fasting and sabbath celebrations that have improper motivations.

Isaiah 57:6-13 presupposes the language of harlotry and adultery used in the preceding unit to confront the people (57:3), and in so doing it condemns Zion's idolatry. This trope appears frequently in prophetic poetry and here assumes that any gift offered to a power other than YHWH represents idolatry: a betrayal of the marital bond that should exist between YHWH and Lady Zion. Verses 6-13 cohere around the direct address to Lady Zion using second feminine singular forms. Isaiah 57:6 accuses her of pouring out drink offerings and grain offerings and seducing her illicit lovers (57:7-8). The next verses (9-10) delineate further seductive actions in metaphorical terms as the sending of oil and perfumes to the (foreign) king.[75] The imagery in these verses also hints at the condemnation of funerary cults.[76] The fact that the idolatry carries both political *and* religious dimensions should not be surprising as it features prominently in the prophetic texts that utilize the infidelity of a feminine persona to condemn the idolatry of Israel (Hos 2) or Jerusalem (Jer 2–4; Ezek 16; 23). What stands out starkly in Isaiah 57 is the change in attitude toward Lady Zion that this passage represents compared to the role she plays in Isaiah 40–55 (and 60–62). There she was a symbol of promise; here she is condemned for seducing a king. As with the condemnation of the people and the sentinels accused of tending to their own desires (56:9-12 and 57:1-3), the castigation of Lady Zion in 57:6-13 for idolatry reinforces a radical change of message that began in 56:9.

The condemnation of fasting and sabbath celebrations takes center stage in Isaiah 58. Isaiah 58:3-6 refers seven times to the fasting, which the people do in hopes of finding YHWH's righteous judgments (58:2). YHWH assumes that the people are "trampling the sabbath" in 58:13-14, as he proceeds to exhort them to change using a series of conditional statements (note the "if" in 58:13 and "then" at the beginning of 58:14). YHWH challenges their celebration because they dishonor it by "serving their own interests." They do not recognize the holiness of YHWH's day (58:13). Apart from the fact that these units (58:3-6 and 58:13-14) challenge the cultic behavior of the people, the rhetoric of the passages, as well as the intervening and surrounding material in 56:9–59:21, makes clear that the problem lies not in the practices of sabbath and fasting themselves but in the people's motivation and their ignoring of social justice and ethical behavior.

The ethical charges in these chapters lie at the heart of the arguments made by YHWH for what is wrong with their cultic observance. The questioning of the efficacy of fasting (58:3) does not condemn fasting as such. It condemns fasting because the practitioner thinks fasting will gain them something. The sarcastic tone drips from the rhetorical questions that open and close the challenge of the current situation: "Why do we humble ourselves when you don't notice?"

(58:3a) . . . Will you call this a fast, a day acceptable to YHWH?" (58:5bβ) In between (58:3b–5bα), YHWH answers these questions, essentially telling the people, "You serve your own interests on *your* fast day; your fasts lead to verbal and physical fights." No wonder YHWH pays no attention. Verses 6-8 flip the argument and describe the kind of fasting YHWH does desire: a day to confront injustice, to challenge oppression, to feed and shelter the poor and homeless.

The bulk of the remaining material in these chapters challenges the wicked who fail to exhibit justice and righteousness, but offers hope to the lowly and contrite: 57:14-21; 58:7-12; 59:1-15a. YHWH confronts those who exert power over the contrite of heart (57:15, 20-21). YHWH accuses the wicked of not practicing righteousness and justice except when they pretend to do so (58:2).

Even the last passage (59:15b-21), which pronounces YHWH's impending wrath in terms of vengeance against his enemies (59:18), concludes with a promise of a redeemer for Zion and Jacob "for those who turn from transgression" (59:20). Beyond these basic statements, however, it remains difficult to create a consensus for dating the chapters. The majority of recent scholars have tended to argue for some time in the mid-fifth century, though significant scholars argue strongly for the late sixth or early fifth century, and a number of scholars date these chapters to the late Persian or early Hellenistic period.[77] Berges's arguments for a date in the second half of the fifth century appear the most plausible at this point.

Isaiah 63–66: Victory over Edom and Calls to the Servants

Scholars have attained something of a consensus regarding both the chronological relationship between Isaiah 63–66 and the rest of the book and its function as the literary conclusion to Isaiah.[78] Nevertheless, disagreement continues concerning the absolute date. The largest percentage of scholars date these chapters to the middle of the fifth century BCE, but a significant number of scholars date the materials to the late sixth century, the Hellenistic period, or points in between.[79] A date sometime in the fourth century seems most likely. Most recent treatments recognize that chapters 63–66 draw upon formulations within Isaiah to conclude the book as a whole. These chapters develop a certain logical progression, while simultaneously creating thematic and allusive connections to other parts of Isaiah (especially to chapters 1, 2, 11, 34, and 56).

The units constituting these chapters stand out clearly: 63:1-6; 63:7–64:11; 65; 66. Isaiah 63:1-6 represents a theophany describing YHWH's victorious return from battle against Edom.[80] As a number of scholars have noted, this passage connects to Isaiah 34, a text that anticipated that YHWH's judgment against the nations would begin with punishment for Edom (see especially 34:5-15). Just as

Isaiah 34:5-6 anticipates a future event when YHWH's sword will be sated with blood in a battle with Edom/Bozrah, so 63:1-6 describes YHWH's return from a battle with Edom/Bozrah. The fact that the battle in 63:1-6 has just occurred (YHWH's garments are still stained with blood) serves both to fulfill the expectation of Isaiah 34 and to raise the expectation that YHWH's judgment against other nations will now ensue (thus continuing Isa 34:2-4).

Isaiah 63:7–64:11 stands apart as a literary unit on stylistic and form-critical grounds. Stylistically, the speaker's combination of the language of "I" and "we/us" (particularly at the beginning and end of the unit) distinguishes these verses from the preceding verses where the "I" who speaks is YHWH. In 63:7–64:11, the people recount a communal complaint and confession by moving from an introductory word of praise (64:7), to a historical reminiscence of the deliverance from Egypt (64:8-14a), to an extended petition for YHWH to change the current situation of suffering (63:14b–64:11).[81] Scholars have not agreed entirely upon whether or not these verses represent a preexisting composition that has been inserted here or whether the communal complaint was written for this position.[82] A number of scholars date this composition to the exilic period because it focuses upon the descriptions of punishment (64:12), which has left Jerusalem and the cities of Judah destroyed (64:10).[83] Those references notwithstanding, the emphasis in the petitions frequently has to do with the lengthy duration of the punishment. Given this emphasis, and given the fact that the walls of Jerusalem in the biblical narratives were not rebuilt until the time of Nehemiah (445 BCE), some seventy years after the initial construction of the Second Temple, one can easily imagine that this complaint language could have been relevant at virtually any point in the fifth century, and even beyond. Consider, for example, Nehemiah 9:32, which recounts a speech of Ezra in the time of Nehemiah that offers a very similar perspective. This prayer contains a lengthy rehearsal of Israel's history (Neh 9:9-31) followed by a petition to remove the current hardship that has lasted from "the time of the kings of Assyria until today" (Neh 9:32). This Nehemiah text portrays the mid- to late-fifth century as a time when Judah still suffered under YHWH's punishment.

Isaiah 65 changes speakers once again and functions as the divine response to 63:7–64:11. This response takes place in three rhetorical movements (65:1-7, 8-16, 17-25). In 65:1-7, YHWH affirms his willingness to respond, yet describes the actions of those currently provoking him through a series of abominable practices (sacrificing in their gardens, burning incense, spending the night in tombs, eating pork and other defiled food).

The second section (65:8-16) offers a promise to the servants that draws upon a number of other texts (both inside and outside Isaiah). Recent treatments of Isaiah have also cited this passage as the means by which the servant character in Isaiah 40–66 changes identity from the servant to the servants of YHWH. References to the servants appear seven times in these verses (65:8, 9, 13 [3 times], 14, 15). The promise consists of both positive and negative imagery in that the land will become fertile for the servants of YHWH, but YHWH will also annihilate those who have forsaken him (65:11-12).

The third section (65:17-25) continues the promise to the servants with a change in theme to YHWH's imminent creation of a new heaven and new earth (65:17). This promise focuses less on fecundity and more upon endurance, endurance of joy in Jerusalem (65:18-19), longevity of life (65:20, 22b), longevity of dwellings (65:21-22a), and permanence of the good life of enduring work and descendants (65:23-24). Here, the good life appears in a quote from the Deuteronomic blessing and curse (Deut 8:12; 28:30; see also Jer 29:5). Finally, the concluding verse of the chapter (65:25) concretizes the new heaven and earth with a citation of the peaceable kingdom from Isaiah 11:6, 9.

Isaiah 66 closes the book of Isaiah by returning to some of the themes that open Isaiah 1–2. The house of YHWH serves as a place where what one sacrifices is less significant than how one behaves toward the poor (66:2-4; cf. 1:11-17). Similarly, the reference to the temple as YHWH's resting place (66:1) immediately after a reference to the peaceable kingdom (65:25) offers a suggestive parallel to the peaceable kingdom (11:6-9) followed by the temple as YHWH's resting place (11:10). These and other allusions illustrate the function of chapter 66 as the conclusion to the book.[84] Relatedly, the openness to the inclusion of foreigners in 66:18-23 links the end of Isaiah 66 thematically with 56:1-8 (a passage increasingly associated with the same redactional layer as chapter 66) and 2:2-4.

In short, Isaiah 66 exhibits a keen awareness of the whole book of Isaiah, but adds a distinctive theological agenda as well. The need for repentance and fear of YHWH's word is presupposed (66:5) before YHWH's judgment comes (66:6). Distinctive, however, is the fact that Isaiah 66 anticipates the judgment that will come on the enemies of YHWH, both inside Judah and outside Judah. The wicked to be judged, thus, are not merely foreign nations, and foreigners will be among those saved on Zion (66:18-23). The group with whom the author of this chapter identifies (those trembling at YHWH's word in 66:5) has suffered at the hands of another group ("Your own people hate and reject you," 66:5). This antagonism reflects a division within the postexilic community that was particularly acute when it came to the attitudes toward foreigners and the role of Israel to the nations. The author of Isaiah 66 (probably along with 2:2-4 and 56:1-8) is open to the involvement of foreigners *who profess allegiance to YHWH* (66:19-20) and even includes the possibility they will serve in the temple (56:3-6; 66:21).

Some have also noted that the latest work on Isaiah also brought about a number of thematic parallels to other parts of the prophetic canon. Above all, these include the parallel themes of Isaiah 66 and Zechariah 14.[85] By the latest stage of the editorial work, Isaiah's role as a compendium of prophecy from the Assyrian to the Persian period served to help structure the book and its topoi. Like the Book of the Twelve, this long duration of the prophetic encounter between YHWH and YHWH's people structures the book as a whole and helps provide the context by which it is to be understood. Repeatedly, it forces the reader to reorient to changing settings. Isaiah 32–35 looks beyond the eighth-century events dealt with in 28–31, but 36–39 forces the reader back to the time of Hezekiah, before the remainder of the book requires the reader to envision the return from Babylon (40–48) and Zion's restoration (49–55) before exploring the resistance encountered by YHWH's servants once back in the land. Nevertheless, Isaiah conveys a sense of promise for the future for "the poor, the contrite in spirit, and the one who trembles at my word" (66:2).

Discussion Questions

1. What is the "Isaiah Memoir" and how does it function in Isaiah 4–12?

2. How do the collections and compositions in Isaiah 1–12 introduce the themes of Isaiah in relationship to the Syro-Ephraimite War and its aftermath?

3. What role does Isaiah 24–27 play for the reader of the book?

4. Describe the four vignettes in chapters 36–39 and their relationship to 2 Kings 18–20, to 2 Chronicles 29–32, and to the early portions of Isaiah dealing with Hezekiah.

5. Explain the different perspectives of Isaiah 40–48 and 49–55.

6. Describe the relationship of the cult and ethics in Isaiah 56–66.

Jeremiah

Historical Backdrop

The books of Jeremiah and Ezekiel cannot be understood without appreciating the dramatic changes happening in Mesopotamia and Egypt, as well as Judah. Whereas Isaiah and the Twelve focus more extensively upon the rise and fall of Assyria, Jeremiah and Ezekiel deal with the competing powers of Babylon and Egypt. If Isaiah and the Twelve largely skip over the events of Jerusalem's destruction and its exiles, Jeremiah devotes considerable space to assessing the events leading up to Jerusalem's first deportation (597 BCE), its destruction (587 BCE), and the aftermath from the perspective of those who remained in Judah. By contrast, Ezekiel begins its message in the midst of the first deportation, but the prophetic action takes place among communities deported to Babylon. To understand the books of Jeremiah and Ezekiel, therefore, one needs a certain amount of information regarding the external and internal political situation at the end of the seventh and beginning of the sixth centuries BCE.

Competing Regional Powers: Assyria, Babylon, Egypt, Others

The events narrated in the book of Jeremiah concerning the life of the prophet reflect knowledge about and interpretation of events from the last quarter of the seventh century BCE and the first two decades of the sixth century (approximately 626–582 BCE). The political and social events taking place in Judah and beyond during this period significantly reshaped the power dynamics of the region. To put these events in context, one needs to understand some of the large-scale

39

political movements of the previous century. Three large powers, Assyria, Babylon, and Egypt, attempted to control the region with varying degrees of success, but each in its own way set in motion events that had a profound effect upon the political and religious life of Judah.

Assyrian Expansion and Decline

The end of the eighth century saw the rise of Assyria as the first truly regional superpower controlling land from Mesopotamia to the Mediterranean. Assyrian expansion down the Mediterranean coast and into Egypt continued well into the seventh century, culminating in the capture of Thebes in 663 BCE. Thebes essentially functioned as the capital of Egypt at the time, and its capture gave Assyria unbridled access to the entire eastern seaboard of the Mediterranean and passageway up the Nile River. Gaining power and keeping it, however, proved to be two very different tasks. Within forty years, Assyrian control of Egypt was no longer a political reality, though the two remained allied rather closely. Egypt controlled its own borders and most of the southern trade routes from the Mediterranean to the Red Sea. Assyria had overstepped its ability to control the territory directly. It also began suffering internally as warring factions and rival claims to territory weakened its ability to collect taxes, to wage war, and to keep its many people groups under control. In 627, the death of the Assyrian monarch Ashurbanipal exacerbated these tensions, and a prolonged civil war created a political vacuum that encouraged several nations (ultimately including Judah) to seek greater autonomy from Assyrian hegemony. These events weakened Assyria, and in 612 BCE the Babylonians conquered the Assyrian capital, Nineveh.

Babylonian Usurpation

In the last quarter of the seventh century BCE, following the death of Ashurbanipal, Babylon sought to fill the power vacuum. The king of Babylon led a revolt against Assyria that succeeded in destroying the last vestiges of Assyria as a regional power. Following Nineveh's destruction, Babylon moved to solidify its holdings in Mesopotamia, but it also had to deal with lingering pockets of resistance from the former Assyrian monarch. Not surprisingly, many of the territories in the outlying western regions of the former Assyrian state made moves to create, or reestablish, their own autonomous nations. These actions put Babylon on a collision course with Egypt as well as smaller countries that had their own ambitions, such as Philistia, Judah, Phoenicia, and Syria, all of whom sought independence. Babylon, as the victorious power, felt entitled to lay claim to the territories formerly controlled by Assyria. Many of these territories, however, which had suffered economically while paying high taxes to Assyria, would resist attempts by Babylon to impose tribute on them. As these territories revolted, Babylon would launch military campaigns to bring them under control. In addition to Babylonian incursion, Egyptian influence had grown in the region in the decades leading up to Nineveh's destruction, and Egypt continued to use its power to resist Babylon's goal of taking Egypt.

Egyptian Defense and Intrigue

In the decades prior to Nineveh's destruction in 612 BCE, Egypt served as a loyal ally to Assyria. Assyria, in turn, provided Egypt with more control of the trade routes leading from the Red Sea to the Mediterranean. As war between Assyria and Babylon weakened Assyria after the death of Ashurbanipal in 627, Egypt also sought to control the eastern Mediterranean seaboard as far north as Syria. After the fall of Nineveh in 612 BCE, Egypt continued to serve the interests of the Assyrian king who had fled the Babylonians. In 609, the Egyptian pharaoh Neco II killed King Josiah of Judah (2 Kgs 23:29), presumably because Neco considered Josiah a threat to Egyptian interests in the region. Almost immediately, Egypt inserted itself into Judean politics by installing one of Josiah's sons, Jehoiakim, on the throne in Jerusalem in place of Josiah's youngest son, Jehoahaz, who had reigned for three months after his father's death. Babylon continued to seek control of the eastern Mediterranean seaboard, until 605 at the battle of Carchemish (in Syria), when Nebuchadnezzar II of Babylon defeated Egypt. This defeat forced Egypt to retreat to its own territory, where it successfully maintained a policy of retrenchment that kept Babylon from capturing Egypt as Assyria had done. Even though Nebuchadnezzar periodically tried to capture Egypt, he was never able to do so. Egypt's policies toward the Levant region were designed to use those countries as buffers against Babylon. By encouraging dissatisfaction with Babylonian rule, Egypt sought to weaken Babylon's ability to mount an effective campaign against its territory.

In summary, the downfall of Assyria and the rise of Babylon in the East coincided with the economic and military rise of Egypt—first as an ally to Assyria and then on its own. These two larger powers subsequently sought political and economic control of the Mediterranean seaboard and surrounding countries like Judah in order to solidify control of trade routes to and from the Mediterranean. These competing ambitions created politically unstable conditions for the entire region between Egypt and Babylon in the last decade of the seventh century and the first two decades of the sixth. Jeremiah was active as a prophet during much of this time.

Judah's Neighbors

Judah's neighbors faced the same trials as Judah and were every bit as vulnerable to being caught in the vise between the two larger powers of Egypt and Babylon. They did not all respond the same way. The countries surrounding Judah included Philistia, Phoenicia, Ammon, Moab, and Edom. According to Jeremiah 27:3, representatives of these powers (excluding Philistia) met in 593 in Jerusalem in hopes of coming to some kind of unified strategy to protect themselves from Babylonian incursions. The text does not say whether they reached an agreement, but subsequent events suggest they did not. Philistia rebelled against Babylon in 604, causing Babylon to retaliate and take over its territory and kill or exile the kings of Ashdod, Ashkelon, Ekron, and Gaza. Babylon laid siege to Tyre, the main city of Phoenicia, as well. The siege began around 585 and lasted thirteen years. Even though Babylon did not succeed in destroying Tyre, Phoenicia was effectively isolated. Moab and Ammon appear to have been slower to rebel, but shortly after Jerusalem was destroyed a group of armed Ammonites murdered the Judean governor, Gedaliah, who had been appointed by Babylon after it conquered Jerusalem. The Babylonians subdued the Ammonites and the Moabites according to Josephus (*Ant.* 10.181–183). By contrast, it appears from several texts that Edom may have allied itself with Babylon and even participated in the overthrow of Jerusalem (cf. Obad 7, 10–14; Lam 4:21-22). Edom thus appears to have escaped military invasion by Babylon by aligning itself politically with the Babylonians, but it would face attacks from Arab tribes beginning in the sixth century that would ultimately force them out of their traditional territory and into land vacated in southern Judah.

Judean Kings in the Seventh and Sixth Centuries BCE

From Hezekiah to Manasseh: A Change of Focus

Whereas the Judean king Hezekiah revolted against his Assyrian overlords in 701, most scholars recognize that Jerusalem's deliverance probably involved payment of tribute to Sennacherib and a reduced role for Judah's monarch. When Hezekiah died a few years later, his youngest son and successor, Manasseh (696–641 BCE), developed a closer relationship with the Assyrians. Manasseh's genius appears to have been his ability to adapt to Assyrian demands. He provided soldiers from Judah to the Assyrians in Egypt and elsewhere, and he also incorporated Assyrian religious practices more overtly into Yahwistic worship at the temple. His lengthy reign came to an end as Assyrian power was beginning to wane and Egypt's power was rising.

From Manasseh to Josiah: A Return to Hezekiah's Vision?

Manasseh's son, Amon, was assassinated in an internal coup two years after he took the throne. The perpetrators are called "the servants of Amon" in 2 Kings 21:23, but the "people of the land" killed those responsible and placed his eight-year-old son Josiah on the throne (2 Kgs 21:24). The implications of this change prove significant. As a young child, Josiah had to be mentored. A co-regent is not named in Kings, but Shaphan the scribe communicated directly with the priests in the temple in Josiah's eighteenth year as king (2 Kgs 22:3), suggesting that a group of elite scribes, priests, and landholders joined forces to prepare Josiah for leadership.[1]

Kings and Chronicles depict Josiah as a political and religious reformer. The religious reforms begin in the eighteenth year of his reign (622 BCE), when Josiah was only 26 (2 Kgs 22:3; cf. 22:1). While religious reforms likely occurred under Josiah's kingship, the Kings account of the finding of the book of the covenant has also been colored with theological drama (a group of priests find the book of the covenant while cleaning the temple). Scholarship has long equated this book of the covenant with some form of the book of Deuteronomy. The priests take the scroll to the king and read it in his presence (2 Kgs 22:10). Josiah then tears his clothes (a sign of penitence) and sends a delegation of priests, scribes, and government functionaries to consult with the prophetess Huldah concerning how to avoid YHWH's wrath, since the book of the covenant essentially formed an indictment against the current religious practices (2 Kgs 22:11-14). Huldah predicts disaster for the people, but Josiah makes drastic changes. He commits to following the covenant (23:1-3), then destroys all the vessels used for the worship of other gods in YHWH's temple (22:4, 6-7), removes government support for non-Yahwistic priests that previous kings had provided (22:5), destroys the religious shrines in towns outside Jerusalem, and eliminates various cultic paraphernalia previous kings had installed (23:8-15). According to the Kings account, Josiah also killed priests and other functionaries who performed rituals at the high places or performed other idolatrous acts (23:20, 24).

These religious reforms had political implications as well. By eliminating public shrines from Judah (and Bethel, according to 23:15) and purifying the Jerusalem temple and its personnel, Josiah also returned to a more centralized form of government that appears to have been the goal of Hezekiah. In the ancient world, temples were not only religious establishments, temples were also involved in the collection of taxes.[2]

From Josiah to Jerusalem's Destruction: Power, Intrigue, and Rebellion

Josiah likely benefitted from Assyria's loss of power during the 620s, since there does not appear to have been any Assyrian resistance to his reforms or his incursions into the Ephraimite territories (the central region of the former Northern Kingdom). In 612, Nineveh (the capital of Assyria) fell to Babylon. Babylon and Egypt then fought for control of the region. In 609, the Egyptian pharaoh, Neco II, killed Josiah of Judah at Megiddo in northern Israel (2 Kgs 23:28). No reasons are stated, but either Josiah confronted Neco directly, or Neco considered Josiah a threat to his own domination of the region. Josiah's son Jehoahaz was placed upon the throne by those in Jerusalem at Josiah's death, but Neco removed Jehoahaz (and exiled him to Egypt), then put Jehoiakim in his place. Jehoiakim was also Josiah's son. However, with the battle of Carchemish in Syria (in 605), Babylon established control over the region, though they never succeeded in taking control of Egypt as Assyria had done.

Jehoiakim had been appointed by the Egyptian pharaoh, but he initially acquiesced to Babylon's control after 605 until he thought he could stop paying tribute not long after a new king in Babylon took over. Not surprisingly, Jehoiakim's rebellion (three years after Nebuchadnezzar became king of Babylon) resulted in a siege of Jerusalem. After three months of siege, Jehoiakim died. His son Jehoiachin surrendered to Nebuchadnezzar and was exiled to Babylon along with a significant part of the elite of Judah (priests, scribes, and royal officials). The deported population included a priest named Ezekiel who would take on the role of prophet to the exiles in Chebar beginning in the fifth year of exile (Ezek 1:2). In Jerusalem, Nebuchadnezzar installed Zedekiah—a brother of Josiah—on the throne in 597, presumably because he considered him loyal to Nebuchadnezzar himself. By 593, however, Zedekiah was also plotting ways to get out from under Babylonian control. When he did revolt in 588, Nebuchadnezzar's response was swift and violent. He laid siege to Jerusalem, a siege that lasted eighteen months before Nebuchadnezzar breached the city wall and destroyed Jerusalem and the temple (2 Kgs 25:1-12). Zedekiah was caught trying to flee. His sons were slaughtered in front of him, and his eyes were gouged out, so that the death of his sons was the last thing he saw before he was bound and taken to Babylon in chains (2 Kgs 25:7). The temple treasures were taken to Babylon before the temple itself was destroyed (2 Kgs 25:14-17).

Neither Jehoiakim nor Zedekiah could ever shake free of foreign rule. Though both came from the house of David, both were placed on the throne by foreigners (Jehoiakim by Egypt and Zedekiah by Babylon), and both instigated failed rebellions against Babylon. These last decades of the seventh century saw the rise and fall of empires, and hope for a strong, independent Judah—a hope that was dashed with the death of Josiah. This political situation shapes much of Jeremiah's confrontations with kings. While Jeremiah grieves the passing of Josiah (22:10), he has little positive to say for Jehoahaz, Jehoiakim, Jehoiachin, or Zedekiah.

Introductory Issues for the Book of Jeremiah

The Prophet and the Book

Any discussion of the authorship of the book of Jeremiah involves a complex interplay of several factors, including the portrait of the prophet himself, Jeremiah's relationship with the scribe Baruch (and others who come to his aid), and decisions regarding the relationship of the MT (Masoretic text) version of Jeremiah compared to the Greek tradition.

The prophetic figure of Jeremiah plays a much more prominent role in the book than does the prophetic figure in Isaiah or any of the Twelve except Jonah, but his character reflects the literary qualities of those who transmitted and edited the sayings, sermons, and narratives about him. Additionally, while we know more about Jeremiah than any other prophet, we know little about him. We know that he came from Anathoth, three miles northeast of Jerusalem. We are told that Jeremiah's father was a priest in Anathoth (Jer 1:1), a priestly lineage that traced its ancestry back to Eli (1 Kgs 2:26-27), but which had been expelled from temple service in Jerusalem under Solomon.

Jeremiah's relationship to Judah's elite is decidedly complex, yet he remains a central figure with whom they have to deal. Jeremiah is almost always portrayed as adversarial toward Judah's kings because of their policies. Despite this conflict, he was enough of an insider that the kings knew him, and Zedekiah even sought his help (see Jer 37:1-3; 17-21; 38:14-28). Jeremiah's relationship to the powerful families of Anathoth was no more positive than his relationship to Judah's kings since Jeremiah was the object of threats from Anathoth's leaders (e.g., 11:21-23; 12:6-7).

Jeremiah did, however, have the trust of one influential scribal family that was a key political player in Jerusalem's power structure. The family of Shaphan played an intricate role in the politics of Jerusalem as scribes and political consultants from the time of Josiah through Gedaliah. Shaphan had been present when the book of the covenant was found in the reign of Josiah and had been part of the delegation that consulted Huldah regarding YHWH's message to the king (2 Kgs 22:14). The book of Jeremiah mentions at least three sons of Shaphan who play roles in the narratives regarding Jeremiah's dealings with various Judean kings: Ahikam (26:24), Elasah (29:3), and Gemariah (36:10-12). In addition, Shaphan's grandson Gedaliah served as governor of Judah in Mizpah until he was assassinated (39:14; 40:5, 9, 11; 41:2; 43:6).

45

Jeremiah is portrayed as having deep internal struggles concerning the message he was commissioned to deliver, though some question whether these "confessions" represent the actual words or a literary portrayal of the prophet. Relatedly, the physical suffering of the prophet cannot be ignored in the stories regarding his imprisonment when he was thrown into the bottom of a muddy cistern without food or water.

For all of this information regarding the prophet Jeremiah, the models developed by critical scholarship for understanding the book as we have it do not assume that Jeremiah was the author of the scroll. For one thing, the book of Jeremiah recounts a number of events from the life of the prophet, most of which are located in chapters 26–52, and these narratives refer to Jeremiah in the third person, though some contain dialogue in which the character Jeremiah speaks in the first person. Relatedly, one of these narratives recounts the story of the first scroll of Jeremiah as a work that the prophet dictated to the scribe Baruch (36:1-32). According to this narrative, King Jehoiakim burned Jeremiah's scroll as it was read to him, creating the need to reproduce the scroll that had been destroyed (36:22-32). A great deal of time and energy has been spent trying to isolate the contents of this first scroll, but such endeavors have not succeeded. The fact that this account takes place in the fourth year of Jehoiakim (605 BCE) eliminates a great deal of the book, since most of the superscriptions involving the prophetic narratives in chapters 26–52 date the events they introduce after 605 BCE. In addition, whereas the book ultimately reports that Jeremiah was taken to Egypt (largely against his will) in the aftermath of Gedaliah's assassination (chapters 42–43), evidence suggests that those responsible for creating the book (perhaps with the help of the scribal family of Shaphan) remained in the land and continued to gather traditions regarding Jeremiah.

Baruch the scribe played an active role in helping Jeremiah record his speeches (Jer 32:11-16; 36; 43:1-7; 45:1-5). These narratives state that Baruch was taken to Egypt with Jeremiah (43:6), where he presumably continued to transmit correspondence from the prophet (43:8–44:30 contain material set in Egypt). Yet Baruch was only part of the scribal alliance that tried to persuade Judah's leadership to acquiesce to Babylonian demands. At some point, traditions about the prophet were recorded and preserved in these circles. Smaller collections were gathered together and ultimately linked with one another, though with a relatively loose structure. Later shapers of the Jeremiah tradition continued to update the contents, as evidenced by the continuing growth of the Hebrew tradition in comparison to the Greek tradition (see the discussion of the unity of Jeremiah below).

Debates continue regarding where the Jeremiah scroll was compiled, and these discussions also relate to disagreements regarding the geographical location of work on the Deuteronomistic History. The book of Jeremiah shares characteristics with the Deuteronomistic accounts in Kings. These verbal and literary similarities suggest a sustained relationship, but Jeremiah's theological perspective differs on some issues.[3] Several scholars locate the composition of Jeremiah in Babylon, but Mizpah seems a more likely location for the preservation of the largest percentage of smaller collections. While some passages address the issue of those living in Babylon, the orientation and general tone of these passages concern the role of that group *in the land* after a period of exile. One group of returnees included Zerubbabel, the grandson of Jehoiachin who was appointed as governor. Several texts in Jeremiah privilege this group as the portion of YHWH's people whom YHWH wants to use to resettle the land.[4]

Increasingly, evidence from recent archaeological work suggests that the administrative center of Mizpah—which Jeremiah 40–43 assumes as the place of Gedaliah's administration after Jerusalem's destruction—remained the administrative center of Judah (along with Samaria) during the time of Babylonian control. Gradually, Ramat Raḥel replaced Mizpah as the main administrative center in the Persian period before the temple complex grew to the point it could sustain the administrative functions.[5] That being said, the evidence suggests that the Jeremiah traditions grew in stages (see "Sources and the Final Form" below). Several specific texts indicate the presence of these smaller collections when they refer to documents or smaller collections of the words of Jeremiah.[6]

Dates of Composition

Superscriptions with dates tied to the reigning monarch appear in quite a number of the prophetic narratives. These stories do not, however, appear in chronological order. In addition, chapters 39, 40–44, and 52 contain narrative material that parallels narratives in Kings. The narratives in Jeremiah 39 and 52 contain parallel accounts of the destruction of Jerusalem, and each of these bears a striking resemblance to the material in 2 Kings 25. Neither of these accounts in Jeremiah is identical to 2 Kings 25, but the wording is too similar to suggest an entirely independent transmission. Portions of chapters 40–41 contain a parallel account of the assassination of Gedaliah that also appears in 2 Kings 25, but the account is expanded with additional material that focuses upon Jeremiah (e.g., 42:7-22). Gedaliah's assassination occurred sometime after Jerusalem's destruction, and fearing Babylonian reprisals, a contingent of refugees fled to Egypt, taking Jeremiah and Baruch.[7] The book of Kings cannot have been completed prior to 560 BCE since the end of 2 Kings 25 refers to the release of Jehoiachin thirty-seven years after being deported to Babylon. The fact that the parallel account in Jeremiah 52 also contains this reference to Jehoiachin's release means that Jeremiah cannot have been completed prior to the mid-sixth century BCE.

Yet, further considerations suggest that Jeremiah was not completed in the form we have it until much later. Most significantly in this respect, the book of Jeremiah is considerably longer in the Hebrew tradition than in the Greek tradition, and the relationship of these two recensions of Jeremiah has implications for understanding the growth of the book.

Unity

Questions about the unity of Jeremiah are complicated by its divergent recensions (represented by the Masoretic Text [MT] and the Septuagint [LXX]), the underlying sources from which it draws, and its lack of a governing structure. These factors create the impression of Jeremiah as an anthology that is updated over time. Its unity derives more from rough thematic groupings than it does from a clear and cogent design for the scroll.

Two distinct but interrelated textual traditions exist for Jeremiah. The Greek version of Jeremiah translates a Hebrew *Vorlage* (or prior version of the text) that scholars estimate is roughly one-seventh to one-eighth shorter than the MT, which serves as the base text for most English translations. With a few notable exceptions in recent years, the most common explanation for these variations is that the MT represents a text tradition that continued to develop (primarily through insertions, redactional updates, and rearrangements of the book's contents). Both versions reflect ancient texts. The LXX was likely translated in the third century BCE and mirrors the shorter text. Qumran fragments reflecting both versions exist in Hebrew, with two of these (4QJer[b] and 4QJer[d]) reflecting a Hebrew text that aligns closely with the content of the Greek.[8] The differences between the Greek *Vorlage* and MT appear throughout the chapters and generally include additional material that ranges in size from partial verses to entire paragraphs. The additional material in the MT generally, though not always, functions as a commentary on the existing text that adds information or demonstrates further reflection.[9]

To illustrate the MT expansions, consider two examples: Jeremiah 7:1-2a and the changes to the oracles against the nations (OAN) in chapters 46–51 (which appear after 25:13 in the LXX). Jeremiah 7 contains a notable line which presumes that the prophet is standing in the temple precincts when he condemns those who argue that YHWH's judgment will not come against Jerusalem because YHWH's temple is present. The passage challenges this idea: "Do not trust in these deceptive words: 'This is the temple of YHWH, the temple of YHWH, the temple of YHWH'" (7:4). Verses 1-2a do not appear in the LXX: "The word that came to Jeremiah from YHWH, saying: 'Stand in the gate of YHWH's house and proclaim this word there.'" There is nothing theologically objectionable that would raise the likelihood that someone removed these words from the Hebrew *Vorlage* used to translate the LXX. Rather, these words appear to expand the earlier text and are here inserted for the reader's benefit. The speech in 7:2b-4 takes place at the temple ("*This* is the temple of YHWH"). Yet, this location differs from the speech beginning in 6:16 where the prophet is commanded to "stand in the crossroad" outside the city. An editor has thus inserted a new heading with 7:1 to mark the beginning of a new speech, and that editor takes the command from 6:16 as the model to provide 7:2a with the same command at a different location: "Stand in the gate of YHWH's house and proclaim this word there."

Second, the OAN in 46–51 appear after 25:13 in the LXX, a place where they are thematically at home. The MT alters these six chapters, and the changes involve relocation, resequencing, and reframing of the individual oracles.

Relocation. These chapters were moved as a block to their current location (chapters 46–51), nearly at the end of the scroll. When the chapters were moved, Jeremiah 25:14 was added, which basically summarizes the message of the oracles against the nations: "For many nations and great kings will moreover enslave them, but I will repay them according to their works and the deeds of their hands." This verse anticipates Judah's punishment and YHWH's retribution against the nations (or at least Babylon as a representative of those nations), which also provides a transition to the same two thematic emphases in the rest of chapter 25, which lists numerous nations whom YHWH will punish (25:19-26, 30-38) after first punishing Jerusalem (25:15-18, 27-29).

Resequencing. The order in which the nations appear in chapters 46–51 was also changed. In the earlier order reflected in the LXX, the arrangement of the nations appears random. By contrast, the nations in the MT sequence appear to move in a geographic arc that runs from Egypt to Babylon.[10]

Reframing. In all likelihood, the Hebrew text that served as the basis for the LXX translation reflects a generally earlier form of the corpus that circulated outside Jerusalem (perhaps among the Jewish community in Egypt and elsewhere), while the MT version continued to receive updates (probably from the hands of temple scribes and scholars who maintained the prophetic scrolls). These two texts may have originally diverged in the fourth century, suggesting that the growth of the MT version continued in Jerusalem well into the Persian period. Additional scrolls may also have existed, but these two are the most widely attested. At the same time, the shorter version that served as the *Vorlage* for the LXX also provides evidence that it periodically received its own additions. Consequently, the two versions originally derive from a common source and offer tantalizing glimpses into the history of the text, but these must be evaluated on a case-by-case basis. Reconstruction of the earliest form of the book remains a complicated endeavor. The Hebrew *Vorlage* of the LXX already shows many of the characteristics of the

book and represents a fairly advanced stage of the collection process. Nevertheless, the two recensions diverged, and the longer version (reflected in the MT)
ultimately gained priority for temple readers.

Sources and the Final Form

The book of Jeremiah draws upon preexisting sources to a considerable degree, presumably because these sources were already in some way associated with
the prophet. One need only look to the prophetic narratives in chapters 26–45 to
see how these sources became integrated into the scroll. No fewer than thirteen
of these narratives begin with their own introduction that dates the vignette to
a particular time in the life of the prophet.[11] Unlike Ezekiel, however, those who
collected these stories show no interest in arranging them in chronological order,
meaning that even though these stories about Jeremiah dominate the second half
of the book, recounting a story in narrative sequence was not the primary motivation for the compilers.

In the history of Jeremiah research, the classification by Duhm and Mowinckel of four source documents (Sources A–D) continues to influence the ways
in which one addresses the compositional elements of the book.[12] Source A
(which appears within chapters 1–25) is a collection (or better, collections) that
included sayings of the prophet (Jer 2; 4–6; 21–23; etc.) and first-person narrative accounts (Jer 1; 13; 18; 24; 25:15-26).[13] Source B represents third person
narrative accounts *about* Jeremiah. These accounts appear mostly—but not exclusively—in the second half of the book, and they tend to focus on Jeremiah's
suffering at the hands of government officials (Jer 19:1–20:6; 26–29; 36–44; 45;
51:59-64). Source C consists of prose accounts that have been revised in light
of Deuteronomistic thought and vocabulary.[14] Source D consists of the oracles
against the nations in chapters 46–51.

Recent scholarship has largely rejected the idea that this material existed as
separate written collections in these forms.[15] Nevertheless, these categories remain relevant as functional classifications rather than physical specimens. Even
scholars who do not speak of Mowinckel's sources often continue to use his terminology to classify the material in the book. Yet interest in how the book came
to be has not ceased. Recent redactional studies have forged new ground, though
without providing a clear consensus.

Redactional Models

Redactional models vary widely for the book of Jeremiah. Brief summaries
of the models of Pohlmann, Schmidt, and Allen demonstrate the range of differ-

ences. Pohlmann has won quite a number of followers by isolating texts across Jeremiah that seek to privilege those returning from the Babylonian *golah* (exile) as the only legitimate heirs to YHWH's salvific plan for Israel.[16] He analyzes a series of texts that give preference to exiles who returned from Babylon.[17] Moreover, he demonstrates that the key texts promoting the interests of these exiles generally interrupt the literary context and thus represent a major redactional expansion of the book, which he dates to the fourth century. Pohlmann's work thus offers a model to make sense of texts that show a special concern for those who returned from Babylon well after the life of the prophet. As a result, the number of scholars has increased who see the development of the book lasting well into the Persian period. His fourth-century dating has not, however, gone unquestioned.[18]

Schmidt does not attempt to isolate a systematic outline of the process because he does not find a methodologically convincing set of criteria that would tip the scales toward a consensus.[19] He does, however, outline some of the processes he believes shaped the book over time. Schmidt (like Pohlmann) rejects the A and B sources of Duhm and Mowinckel by denying that these were separate written sources. He thinks that one has to analyze how oral transmission lead to small written compositions and collections, and the extent to which later expansions updated the individual speeches. Additionally, the recollection and creation of scenes for these speeches also shaped the collections. Recollections of individual speeches (in first and third person forms) and narratives have to be evaluated to identify the core speeches over against evidence of later perspectives. Additionally, one should determine how these speeches display awareness of and function within the current literary context. He sees chapters 1, 2–6, 8–10, and 11–20 as examples of smaller collections that were made into compositions by combining individual sayings and speeches that may originally have come from different settings.[20] For Schmidt, the links between the various parts show a protracted literary development. It grew as the Jeremiah-Deuteronomist redaction (JerD) combined the various traditions by creating a "string of superscriptions" that "arrange the book."[21] For Schmidt, the JerD redaction represents the major editorial work that shaped the book, but he emphasizes it was *not* the work of a *single* redactor.

For Schmidt, these materials grew gradually in the context of a JerD school. Hence the individual compositions show a wide range of perspectives on the prophet, his suffering, and specific rationale for what caused the catastrophe. Schmidt's gradual accretion model also accounts for the lack of a uniform structure. He lists at least five additional factors that help account for the shape of the book: (1) generalized additions with a wisdom character;[22] (2) expansions from worship services;[23] (3) post-Deuteronomistic additions;[24] (4) the oracles against the nations (MT 46–51), which seem to be their own collection; and (5) the variations that are reflected in many of the MT expansions over against the LXX *Vorlage*.

Leslie Allen discusses the development of Jeremiah as primarily an exilic work that was "intended for the Babylonian exiles."[25] Allen starts from the existence of the longer and shorter versions of Jeremiah, but he argues that both these versions already attest the major redactional work in the book that provided the "overall structure, superscriptions, assignment of historical settings, and arrangement of material."[26] In this respect, he describes things very closely to the model of Schmidt, but the differences come in the time allotted for the production of the book. One gets a clear sense that Schmidt sees this process taking most of the Persian period, but Allen thinks that the shorter version of Jeremiah was largely completed before the fall of Babylon, while the longer version arose "not long afterward," though he does recognize some texts (e.g., 33:14-26) clearly reflect a postexilic setting in Judah.[27] It seems unlikely that the original compilation of the book took place in Babylon or that the concern for the reincorporation of the Babylonian refugees should be situated so early.

The book of Jeremiah represents a thematically arranged anthology. At some point (or points), independent compositions and narratives about the prophet were combined into smaller collections before they were joined to one another. At a relatively late stage of the collection process, the oracles against the nations were moved, resequenced, and updated with a more eschatological tone. Other updates continued, especially in the version of Jeremiah that eventually became the MT. Sometimes, these updates evince aids to the reader based upon the continuing reading and rereading of the text (see discussion of Jer 7:1-2a). Sometimes, the updates provide additional information from a later time period (as in the Egypt oracle of 46:25b-26, discussed below). Yet, the updates do not often change the central focus of Jeremiah on the events leading up to Jerusalem's destruction and its immediate aftermath. Even in those places where material in Jeremiah expresses hope for the future (e.g., the so-called book of consolation in chapters 30–33), the text still presumes that punishment must come before hope can be realized. In this sense, even the later additions assume a "Jeremianic" setting. Those tradents who updated the prophet's message did so with a conviction that they were extending the words of Jeremiah himself. This process is mirrored in the story of Jehoiakim's burning of Jeremiah's first scroll:

> [27] Now, *after* the king had burned the scroll with the words that Baruch wrote at Jeremiah's dictation, the word of the LORD came to Jeremiah: [28] *Take another scroll and write on it all the former words* that were in the first scroll, which King Jehoiakim of Judah has burned. . . .[32] Then Jeremiah took another scroll and gave it to the secretary Baruch son of

Neriah, who wrote on it at Jeremiah's dictation all the words of the scroll that King Jehoiakim of Judah had burned in the fire; *and many similar words were added to them.* (Jer 36:27-28, 32 NRSV; emphasis added)

Thus, according to the narrative, the destruction of one scroll led to the production of another scroll to replace it, but the replacement was not identical. In fact, as noted in 36:32, the rewriting of the scroll involved the addition of "many words like these." Scholars still debate whether parts of the second scroll can be isolated in the current book of Jeremiah. While most are wisely dubious that we have any solid criteria for reconstructing this scroll, Schmidt argues that the core of chapters 2–6 likely perhaps contains the second scroll.[28] Such debates and presuppositions regarding how to explain the complex processes that led to the book of Jeremiah as it exists today in both the Hebrew and Greek traditions show no signs of resolution anytime soon.

The Structure and Contents in Jeremiah

The book of Jeremiah does not manifest a grand design, but that does not mean that there are no structural and thematic turning points. Chapters 1–25 contain mostly poetic materials (with a few narrative vignettes) while chapters 26–45 and 52 represent mostly narrative materials (with a few poetic passages). The third major block is the collection of oracles against the nations, which contains its own thematic development as a collection, in both the Greek and Hebrew traditions.

Jeremiah 1–25: Accusations, Laments, and Failed Leaders

These chapters contain mostly poetic materials that have been placed and/or edited in loose thematic sections, some of which may have circulated independently as smaller collections. Additionally, the MT contains numerous short sections that do not appear in the Greek tradition, and most (but not all) of this additional material represents later supplements to an earlier version of the book, some form of which served as the *Vorlage* for the LXX.[29] Frequently, scholars recognize thematic groupings within chapters 1, 2–10, 11–20, and 21–25.

Jeremiah 1: Setting the Stage

Chapter 1 functions as the introduction of two prominent themes: YHWH's commission of the prophet as messenger and the impending devastation caused by the "enemy of the North." The book begins with an extended superscription dating Jeremiah's ministry from the thirteenth year of Josiah's reign until the fall of Jerusalem (1:1-3). This superscription introduces the book, not just the first units, since it covers almost the entirety of the prophet's ministry.

Two major sections dominate the remainder of the chapter to portray the prophet's call narrative (1:4-10) and the two vision reports along with interpretive comments (1:11-13, 14-19). The call narrative opens a recurring motif regarding the difficulties the prophet will face, yet it also affirms his power to overcome those difficulties. It recounts YHWH's commission to be a prophet to the nations (1:4, 10) alongside the prophet's sense of inadequacy to fulfill the task on his own (1:6) and YHWH's response to the prophet (1:7-9). The second motif, judgment against Judah and the nations, already appears within the call narrative but becomes the focus of the second half of the chapter. The prophet reports two visions—the branch of an almond tree and a boiling pot tilted away from the north (1:11, 13). The first object serves as a wordplay, in much the same way as the third and fourth vision reports of Amos (7:7-9; 8:1-3). Jeremiah sees the branch of an almond tree (*shāqēd*, 1:11) and YHWH announces (1:12) that he is "watching" (*shōqēd*), implying that he is just about to bring about judgment.

The second vision report recounts a more direct threat, much like the first two vision reports of Amos (7:1-3, 4-6). The prophet sees a boiling pot tilted away from the north (1:13), and YHWH's lengthy interpretation of the vision (1:14-16) describes disaster coming from the north against all the inhabitants of the land. The prophet does not say that the judgment is like boiling water poured upon the land, but the interpretation links to the vision for the catchword "from out of the north" (1:14, 13).

Jeremiah 2–10: Laying Out the Problems

Chapters 2–10 convey lengthy accusations against Judah, Israel, and various leaders. The charges indict the people, the personified city, the poor, the wealthy, the kings, priests, prophets, scribes, the wise, and Judah and Israel. No group goes unmentioned. Charges include the rejection of YHWH's expectations (3:13, 23, 25; 6:10), the veneration of idols or other deities (1:16; 2:28; 5:7, 19; 9:12-14; 10:1-16), the inability to distinguish good from evil (4:22; 5:21; 7:30), lies (8:4-6, 8-10), and the oppression of the poor (5:26-29). Like Hosea, Jeremiah often compares disobedience to an adulterous wife (2:20; 3:1-11). Such accusations appear throughout these chapters, and some compositions consist almost entirely of accusations (5:1-9; 8:4-12). Increasingly, however, accusations include descriptions of impending destruction, including accounts of the attacking enemy (4:13-18, 29-31; 5:10), accounts of the devastation of the land (4:19-28), and chapter 7's depiction of the coming destruction of the temple (7:1-15).

These chapters also contain passages that deal with the pathos of the prophet and YHWH, motifs that will play a bigger role in chapters 11–20. By the end of chapter 1, the prophet learns from YHWH that the people will turn against him personally (1:19) and that the prophet will have to rely upon YHWH's strength (1:17-18). This image includes both the rejection of the prophet's message (7:27) and prophet's laments over the fate of his own people (e.g., 8:18-22).

Additionally, in the beginning, YHWH vacillates between hard words of judgment and offers to allow the people to return if only they change their behavior (3:12-16). These calls to return are not heeded (3:10). By the end, YHWH testifies to his own disappointment at having to implement judgment against his own people because they refuse to pay attention (10:18-21).

Chapter 10 concludes with an idealized speech placed in the mouth of an individual speaking on behalf of the entire people. The speaker accepts YHWH's judgment as correction, asking only a measure of mercy that will allow the speaker to survive (10:23-24) before asking YHWH to punish the nations who have "devoured Jacob" (10:25). This speech perhaps functioned as the conclusion to an earlier collection, but it also creates a dramatic pause for the reader.

The coherence of chapters 2–10 derives more from poetic form and repetition (repeating vocabulary, speakers, and recurring themes) than it does from any particular plot line. Poetic materials dominate, though prose materials do appear (most extensively in 7:1–8:3). Some thematic groupings of short speeches can be observed (e.g., the collection of materials regarding idolatry in 10:1-16), and some concatenation of materials through catchwords (e.g., adjacent compositions recounting the failure of Israel/Judah to return to YHWH in 3:1-5, 6-10, 11-13, 14-16). The logic, therefore, of Jeremiah 2–10 conveys the logic of an anthology: repetition and variation work together to create an emphatic, undeniable, and dramatic picture with a clear message. YHWH's people repeatedly turned their backs upon YHWH, ignored his instruction, and worshiped other deities, leaving YHWH no choice but to take action against YHWH's own people. This repetition leaves no doubt for the reader about what has happened, what will happen, and why. The informed reader knows that Jerusalem was defeated not once, but twice by the Babylonians. These speeches in chapters 2–10 repeatedly recount the recalcitrance of YHWH's people in all its breadth: from north to south, from rich to poor, from king to priest, from prophets to scribes.

Jeremiah 11–20: Complaints and Conversations

Chapters 11–20 continue to visit many of the same themes as 2–10, but the lament elements (which played a smaller role in 2–10) increase in volume and frequency. The laments are spoken by the prophet and YHWH, but the contents concern most of the major characters of prophetic literature: the prophet, YHWH himself, the personified city, and the people. Also, the recurring themes within these chapters become progressively bleak.

Chapter 11 begins with a series of three increasingly pessimistic passages (11:1-5, 6-8, 9-15) in which YHWH commands the prophet to require obedience of "this covenant" from the people (cf. 11:2, 3, 6, 10). The first admonishes the people to hear this covenant (v. 2) because those who do not will experience the curse (v. 3). The second covenant passage also admonishes the people to keep this covenant (v. 6) and not be like their ancestors whom YHWH brought into the land. The third covenant passage states explicitly that the current generation has in fact "broken the covenant that I made with their ancestors" (11:10), leading to YHWH's judgment against them (11:11-13). The effect of this covenant collection sets the tone for a number of ways in which the themes of the book manifest a significant decline in the relationships between YHWH and the other characters in the ongoing dialogue. This deprecation continues throughout 11–20 as YHWH addresses other characters and even delivers several monologues that function as divine laments.[30]

Divine laments appear in at least four places in 12–15, characterizing YHWH's sorrow at the judgment he was forced to implement (12:7-13; 13:15-17; 14:17-18; 15:5-9). In the first divine lament in these chapters, YHWH mulls the implications of turning "the beloved of my being" over to her enemies (12:7), but he also indicates she left him no choice because she turned on him like a lion in the forest (12:8). The terms that YHWH uses to refer to the land of Judah (beloved, heritage) convey a sense of intimacy that makes the betrayal all the more dramatic, especially in that it follows directly upon the first "confession" of the prophet who brings to YHWH's attention that his own family in Anathoth has turned against him. The passage draws upon the imagery of Isaiah 5 to condemn the many shepherds (i.e., kings) who have destroyed "my vineyard" (12:10-11).

The second (13:15-17) and third (14:17-18) divine laments both speak of YHWH's tears. Many scholars assign the first of these passages to the prophet, but at its center, the speaker rues the loss of the land if the people do not change. The third lament indicates that there is no way out and even elicits a communal response (14:19-22), where the people ask whether YHWH has "completely rejected Judah." The fourth divine lament (15:5-9) addresses Lady Zion directly, stating he is "weary of relenting" (15:6). This phrase presupposes knowledge of a recurring biblical theme. Beginning in Exodus 32:14, a lengthy string of texts recounts how many times YHWH "relented" (i.e., changed his mind) concerning his decision to destroy his people.[31] Thus, Lady Zion, the personified city, makes a dramatic appearance in chapters 11–20, as she does in 2–6 and the other prophetic collections. YHWH confronts her with a charge that she is incapable of change because of her political and religious infidelity, causing YHWH to reject her (13:20-27). She is also addressed by YHWH (15:5-9), conveying that her punishment is unavoidable and no one will lament her passing.

The so-called confessions of Jeremiah (11:18-23; 12:1-6; 15:10-21; 17:14-18; 18:18-23; 20:7-12; 20:14-18) surround YHWH's laments. These confessions express in increasingly graphic terms the inner turmoil the prophet suffers as a result of having to deliver YHWH's message of judgment. As such, these confessions function much like complaint songs in the Psalter. They lay grief and problems before YHWH in hopes that he will address the ongoing turmoil. The first three complaints include a divine response that follows the prophetic complaint and explicitly reassures the prophet that his enemies would be punished (11:21-23) or exhorts him to stay strong (12:5-6) because his enemies will not prevail (15:19-21). By the end, however, the prophet who had been called even before his birth (1:5) despairs so greatly that he curses the day he was born (20:14-18). The cessation of divine response across these complaints from the prophet adds to the characterization of the prophet as increasingly isolated.

Chapters 11–20 also recount a number of sign acts, and these actions exhibit an increasingly negative message. For example, Jeremiah 16 begins with a command for Jeremiah not to marry or have children so that they will not suffer the fate of other wives and children when Jerusalem is destroyed. Jeremiah 18 describes YHWH's command to Jeremiah to go to the house of a potter and watch him work. The rhetorical interpretation of this visit underscores YHWH's power to determine the fate of nations (18:7-10). Like the potter, YHWH can destroy a nation and start over. YHWH announces an end to Judah. In chapter 19, YHWH commands Jeremiah to go to the valley of Hinnom and announce judgment (19:1-9). There he shatters a jug on the rocks to symbolize how YHWH will destroy Judah (19:10-13).

Jeremiah 21–25: Charges against the Leadership

Chapters 21–25 collectively condemn the leaders of Judah and Jerusalem. The block begins a new thematic unit in Jeremiah with a "word of YHWH" superscription.[32] The theme of failed leadership takes center stage in these chapters. First, these chapters address all the kings of Judah following Josiah by name (though not in chronological order): Zedekiah (21:1), Jehoiakim (22:18), Shallum (= Jehoahaz, 22:11), and Coniah (= Jehoiachin, 22:24). For the first time since 1:3, several texts mention Jehoiakim and Zedekiah by name, fore-shadowing the narratives in 26–40, where they become central players in the dramatic narratives recounting events from Jeremiah's life. In 21–25, these kings and the entire house of David are condemned for disobeying YHWH. In chapter 21 YHWH tells Zedekiah he will die a terrible death (v. 7), and then warns the entire house of David that their time has all but run out (v. 12). According to chapter 22, Jeremiah tells Jehoiakim that Josiah's son Shallum (who had been exiled to Egypt after the pharaoh placed Jehoiakim on the throne) will never return to Judah (v. 11), and that YHWH will reject Jehoiakim's son Coniah (= Jehoiachin) from being king (v. 24). Thus, YHWH rejects every king after Josiah according to Jeremiah 21–22.

Additionally, an editor has inserted a collection of sayings about the prophets who abused their positions (23:9–40). The preexisting collection begins with a superscription ("concerning the prophets") that sets it apart from the surrounding text. Chapter 24 represents a vision report in which Jeremiah sees two baskets of figs, one that had "very good" figs and the others that had rotted. The good figs represent the group taken to Babylon who will form the basis of the returnees (v. 6), while the bad figs include those who remained in the land *and* those who fled to Egypt (24:8).

Finally, in chapter 25, Jeremiah presents a judgment oracle that begins with a summary of his own work, according to which he has preached for 23 years (v. 3), but no one had listened (v. 5). Consequently, YHWH will devastate the land and the people will serve Babylon for seventy years (v. 11). This portion of the chapter then reaches back to the themes of chapter 1: the strength of the prophet to fulfill his task and the threat from the enemy from the north. Verses 12-13 transition to the ultimate fate of Babylon and all the nations. Jeremiah 25:13 refers to the previous material as "this book," suggesting that, at one point, 25:12-13 ended a collection, but 25:12 also appropriately mentions judgment against Babylon and the nations since the oracles against the nations that appear in chapters 46–51 in the MT tradition originally appeared right after 25:13, and oracles against Babylon take up most of five chapters (26–30 in the Old Greek tradition; see the discussion of chapters 46–51 below).

Jeremiah 26–45 + 52: Reports, Illustrations, and Repetition

Chapters 26–45 + 52 contain mostly (but not exclusively) narratives regarding episodes from Jeremiah's life. The structure of these narrative (and other) materials is, however, complex. A number of the narratives are dated by superscriptions or narrative logic to particular times in the reigns of Judah's final kings, but these dated narratives do not appear in a strict chronological order. Rather, the superscriptions flow in three episodic cycles that recount events in the reign of Jehoiakim to Zedekiah and beyond (chapters 26–34, 35–44, 45 + 52). That movement, however, does not mean that these three cycles represent three original compositions.

Three Cycles of Tragedy

This triple chronological movement creates an ominous sense of foreboding regarding the fate of Judah. Remarkably, Jeremiah stands as the longest of the four prophetic scrolls, but its dates cover the shortest time span. Moreover, the narrative cycles after chapter 26 force the reader to relive the events leading up to Jerusalem's destruction three times, and they create parallels between the reigns of Jehoiakim and Zedekiah that lead to the deportation and destruction of Judah in 597 and 587 respectively.

Dated Superscriptions in the Narrative Sections of Jeremiah

CYCLE 1

Jer 26:1 starts with the beginning of the reign of Jehoiakim (608).

Jer 27:1 tells of the beginning of the reign of Zedekiah (597).

Jer 28:1 reports the confrontation "in the same year" between Jeremiah and Hananiah and its aftermath (597/593?).

Jer 29:1 begins Jeremiah's letter to the leaders of those in the first exile (597, cf. 29:2).

Jer 30–31 contains predominately poetic materials of comfort (no date).

Jer 32:1 dates the material to the 10th year of Zedekiah (587).

Jer 33:1 brings a "second" word to Jeremiah during this period (587).

Jer 34:1 dates to the time when Nebuchadnezzar laid siege to Jerusalem in the reign of Zedekiah (post-588).

CYCLE 2

Jer 35:1 dates the message to the reign of Jehoiakim (609–598).

Jer 36:1 dates the confrontation between Jeremiah and Jehoiakim to the 4th year of Jehoiakim's reign (605).

Jer 37:1 sets the scene in the reign of Zedekiah after Nebuchadnezzar of Babylon had made him king (post-597).

Jer 39:1 marks the time when Nebuchadnezzar laid siege to Jerusalem in the 9th year of Zedekiah's reign (588) and contains a parallel account to 2 Kgs 25.

Jer 40:1 is set after the destruction of Jerusalem, when Jeremiah was released from Ramah (post-587), but before the assassination of Gedaliah.

Jer 41:1 provides a date for the assassination of Gedaliah in the 7th month (587).

Jer 44:1 identifies the following as Jeremiah's letter to the refugees in Egypt after Gedaliah's death (587).

CYCLE 3

Jer 45:1 dates to the 4th year of Jehoiakim when Jeremiah dictated to Baruch (605).

Jer 51:59 dates a message to Seraiah in the 4th year of Zedekiah's reign (594).

Jer 52:1 summarizes the reign of Zedekiah from his accession through Jerusalem's destruction (587) in his 11th year, with parallel material from 2 Kgs 24–25.

The dated events within the three cycles present biographic episodes arranged chronologically, but each cycle begins in the reign of Jehoiakim. The three cycles also draw parallels between Jehoiakim and Zedekiah. In the first cycle, 26:1 and 27:1 are dated to "the beginning of the reign of" Jehoiakim and Zedekiah respectively, while chapter 28:1 also sets its narrative in the same time as 27:1 (at the beginning of Zedekiah's reign). Then, 29:1 has no date but introduces a letter sent to the exiles in Babylon, which would have been after Jehoiakim's death but still in the early reign of Zedekiah. The superscriptions in the so-called book of consolation (30–33) do not contain many dates, and they deal with promises about the future restoration of the land, so they transcend the time of Jeremiah. Yet, 32:1 dates Jeremiah's affirmation of Zedekiah's death to the tenth year of his reign, and 34:1 sets the time during Nebuchadnezzar's siege of Jerusalem in 587 BCE. Thus, 26–34 exhibits a chronological movement from the time of Jehoiakim to Jerusalem's destruction, but 35:1 and 36:1 go back to the reign of Jehoiakim.

Many of the narrative accounts are episodic, but a significant number of scholars treat 37–44 as a continuous narrative. That being said, portions of chapters 37–44 contain nearly verbatim parallel accounts of 2 Kings 25, meaning it is nevertheless a composite narrative that incorporates multiple sources. Both chapters 39 and 52 contain accounts of Jerusalem's destruction that offer lengthy parallels with 2 Kings 25. Scholars continue to debate the precise relationship of 2 Kings to Jeremiah, since the parallels contain some notable differences and Jeremiah the prophet is not mentioned in Kings.

The third chronological cycle frames the oracles against the nations in the MT with two narrative accounts of oracles that underscore YHWH's decision to destroy the land (45:1-5) and Babylon (51:59-64) before the final account of Jerusalem's destruction in chapter 52. According to 45:1, the narrative material jumps backward in time again, from the aftermath of Gedaliah's death (chapters 43–44) to the fourth year of Jehoiakim when Jeremiah dictated the scroll. Instead of recounting those events, however, chapter 45 records a lament from Baruch (45:3), Jeremiah's scribe, along with YHWH's word to him (45:4-5), which re-iterates YHWH's decision to uproot the entire land even while sparing Baruch's life. Jeremiah 51:59-64 appears at the end of the oracles against the nations and records an oracle to Seraiah from the fourth year of Zedekiah that also concerns a scroll that Jeremiah dictated. This scroll, however, contains a hopeful message for those who will be taken to Babylon after Jerusalem's destruction in the eleventh year of Zedekiah. They learn that Babylon will also be destroyed. Hence, the end of the Gedaliah story condemns those who fled with Jeremiah to Egypt (43–44) before reconfirming the destruction of the land in advance (45:3-4), while the oracles against the nations pronounce a final assurance of Babylon's destruction (51:59-64) before recounting Jerusalem's destruction one final time (52). This emphasis on the destruction of both Egypt and Babylon at the beginning and end of the OAN happens only in the MT version.

Recurring Themes in Jeremiah 26–45 + 52

The contents of the narratives in Jeremiah 26–45 + 52, in many respects, recapitulate the same themes (and in some cases, even the same speech settings) as the material in chapters 1–25. The narrative episodes document the hostility directed toward the prophet by various political and religious leaders; they confront Judah with the people's offenses; they provide Jeremiah's message to the exiled communities in Egypt and Babylon; and they provide words of hope for a remnant people after Jerusalem's destruction.

Hostility toward the Prophet by Judah's Leaders. As already noted, the narrative episodes in chapters 26–45 highlight the resistance of Judah's leaders toward Jeremiah's words from YHWH. In most cases, Jeremiah also had advocates who spoke or acted on his behalf. The picture that develops portrays a dynasty in turmoil.

When chapter 26 presents Jeremiah offering the people a chance to repent at the beginning of Jehoiakim's reign, the "priests and prophets" attempt to kill Jeremiah (26:7-9). These groups refer, in all likelihood, to cultic officials whose livelihood was tied to the temple, which in turn relied upon good relationships with the king. This narrative account appears to refer to portions of the temple speech that appear in Jeremiah 7 in a more expanded form. Chapter 26 focuses more upon the events after the speech than the speech itself. The prophets and priests accuse Jeremiah of spreading political sedition because he proclaimed that Jerusalem would be destroyed. Jeremiah's life is saved only when a group of royal officials and "all the people" draw upon prophetic tradition to save his life by quoting Micah 3:12. This prediction of Jerusalem's destruction is set in the time of Hezekiah and indicates that Hezekiah refused to kill YHWH's prophet Micah (Jer 26:16-19). The dangerous situation is underscored, however, by the report of Jehoiakim's execution of another prophet who prophesied words similar to Jeremiah's (26:20-23). This prophet Uriah was warned that Jehoiakim was seeking his life so he fled to Egypt, but Jehoiakim brought Uriah from Egypt and executed him in Judah. The concluding verse of the chapter credits Ahikam, son of Shaphan, with saving Jeremiah (26:24). The Shaphan family appears to have served the kings from Josiah through Zedekiah as political counselors, and this is not the only time this family allies itself with Jeremiah.[33]

Chapter 28 records an encounter with the prophet Hananiah, who confronts Jeremiah on several levels. He confronts Jeremiah publicly (28:1), claims to have received a word from YHWH that directly contradicts the message of Jeremiah (28:2-4), and attempts to upstage Jeremiah's symbolic action recounted in chapter 27. In that passage Jeremiah put on a wooden yoke (27:2) to symbolize YHWH's judgment against those nations who would try and resist Babylon's power (27:9-12). In chapter 28, Hananiah removes the wooden yoke from Jeremiah's neck and breaks it (28:10a). Hananiah interprets his actions as YHWH's word that he will return Jehoiachin from Babylon within two years (28:11). At first, Jeremiah responds rather mildly, saying essentially that he hoped Hananiah was right, but he remained skeptical and walked away (28:6-9, 11b). Sometime later, Jeremiah receives his own word from YHWH, in which YHWH tells Jeremiah that he will replace the wooden yoke with an iron one and that Hananiah himself would be dead within one year (28:12-16). Finally, the narrator tells the reader that Hananiah died in the seventh month of that year. This account provides several points worth pondering. Prophets were speaking on YHWH's behalf but making contradictory claims. Jeremiah, while skeptical, allows Hananiah's word from YHWH to stand until Jeremiah receives his own message. Jeremiah condemns Hananiah for abusing the power of the word: "Listen, Hananiah, YHWH has not sent you, and you made this people trust in a lie" (28:15).

Jeremiah has a complicated relationship with Judah's last kings. Jeremiah challenges the anti-Babylonian policies of both Jehoiakim and Zedekiah, not because Jeremiah is pro-Babylon, but because he believes YHWH has sent Babylon to punish Judah for its continuing disobedience and its worship of other deities. That being said, the two kings are not characterized in the same way. Jehoiakim comes across as brutish and dangerous. He would have killed Jeremiah if he could, but Jeremiah escaped. By contrast, the narrator portrays Zedekiah more ambivalently. On the one hand, Zedekiah allowed Jeremiah to be imprisoned and Jeremiah nearly died (38:4-6). On the other hand, Zedekiah subsequently showed a level of compassion by putting Jeremiah in a less severe setting and providing him with food and protection (38:14-28). The narrator both records that Zedekiah requested Jeremiah pray for him (37:3) and recounts secret, intimate conversations between the prophet and the king in which the king expresses his own dilemmas (38:14-28). Thus, Zedekiah's relationship with Jeremiah comes across as more complex, and many would even say that Zedekiah is a more sympathetic character caught in the paradox between royal power and its limitations.[34]

Confrontation of Judah's Offenses. In 26–45, accusations against the people are less concentrated than in the poetic accounts, and more of the material conveys a sense that Judah's leadership has failed. The prophets and priests are castigated for misleading the people by lying about messages they have received from YHWH (27:10, 14, 16; 28:15; 29:9, 21, 31). The kings did not listen when prophets spoke to them (e.g., 29:16-19). The leadership refuses to recognize that YHWH will use Babylon to punish Judah unless some change occurs.

Words to the Exiles. Jeremiah's messages to the exiled communities in Egypt and Babylon differ. The exiles in Egypt are condemned for two kinds of disobedience. First, Jeremiah 44 condemns Judean refugees who fled to Egypt because they continue to worship other deities. Second, they are condemned for their fear (42:10-12) that causes disobedience (42:13-17). As a result, Jeremiah warns a group after Gedaliah's assassination not to flee to Egypt since Babylon will ultimately attack it (42:18-22). Rather than listen, they force Jeremiah to go with them. Additionally, Jeremiah 24 depicts the Egyptian refugees in the time of Zedekiah as bad figs (24:8-10), along with those who remain in Jerusalem and align themselves with Zedekiah. Ironically, Babylon never conquered Egypt, which does not seem to have disqualified Jeremiah as a true prophet, despite the close association of Jeremiah with Deuteronomic traditions.[35]

The refugees in Babylon are not condemned, but they are told to prepare for a lengthy sojourn of seventy years (29:1-11). At the end of the OAN, 51:59-64 contains a brief account of Jeremiah's letter to Seraiah in the fourth year of Zedekiah's reign. Jeremiah tells Seraiah that he will be taken to Babylon where he is to open the scroll and read it. It contains a judgment pronouncement that Babylon itself would be destroyed. Seraiah is then to throw the scroll into the Euphrates to symbolize the coming end of Babylon's power. This final word from

Jeremiah does not appear as the last message in the early version of the oracles against the nations, but it has a prominent role in the MT as the final speech of Jeremiah.[36]

Hope and Consolation. Words of hope do not appear frequently in Jeremiah, but editors have compiled most of these hopeful messages together in chapters 30–33. Thematically, this section follows closely on Jeremiah's message to the exiles in Babylon that contained a message of hope that YHWH spoke:

> [10] For thus says the LORD: Only when Babylon's seventy years are completed will I visit you, and I will fulfill to you my promise and bring you back to this place. [11] For surely I know the plans I have for you, says the Lord, plans for your welfare and not for harm, to give you a future with hope. (Jer 29:10-11 NRSV)

The end of chapter 29 also contains words of judgment against specific leaders in Babylon who were speaking contrary to Jeremiah's message from YHWH regarding the exiles in Babylon (29:15-32). Nevertheless, chapters 30–33 owe their location to this topic of YHWH's plans after the destruction of Jerusalem. These chapters contain a series of speeches addressed to or concerning groups addressed in the book already: Israel and Judah, the personified Lady Zion, and the people as a whole. Additionally, these chapters contain numerous introductory formulas that can begin new speeches.[37] As a result, these chapters (like Amos 3–6 and Zech 7–8) read like an anthology. They serve a rhetorical purpose since they are gathered together, but they do not show any real logical progression. They drive home the idea that YHWH has not finished with the remnant, variously labeled as Judah, Israel, Jacob, and Jerusalem.

Several of these sayings address those already in exile, while others focus upon conditions in the land. For example, 30:3 refers to restoring "the fortunes of my people, Israel and Judah" and delineates that action as bringing "them *back* to the land." The same is true for Jacob in 30:10; 31:8, 11-15. By contrast, 30:12-17 addresses a feminine entity (Lady Zion) who is reminded why she is being punished before she is told that YHWH will also punish those who attack her and that he will restore her as well. The resulting picture is one in which YHWH clears Jerusalem in order to start over with a new generation. Similarly, 30:18 promises to rebuild the city over the mound of its destruction.

The contents of the hope units offer different portraits of when and how restoration will occur. For example, chapter 32 contains a prophetic narrative in which Jeremiah is told to buy a piece of property in Anathoth that is intended to symbolize that YHWH's people will have a future when houses and vineyards will be purchased again (32:15). At the same time, the remainder of the chapter goes to considerable lengths to remind the people of YHWH's great acts and that their disobedience has caused the disasters, including the siege ramps that have been laid by the Babylonians (32:16-24). YHWH then recounts the misdeeds of the people as a defense of why he must give Jerusalem to the Babylonians (32:27-36). Only after both the prophet and YHWH rehearse the sins of the people does YHWH offer a word of hope that the people will be gathered from where they have been sent so that life in the land can resume (32:37-44).

Jeremiah 46–51: The Oracles against the Nations

The OAN in Jeremiah 46–51 (MT) have a complex history that involves the selection and arrangement of the individual sayings against select nations into a block that was originally placed in the middle of Jeremiah 25 (specifically, after 25:13bα).[38] The individual sayings against these nations were likely not all composed at one time. In other words, the oracles against Edom in 49:7-22 include several existing short sayings against Edom that the compiler grouped together. Relatedly, much of the material against Moab (48:1-47) appears to be rephrasings of oracles that appear elsewhere.[39] The compiler of the OAN gathered these collections together to affirm in Jeremiah that YHWH controls the fate of all nations. This block was originally placed after 25:13bα where it fit thematically.

A later editor moved the collection from the middle to the end of the corpus, between Jeremiah 45 and 52. Simultaneously, the order of these oracles was changed, and some of the nations received qualified promises. The change of order reflects a general geographic pattern that moves from the south and west eastward. In short, the rearranged oracles move from Egypt to Babylon. The grouping in the MT tradition manifests a more logical progression. Further, by starting in Egypt and concluding with Babylon, the order begins and ends with the two centers of servitude which figure so prominently in the Torah narrative (explanation of Israel's arrival in Egypt, as well as its escape from slavery in Egypt in Exodus) and the Deuteronomistic History (devastation of Judah and exile to Babylon in Kings). Relatedly, Egypt and Babylon represent the two historical powers which changed the course of Judah after the downfall of Assyria.

In addition to the rearrangement, nearly half of the nations receive promises of restoration in the MT tradition, most of which do not appear in the shorter text reflected in the Greek. The oracles against Egypt (46:25b-26), Moab (48:40-47), Ammon (49:6), and Elam (49:39) contain brief promises (along with other updates) in the MT, while the oracles against Philistia (47:1-7), Edom (49:7-22), Syria (49:23-33), Kedar (49:28-32), and Babylon (50:1-46) do not. The qualified promises for some of these nations and not for others reflect different theological and historical perspectives and later vantage points for the collection when compared to the shorter text. Only the Elam oracle contains a promise in the shorter Greek tradition. By contrast, the oracles for Egypt, Moab, and Ammon speak of restoration after punishment.

Consider the following addition to the oracles against Egypt in 46:25b-26 (where the underlined text does not appear in the shorter Greek tradition).

> 25 The LORD of hosts, the God of Israel, said: See, I am bringing punishment upon Amon of Thebes, and Pharaoh, and Egypt and her gods and her kings, upon Pharaoh and those who trust in him. 26 I will hand them over to those who seek their life, to King Nebuchadrezzar of Babylon and his officers. Afterward Egypt shall be inhabited as in the days of old, says the LORD. (NRSV)

The added material in MT 46:25b-26 does not eliminate judgment against Egypt, but it anticipates a different, positive outcome after judgment by Babylon. In other words, the MT anticipates a two-stage process: Babylon will punish Egypt, but then Egypt will be inhabited as before. This second stage is not reflected in the earlier Greek tradition. The shorter text only promises destruction for Egypt and consolation for Jacob (= Israel).

The oracle against Moab in 48:40-47 shows similar signs of expansion that includes a positive, hopeful ending (48:47):

> 40 For thus says the LORD: Look, he shall swoop down like an eagle, and spread his wings against Moab;41 the towns shall be taken and the strongholds seized. The hearts of the warriors of Moab, on that day, shall be like the heart of a woman in labor. 42 Moab shall be destroyed as a people, because he magnified himself against the LORD. 43 Terror, pit, and trap are before you, O inhabitants of Moab! says the LORD. 44 Everyone who flees from the terror shall fall into the pit, and everyone who climbs out of the pit shall be caught in the trap. For I will bring these things upon Moab in the year of their punishment, says the LORD. 45 In the shadow of Heshbon fugitives stop exhausted; for a fire has gone out from Heshbon, a flame from the house of Sihon; it has destroyed the forehead of Moab, the scalp of the people of tumult. 46 Woe to you, O Moab! The people of Chemosh have perished, for your sons have been taken captive, and your daughters into captivity. 47 Yet I will restore the fortunes of Moab in the latter days, says the LORD. Thus far is the judgment on Moab. (NRSV)

The Moabite oracle in 48:40-47 has been expanded significantly compared with the shorter tradition that goes only through 48:44. The MT contains two additional half-verses (48:40b, 41b) plus three additional verses (48:45-47) that are not part of the shorter text. The additional material in MT does three things: (1) it strengthens the imagery of judgment upon Moab (48:40b, 41b)—including using language found elsewhere in Jeremiah (cf. the "woman in labor" imagery in 48:41b with Jer 4:31; 6:24; 13:21; 22:23; 30:6; 48:41; 49:22, 24; 50:43); (2) it anticipates a distant time of judgment (using "on that day") that colors the oracle with eschatological overtones; and (3) it allows for a restoration of Moab after it has been punished (48:47).

The Ammonite oracle adds 49:6 using the same phrase that 48:47 used for Moab:

> [5] I am going to bring terror upon you, says the Lord GOD of hosts, from all your neighbors, and you will be scattered, each headlong, with no one to gather the fugitives. [6] But afterward I will restore the fortunes of the Ammonites, says the LORD. (NRSV)

The MT adds a promise of restoration for the Ammonites in 49:6. Unlike the previous examples, the MT does not expand upon the judgment sayings in the remainder of the oracle. Jeremiah 49:6 does, however, anticipate a complete restoration for the Ammonites, as with Egypt and Moab, but only after a period of punishment. The addition even uses the same language of restoration used for Moab (48:47), Elam (49:39), and YHWH's own people (30:3, 18; 33:7). The extra material thus extends the oracle to include a more distant time frame ("but afterward") and an eventual time of restoration.

Consequently, this updated version of the OAN (with its new arrangement and its new location) conveys a more eschatological tone at the end of the book than it did in the middle of the corpus, and it allows for an ultimate return of some foreign nations to create a more peaceful situation.

Despite the brief messages of hope for some of the nations, the primary thrust of the OAN remains the pronouncement of judgment against the nations engaged in the political intrigue of the late seventh and early sixth centuries. Several commentators have noted that these oracles do not primarily express the reasons for judgment as theological concerns.[40] The OAN contain no condemnations of idols, for instance. Rather, the oracles proclaim judgment against the nations because of their own evil and pride. In other words, they are condemned for acts of violence against others and for acting without regard for the consequences of their actions.

Major Themes in Jeremiah

The contents of the book of Jeremiah take many forms, but major themes recur across the portions of the book no matter where one divides the sections. These recurring themes include accusations of religious infidelity, injustice against the poor, political miscalculations, the price paid by YHWH's emissaries, a qualified hope for the future, and words of judgment aimed at the foreign nations who contributed to Judah's suffering.

Religious infidelity plays a major role in the accusations against YHWH's people that they broke the covenant (e.g., 11:6-8) and worshiped other deities (e.g., 1:16; 5:7; 44:3-5). The texts document past and present attempts to call the people to repent of their misdeeds, but they (and especially their leaders) prove incapable of acting to repair their relationship with YHWH (e.g., 8:6; 9:5).

A second recurring theme involves the numerous ways that the rich and powerful ignore YHWH's expectation for social justice. Greed and violence motivate the groups (e.g., 22:15-18). These charges are leveled against Lady Zion (2:34), as indicated by the feminine address, and the wealthy (5:28) who abuse the poor, the sojourner, the widows, and the orphans (see 7:6; 22:3).

Third, YHWH's foes suffer from political myopia. From the outset, the message is clear. YHWH has commissioned the foe from the north (whom the reader soon learns is Babylon) to take control of Judah and ultimately to destroy Jerusalem. At times, Judah's kings (Jehoiakim and Zedekiah) think they can succeed on their own, or they turn to others to help resist Babylon. Portions of Jeremiah echo the words of Hosea to underscore that Egypt will not deliver Judah from Assyria or Babylon (e.g., 2:18, 38). According to Jeremiah, Egypt will be overrun by Babylon and will be of no help to Judah or its refugees (see 43:7-13). When addressing these political follies, the book portrays the prophet speaking truth to power in the name of YHWH.

Fourth, the cost of proclaiming God's word plays a major role in the life of the prophet. From the opening admonition to stand firm in the face of opposition, Jeremiah confronts an array of powerful enemies: battles with kings Jehoiakim and Zedekiah, challenges to and from cultic personnel, threats from his own family, plots by the leaders of his hometown, and finally being taken to Egypt against his will after Gedaliah's assassination by those who feared Babylonian reprisals. The prophet survives all but the last of these confrontations, but the laments of the prophet (in 11–20) and the accounts of his imprisonments and close calls (in 26–44) document the dangers of being a true messenger of YHWH.

Foreign nations play an important role from the beginning of the book, where Jeremiah is proclaimed as a prophet to the nations (1:4). The enemy from the north functions as a threat sent by God against Judah. The enemy (Babylon) will attack Judah at YHWH's command. Yet, Babylon will also experience divine justice along with the nations surrounding Judah for the way they have behaved (46–51). The nations are not condemned because they are foreigners, but because of their behavior. This aspect represents an important part of the book's theological hope. The cup of wrath imagery (e.g., 25:15-17, 28; 49:12; 51:7) assumes that punishment represents an act of justice. If Jerusalem must be punished for its behavior, then YHWH must also hold the surrounding nations accountable for theirs.

Finally, on a sociological level, one finds that a recurring sense of hostility and partisanship lies behind many of the stories. Jeremiah confronts the powers of the palace and the temple, but he is not entirely alone. He has well-placed allies, including most of those in the Shaphan family; Baruch the scribe; Gemariah, son of the high priest Hilkiah (29:3); Zedekiah's court eunuch, Ebed-melek (38:7-13; 39:16-18); and Nebuzaradan, the captain of the guard who helps arrange Jeremiah's release to Gedaliah, Shaphan's grandson appointed governor in the aftermath of Jerusalem's destruction (Jer 39:11-14). These allies appear at key points in the narratives to help Jeremiah escape his enemies. As for those enemies, the prophet takes on the priests and the prophets at the temple in numerous places (e.g., Jer 7; 23; 26; 28). He confronts Jehoiakim and Zedekiah over the misuse of their power and their misconceived political policies. At the same time, the portrait of the prophet consistently takes sides against those pushing political folly. He also privileges some groups over others. For example, the prophet offers words of comfort and hope to those in exile in Babylon (29), but he offers little hope or comfort for refugees in Egypt (42:15-22). The hope for those in Babylon is not a quick fix, but suggests that those who transmitted the tradition incorporated a pro-*golah* stance into the message of Jeremiah, which continued to have social implications well into the Persian period. For many, an early Persian-period setting makes better sense of this theological agenda by interpreting such passages as "texts undergirding the theological legitimation of those returning from exile who wanted to see their leadership claims anchored in prophecy."[41]

The book of Jeremiah thus presents the end of the seventh and the beginning of the sixth centuries BCE as a tragic time of punishment from YHWH. YHWH had run out of patience because of the depth of the problem that cut through every segment of society. For his enemies, Jeremiah is a purveyor of treason who should be imprisoned or killed. He refuses to follow the party line because he speaks for YHWH, and he pays a price as a result. For those who collected and shaped the traditions, Jeremiah becomes the prime example of a prophet who courageously confronts the power structures with a genuine, but unpopular, word from YHWH.

The role of the book within the prophetic corpus can hardly be overestimated. Through repetition and testimony, the scroll of Jeremiah represents a collection of oracles and narratives that tell a story by underscoring the need to follow YHWH and YHWH only. This book serves a didactic function: to train Judah's elite following Jerusalem's destruction. In many ways, it represents a continuation of Josiah's reforms by emphasizing the need for keeping the covenant and avoiding the worship of idols. It also demonstrates the limits of kingship. The obstinacy of Jehoiakim and the weakness of Zedekiah brought Jerusalem to ruin. Those who transmitted the scroll learned this lesson well and taught it over a lengthy process of collection and revision to testify about the need to follow YHWH. The scroll focuses upon a brief time period, but it documents the tragedy that occurs when power and religion become enmeshed in the egos of those in charge. It provides its readers with a front row seat from which to view the events that led to Jerusalem's destruction. The prophet who remained in the land and spoke on YHWH's behalf could not change the events, but the scroll presents him as the voice of YHWH who stood against the great religious and political powers of his day with a last-ditch effort to stop the madness. Ezekiel will cover some of the same territory, but from the perspective of those outside the land. Isaiah and the Twelve largely skip the time covered by Jeremiah and Ezekiel, but they testify to the longevity of the problem and to life beyond Jerusalem's destruction.

Discussion Questions

1. Explain the relationship of the prophet Jeremiah to the kings, priests, and scribes of Judah.

2. Describe the relationship of the MT and LXX versions of Jeremiah to one another. How do these two versions affect your understanding of the concept of scripture?

3. Describe the issues that complicate reaching a consensus about how the book of Jeremiah came to be.

4. Compare the thematic development of Jeremiah 2–10 with chapters 11–20.

5. Explain the changes to the oracles against the nations in Jeremiah and how to account for them.

6. Name and illustrate the recurring themes of Jeremiah 26–45 + 52.

Chapter 3
Ezekiel

Historical Backdrop

Ezekiel was a contemporary of Jeremiah, which means that they share knowledge of quite a number of historical events (see the historical background at the beginning of the chapter on Jeremiah). Nevertheless, the books recount very different expectations and attitudes about the experience of those events. The biggest difference between the two is that Jeremiah remained in the land where he suffered attacks by kings, priests, and prophets, while Ezekiel functioned as a prophet to the exiles from 597 BCE who were forcibly relocated when Jehoiachin surrendered to Nebuchadnezzar. Ezekiel reflects on the fate of those exiled in 597. A second difference lies in the educational backgrounds of the groups who transmitted the two scrolls. Jeremiah's scroll reflects the language and thought world of the Deuteronomistic movement, one that likely has roots in Levitical circles, while Ezekiel regularly draws upon priestly traditions, especially from the Holiness Code.

We know few details about Ezekiel prior to his deportation except the name of his father, Buzi, and that he was educated to be a priest in the Jerusalem temple (1:3). The opening superscription (1:1-3) refers to the fifth year of Jehoiachin's exile (593 BCE) and an enigmatic reference to "the thirtieth year" that is variously interpreted as the thirtieth year after Josiah's reforms, the thirtieth year of the prophet himself when he could begin fulfilling priestly duties, or the thirtieth year of Jehoiachin's exile (568).[1]

Ezekiel was exiled to Tel-abib on the river Chebar, southeast of the capital in Babylon. Various suggestions have been put forward regarding his role as prophet among these Judean exiles. Some suggest that the prophet/priest served in a leadership capacity in the workgroups of Judeans tasked with digging canals, while others argue that Ezekiel's community served agricultural needs for Babylon's economy.[2] Recent studies have complicated our understanding of these communities, in part because of differences between the cross-deportation policies of neo-Assyrians and the neo-Babylonians.[3] The Babylonians exiled populations back to Babylon and tended to settle them in ethnic pockets. Additionally, Nebuchadnezzar appears to have scaled back the number of exiles he brought into the kingdom in comparison to his predecessors.[4] The prophetic oracles in the book do not focus on daily life. Rather, they present Ezekiel's prophetic activities, particularly in terms of his visions and his symbolic actions. Nevertheless, the theological outlook of the book of Ezekiel is often associated with the outlook of the Zadokite or the Aaronide priestly group who ultimately took control of the priestly leadership of the temple in the early years after its reconstruction.[5] Somehow, dialogues took place regarding the composition of the Torah and the Former and Latter Prophets and Ezekiel was included among the prophetic scrolls. These dialogues required no small measure of compromise on the part of the theological stakeholders. In many respects, the theology of Ezekiel represents a minority voice in these prophetic conversations. Ezekiel's exclusionary tone, which sought to maintain a strong religious identity for the exiles of 597 BCE, seems strangely out of place among the other three prophetic scrolls whose final shaping was largely accomplished within the confines of Judah. By contrast, most recent commentators agree that the book of Ezekiel, while fixated upon events in Jerusalem, nevertheless largely took shape in Babylon.

Kings of Judah Relevant for Ezekiel

Josiah (640–609 BCE): Placed on the throne at the age of eight, instituted reforms (622 BCE), killed by Pharaoh Necho II (609).

Jehoahaz (609 BCE): Son of Josiah, made king at his father's death. Ruled three months before being exiled to Egypt by Necho II.

Jehoiakim (609-597 BCE): Son of Josiah placed on the throne by Necho II. Jehoiakim rebelled against Babylon in 597 causing Nebuchadnezzar to lay siege to Jerusalem. Jehoiakim died during the siege.

Jehoiachin (597–560?): Son of Jehoiakim, grandson of Josiah. He negotiated an end to the siege begun by his father and was exiled to Babylon where he was imprisoned until at least 560 BCE when he was released (2 Kgs 25:27–30). The dates in Ezekiel refer to the reign of Jehoiachin. Jehoiachin's grandson, Zerubbabel, was appointed governor in the time of Haggai.

Zedekiah (597–587 BCE): Son of Josiah, appointed king in Jerusalem by Nebuchadnezzar II of Babylon after the failure of Jehoiakim's revolt and Jehoichin's exile to Babylon. Zedekiah rebelled against Nebuchadnezzar in 588/587 leading to Jerusalem's destruction. After thirty months of siege, Zedekiah tried to escape through a hole in the wall of Jerusalem, but was captured by Babylon in the plains of Jericho. Zedekiah's sons were killed in front of him, and then he was blinded before being taken in chains to Babylon.

Introductory Issues for the Book of Ezekiel

The Prophet and the Book

An autobiographic style permeates Ezekiel, which gives the impression of direct access to the prophet in ways that supersede the other three scrolls. The dramatic qualities embedded in the material also represent a distinguishing characteristic of the Ezekiel tradition. Vision reports and symbolic-action reports dominate much of the book, but they require explanatory material that also contributes to the book's distinctive qualities. Visions have to be interpreted, and frequently that interpretation takes the form of divine speech explaining the visions. Symbolic actions also include interpretation, often explicitly delivered from the mouth of the prophet as the word of YHWH. In addition, several passages are structured as priestly instruction using a casuistic style where several cases are laid out to clarify the complexity of an issue or to drive home a particular point.

A sense of holiness and purity also pervades the book. The exile is seen as punishment for abominations committed in the temple. These abominations continue a long history of rebellion on the part of the people and their leaders that the prophet traces back to the time in the wilderness. For Ezekiel, YHWH decides to stop these abominations, which requires the complete destruction of the land and the decimation of its population through war, pestilence, and exile. For Ezekiel, YHWH decided to begin again, and the exiles of 597 essentially form the exclusive core of the remnant population. This decision does not mean, however, that all exiles will constitute the remnant. For Ezekiel, even the exiles of 597 must still be purified. They must reject idolatry and pay for their sins, and some will refuse to do so. Nevertheless, the prophet largely excludes the citizens of Judah and Jerusalem who were exiled after 587 and 582. For Ezekiel, YHWH rejects the idea of a core group living in the land. In many respects, these exclusionary attitudes put Ezekiel in conflict with the other three prophetic scrolls.

Dates of Composition

Fourteen times in the book of Ezekiel dated superscriptions introduce new material. Most of these headings appear in chronological order, giving the book a sense of sequential progression that runs from 593–571 BCE (see table below). In other words, the superscriptions provide a major structural element of the book.

Date Formulas in Ezekiel

Verse	Approximate Date	Subject
1:1-3	June 593	Chariot vision
3:16	June 593	Call to be a watchman
8:1	Aug 592	Temple vision
20:1	Aug 591	Discourse with elders
24:1	Jan 588	Second siege of Jerusalem
26:1	Mar 587	Judgment on Tyre
29:1	**Jan 587**	Judgment on Egypt
29:17	**Apr 571**	Judgment on Egypt
30:20	Apr 587	Judgment on Egypt
31:1	June 587	Judgment on Egypt
32:1	**Mar 585**	Lament over Pharaoh
32:17	**Mar 585**	Lament over Pharaoh
33:21	Dec 586	Fall of Jerusalem
40:1	Apr 573	New temple vision

The superscriptions that do not follow in chronological order can be explained by thematic placement. These superscriptions that do not appear in chronological order appear as part of the oracles against the nations (chapters 25–32) and specifically as oracles directed against Egypt. The majority of Ezekiel scholarship today approaches these dates as more reliable than did critical scholars in the early part of the twentieth century.[6] The role that the superscriptions play in the literary structure and thematic development of Ezekiel is not, however, always considered. Scholars frequently merely assume that the superscriptions were transmitted with the materials they introduce, but their presence in key locations suggests they are also part of the book's conceptual framework, so readers should recognize their literary implications as well.

Unity of Ezekiel

The question of the unity of the book of Ezekiel involves a complex set of issues that ultimately depend upon one's definition of unity. On the one hand, much of the book puts forward a consistent theological program that focuses upon punishment for sin, cleansing of the land and a remnant of the people, retribution against the foreign nations who take advantage of Judah's trouble, and finally, restoration of the people, reconstruction of the temple, reorganization of its personnel, and redistribution of tribal territories.

On the other hand, the Old Greek translation that forms the basis of the Septuagint (LXX), as with the book of Jeremiah, demonstrates that the book of Ezekiel as we now have it did not result from the work of a single author. The Greek version, when retroverted back into Hebrew, represents a considerably shorter text than the MT. As with Jeremiah, detailed comparisons of these two traditions show a complex process in which the MT generally represents the continued growth of the tradition (though not in every case) while the shorter Greek text generally represents an earlier version of the corpus. Yet, even this shorter version has experienced updates both in its Hebrew *Vorlage* and among the Greek translations themselves.

In addition to the issues of length, transposition of passages complicates the issue of unity. The clearest example appears when comparing chapters 37–39 in the MT with the LXX. In the Greek tradition, likely the earlier version, the account of the defeat of Gog's army in chapters 38–39 precedes chapter 37 with its anticipation of the reunification of Judah and Israel. The change derives from someone's conviction that the defeat of Gog offers a better transition to the restoration of the temple that begins with chapter 40, but one can only speculate as to why.

Finally, the book of Ezekiel presents conflicting messages on some issues. For example, the majority of Ezekiel 34 rejects Israel's shepherds (i.e., its kings) entirely. The text condemns them for their greed, violence, and idolatry. Yet, two verses (34:23-24) claim that YHWH will establish David as his prince in the land, largely undercutting the message of chapter 34. These two verses, however, coincide with the symbolic action of Ezekiel 37:15-28 where sticks with the name of Judah and Israel are joined together under one king (37:22), and that king comes from the line of David (37:24), giving preference to the royal lineage of Judah (especially through Jehoiachin).[7] The pro-David message in 37:22, 24 almost certainly comes from a later hand than the prophet, but its location is no accident and it coheres with 34:23-24.[8]

Sources and the Final Form

More than any of the other scrolls, the book of Ezekiel is known for its *Fortschreibungen* (comments inserted by later readers to clarify, qualify, or correct something in the text). As will be seen in the discussion of the redactional models, as well as comparisons of the text-critical evidence, Ezekiel has a history of additional comments embedded in its message. Some argue that the prophet himself expanded upon the descriptions of the visions and the symbolic actions. Others ascribe more of this reflection to the tradents who transmitted and reflected upon the book. The extent of such material differs according to the scholar who attempts to describe it, but almost all the redactional models and the differences between the Greek and Hebrew traditions lend themselves to such arguments.

Two illustrations of widely recognized *Fortschreibungen* can demonstrate these various functions. First, consider the lengthy passage of 36:23c-38 that emphasizes the need for the people to undergo a process of cleansing and purification. This passage is missing from the Old Greek and from a late second-century Greek manuscript (P967). Recent studies continue to assess this passage as a later addition to the text. This passage adds considerable detail to the cleansing of the people that involves sprinkling with clean water, renewal of the spirit, removal of intransigence, and a spirit of obedience toward YHWH's ordinances. This cleansing of iniquity hardly runs counter to the theology of Ezekiel, but its inclusion at a later date implies that someone thought it needed explicit articulation at this point in the discourse.

Second, the pro-David insertion in Ezekiel 34:23-24 mentioned above seeks to *correct* a straightforward reading of chapter 34 regarding the rejection of the shepherds. It undercuts YHWH's rejection of royal leadership with an affirmation that the Davidic descendant will continue to function as king back in the land. In fact, no Davidic king ever ruled in Judah again (though the Persians appointed Jehoiachin's grandson Zerubbabel to administrate the land on their behalf along with the high priest Joshua, according to Haggai and Ezra).

Redactional Models

Scholarship on Ezekiel falls into two general camps when talking about how the book arose, alongside the question of when individual speeches and vision reports may have been composed.[9] The larger group argues that the book arose gradually as a collection of individual pieces of tradition that documented the prophetic activity of Ezekiel. This group argues that, to varying degrees, recollections of speeches and the prophet's activity contain material that goes back to the prophet, but that the selection and organization of these pieces should probably be attributed to the prophet's followers.[10]

A second group emphasizes the unifying conceptual markers of the book and attributes them to the prophet. The predominance of first-person language almost certainly plays a role in these decisions. For example, Moshe Greenberg operates with what he labels a "holistic" interpretive method that assumes that *if* one can find a way to explain apparent tensions, *then* one should do so and attribute the book to the prophet.[11] Not surprisingly, Greenberg manages to find explanations for most tensions noted by other scholars. While Greenberg represents an extreme case, and even he speaks of editors on occasion (as in 34:23-24), many treatments in the last forty years have concluded that the book of Ezekiel provides reliable information about the prophet and about the community in which he was active.

Even the first group of scholars often admits to difficulties distinguishing the prophet's words from later explanatory material that could come from the prophet or those who transmitted the scroll. Yet, the second group often downplays or ignores the chronological distance between the earliest (593 BCE) and the latest (571 BCE) material dated in the book. The chronological structure created by the networks of material introduced by these superscriptions, combined with the thematic blocks of judgment against Israel (1–24), oracles against foreign nations (25–32), and restoration (33–48) provides an overarching schema that begs to be taken seriously. The fact that one of the latest superscriptions (40:1) introduces material that interacts specifically with one of the earliest portions of the book (the departure and return of YHWH's glory in chapters 11 and 43), presupposes that the author of the scroll intends the readers to be aware of the scroll's preceding material. Consequently, the literary character of the scroll cannot be gainsaid. In fact, this unifying vision actually extends the crucial period of the composition to the latest of these dates, not the earliest. The book as we have it includes interrelated vision reports, ostensibly separated by some twenty years, and these reports reflect upon the vision's significance in ways that show some distance from the events themselves. It therefore seems less likely that the form we possess comes directly from the hand of the prophet. On the other hand, the structure of the book and its theology argue for an idealistic vision of the returning exiles from the time of 597 BCE that does not appear to align well with other accounts of life in Judah in the early Persian period. This discontinuity suggests to many that Ezekiel took its initial shape before the events of 539 enabled the return of several different groups of exiles.

The Structure and Contents in Ezekiel

Scholars largely agree that the book of Ezekiel exhibits three structural and thematic sections: the pronouncements of judgment against Israel in 1–24, the oracles against foreign nations in 25–32, and the pronouncements that focus upon restoration in the land in 33–48.

Ezekiel 1–24: Judgment against Israel

Ezekiel 1–3: Throne Vision and Commission

The first major structural block (chapters 1–24) largely pronounces judgment upon YHWH's people, primarily those in Jerusalem but also certain groups among the exiles. Chapters 1–3 open with the most extensive call narrative among the prophets. Chapter 1 describes the divine chariot and throne, beginning with a brief description of the whole (1:4-5) as a fiery cloud coming from the north with "something like amber" inside the cloud that stood on top of four creatures (whose identity as cherubim is ultimately made known in chapter 10).

Following that brief description, the prophet provides a detailed description that moves from the ground upward. It starts with the cherubim carrying the throne, moving from their feet (1:7) to the hands under their wings (1:8), to their four faces (1:10), to their wings (1:11). Each cherub had four faces: one that looked like an angel, a human, a lion, and an ox. Each cherub had four wings, two that rose above them and two that covered their bodies.

Beside each of the cherubim the prophet describes an elaborate "wheel within a wheel" that looked "like gleaming beryl" (1:16, or topaz), a translucent mineral that can appear in shades of green, yellow, and amber. The rims of the wheels were dotted with eyes. The wheels moved freely in any direction (including horizontally and vertically). When the chariot moved, the wings made the sound of "mighty waters" and "the thunder of the Almighty" (1:24).

Continuing the upward movement, the prophet describes "something like a dome" above the heads of the cherubim (1:22) that shone like crystal. The word "dome" has cosmic overtones as it represents that part of creation that, according to the Priestly creation tradition, separates the waters above from the waters below the earth even before the creation of dry land (see Gen 1:6-8). Above the dome stood "something like a throne," upon which sat something that seemed "like a human form" (1:26). Above the loins, this form glowed like burning amber and below the loins of this human-like form emanated "something that looked like fire" (1:27). The entire scene looked like a rainbow, and the prophet finally states that he is gazing upon the "likeness of the glory of YHWH," a realization that forces him to fall on his face immediately (1:28).

The purpose of YHWH's appearance is the subject of 2:1–3:3. YHWH commands the prophet to get back on his feet (2:1), and then YHWH announces he is sending Ezekiel to speak to a rebellious and sinful nation (2:1-3). In this commission, YHWH tells the prophet that it makes no difference whether the nation listens or not, but YHWH does not believe they will listen (2:5; 3:7). The prophet's role, however, is to make sure that they know a prophet has been among them (2:5). He tells Ezekiel not to fear the people (2:6; 3:9). YHWH then spreads open before the prophet a scroll covered with writing on the front and the back (2:8-10) and commands Ezekiel to eat the scroll, which the prophet reports tasted as sweet as honey (3:1-3).

The remainder of chapter 3 contains four units that create a sense of discontinuity (3:4-11, 12-15, 16-21, 22-27). The first (3:4-11) essentially repeats the message of 2:3-7, except it articulates the conviction that the people of Israel will refuse to listen, whereas 2:3-7 conveys a more open-ended response.[12] The second unit (3:12-15) then recounts how the spirit of YHWH brought the prophet to the exiles at Tel-abib by the river Chebar, where he sat stunned for seven days (3:12-15). The passage could represent the original conclusion to either of the two commissioning accounts, but it now serves that function for both.

In the third unit (3:16-21), the word of YHWH comes to Ezekiel after seven days and tells him he shall be a sentinel for the people. The role of sentinel as defined in this passage is to warn the wicked and the righteous among YHWH's people of impending judgment. The passage describes the scenario in the "if . . . then" style of casuistic law. It emphasizes that those who receive the message bear responsibility for how they respond, including the prophet. The prophet fulfills his role by providing the warning. The wicked are warned in advance, but the text assumes they will ignore the warning. It also suggests that at least some of the righteous will ignore the message (3:20-21).

In the fourth unit (3:22-27), YHWH commands the prophet to go to the valley for further instructions. There, YHWH tells Ezekiel to shut himself off, bind himself with cords, and remain speechless until YHWH tells him otherwise. This unit creates a clear dichotomy in the portrait of the prophet. On the one hand, chapters 1–3 consistently portray Ezekiel's role as one who shall deliver YHWH's message, but 3:22-27 commands the prophet to be silent. The prophet's silence comes up again when he is finally told to speak (33:21-22), just prior to the point in the book where Ezekiel begins to offer words of restoration in chapter 34. This juxtaposition undoubtedly derives from compiling diverse prophetic traditions, since in chapters 4–7 there are several symbolic-action reports where the prophet speaks. The reports contain interpretive commentary to

79

explain the action's meaning as well as commands for the prophet to speak.[13] The prophet appears to speak routinely, further complicating any explanation of the conflicting commands to speak and not to speak. Those tensions do not disappear and are not easy to explain.[14]

Ezekiel 4–7: Symbolic-Action Reports and Oracles

Chapters 4–7 continue directly from the speech in chapter 3 but recount a series of symbolic actions commanded by YHWH to the prophet. These actions include creating a brick model of Jerusalem under siege (4:1-3), lying on his left side for 390 days (4:4-5) and then on his right side for forty days (4:6) while being bound with cords (4:8), eating bread that is ritually impure (4:9-15), and using a sword to shave his head and beard (5:1-4). In addition to the reports of the symbolic actions, chapters 4–7 also contain passages that interpret the acts and present additional oracles. For example, YHWH explains the meaning of the bread to the prophet in 4:16-17, and 5:5-17 explains why the hairs are divided into three parts representing the population. By contrast, chapters 6–7 deal mostly with accusations against those who remain in the land. Chapter 6 conveys two prose divine speeches (6:1-10, 11-14) that have a loose thematic association with chapter 5 but are addressed to the "mountains of Israel," while chapter 7 contains a series of poetic compositions and sayings that consistently pronounce the imminent end of the land. The formulations in chapters 6–7 recount commands to the prophet to speak to the people (e.g., 6:2-3, 11; 7:9), to the land personified (the bulk of 7:1-10), and about various groups (7:10-27) concerning "the end" which is coming. Chapter 6 mentions idolatry for the first time in the book (6:4, 5, 6, 9, 13), which constitutes a major focus of the accusations against those in the land. According to Ezekiel, those in the land and some in exile have worshiped idols and offered sacrifices on the high places thereby defiling the temple and the land itself.[15]

Ezekiel 8–11: Vision of Jerusalem's Guilt and YHWH's Departure

Chapters 8–11 recount a second vision that, according to 8:1, is dated a little more than a year after the call narrative (cf. 1:1). The setting of this visionary account takes place while the "elders of Judah" visit Ezekiel at his house in Babylon (8:1). The vision recounts the prophet being physically carried by the hair to Jerusalem by the same "glory of YHWH" he saw in chapter 1. He is taken to the north entrance of the inner court of the temple (8:3), a space reserved for the priests. God then reveals a series of "great abominations" (8:6) that include an "image of jealousy" north of the altar, seventy "elders of the house of Israel" worshiping images and idols inside the inner court (8:3, 7-13), women weeping for the Mesopotamian God Tammuz (8:14-15), and twenty-five men in the temple courtyard worshiping the sun (8:16). YHWH interprets these abominations as a sacrilege that cannot go unpunished because they have defiled the temple itself (8:17-18).

Chapter 9 describes YHWH's preparation for destroying the city. Six executioners come at YHWH's command (9:1-3), and a scribe is commissioned to go through the city and place a mark upon those who lament these abominations so that they will not be destroyed (9:3-4, 11). The remainder of YHWH's executioners set about slaughtering those in the city. One can hardly miss the allusion to the Exodus story, where the homes of the Israelites were marked for deliverance before the firstborn sons of the Egyptians were struck (Exod 11:1-10; 12:29-32). The prophet responds like Amos in his first two visions (Amos 7:2, 5), interceding on behalf of the people that the punishment is too severe (9:8), but YHWH rejects the prophet's plea because of the severity of the crimes (9:9-10).

Chapter 10 adds three narrative elements. First, it recounts the command and execution of the burning of Jerusalem using fiery coals that come out of the burning sections of the chariot (10:2, 6-7). Second, most of the chapter (10:1, 3-5, 8-17, 20-22) rearticulates the description of the chariot and the dome, anchoring this vision with chapter 1. Chapter 10 clarifies that the four creatures propelling the chariot are cherubim (10:15, 20, 22). Third, the vision recounts the departure of YHWH's glory from the center of the temple to the east gate (10:18-19).

Chapter 11 focuses on the twenty-five men at the east gate who were described in 8:16-18 as worshiping the sun. The second account mentions two of these by name and commissions the prophet to pronounce judgment upon them for their betrayal of the city (11:1-12). One of these two leaders, Pelatiah, dies while Ezekiel is speaking, causing the prophet to question again whether YHWH's punishment is too severe (11:13). The fact that this segment of the vision seems to know nothing of the destruction of the city, which was described in chapter 10, again shows how the incorporation of individual speech-blocks both taps into the progression of the broader narrative (hence, the pause at the east gate of the temple) and creates irresolvable tensions within the details of the narrative flow. Two additional units provide the climax to chapter 11 with YHWH describing his plans (11:14-21) followed by a report of YHWH's departure from the temple to the mountain east of the city and of the prophet's return to the exiles in Babylon (11:22-25). The programmatic description of YHWH's plans (11:14-21) marks a major speech by YHWH in which the deity announces that the exiled community that was removed from the land (i.e., those deported with Jehoiachin in 597 BCE), and not those who remained behind, represent the group with whom YHWH will work in the future.[16] Rather than abandoning the exiles to an unclean land, YHWH announces that he has been a "sanctuary" for them where they have been scattered and that he will restore the land to them once it has been cleansed of the abominations (11:18). By contrast, those involved with the abominations will be brought down (11:21).

Chapters 8–11 represent the foundational message of Ezekiel in a nutshell. The vision takes place in a public setting in Babylon as indicated by the opening and concluding verses (8:1; 11:25), yet the prophet receives a tour of the temple in a vision where YHWH shows him the depth of Jerusalem's problems. The abominations at the temple have profaned the temple and the land. As a result, YHWH determines to destroy both the city and the temple. The superscription dates the vision five years before Jerusalem's destruction, but it also encourages the exiles, who are told that they represent YHWH's hope for the future. This negative attitude toward those in Jerusalem represents a consistent theological outlook in the book of Ezekiel.

Ezekiel 12–19: Symbolic Acts, Allegories, and Contemplations

Ezekiel 12–19 presents a stream of allegories and oracles that in many ways serves to reinforce the message of the vision of 8–11. Collectively, this material illustrates why the abominations practiced in the land have doomed Judah and its leaders to destruction and why the exiles of 597 BCE shall serve as the remnant that shall return to take control of the land.

Chapter 12 presents four units (12:1-16, 17-20, 21-25, 26-28) directed to the exiles in Babylon, the first two reporting symbolic actions (and related interpretations) and the second two emphasizing the truthfulness of Ezekiel's message despite the apparent delay in its fulfillment. In the first symbolic-action report, YHWH commands the prophet to put together the baggage of exile and then to dig through a wall at night. He is commanded to perform both acts in front of the exiles (12:1-7), and then he receives a word from YHWH to interpret the action so that Ezekiel's audience will understand that YHWH intends to send the population of Jerusalem into exile and to thwart the attempt of Zedekiah to flee the Babylonians (12:8-16).

Following an introduction (13:1-2), chapter 13 contains a series of oracles against false prophets. Five messenger formulas create the impression of distinct oracles (13:3-7, 8-12, 13-16, 17-19, 20-23). One of these oracles (13:13-16) represents an expanded duplicate of the preceding. Three of these oracles are directed against male prophets who "prophesy out of their own imagination," while the last two condemn female prophets who "prophesy out of their own imagination," clearly drawing an intentional parallel (13:2, 17).

Ezekiel 14–15 contains a series of warnings against idolatry and against future exiles who come to Babylon. Chapter 14 begins with admonitions addressed to certain "elders of Israel" who approached Ezekiel for consultation (14:1), but YHWH rejects their consultation because this group of leaders was worshiping idols (14:3). Ezekiel 14:1-20 thus contains a series of diatribes against idolatry as warnings to the exiles. This chapter concludes with a short vignette (14:21-23) admonishing Ezekiel's exiles to take comfort in YHWH's justice when survivors from Jerusalem arrive as exiles in Babylon. This short word leads to a longer allegory concerning the uselessness of a vine that has been burned (15:1-5), followed by an interpretive comment (15:6-8) that equates the charred vine with the inhabitants of Jerusalem, creating the connective logic between 14:21-23 and 15:1-5. Ezekiel condemns idolatry among the exiles in the strongest terms possible, but the purpose of the condemnation of Jerusalem's exiles derives largely from the charges in the vision of chapters 8–11 that condemned idolatrous practices at the temple. Ezekiel's theology demands the rejection of idols, but considers those in Jerusalem as having been unequivocally tainted by such practices. It is the righteous among Ezekiel's exiles who will be purified, not subsequent groups of exiles from Jerusalem.[17]

Ezekiel 16 contains the first of two extended allegories concerning personified Jerusalem (chapter 23 is the other). These allegories contain shocking images of a disturbing, misogynistic theological expression that, in our time, should raise numerous questions about a text that needs to be challenged. To be sure, the imagery would have been shocking in Ezekiel's time, but the assumptions of this text raise theological and ethical problems beyond recognizing that Ezekiel uses the imagery of an unfaithful spouse to depict the severity of idolatry. The chapter portrays Jerusalem as the wild, orphaned daughter of an Amorite father and a Hittite mother (16:3) who was left naked and abandoned in an open field from the time of her birth (16:4-5). YHWH saves her, and when she grows into a woman, YHWH takes her as his wife (16:6-8), then bathes her and presents her with jewelry and fine clothing until she is beautiful enough to be a queen who radiates the splendor that YHWH bestowed on her (16:9-14). There, the honeymoon ends. YHWH accuses her of trusting in her own beauty, and of fornicating with anyone, anywhere that she desires (16:15-22). Consequently, YHWH turns her over to the Philistines, the Assyrians, and the Chaldeans, to whom she also gave herself (16:23-29). YHWH accuses his adulterous wife of being worse than a prostitute because she gave gifts to her lovers rather than being paid for her services (16:30-34). YHWH then turns her over to a mob to strip and stone her (16:34-43). Her behavior is compared unfavorably to the behavior of her sisters who have already been punished, specifically Samaria and Sodom (16:44-52). Finally, YHWH announces he will restore the fortunes of all three sisters (Sodom,

Samaria, and Jerusalem) in order to shame her further, but only after they have borne the penalty for their behavior (16:53-58). YHWH then pats himself on the back for reestablishing his covenant with her, knowing that she has been suitably shamed so that he might forgive her (16:59-63).

Such charges regarding the illicit behavior of YHWH's spouse appear elsewhere in prophetic literature to condemn idolatry, most notably against Israel in Hosea 2 and against Jerusalem personified in Jeremiah 3:1-8, Isaiah 1:21, and 23:15-17. Hence, this motif appears in each of the four prophetic scrolls, but the graphic quality of Ezekiel's rhetoric outpaces all the others. This theology is dangerous for several reasons. First, it presupposes an ancient view that a man's wife was his property and transposes that unhealthy image onto the relationship between YHWH and YHWH's people. Second, descriptions of the brutality leveled against the spouse diminish the portrait of God into little more than a jealous bully whose wounded ego cannot be sated until he has acted violently himself. In our culture, we call that spouse abuse, and it hardly represents a deity worthy of worship. Third, ethically, leaving this portrait of God unchallenged makes us complicit. If violence against one's spouse represents acceptable behavior for the deity, then by extension any jealous spouse may feel entitled to behave similarly.

Ezekiel 17 explicitly presents itself as a riddle and an allegory (17:1) designed to reject Zedekiah as king in Judah in favor of Jehoiachin, who had been exiled to Babylon in 597 BCE. The allegory tells a story (17:3-10, 22-24) interrupted by an explanatory word from YHWH (17:11-21). An eagle (= the king of Babylon) removed the top branch of the cedar (= Jehoiachin) and took it to a foreign city. The eagle then planted a seed (= Zedekiah) that became a vine. The vine, however, reached out to another eagle (= the king of Egypt), hoping that it would provide the vine with the ability to bear fruit. A series of rhetorical questions casts doubt upon the ability to prosper under the second eagle (17:11-21). In the epilogue to the story (17:22-24), YHWH promises to take the branch from the top of the cedar (= Jehoiachin) and plant it on a high and lofty mountain so that the seed will produce fruit and protective shade for all kinds of birds. Again, the driving theological conceptions privilege those associated with the exile under Jehoiachin while anticipating failure for Zedekiah and devastation for Jerusalem.

Chapter 18 presents a theological treatise that provides an extended exploration of guilt. This composition begins with a question regarding an axiomatic parable that was undoubtedly used to explain why children were sent into exile when they had not abandoned YHWH: "The parents have eaten sour grapes, and the children's teeth are set on edge" (18:2). One could interpret this adage essentially as a summary of the Deuteronomistic explanation of Jerusalem's destruction that blamed YHWH's decision to destroy Jerusalem on the sins of Manasseh (2 Kgs 21:11-12), even though he ruled for fifty-five years and died more than fifty years before Jerusalem's destruction. Using a series of casuistic vignettes, Ezekiel 18 argues against this idea. Rather, this composition argues that punishment comes to those who have sinned, not to their descendants. Further, punishment is reserved for the wicked who do not turn from their sins.

Chapter 19 presents two additional allegories as lamentations for the leaders of Israel (19:1, 14b). The first tells the story of the end of Judah's kings as a story of a lioness and the tragic fate of her cubs (19:2-9). The second uses the imagery of a vine whose branches are destroyed (19:10-14a). Both assume YHWH's rejection of Judah's kings.

Ezekiel 20–24: Judgment Comes Closer

Chapters 20–24 continue to pronounce judgment on certain groups in exile and upon Judah and Jerusalem. The literary characteristics do not differ radically from the material in chapters 12–19, but a new superscription in 20:1 dates this material about a year later than the superscription in 8:1. The attentive reader thus knows that the time of Jerusalem's destruction is creeping nearer. In fact, the next superscription (24:1) dates to the day that Nebuchadnezzar laid siege to Jerusalem before destroying the city, burning the temple, and forcibly removing its rebellious king Zedekiah. Redactors have arranged the chapters thematically, creating a composition from short speeches addressing various groups (the elders of the land, sanctuaries of Jerusalem, city of bloodshed, and the lusty adulteress). Repetition plays a role within these compositions, as does the fact that the recipients themselves have been addressed before.

Chapter 20 opens with a second visit from the "elders of Israel" whom YHWH rejects because of their idolatry. Undoubtedly, this group represents leaders among the exiles who have either accommodated to religious expression in Babylon or who have retained the idolatrous practices in which they participated in Jerusalem.[18] In either case, YHWH announces through the prophet his rejection of their overtures to consult him (20:3, 32) because of the extensive history of such abominations from the time of Jacob forward. The chapter retells the story of Israel's recalcitrance through the use and repetition of key phrases, such as the priestly terms "abominations" (20:4), "detestable things" (20:7, 8, 30), and "idols" (20:7, 8, 16, 18, 24, 31, 39). They forgot YHWH's "statutes," "ordinances" (20:11, 13, 16, 18, 19, 21, 24, 25), and sabbaths (20:12, 13, 16, 20, 21, 24), which they were to keep "for the sake of my name" (20:9, 14, 22, 44). The chapter retells the story of Israel: how the family of Jacob went into slavery in Egypt (20:5-10); how YHWH brought them out of Egypt and provided them with statutes, ordinances, and sabbaths (20:11-12); how they rebelled in the wilderness (20:13-17); how their children did the same (20:18-22); how they

85

were warned of the consequences of disobedience (scattering among the nations) before they entered the land (20:23); and how they rebelled once in the land (20:24-26). Only YHWH's decision not to destroy Israel for the sake of his name allowed them to continue, but now the exiles have been removed from the land in order to purge themselves of idolatry while YHWH destroys the land that has been profaned (20:27-32). Only then will YHWH bring them back into the land, where the shame of the knowledge of their former behavior will stop them from repeating it (20:33-44).

Ezekiel 21–23 turns its attention to Jerusalem's destruction, a theme driven home by the repetition of the word *sword* some twenty-one times in chapter 21. Unlike the previous chapter's focus upon the sins of the ancestors, chapter 21 focuses upon the coming judgment, not the rationale (idolatry and covenant disobedience). Chapter 22 fills this gap when it begins with a long list (22:2-13) of charges against the city of "bloodshed" (22:2). Charges include ethical and cultic violations: shedding blood (22:3-4, 6, 13), worshiping idols (22:3-4), disrespecting parents (22:7), mistreating resident aliens, orphans, and widows (22:7), profaning the sabbath (22:8), committing slander (22:9), sexual impropriety (22:10-11), bribery (22:12), and usury (22:12-13). The conclusion of this list pronounces YHWH's decision to scatter those in the city among the nations (22:14-16). The chapter ends with an allegory (22:17-22) and condemnation of Jerusalem's leadership (22:23-31). The allegory explores the imagery of smelting to refine the dross from the metal, while 22:23-31 condemns the unclean state of Jerusalem's royalty (22:25 LXX and most of the English versions), its priests (22:26), and its prophets (22:28, 25 MT).[19]

Chapter 23 offers a second allegory regarding the adultery of Jerusalem personified. Like Ezekiel 16, the sexually charged rhetoric personifies Jerusalem and Samaria as two sisters symbolically named Oholah (the tented one) and Oholibah (my tent is in her), where *tent* alludes to a temple.[20] Both sisters prove themselves to be adulterers, but the text condemns Jerusalem's actions as more egregious than her sister's (23:11) because she lusted after the Assyrians (23:12), the Babylonians (23:14), and the Egyptians (23:19). Subtle differences between chapter 23 and 16 appear in the cultic focus of 16 versus the more political focus of 23. One cannot draw too great a distinction, however, since the state was closely associated with its deities in the ancient Near Eastern thought world, and since YHWH's speech also interprets adultery in chapter 23 as idolatry and a defilement of YHWH's sanctuary (23:38-39).

Chapter 24 offers a climax to the words of judgment against Israel that have dominated chapters 1–23. It contains three parts: the dated superscription placing the message on the very day that Nebuchadnezzar laid siege to Jerusalem (24:1-2), the allegory of the pot pronouncing the destruction of Jerusalem (24:3-

14), and the symbolic-action report of YHWH's command that Ezekiel refuse to mourn the death of his wife to symbolize how the exiles should respond to Jerusalem's destruction (24:15-27). Again, the driving theological foundation of most of the judgment sayings in Ezekiel seeks to create an identity among the exiles as a purified remnant that rejects idolatry and to create a sense of distance between themselves and those in Jerusalem or those who are exiled to Babylon after Jerusalem's destruction in 587. In other words, the exiles of 597 BCE, for Ezekiel, constitute the remnant with whom YHWH will restore the land.

Ezekiel 25–32: The Oracles against the Nations

Chapters 25–32 form the middle section of the book, which pronounces judgment upon seven foreign peoples, first those east of Israel (Ammon, Moab, and Edom), then to its west (Philistia, Tyre, Sidon), and finally, to the south (Egypt). Collectively, this geographically patterned arrangement effectively surrounds Judah and Israel, but one should also note the omission of Babylon as a subject of judgment, a gap that contrasts markedly with Jeremiah's oracles against the nations. In fact, Nebuchadnezzar and Babylon factor positively in the pronouncement of judgment against both Tyre (26:7) and Egypt (29:18, 19; 30:10, 24, 25; 32:11).

In addition to this geographical pattern, however, the sheer volume of pronouncements emphasizes judgment against Tyre and Egypt. Four countries (Ammon, Moab, Edom, and Philistia) appear in the first chapter before the focus changes to Tyre for nearly three chapters (26:1–28:19), followed by a brief oracle against Sidon, Phoenicia's other major city (28:20-26). Finally, the collection devotes its final four chapters to the condemnation of Egypt (29–32). The emphases of these chapters reflect events from the early sixth century. Nebuchadnezzar laid siege to Tyre for thirteen years from 586–573 BCE. Despite Ezekiel's confidence that the city would fall, Nebuchadnezzar never conquered it.[21] Similarly, several of the pronouncements against Egypt predict Nebuchadnezzar's conquest of Egypt (e.g., 30:10), but Babylon never defeated Egypt inside its own territory the way the Assyrians had done. Ezekiel's antagonism against Egypt is quite understandable since the Egyptians clearly pursued policies at odds with the Babylonians and used the kings of Judah to foment resistance. Yet, when the chips were down and Babylon entered the Levant, Egypt chose to pursue policies of protecting their border rather than helping their allies.

Chapter 25 contains a number of similarly styled oracles that begin with an accusation ("because you have done *X*") and then move to a verdict (introduced by the phrase "therefore thus says the Lord"). Ammon and Moab are both judged for enjoying Judah's destruction (25:3, 6, 8). Their punishment is described in terms of overthrow by the Arab tribes of the desert (25:4-5, 7, 10). Edom, by contrast, is condemned for the violent action it took against Judah (25:12), which leads to the pronouncement of YHWH's vengeance against that country until its inhabitants are utterly destroyed (25:13-14). This brief note coincides with other allusions to Edom's involvement in Jerusalem's destruction or its aftermath (see Obad 11–14 and Ps 137:7). The oracle against the Philistines condemns them for their historic animosity, but it also hints that they took advantage of Judah after the destruction of Jerusalem (25:15). Each oracle ends with a purposive statement indicating that action will be taken "so that they will know that I am YHWH" (25:5, 7, 11, 17; cf. 25:14). This refrain continues into the oracles against Tyre and Egypt, though in a less consistent and stylized fashion (25:5, 7, 11, 17; 26:6; 28:22, 23, 24, 26; 29:6, 9, 16, 21; 30:8, 19, 25, 26; 32:15). Hence, the oracles against all four entities in chapter 25 pronounce judgment in the assumed aftermath of Jerusalem's destruction. Most of the oracles against Tyre (chapters 26–28) and Egypt (chapters 29–32) spend more space pronouncing judgment than stating a rationale for the destruction, but these oracles presuppose that the judgment comes against Tyre because of her pride and her wealth and against Egypt because of her continued resistance to Babylonian control.

Ezekiel 33–48: Restoration of the People, the Temple, and the Land

The third and final segment of the book begins with a redactional composition (chapter 33) that refers back to the prophet's call narrative in chapter 3 (a reprisal of the motif of the sentinel from 3:16-21 and the cessation of YHWH's command of silence from 3:22-27), along with citations and allusions to Ezekiel 18 and 24. At the same time, news of Jerusalem's destruction allows the prophet to speak, and his first words reject the survivors of Jerusalem's destruction before turning to an exploration of what restoration should look like. The restoration section begins (chapters 34–37) with several distinctive oracles. It moves to a vision of YHWH's defeat of the mythic enemies (38–39), which results in the cleansing of the land, and then finally presents a programmatic description of a new temple, a new temple hierarchy, and a new division of the land into tribal territories (40–48).

Ezekiel 33–39: Hope for Cleansing and Restoration

Ezekiel 33: Sentinel, Silence, and Survivors of the Destruction of Jerusalem

Ezekiel 33 unfolds in three important thematic units (33:1-20, 21-22, 23-32). As already noted in Ezekiel 3, chapter 33 reiterates the commission of the prophet as the sentinel (33:1-20) but cancels the command to be silent (33:21-

88

22). The first part of this chapter quotes from and alludes to the theological treatise in Ezekiel 18 quite extensively.[22] At least in part, these citations affirm that
Ezekiel's role as a sentinel to warn the people should begin again.

Questions remain regarding the meaning of Ezekiel's silence, since clearly the
prophet has spoken on numerous occasions between chapters 4 and 33, after he
was told to be silent in 3:22-27. Just as clearly, however, the links between 3:22-
27 and 33:21-22 cannot be ignored. These passages suggest the reader should
understand the repetition as a dramatic redux of his prophetic commission to
mark a change in the prophet's message that is about to occur. From chapter 34
onward, the prophet's message concerns his vision of hope and restoration in the
purified land.

The third thematic block (33:23-33) raises the question of the relationship
between the survivors of Jerusalem's destruction and the exiles of 597 BCE and
reiterates Ezekiel's strong conviction that only his group represented the true
remnant of Israel. This speech divides into four parts: the introduction of the
question regarding whether the refugees of Jerusalem's destruction should be
considered owners of the land of Abraham (33:23-24), a two-part response that
recounts the sins of the group (33:25-26) and announces YHWH's verdict to lay
waste the land and exterminate the survivors (33:27-29), and finally a warning to
the prophet not to get caught up in his own celebrity (33:30-33). The restoration
oracles in Ezekiel do not merely pronounce a word of unqualified hope. Rather,
they still convey words of admonishment about the past as they look toward the
future.

Ezekiel 34–37: Restoration Oracles

Each chapter in 34–37 presents a new venue for a thematic discussion. Ezekiel 34 deals with the issue of leadership through an allegory about shepherds
and their flock. The shepherd metaphor appears across the ancient Near East as a
designation for the king. At issue here is YHWH's rejection of the Davidic covenant. The basic structure of the chapter unfolds clearly: first, YHWH rejects the
current "shepherds of Israel" (34:1-10); then YHWH announces his intention
to retake the role of shepherd (34:11-16); this decision leads to a reevaluation
of the flock to separate the clean from the unclean (34:17-22); and the passage
concludes with a promise to restore a covenant of peace, depicted as security from
marauding nations and fertility of the land (34:25-31).

The promise in 34:23-24 stands out dramatically since, therein, YHWH reaffirms his intention to put in place a shepherd with a Davidic lineage. These verses
undercut the entire argument of the rest of the chapter because it is hard to see
how the condemnation of the "shepherds" would not have included Jehoiachin.

Two possibilities account for verses 23-24: diachronic and literary. One can understand 34:23-24 as the insertion of a later editor who did not disavow the promise of Davidic kingship. Haggai 2:20-23 shows that this perspective existed in Judah at the time of Zerubbabel. This diachronic explanation can account for *how* verses 23-24 entered the corpus, but a literary explanation is required to explain *why* the Davidic promise appears in 34:23-24.[23] Three suggestions focus on distinctive elements: the verses' location, terminology, and function.[24] First, verses 22-23 do not appear in a vacuum. Their literary context presupposes that YHWH has retaken the position as shepherd (34:11-16), and has begun separating the flock based on the sheep's fitness (34:17-19, 20-22). The logic, therefore, of this Davidic promise would *assume* that a reader would infer that this Davidide passed YHWH's test to be counted among the good animals of the flock. Second, some infer from the terminology that a line of authority is presumed in 34:22-23 wherein the king is subject to YHWH. Consequently, they argue that the editor avoids the term *king* for David's representative.[25] For these interpreters, the crucial element in this promise is that the promise calls David's descendant a prince, not a king. YHWH is king, so the prince rules under the authority of the king.[26] The problem with this interpretation is that it overlooks another passage (37:15-28) that does refer to "my servant David" as "king" (37:24). A third option focuses on function. Perhaps 34:22-23 merely attempts to reconcile the very diverse message that forms the core of Ezekiel 34, rejecting Israel's shepherds and the message of Ezekiel 37:15-28, a symbolic-action report commending the reunification of Judah and Israel under a single Davidic king.

Ezekiel 35 provides an extended condemnation of Edom. We do not know why this chapter does not appear with the OAN, except to emphasize the strong sense of betrayal of this brother kingdom.[27] Ezekiel 35 condemns Edom for two reasons: because they "cherished an ancient enmity" (35:5) and because they attempted to take Judah's land (35:10: "because you said, 'these two nations and these two countries shall be mine, and we will take possession of them'"). These descriptions fit other accounts describing Edom working with Babylon in some capacity following the events of 587 BCE when Jerusalem was destroyed. By condemning Edom within the restoration texts, the book emphasizes Edom's betrayal. Thematically, Edom also serves as a specific illustration of the motif that YHWH's people will no longer be plunder for the nations nor be the subject of their taunts—hopes expressed in the promise of restoration in Ezekiel 34:25-31 (see specifically 34:28-29) and the beginning of chapter 36.

Ezekiel 36 begins by expanding upon two motifs articulated in the blessing described in Ezekiel 34:25-31: judgment upon all the nations who have taken YHWH's land (36:1-7), and restoring the fertility of the land and rebuilding its cities in order to remove the taunts of the nations (36:8-15). The remainder of the chapter deals with the content of the nations' taunts by reestablishing YHWH's holy name (36:20-23) and by describing the cleansing of the people that will enable them to return to the land (36:24-35). As a result of this cleansing, the house of Israel will ask YHWH to increase the population in Jerusalem and the destroyed towns (36:37-38).[28]

Ezekiel 37 also consists of two distinct parts (37:1-14 and 15-28), a vision report and a symbolic action, thematically related by their focus upon the nature of the new community that will return to the land. The first part of the chapter arguably contains Ezekiel's most famous vision report regarding the valley of dry bones (37:1-14). In this vision, the prophet speaks directly with YHWH who asks the prophet whether he thinks the bones could live, and the prophet cryptically replies, "Lord God, you know" (37:3). Curiously, YHWH does not simply reinvigorate the bones himself. Rather, YHWH commands the prophet to prophesy not once but twice (37:4, 9) so that the *rûaḥ* will come and bring life to the bones. This Hebrew word, *rûaḥ*, has a wide range of meanings that include spirit, wind, and breath. The first time that the prophet prophesies to the bones, he hears a loud noise as the bones come together and are joined with sinews and flesh. Yet, the *rûaḥ* was not yet in them (37:8), so YHWH commands the prophet to prophesy a second time asking the four winds (the plural of *rûaḥ*) to come and bring *rûaḥ* to them. The prophet did as he was told, and the *rûaḥ* enters the bones, and they come to life. The final part of this vision report (37:11-14) provides the interpretation. The bones represent the "whole house of Israel" that had become dried up from lack of hope. Two things stand out. First, the prophet is needed to revive the hope of the people, and this vision report essentially re-orients the mission of the prophet from that of sentinel to that of a purveyor of hope. It paints a picture of a community in crisis, forced to live in a foreign land and work for a foreign king. Second, the "whole house of Israel" takes on added significance as the thematic touchstone to what follows. Ironically, the prophet who rejected the exiles of 587 BCE and 582 BCE is tasked with reinvigorating the whole house of Israel. The parable that follows makes clear that the compilers of the book understood restoration to include the territory of the former Northern Kingdom.

The remainder of the chapter (37:15-28) narrates a symbolic action regarding the reunification of Judah and Israel into a single political entity. YHWH commands the prophet to label two sticks, inscribing one "for Judah and all the Israelites associated with it" and the second "for Joseph (the stick of Ephraim) and all the house of Israel associated with it" (37:16). When asked by the people the meaning of the two sticks, he is to join the two sticks together by putting Judah on top of Ephraim and telling them that YHWH will soon bring the people of Israel back to the land from where they have been scattered. "Joseph" stands for the political entity of the Northern Kingdom. The sticks thus represent the reunification of the two kingdoms that YHWH intends to unite into a single nation with one king over them all (37:22). This king will be a descendant of David (37:24), and YHWH will dwell among them (37:27).

Ezekiel 38–39: Grand Defeat of the Enemies

Contrary to later usage in the book of Revelation, *Gog* and *Magog* in Ezekiel represent a king and a country centered in Asia Minor. In Ezekiel, Gog lives in Magog. Two approaches have dominated the discussion of the identity of Gog. One focuses upon the similarity of the name with a famous king Gyges, who ruled Lydia in western Asia Minor at the end of the seventh century BCE. The second group focuses upon the number of names in this passage that appear in Genesis 10, where they are associated with the sons of Japheth.[29] These two approaches are not mutually exclusive. In their totality, chapters 38–39 envision an attack against the mountains of Israel led by Gog, but the army includes peoples from virtually every territory from the far western parts of Asia Minor to the eastern ends of Persia. To be sure, some of the names are more cryptic than others, but Ezekiel 38–39 fundamentally describes an end to the enemy from the north, a tradition known in both Ezekiel and Jeremiah. Mention of Put and Cush (38:5) involves lands to the south and west of Egypt. It is hard to imagine an army more massively conceived in the ancient world, and the fluidity of these chapters in the transmission of Ezekiel suggests that multiple understandings of the enemy could have played a role in their position.

The story of Gog unfolds across chapters 38–39 in seven phases: 38:1-9, 10-13, 14-16, 17-23; 39:1-16, 17-24, and 25-29. The treatise begins with Ezekiel's common revelatory formula (38:1), and each oracle contains a messenger formula ("Thus says the LORD God" in 38:3, 10, 14, 17; 39:1, 17, 25). Each of the seven passages moves the action of the battle forward, but evidence suggests these chapters entered the book after its initial composition.[30] Ezekiel 38:1-9 introduces Gog and commands the people to be ready when he attacks, while 38:10-13 warns the king not to seek plunder in Israel, and 38:14-16 predicts his army's defeat. Next, 38:17-23 describes the imminent battle in terms of creation itself, while 39:1-16 describes the destruction of Gog's army on a massive scale as well as a burial site for Gog himself. Ezekiel 39:17-24 describes the defeat on the mountains of Israel as a massive feast (39:17-20) that will manifest the glory of YHWH (39:21-24). Finally, 39:25-29 connects back to the themes of chapter 36–37, restoring the whole house of Israel, the holy name of YHWH, and the security of the land.

Ezekiel 40–48: Vision of a New Temple, YHWH's Return, and New Tribal Allotment

Chapters 40–48 conclude Ezekiel with a series of vignettes setting forth a visionary program for restoring the cult and reorganizing the land. This vision depicts one of YHWH's messengers as the prophet's guide who also measures the dimensions of the temple complex (40:3).[31] These chapters unfold in thematic blocks, beginning with 40:1–44:3, that systematically describes the building of the temple complex from the outer gates to the inner gates, to the temple building, and to the inner regions of the temple. One passage (43:1-9) interrupts the description in order to narrate the return of YHWH's glory through the east gate and back into the temple recesses. This narrative reaches back to the visions of chapters 8–11, where the glory of YHWH departed the temple and the city because of its abominations, but 43:4-5 dramatically depicts YHWH's return at the very point the temple is cleansed. It provides evidence that the compilers of Ezekiel intended the scroll to be read from start to finish. Within the larger contextual flow, YHWH's glory returns immediately after the building of the temple and the confirmation that it is a perfectly square 500 cubits on every side (42:15-20). Following YHWH's return, the narrative describes the sacrificial altar (43:13-17) and a series of sacrifices lasting seven days that consecrate the altar and atone for the sins of the Zadokites (43:18-27). The significance of this element cannot be overstated from a priestly perspective, since the altar had been defiled. Finally, a brief passage sets up a special entrance at the east gate so that the prince has a place (44:1-3).

With the temple structure complete and YHWH's glory returned, 44:4–45:9 deals with the temple personnel and the holy district of land to support the priests, Levites, and royal interests. The section begins with exclusionary pronouncements that foreigners will be excluded from the temple (45:4-9) and that the Levites (except for the family of Zadok) will be excluded from the priestly duties inside the temple building (45:10-14). Service inside the temple will be strictly limited to the descendants of Zadok, and they are provided with a number of stipulations governing their behavior (44:15-31). Relatedly, Ezekiel envisions a holy district around the temple that includes lands for the priests, the Levites, and the royal representative.[32]

The third thematic section includes 45:10–46:24. It concerns the regulation of cultic activity, including weights and measures (45:10-12), allotments of the priestly portions (45:13-17), and a lengthy series of regulations concerning offerings and festivals (45:18–46:24).

The fourth and final thematic block concerns allocation of the land (47:1–48:35). The description of the land begins with the temple at the center. In the first segment (47:1-12), the prophet describes a river flowing from the temple eastward, getting deeper as it crosses the land so that it can water the desert and refresh the "sea of stagnant waters" (47:8), a reference to the Dead Sea. This image of abundant freshwater teeming with fish flowing from the temple complex hardly corresponds to actual topography. The remainder of the text describes the ideal boundaries of the land (47:13-20) and then presents a renewal of the allotment of the land by tribal regions (47:21–48:7, 23-29), plus the addition of a holy district in 48:8-22 (see 44:4–45:9). The final passage describes Jerusalem's massive walls and the twelve gates of the city, each named for one of the tribes. The organization by tribal regions stands in a significant conflict with the model of Davidic kingship that appears in 34:23-24 and 37:24-25.

Important Themes in Ezekiel

Several important themes should be noted in the book of Ezekiel: the role of YHWH's glory, its avoidance of the term Zion, its teachings about kingship, and its priestly orientation. The glory of YHWH plays a major role in the message of the book. Its mobility (see chapters 1, 10, 43) and its location (chapters 11 and 43) emphasize the message of judgment against Jerusalem, YHWH's availability to the exiles in Babylon, and finally, the restoration of a purified land.

Royal imagery also undergirds the portrait of YHWH. Even though the text explicitly mentions YHWH as king only once (20:33), that text makes clear that kingship lies at the heart of the vision for the future in the book of Ezekiel. Chapter 34 portrays YHWH as shepherd, a metaphor with royal connotations. The chariot envisioned by Ezekiel carries a throne. YHWH's glory rises above the throne carried by the cherubim (1:26), but YHWH's glory also leaves the temple on this throned chariot (11:22-23) and does not return until Jerusalem has been cleansed (43:2-7).

The movement of YHWH's glory has significant literary and theological implications. The departure from and return to Jerusalem (in chapters 11 and 43 respectively) symbolizes YHWH's rejection of Jerusalem and its temple because of its abominations (chapter 11) and YHWH's acceptance of Jerusalem after the temple has been rebuilt and reconsecrated (chapter 43).

The book of Ezekiel avoids the term *Zion* altogether and only mentions Jerusalem in the judgment section of the book, with two exceptions (33:21; 36:38), but both of those references involve polemic against Jerusalem. This avoidance of *Jerusalem* is no accident. In the priestly perspective, Jerusalem has become a place of defilement, and until the land and the inhabitants are made clean, no true remnant community can live in that city. Ezekiel dismissively refers to Jerusalem more than thirty times as "the city" or "this city."[33]

The temple plan of Ezekiel is not the one that was constructed. This fact points to the complicated nature of prophetic books, predictions embedded in them, and the historical realities on the ground. A number of scholars argue that the unfulfilled plan of the temple suggests this idealistic plan was composed prior to the time that temple reconstruction began.[34] Just as importantly, the book of Ezekiel represents a faith document for one of the groups of returning exiles who had a vested interest in pushing the theological agenda of the book. The book continued to be adapted for generations, as we know by comparing the versions represented by the shorter (and generally earlier) version that appears in the Old Greek with the version that resulted in the Masoretic Text. Inconsistencies occur in the theological statements of the final form, and the specifics of several prophetic predictions failed to materialize (the most obvious being no Davidic king ever ruled again and Nebuchadnezzar never defeated Tyre). Yet, the boldest prediction that Jerusalem would fall seems to have overcome all other issues. Armed with this message, those who returned from Babylon with this prophetic book undoubtedly used its message of preference for the exiles from 597 BCE to their advantage. Additionally, the preference for the Zadokite priests and the demotion of the Levites to the status of secondary clerics largely coincides with the portrait of the temple personnel in Ezra, Nehemiah, and Chronicles (though each of these works document a certain fluidity in the status of the Levites as well, probably because the temple bureaucracy continued to grow).

Ezekiel's priestly outlook colors the book in numerous ways. Ezekiel functioned as a prophet to the exiles in Tel-abib, and he assiduously uses prophetic speech formulas (e.g., "the word of YHWH came to me") and forms (e.g., judgment oracles). At the same time, virtually every commentator notes that the book of Ezekiel displays a strong sense of priestly traditions, forms, and theology. Most attribute this orientation to his education as priest, which would have been years in the making. Recent studies have begun to clarify which priestly traditions appear in Ezekiel. Steven Cook suggests that Ezekiel shows a marked affinity with the Holiness School.[35] According to Cook, the Holiness School represents a continuing sociological tradition that aligns closely with the Zadokite traditions in Ezekiel. Further, Ezekiel's priestly theology puts him in conflict with both the Aaronide Priests (whose influence he finds represented in Isaiah 40–55 and in the Priestly Torah [PT]) and with the spectrum of Deuteronomistic traditions that one finds in Deuteronomy, the Deuteronomistic History, and Jeremiah and that had closer ties to the Levites. According to Cook, the Holiness School (HS) and Ezekiel have a much more hierarchical view of priestly organization:

Similarly, the PT strand is uninterested in functional distinctions among the priestly lineages of Levi, Aaron, and Zadok (see Knohl, *Sanctuary of Silence*, 66, 85, 192, 209–12). Things are far different in both HS and Ezekiel. Ezekiel 40:44-46 differentiates two types of priests serving within the temple's restricted inner court, where the Levites are not allowed.[36]

The Jerusalem priests exiled with Jehoiachin largely reflect the Zadokite tradition whose control of the Jerusalem temple they claimed went back to Zadok's appointment by David and Abiathar the priest's exile to Anathoth by Solomon for supporting Adonijah as king.[37] The observations of Cook suggest that priestly groups also had vested interests in preserving prophetic traditions. Ezekiel's inclusion among the prophets represented the interests of the Zadokites, but these interests were neither the only nor the dominant voice in the prophetic corpus.

Discussion Questions

1. Compare the function of the dated superscriptions in Ezekiel with those of Jeremiah, Isaiah, and the Twelve.

2. Explain the interplay between signs of unity and disunity in Ezekiel.

3. How do scholars wrestle with the redactional processes of Ezekiel?

4. Explain the tripartite structure of Ezekiel.

5. Compare the call narrative of Ezekiel (chapters 1–3) with the call narratives of Jeremiah (chapter 1), Isaiah (chapter 6), and Hosea (chapters 1–3).

6. How do you interpret the commands to speak versus the commands to be silent in Ezekiel?

7. Explain the literary, chronological, compositional, and theological issues associated with the departure and return of the "Glory" of YHWH in Ezekiel 8–11 and 40–43.

8. Explain the problems of the misogynistic images in Ezekiel 16 and 23 along with similar imagery in the other three prophetic scrolls.

9. Describe and illustrate the role of the purified remnant in Ezekiel.

10. How does Ezekiel 33–48 portray restoration?

11. How does Ezekiel's priestly background color the book?

Chapter 4

The Beginnings of the Twelve

Introduction

Ancient Traditions

Hosea–Malachi go by a number of names: the Book of the Twelve, the Twelve Prophets, the Twelve, and the Minor Prophets. Ancient traditions have made clear that these writings were deliberately transmitted together on a single scroll and were counted as one book, not twelve. Christian interpreters largely ignored this tradition after the production of the Vulgate, but scholars in the last thirty years have showed renewed interest in what happens when one interprets the Twelve as a deliberately arranged scroll. Scholars in the last thirty years also believe that the meaning one derives from reading the corpus involves more than merely placing completed writings side-by-side. Rather, a sustained conversation has developed regarding the process by which these writings came together, the degree of editorial shaping that they received, and the role of the individual books in the thematic and theological development of the Twelve.

The earliest reference to the canonical collection of the Twelve Prophets appears in Sirach 49:10, from the early second century BCE, as part of the Hymn of the Ancestors (Sir 44–49). This passage rehearses the history of God's people through the major characters (individually and collectively), but it follows a particular order that coincides with the MT order of the canonical books: Judges

97

(46:11), Samuel (46:13), Isaiah (48:23), Jeremiah (49:6), Ezekiel (49:8), and the Twelve Prophets (49:10).

During the third and second centuries BCE, the prophetic corpus was translated into Greek. This Greek translation is typically called the Septuagint (meaning "the seventy"; abbreviated as LXX), though it actually has a very complex history of its own. Most LXX manuscripts manifest a different order of the first six writings:

MT	Hos	Joel	Amos	Obad	Jonah	Mic	Nah, Hab, Zeph, Hag, Zech, Mal
LXX	Hos	Amos	Mic	Joel	Obad	Jonah	Zeph, Hag, Zech, Mal

The LXX order changes the original MT order by pulling the three eighth-century prophets to the front (Hos-Amos-Mic) and leaving the others in the same order in which they existed (Joel–Obad–Jonah). This rearrangement keeps the individual writings together, underscoring their existence as a single unit. In the first century CE, Fourth Ezra and Josephus state that 24 and 22 books respectively are authoritative for all Jews. Neither number is the same as the thirty-nine books counted in English Bibles, but both require counting the Twelve as a single book.

Jerome completed his translation of the Vulgate around 400 CE, and in his introduction to Hosea, he writes specifically that "the Twelve Prophets are one book."[1] He also articulates a reading strategy in that one should consider the undated writings as coming from the time of the last king mentioned.

The Masoretic notes in the Leningrad Codex also testify that the Twelve was still considered a unit between 700–900 CE. The note at the end of the Twelve indicates that the Twelve has 1025 verses, and the Masoretic note in the margin of Micah 3:12 indicates that this verse represents the middle of the Twelve by verses.

All this evidence suggests a strong tradition that the Twelve was written on a single scroll and counted as a single book. However, another tradition emphasized the size of the individual writings. Augustine and others called this collection the Minor Prophets because the individual writings were small in comparison with Isaiah, Jeremiah, and Ezekiel.[2] Over time, this tradition became dominant, and by the twentieth century very few people had ever heard of the Book of the Twelve or the Twelve Prophets.

Recent Investigations

In the first half of the twentieth century, Karl Budde and Rolland Emerson Wolfe postulated that redactional activity in and among the Twelve helped to account for its character as a single scroll.[3] Budde described this activity as deletions that removed narrative elements from these books. Wolfe proposed thirteen distinct redactional levels that gradually accounted for the inclusion of the twelve books. Contemporaneously, Umberto Cassuto made an important series of observations leading him to conclude that the writings of the Twelve were placed in their positions by scribes who noticed the shared catchwords between the writings.[4]

Scholarly investigations on the Book of the Twelve have increased dramatically from the late twentieth century onward. These investigations have recognized the Book of the Twelve as a canonical unit. This work began with treatments by Dale Schneider and Andrew Lee, both of whom wrote dissertations influenced by canonical criticism.[5]

Redactional investigations of the Book of the Twelve by Nogalski, Schart, Zapff, Bosshard-Nepustil, Wöhrle, and others have created a considerably different picture from earlier theories. Nogalski investigates catchwords between the writings and argues that they accentuate connections between adjacent writings.[6] He demonstrates that many of the catchword connections were deliberately created as editorial insertions. Schart agrees with Nogalski in many ways, but differs in three respects: he uses Amos as his starting point; he traces a more complicated series of stages leading to the Twelve;[7] and he argues that Malachi was attached to the end of Zechariah 14, whereas Nogalski argues that Zechariah 9–14 was inserted between Zechariah 8 and Malachi.[8] Like Nogalski, Schart argues that Hosea, Amos, Micah, and Zephaniah existed as a book of four prophets, and that Haggai and Zechariah 1–8 also existed as a book of two originally independent writings that were redacted together. Zapff largely concurs with Schart, but works outward from Micah rather than Amos.[9]

Bosshard-Nepustil emphasizes the development of the Book of the Twelve as a process that created a deliberate parallel with the book of Isaiah by redactional compositions designed as thematic mirrors in the two prophetic collections.[10]

Wöhrle critiques the existing models for not taking full account of the developmental histories of each book prior to asking how it relates to the Twelve.[11] Wöhrle analyzes each book for its redactional history, except Hosea, and withholds judgment on the interrelationships until he determines the foundational layer and subsequent additions. Nevertheless, he also finds layers that link the writings, and also concludes that a four-prophets book included Hosea, Amos, Micah, and Zephaniah. Wöhrle describes the origin of the individual writings in more developmental terms than compositional terms, positing a number of thematic layers within the corpus: the foreign-nations corpus 1 and 2, the grace layer, and so forth, each having its own characteristics.

Some commonalities result from these investigations. Most agree that two preexisting collections were edited together and that their dated superscriptions form the chronological backbone to the Book of the Twelve. The Book of the Four links Hosea, Amos, Micah, and Zephaniah by patterns in the kings mentioned in the superscriptions.

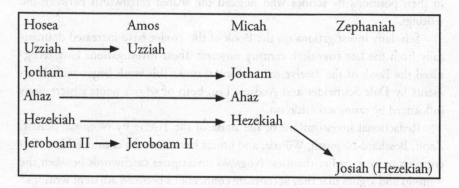

Hosea lists four Judean kings and Jeroboam II, king of Israel. Amos lists the first and last kings mentioned in Hosea, who are contemporary with each other. Micah lists the three Judean kings not mentioned in Amos, culminating in Hezekiah. Zephaniah dates to the reign of Josiah, but the prophet is linked to Hezekiah by a five-generation genealogy.

Moreover, these books share common macrostructural patterns. Hosea and Amos direct their message primarily toward the Northern Kingdom while Micah and Zephaniah focus upon the Southern Kingdom. Also, the first of these two pairs (Hosea and Micah) regularly alternate words of judgment with words of hope while the second two books offer no real words of hope or promise until the very end of the writings (in Amos 9:7-15 and Zeph 3:9-20), with most scholars treating these passages as later additions to the early forms of the books of Amos and Zephaniah. The second of these pairs (Amos and Zephaniah) offers a section of OAN that concludes with a word of judgment against the Northern Kingdom and against Jerusalem respectively (Amos 1–2; Zeph 2:4–3:7). Finally, the transition from the message to the Northern Kingdom to the Southern Kingdom takes place in the significant passage of Micah 1:2-7 where Samaria's destruction appears as a warning to Judah. Nogalski argues that this line of reasoning draws upon knowledge of Kings, since it represents the only literary source containing this particular slant on the history of Judah (see especially 2 Kgs 17).

The second preexisting collection is Haggai-Zechariah 1–8. These two prophets also share a similar dating pattern that dates the prophetic speeches to particular days and months in the reign of Darius, king of Persia.[12] These date formulas create an overlapping chronology that situates the vignettes in each book to specific dates from 520–518 BCE. In addition, these two writings focus on motivational speeches and cultic expectations surrounding the works of Haggai and Zechariah in helping to rebuild the temple (Haggai) and establish its role in the community (Zechariah 1–8).

The remaining six writings do not exhibit dates in their superscriptions, but their placement in the order of the MT is by no means random. The role of each writing in the Book of the Twelve will be addressed below. For Nogalski, the majority of these undated writings show deliberate use of a paradigm of history related to the imagery and themes of Joel. Many of the catchwords inserted into the writings at this point draw upon Joel and the existing writings. Nogalski calls this expansion of the collections the Joel-related layer. He refers to Joel as the literary anchor of the larger collection that includes every book except Jonah and Zechariah 9–14, which were added subsequently.

These different redactional models will have to be sorted out over time, but cumulatively they make a strong case that the Book of the Twelve came together gradually, involved considerable theological reflection upon the texts, and included the work of editors who used various means to connect the writings to one another. All these scholarly works largely agree upon two primary conclusions: (1) the six writings containing chronological elements in their superscriptions did not all arise simultaneously, but do provide the Book of the Twelve with a chronological framework that moves from the eighth century to the Persian period; (2) those writings that do not contain chronological elements in their superscriptions nevertheless owe their location in the larger corpus to thematic considerations. Issues related to this chronological macrostructure and to recurring themes should thus receive attention. It follows, then, that any reading of the Twelve as a corpus should consider how the location and message of the individual prophetic writings add to the meaning of the whole.

Individual Writings and the Collective Whole

The individual writings of the Twelve have a history of development prior to their inclusion in the developing corpus. That being said, many scholars now recognize that the placement and editing of the individual writings adds meaning to the individual collections because of the intentional interplay between them.

Debates continue over the nature of the redactional work on the individual writings and the extent to which they manifest cognizance of their location in the Twelve. Some redactional models rely more heavily upon the idea that the author/compiler/editor combined preexisting sources to create the majority of the book. These models see literary tensions as a result of the source blocks used

101

in combination with editorial transitions and commentary. Other models explain the same literary tensions as resulting from a longer series of updates. The former tends to produce a smaller number of editorial stages.

Details regarding individual books will enter the discussions below, but attention will also be given to the question of the literary function of each of the twelve prophetic collections within the scroll. Special attention will be given to the chronological structure that shapes the final form of the Book of the Twelve and to the thematic overlap between adjacent writings. Accordingly, the discussion will begin with Hosea, Amos, Micah, and Zephaniah (which scholars now frequently label the Book of the Four Prophets). We then will turn to Haggai-Zechariah-Malachi. These chapters reflect the conviction that the two preexisting collections (the Book of the Four and Haggai-Zechariah 1–8) create the chronology that guides the reading of the scroll of the Twelve Prophets. Finally, the final chapter will deal with the remaining writings (Nahum, Habakkuk, Joel, Obadiah, and Jonah) which are thematically linked to their adjacent writings.

Hosea

The Prophet and the Book

Explicit biographical data in Hosea includes only the names of kings who reigned contemporaneously with the prophet (1:1), the name of the prophet's father Beeri (1:1), the name of his wife Gomer (1:3), and the symbolic names of three children (Jezreel in 1:4; Lo-Ruhamah in 1:6; and Lo-Ammi in 1:8). That said, scholars agree that the early texts in Hosea suggest that this prophet preached in the Northern Kingdom of Israel (and likely originated there). Most concrete historical references in the book refer to the time surrounding the Syro-Ephraimite War (734–732 BCE). Most of the redactional models conclude that the transmission of the book shifted to Judah after the events of 722 BCE when the Northern Kingdom was destroyed and a significant number of refugees made their way south to Judah to escape the Assyrians. The application of texts to Judah throughout the book, especially those which reflect positively upon the Judean monarchy, provide the primary evidence for this perspective.[13]

The rhetoric of Hosea generally addresses the Northern Kingdom, and for the most part warns them of the coming catastrophe if they do not change their ways. One would therefore assume that the editors of the book expected the reader to situate these verses prior to 722 BCE when the Assyrians destroyed Samaria and exiled its leadership. Nevertheless, portions of Hosea postdate 722 in all likelihood, and nowhere is this clearer than in the places where words addressed originally to an audience from the Northern Kingdom have been updated with specific statements including Judah as well.

Despite the fact that Hosea begins the Book of the Twelve in all the variant orders, critical scholarship has determined with an unusually high degree of unanimity that Hosea is not the earliest of the eighth-century prophets represented in either the Latter Prophets or the Book of the Twelve. Both Isaiah and Amos likely appeared before Hosea, and Micah is considered the youngest of the four. This critical consensus raises the question why Hosea consistently appears at the beginning of the Book of the Twelve, especially since the chronology appears to have been a factor in compiling these writings into a collection. Two suggestions appear with some frequency, the one ancient and the other suggested by recent critical scholarship. Ancient Jewish sources (e.g., Baba Batra, 14b) explain the location of Hosea at the beginning of the Twelve as a result of the opening incipit in the book (1:2): "when the Lord *first* spoke through Hosea . . ." Recent investigations suggest the rationale for placing Hosea in the opening position has more to do with thematic considerations. One of the key structural components of Hosea is its deliberate alternation of words of judgment with words of hope and its rather frequent inclusion of calls to return to YHWH. The book of Hosea seems deliberately designed to show that Israel was given numerous chances to change its behavior. The book of Amos, by contrast, offers its readers no such ambiguity. From the beginning, the prophetic and divine pronouncements in Amos announce impending judgment against Israel that cannot be averted.

The Structure and Contents of Hosea

Scholars have long noted transition points in Hosea that may reflect earlier collections or editorial tendencies to juxtapose texts that announce judgment against those of a more hopeful future. Chapters 1–3 contain marriage metaphors regarding the relationship of Israel and YHWH. Each of the three core units also begins with words of judgment and ends with words of hope. The majority of chapters 4–6 pronounce judgment upon Israel, yet chapter 6 begins with the voice of the people calling for a return to YHWH (6:1-3). Judgment dominates chapters 7–10, but Hosea 11 offers a divine soliloquy portraying YHWH's inner conflict before deciding *not* to punish Ephraim. Chapters 12–13 again condemn Ephraim's inability to remain faithful, but the book ends optimistically when the prophet calls the people to return to YHWH (14:1-3) and YHWH responds with a contingent promise of restoration. In other words, each of the major sections (1–3; 4–6; 7–11; 12–14) vacillates between words of judgment and a desire for restoration.

Chapter 4

Hosea 1–3: Marriage Metaphors and Symbolic Actions

Hosea 1–3 begins the book with three literarily distinct units (chapters 1, 2, and 3) that explore the relationship between YHWH and Israel using marriage motifs. These metaphors create troubling theological images for modern readers because of the violence they condone against women.[14] Chapter 1 narrates a prophetic sign act in which YHWH commands Hosea to marry a woman named Gomer, described as a woman of fornication, and to have children with her.[15] Three scenes (1:3-5, 6-7, 8-9) recount the birth of these children, each of whom is given a name symbolizing judgment: Jezreel (the name of a valley that was the location of a famous defeat for Israel), Lo-Ruhamah (meaning "not pitied"), and Lo-Ammi (meaning "not my people"). Chapter 1 ends with a promise that contains a play on words for each child (1:10–2:1). Notably, these promises display a decidedly Judean conceptualization.[16]

Chapter 2 poetically describes the relationship between YHWH and his promiscuous wife, now personified as the land of Israel (not the wife of the prophet). In Hosea 2, YHWH describes his sense of betrayal because his wife chases after other "lovers," erroneously attributing to her paramours gifts given by YHWH (2:8 [Heb. 2:10]). YHWH disturbingly responds with threats of violence against his wife: he will strip her naked (2:5, 10 [Heb. 2:7, 12]) and attempt to hold her captive while he tries to win her back (2:14 [Heb. 2:16]). The ancient author penned such images to convey the idea that punishment leads to restoration (2:15-23 [Heb. 2:17-25]). Such imagery works against itself for modern readers because it describes YHWH's behavior in terms analogous to spousal abuse.

At least three distinctive elements can help contextualize the theological claims, though they cannot redeem the imagery: the cultural context, the metaphorical language, and the alternation of judgment and restoration. First, these images do not condone human violence in the name of God, and one can contrast these images against the background of ancient Near Eastern culture, including Jewish tradition, where adultery was considered a crime punishable by death (cf. Lev 20:10-14). Ancient audiences could have thus found them disturbing, but for very different reasons: because the woman does not die. Second, Hosea 2 depicts the relationship between YHWH and Israel in metaphorical, almost allegorical, terms. The promiscuous lover imagery dominates the chapter. Nevertheless, the chapter uses rhetoric that targets Israel as the actual recipient of judgment and restoration much like other expressions of prophetic judgment. Third, like Hosea 1, chapter 2 structures its message paradigmatically to include judgment and the promise of restoration. The first of these promises (2:14-20 [Heb. 2:16-22]) reverses the punishment announced in 2:1-13. After YHWH announces he will entice her to the "door of hope" (2:14-15 [Heb. 2:16-17]) and restore the vineyards as in the days of her youth, she will cease to call upon the Baals (2:16 [Heb. 2:18]) and will become a faithful wife (2:20 [Heb. 2:22]). The second promise (2:21-23 [Heb. 2:23-25]) returns to Hosea 1 and uses the names of the prophet's children (Jezreel, Lo-Ruhamah, and Lo-Ammi) as word plays with messages of restoration.[17]

Most scholars recognize that a redactor added at least the second section of these promises as a later insertion to connect the two chapters more closely.[18] These chapters do not exhibit the explicit pro-Judean agenda as do the promises in chapters 1 and 3, but 2:18 (Heb. 2:20) uses language closely associated with the Priestly creation story (Gen 1:20-25) and the flood account (Gen 6:18-20). Thus, these verses equate YHWH's promises with the re-creation of the land and make a deliberate point to reverse the judgment of chapters 1–2.

Hosea 3 concludes the extended marriage metaphors with another narrative about the prophet and a lover. Several things set the narrative apart from chapters 1 and 2. First, Hosea 3 tells of a symbolic action, in a way similar to chapter 1, with chapter 3 using an autobiographical style. Thus, the "I" speaking in chapter 3 is the prophet while the "I" in chapter 2 is YHWH. This autobiographical style also differs from the report style of Hosea 1, where the voice of a narrator speaks about both YHWH and the prophet. Second, the woman in Hosea 3 is unnamed and is called an adulteress (3:1), not a prostitute as in Hosea 1. Third, this chapter never mentions the children. Instead, the prophet tells the woman that she and he will not have sex for an extended period of time (3:3). These differences have led many scholars to argue Hosea 3 represents a variant version of the prophetic call narrative in Hosea 1 that would have been transmitted independently before it was joined with the other two marriage accounts.[19] Many have wondered whether Hosea 3 refers to the same woman as Hosea 1, or whether the "again" in 3:1 implies a second woman.

Despite the stylistic differences, Hosea 3 conveys a similar message to chapters 1–2. Like chapter 1, it depicts the prophet's marriage (not YHWH's) as a symbolic action to make a theological point. Like Hosea 2, it depicts the spouse (not the children) as a metaphor for the people (3:1, 4-5). Like chapter 1, Hosea 3 ends with a decidedly Judean promise of restoration when the Israelites "will return and seek the LORD their God, and David their king" (3:5).

Hosea 4–6: Accusations, Judgment, and Calls to Return

Hosea 4–14 exhibits characteristics of an anthology of prophetic speeches of varying lengths, and contains three cycles that vacillate between judgment and restoration (chapters 4–6; 7–11; 12–14). The arrangement involves loose thematic associations of accusation and pronouncements of judgment that lead

105

periodically to a reflection of hope that the people will return to YHWH. The verb *return* (*shûb*) functions as a major *leitmotif* for the book.[20] Hosea 4:1–5:7 throws a litany of accusations against the people and priests involving ethical and cultic misdeeds, punctuated with pronouncements of judgment (4:5, 10, 19; 5:2, 6, 7b). Hosea 5:8-10 takes a more political turn as commentary on the Syro-Ephraimite War and its aftermath. Hosea 6 concerns whether or not Israel/Ephraim can truly return to YHWH. The chapter assumes that Israel's departure from YHWH concerns the cultic misdeeds of chapters 4–5. YHWH's covenant expectations, however, also focus upon ethical behavior (6:7-9) and cultic infidelity (= Israel's promiscuity in 6:10). YHWH articulates concerns for fidelity in one's actions and orientation: "For I desire steadfast love and not sacrifice, the knowledge of God rather than burnt offerings" (6:6).

Hosea 7–11: Politics, Idolatry, Punishment, and Reprieve

Hosea 7 returns to the theme of the condemnation of political entities, including the king and the king's family, Israel randomly turning to Egypt and Assyria, and Israel's abandonment of the worship of YHWH. Chapter 8 blends the themes of idolatry and kingship by referring to transgression of the law (8:1), the calf of Samaria (8:5, 6), sacrifice upon non-Jerusalem altars (8:11), and reference to Egypt and Assyria (8:9, 13).

Chapters 9–10 primarily announce a series of punishments for Israel because of its cultic infidelity.[21] These chapters level charges against Israel/Ephraim (9:1, 3; 10:1, 6b-11), its prophets (9:7, 8), and its idolatrous priests at Bethel (10:5).

Chapter 11 concludes this third section with YHWH's dramatic soliloquy in which he speaks about his internal conflict over whether or not to punish Ephraim or allow the people to return (*shûb*). The end of this soliloquy does not resolve this tension. On the one hand, 11:9 suggests YHWH's inclination toward deliverance: "I will not execute my fierce anger; I will not again destroy Ephraim for I am God and not man, the holy one in your midst, and I will not come in wrath." Verses 10-11 depict the future return of the people from the land of Assyria. On the other hand, the very last verse of the chapter (11:12) changes course dramatically and begins to accuse Ephraim/Israel once again of lying (11:12).

Hosea 12–14: Judgment and a Call to Return

The final extended block in Hosea also moves from judgment to potential promise. The rhetorical logic of the placement of smaller units provides this section with a juridical and dialogical character. The rhetorical elements include indictments and accusations (12:1-6; 13:1-3), Israel's denial of guilt (12:7-8), and verdicts in the form of pronouncements of divine judgment (12:9-14; 13:4-8). In addition, Hosea 12–14 includes two calls to repent (12:6; 14:1-8 [Heb. 12:7; 14:2-9]) before the final motto of the book that admonishes those who are discerning to take the words of the book to heart (14:9 [Heb. 14:10]). Thus, the final chapters of Hosea convey a clear sense of the guilt of Israel combined with YHWH's desire to show compassion.

Chapters 12–13 indict Ephraim (and Judah and Jacob) with a string of accusations.[22] As a result, the prophet delivers YHWH's verdict: Ephraim must pay for his crimes (12:14 [Heb. 12:15]). Hosea 13 then replays the juridical dynamics of chapter 12, though most of Hosea 13 appears in the form of divine first-person speech rather than a prophetic speaker.

Hosea 14 ends the book with a final call to return to YHWH in order to allow YHWH to display his compassion on Israel (14:1-8). Remarkably, following the two trial scenes that increasingly focus upon the judgments that will befall Israel, the last major rhetorical unit of the book yet again offers Israel a chance to return to YHWH and ends with a promise. Jörg Jeremias has conclusively demonstrated, however, that this promise is contingent.[23] The final statement (14:8 [Heb. 14:9]) still awaits Israel's response: "Oh Ephraim, what have I to do with idols?" This call and promise demands a response, a notion underscored by the final verse of the book that calls upon readers to discern how they will respond: "Those who are wise understand these things; those who are discerning know them. For the ways of the LORD are right, and the upright walk in them, but transgressors stumble in them" (14:9 [Heb. 14:10]).

Recurring Themes

Proper cultic and ethical behavior take center stage in Hosea, but one should not lose sight of the fact when reading Hosea that the thrust of the message orients its message toward the Northern Kingdom. The term *Ephraim* refers to the central region of the Northern Kingdom. No other book in the entire Old Testament refers to Ephraim as many times as Hosea. Allusions to eighth-century events remain obscure, but many see references to the Syro-Ephraimite War (734 BCE),[24] the dramatic overthrow of a number of kings prior to the appointment of Hoshea by the Assyrians (732 BCE),[25] and possibly the destruction of Samaria (722 BCE).[26]

Cultic Behavior

Religious terminology plays a central role in the accusations. Priests and prophets are condemned, and texts describing idolatry as whoredom appear frequently. A strong scholarly consensus understands the religious practices that are condemned as more closely reflecting religious practices of the Northern Kingdom. The majority of passages mentioning Judah (but not all) reflect the work of later editors applying critiques against the Northern Kingdom to Judah.[27]

The cultic guilt of Israel/Ephraim dominates the accusations in the book of Hosea, and this element plays out in at least six recurring motifs. First, infidelity serves as a cipher for idolatry. Second, the worship of Baal is first mentioned in the depiction of the promiscuous wife, but it appears in several passages in the rest of the book (Hos 2:8, 13, 16, 17 [Heb. 2:10, 15, 18, 19]; 9:10; 11:2; 13:1). Third, specific mention of the worship of idols appears in a number of different contexts (Hos 4:17; 8:4; 10:5-6; 11:2; 13:2; 14:8). Some of these refer to the calf image established at Bethel by Jeroboam I (10:5-6), while others probably refer to cast images that played a role in the household religion of Israel and Judah (13:2). Fourth, several texts specifically condemn practices of Israel whereby it offers sacrifice at nonsanctioned altars (4:19; 8:11;10:1, 2, 8; 12:11). Fifth, not surprisingly, the prophet condemns improper priestly participation in these rituals and other objectionable actions (4:4, 6, 9; 5:1; 6:9; 10:5). Sixth, a number of passages in this book castigate Israel for its failure to listen to prophets sent by YHWH (6:5; 9:7, 8; 12:10, 13).

Behavioral Expectations

A significant number of texts noted above either accuse Israel of covenant infidelity or pronounce judgment against Israel for violating YHWH's expectations. At the same time, a number of texts articulate YHWH's expectations for Israel's behavior in positive terms. Rather than condemning them for what they did not do, these texts exhort the people to do what they should: show covenant fidelity, practice justice, and demonstrate righteousness. Most notably, among these admonitions one finds these expectations articulated as concrete expressions of recommitment to YHWH: "But as for you, return to your God, hold fast to love (*ḥesed*) and justice (*mišpat*), and wait continually for your God." (12:6 NRSV [Heb. 12:7]) One also finds statements indicating that these relational qualities supersede, or better, serve as the foundation for cultic ritual acts: "For I desire steadfast love (*ḥesed*) and not sacrifice, the knowledge of God rather than burnt offerings" (6:6 NRSV). These expectations reappear consistently within the Book of the Four.[28]

Political Foolishness

The book of Hosea accuses Israel of political nonsense because its leaders continually vacillate between policies that ally them with Assyria and with Egypt

(5:13; 7:11, 16; 8:9, 13; 9:6; 10:6; 12:1). During the eighth century BCE, Egypt and Assyria were enemies, so such policies would result in exile to Assyria in what these texts depict as a return to the slavery of Egypt prior to the time of Moses (9:3; 11:5).

Hosea within the Book of the Twelve

Hosea, Amos, Micah, and Zephaniah were edited and transmitted together as a collection with a didactic purpose. This collection underscores the link between the destruction of the Northern Kingdom of Israel and the Southern Kingdom of Judah that plays an important part in the book of Kings. These four books share interrelated elements, including chronological patterns connecting the superscriptions, macrostructural patterns, unusual endings to OAN, and eschatological optimism. The linking of the superscriptions has been noted. Macrostructural patterns can be seen in the pairing of two writings focusing upon the Northern Kingdom (Hosea and Amos) followed by two writings directed to the Southern Kingdom (Micah and Zephaniah). Each pair begins with a book alternating words of judgment with words of hope (Hosea and Micah) followed by a book that focuses exclusively upon judgment until the end of the book (Amos and Zephaniah) with a dramatic judgment oracle against YHWH's own people.

The Book of the Four does two things quite effectively. First, the superscriptions provide the Book of the Four with a clear sense of chronological progression. Second, Hosea and Micah alternate words of judgment with words of hope to create a dramatic tension in terms of the fate of the two kingdoms, while the consistent pronouncements of judgment in Amos and Zephaniah eliminate any question as to whether Israel and Judah will be punished. The book of Hosea has laid the groundwork that demands a decision from Israel. The book of Amos begins with the assumption that the time for Israel to change has passed. Subsequently, Joel draws conceptually from Hosea 2 and 14.

Amos

The Prophet and the Book

Only a short prophetic narrative (7:10-17) and the superscription (1:1) contain biographical information about Amos. He came from Tekoa (a village about twelve miles south of Jerusalem), where he worked as a shepherd and farmer (cf. 7:14) during the reign Jeroboam II (786–746 BCE). Unlike Hosea, Amos's hometown means he comes from Judah, yet like Hosea, the book directs its message mostly against Israel. This outsider status colors the book from the opening motto (1:2).

Scholars date Amos's prophetic career to the mid-eighth century BCE, making him the earliest of the Latter Prophets. Evidence for an early date derives from explicit and implicit memories. The action of 7:10-17 (cf. 7:9) takes place during the reign of Jeroboam II, though the narrative comes from a later time. Likewise, the social setting of a number of the oracles presupposes a thriving economy in Israel, which aligns well with the time of Jeroboam II, when compared with Hosea and Micah. Micah, for example, speaks of the houses being taken (probably as part of Hezekiah's preparation for war; see Mic 2:1–2) while Hosea references a series of kings who have come to power by force (see Hos 7:7; 8:4). The second half of the eighth century BCE was a more volatile time politically and socially.

The Structure and Contents of Amos

Amos unfolds in four main sections (1–2; 3–6; 7:1–9:6; and 9:7-15). For convenience, these blocks can be labeled by their primary literary characteristics as the OAN, the sayings, the visions, and the promises. These sections came together over time and were updated during the exilic period and beyond. Two of these sections (1–2 and 7:1–9:6) display climactic movement as well as signs of later editorial reshaping. Chapters 3–6 display the characteristics of an anthology (like Hos 4–14), yet the headings at the beginning of each of these chapters suggest that an editor related independent collections to one another. Amos 7:1–9:6 revolves around an early composition of vision reports (7:1-3, 4-6, 7-9; 8:1-3; and perhaps 9:1-4) into which two additional blocks of material have been incorporated at key positions: a prophetic narrative (7:10-17) and a theological summary of the message of the book (8:4-14). Finally, 9:7-15 offers several distinct promises.

Amos 1–2: The Oracles against the Nations

The first major block of Amos contains a superscription (1:1), a motto summarizing the book's message (1:2), and a series of oracles against the surrounding nations (1:3–2:16).

The Superscription (1:1). The superscription provides limited biographical data about the prophet, including his hometown (Tekoa), his occupation (shepherd), and two distinct dating schemes (two contemporary kings and an earthquake). Most critical scholars agree that the superscription grew over time. In all likelihood, the reference to the two kings entered during the exile when the Book of the Four Prophets came to be. Uzziah and Jeroboam II ruled Judah and Israel as contemporaries (786–746 BCE). The coordination of the reigns of kings of Judah and Israel fits the content and the pattern of superscriptions found in the Four Prophets.

The Motto (1:2). Amos 1:2 functions as a thematic summary of the book and is syntactically separate from both the superscription and the OAN. Its four poetic statements represent two pairs of synonymous parallelism:

> The LORD roars from Zion and utters his voice from Jerusalem;

> The pastures of the shepherds wither, and the top of Carmel dries up.

These lines are interrelated by the assumption of cause and effect. The lion roars and the land withers. Further, the geographic terms in the first line name Judean sites while Carmel represents Israel in the second line, meaning YHWH's judgment emanates from Jerusalem, which implies a Judean theological perspective. The judgment affects the land of Israel. The sayings, speeches, and compositions in Amos overwhelmingly pronounce judgment upon Israel, making this opening motto quite appropriate for summarizing the theme of the book. The unrelenting pronouncement of judgment against Israel in Amos 1:1–9:6 differs notably from the continual vacillation between judgment and promise in Hosea, and this quality probably explains why Amos comes after Hosea in every arrangement of the Twelve.

The Oracles against the Nations (1:3–2:16). The OAN in Amos exhibit a clear compositional style and rhetorical agenda. Each of the eight oracles begins identically with the refrain "for three transgressions of [X] and for four, I will not turn it back." From there each of the oracles follows a similar pattern.[29] The geographical locations of these oracles make clear that the composition intentionally encircles Israel before pronouncing judgment against it. The ultimate goal of these pronouncements against other nations reaches its climax when the final and longest oracle uses the same refrain (2:6) to pronounce judgment against Israel.

The oracles against Tyre (1:9-10), Edom (1:11-12), and Judah (2:4-5) differ in small stylistic ways from the other oracles.[30] Also, accusations in these oracles likely presuppose Jerusalem's destruction when an editor updated the collection.

The OAN in Amos grab the reader's attention due to the brutality they ascribe to these neighboring peoples. Surprisingly, these oracles climax in a pronouncement of judgment against Israel using the same refrain that begins the preceding seven oracles. Equally surprising, the prophet does not accuse Israel of war crimes, but graphically describes the callousness of those who ignore the demands of social justice and covenant fidelity. The portrait of Israel depicted by

111

these verses is certainly not pretty. Those in Israelite society who had no protection were sold into slavery by those to whom they owed money (2:6-7a). Debauchery sullies YHWH's name (2:7b). Elite citizens of means treat places of worship as their own party zone when they lay on garments left as pledges for money owed and drink the wine paid as fines (2:8). Such callous behavior shows no respect for YHWH or for the people whom they abuse. Therefore, the prophet announces Israel's punishment (2:13-16) and communicates that YHWH's past decision to redeem Israel from slavery will not protect them from destruction (2:9-12). For YHWH's people, oppression of the poor, ethical misconduct, and profaning what is holy rise to the level of war crimes against foreign nations in the eyes of YHWH.

Amos 3–6: The Sayings

Chapters 3–6 differ from the climactic movement in the oracles against the nations (Amos 1–2) that precede it and in the visions of chapters 7–9 that follow. The units in Amos 3–6 are generally smaller (often only 4 to 5 verses) and reflect various backgrounds. Consequently, they present themselves more as a collection of sayings, or an anthology of the prophet's message. The logic is not climactic but repetitive, in order to emphasize essential themes.

Four subsections begin by addressing a different group (3:1; 4:1; 5:1; and 6:1) and may represent smaller collections that were joined editorially. Three introductory calls to attention demand that the people of Israel, the "cows of Bashan," and the house of Israel pay attention to the word of YHWH (3:1; 4:1; 5:1). The final section begins with a woe oracle against the leaders of Zion as well as Samaria (6:1). This subtle shift coincides with a number of places in Hosea and Amos where the message of judgment against Israel makes a rhetorical point to Judean readers that they are not immune to YHWH's judgment.[31] The introductory calls also present a subtle intensification of the danger. The first three introductory calls all begin with the same phrase ("Hear this word"). One can detect an editorial intensification of danger in 5:1 when YHWH classifies "this word" as a lamentation. The language of lamentation implies death, and 5:2 underscores this image by depicting "virgin Israel" dead on the ground. This language of death changes to funeral language with the introduction in 6:1, which begins with the word *hôy*, often translated as "woe" or "alas." This language evokes funeral settings.[32] Hence, 5:1 and 6:1 show a logical progression from death to funeral, and 6:1 broadens the rhetorical addressee to include "those who are at ease in Zion" as well as "those who feel secure on Mount Samaria." This shift foreshadows the theological focus of the Book of the Four, namely that the sins that engulfed Israel and led to its destruction will ultimately cause the undoing of Judah as well.[33]

Motifs in 3–6 reinforce the major accusations from 2:6-16: mistreatment of the poor and the needy, ethical impropriety, and cultic laxity. The judgment oracle of 3:9-11 accuses Israel of storing up violence and robbery while the elite in Samaria oppress the poor and needy (4:1). Amos 5:6-7 (and 6:11-14) threaten Israel with destruction because of the people's perversion of justice and righteousness, charges that are concretized in 5:10-12 against those who reject justice in the gate, who abuse the poor physically and financially, and who take bribes to rule in favor of the wealthy. The prophet admonishes the people to seek what is good, hate what is evil, and establish justice in the city gate (5:14-15). Chapter 6 also condemns a group who lives lavishly, oblivious to the suffering of others until they themselves will be taken into exile (6:4-7).

As with 2:6-16, Amos 3–6 peppers its accusations of injustice with rebukes of crass and improper behavior at places of worship. The sanctuary at Bethel repeatedly comes into the crosshairs (3:14; 4:4; 5:5-6), which is not surprising given its role in the book of Kings as a symbol of the Northern Kingdom's rejection of Jerusalem as the sole temple of YHWH. It is no surprise, therefore, to see Bethel condemned in Amos because it represents an improper altar from a Judean perspective. Yet, Gilgal is also condemned as a place of illicit worship (4:4) and paired with Bethel as a city doomed for destruction (5:5). Gilgal was one of the oldest sites of worship in the heart of Ephraimite territory, and a central city that plays a significant role in the book of Joshua (Josh 4:19-20; 5:9-10; 9:6; 10:6-7, 9, 15, 43; 14:6; 15:7).

In addition to places of illicit worship, texts in Amos 3–6 condemn certain practices at religious sites in the north, though (in contrast to Hosea) Amos never mentions the worship of Baal explicitly. Amos 4:4-5 condemns the multiplicity of sacrifices at Bethel and Gilgal as ineffective means of protection against YHWH's punishment. Similar charges appear in 5:21-27 without mentioning Bethel and Gilgal by name. In 5:21-22, YHWH rejects the sacrifices in strong terms: "I hate, I despise your festivals, and I take no delight in your solemn assemblies. Even though you offer me your burnt offerings and grain offerings I will not accept them." Amos 5:24 provides the reason for YHWH's rejection of the sacrifices, implying that because those who offer sacrifices pay no attention to justice and righteousness, the sacrifices mean nothing. Instead of accepting their sacrifices, YHWH admonishes: "Let justice roll down like waters, and righteousness like an ever-flowing stream" (5:24). One may infer from this statement a theology that rejects ritual sacrifice if the life of the worshiper does not reflect a commitment to justice and righteousness.

113

Other practices come into view as well. Amos 5:25-26 seems to condemn the worship of idols and astral deities associated with Assyrian practices. In addition, and rather unusually, two texts take exception to the raucous use of musical instruments and songs at these festivals (5:23; 6:5). The exact nature of these practices cannot be reconstructed from these accusations with any clarity, but their presence helps to reinforce the book's image of the prophet as an outsider. Amos comes from Tekoa in Judah, but his accusations address the population of the Northern Kingdom.

Accusations abound in Amos 3–6, but most of the material deals with the certainty of the coming judgment. These oracles and sayings forcefully challenge those who think YHWH will not hold them accountable. Recurring motifs drive home the message of the devastation to come. References to deliverance from Egypt appear periodically as reversals of election (3:1-2; 4:10; 6:1). These statements emphasize that YHWH's past acts of salvation will not protect them from danger now. The severity of the coming devastation also stresses useless remnants: a piece of the ear of a lamb, the corner of a couch, and decimated populations (3:12; 5:3; 6:9-10). One passage (5:15) holds out hope for a remnant for Joseph, but the statement is conditional. A number of passages in these chapters allude to a coming attack from an enemy who will take Israel into exile (3:11; 4:2; 5:27; 6:14), again hardly a promise of well-being for those who survive.

Consistent with these recurring pronouncements about the certainty of coming judgment, Amos 5:18-20 presents another powerful reversal of an old concept, specifically the day of YHWH. The idea arose from the holy war tradition, in which those fighting under the name of YHWH called upon YHWH to act against their enemies. The prophet confronts those who believe that the day of YHWH will protect them. By contrast, Amos 5:18-20 argues that the day of YHWH will offer no protection if the people themselves are the target of YHWH's wrath. The nature of the day of YHWH becomes one of the distinctive recurring motifs in the Twelve (see Joel).

One of the longer units in chapters 3–6, 4:6-12 articulates YHWH's frustration that previous attempts to correct Israel's behavior have failed, leaving YHWH with no choice but to reject Israel. Five times YHWH utilizes a refrain to emphasize a series of punitive measures that failed to change Israel. With each increasingly devastating punitive act (famine, drought, locust plague, pestilence after the manner of Egypt, and devastation like Sodom and Gomorrah), this refrain drives home the point that no matter what measures YHWH took to punish Israel, "yet you did not return (*šûb*) to me, says the LORD" (4:6, 8, 9, 10, 11). This passage plays a critical role in Amos, especially when compared to the use of the verb *return* (*šûb*) in Hosea, which also uses the verb to recount Israel's refusal to return (5:4; 7:10; 11:5), but there articulates a hope that Israel will return (2:9;

3:5; 6:11) or exhorts Israel with a call to return to YHWH (6:1; 12:6; 14:2-5). By contrast, Amos 4:6-12 five times denies that Israel returned. Shortly thereafter, the funeral dirge of 5:1-2 announces that Israel has fallen and will not rise again.

Through accusations, judgment oracles, and descriptions of YHWH's power, Amos 3–6 repeatedly provides short, powerful articulations of the themes of justice, proper worship, and accountability. The rhetorical movement of the headings pronounces judgment against Israel whose behavior threatens Jerusalem.

Amos 7:1–9:6: The Visions

The third extended unit in Amos, like the OAN, begins as a composition that exhibits a climactic movement, but it also appears to have experienced the contribution of additional passages that retard this climax. These later passages, however, play important rhetorical roles in their own right. They are not mere appendages.

Five Vision Reports. The first four visions (7:1-3, 4-6, 7-9; 8:1-3) convey an increasing threat when one pays careful attention to the structure of the conversations and the content of the visions. The fifth vision report (9:1-4) records no conversation, but describes the destruction of Israel's temple. The first two vision reports describe unmistakable threats against Israel: a locust plague (7:1) and a cosmic fire sent by YHWH to devour the land (7:4). In both cases, the horror of the vision itself immediately elicits a call for mercy from the prophet using the same words: "O Lord GOD, forgive, I beg you! How can Jacob stand? He is so small" (7: 2, 5). Both times YHWH changes his mind in response to the prophet's petition (7:3, 6).

The third and fourth vision accounts follow a different pattern. The content of the vision seems far less threatening, but the consequences prove more severe. These visions begin with the prophet seeing an innocuous object, a lump of metal beside a wall (7:7) and a basket of summer fruit (8:1). Twice YHWH asks Amos to tell what he sees (7:8; 8:2), then pronounces devastating judgment. In the third vision Amos replies that he sees a "metal plumb" (*'anâk*); YHWH announces that he is about to place a metal plumb in the midst of Israel and will no longer withhold punishment. He will destroy the high places and the sanctuaries of Israel and send a sword against the house of Jeroboam (7:8b-9). The fourth vision unfolds even more dramatically. Amos sees a basket of summer fruit (*qayits*). YHWH responds with a pun that the end (*qêts*) has come. YHWH will no longer withhold punishment, but the temple songs will become the sound of wailing because of all the dead bodies (8:2b-3).

Debates continue regarding originality of the fifth vision report (9:1-4). A significant number of scholars maintain that the fifth vision was added after the

115

first four.[34] Nevertheless, no one doubts its function as the literary climax of the vision cycle. Dialogue between YHWH and the prophet dominates the first four visions, but the prophet never speaks in the fifth vision. He merely plays the role of a spectator as YHWH stands beside the altar and commands that the temple be destroyed by striking the capitals of the columns so that they are shattered upon the heads of the people (9:1a). The prophet can only watch as YHWH destroys the temple of the Northern Kingdom so that none can escape (9:1b-4). *Growth of the Vision Cycle.* The vision cycle circulated as an independent composition. At some point, the visions were joined with the OAN and the sayings to form the first edition of the book of Amos. Most suggest that these small collections were combined in the early sixth century.[35] Three additional compositions were added for dramatic effect: a prophetic narrative about the expulsion of Amos by the chief priest at Bethel (7:10-17), a series of sayings repeating phrases from the book (8:4-14), and the last of three hymnic doxologies that focus upon the power of YHWH over creation (9:5-6; cf. 4:13; 5:8-9). All three of these inserted pieces appear in locations designed to have a literary impact upon the growing collection.

The narrative in 7:10-17 is unusual in the Book of the Twelve because it recounts a story from the life of the prophet.[36] Nevertheless, the combination of its plot and its placement makes a powerful statement within the visions. This dramatic encounter pits the prophet from Judah against the high priest of Bethel. The narrator conveys the strength of Amos through his dependence upon the power of YHWH's word, while the priest comes across as manipulative, hiding behind the power of the king but powerless against YHWH. Amos takes on the entire political and religious establishment of the Northern Kingdom.

The drama within the narrative increases when this narrative is placed with the visions. In the first two visions, the prophet intercedes on Israel's behalf and causes YHWH to change his mind. In the third vision, YHWH's pronouncement of judgment ends the vision report (7:9), and this narrative appears at precisely the place where the reader would expect the prophet to plead for YHWH's mercy. Instead, Israel's chief priest, with the king's implicit permission, demands that Amos be silent. The narrative's placement could hardly be more emphatic.

Amos 8:4-14 represents a second block of texts inserted into the vision cycle. In several respects, 8:4-14 exhibits the same literary qualities as those that appeared in the anthology (chapters 3–6). Small units (8:4-6, 7-8, 9-10, 11-12, 13-14) convey accusations (8:4-6), affirm impending punishment (8:7-8), and announce what will happen using introductory eschatological formulas: "on that day" (8:9, 13) and "behold the days are coming" (8:11). What sets these verses apart, however, is the way in which they evoke phrases from elsewhere in the book. Almost every line of these verses contains language or imagery that the reader has already encountered.[37] These lexical clusters provide a thematic summary of the prophet's message just prior to the final vision in which the prophet watches YHWH destroy the temple of Israel. It seems plausible that these statements were added here when the three parts of Amos were combined. Cumulatively, these verses force the reader to reflect upon the message of Amos between the announcement that the end has come (8:3) and the destruction of the temple (9:1).

Third, in the history of critical scholarship three texts called the doxologies (4:13; 5:8-9; 9:5-6) have long been treated as insertions into their respective contexts. They stand apart because of their hymnic style and their thematic emphasis on creation. Scholars generally treated them as an independent poem, divided to mark important passages.[38] Recently, scholars question the extent to which the three doxologies really function as a single poem and suggest, instead, that they were composed to fit into their current locations.[39] Undoubtedly, debates about their genesis will continue, but both models agree upon their literary function. By emphasizing the power of YHWH as creator of the cosmos, these verses emphasize YHWH's ability to execute the judgment pronounced in the preceding verses (4:6-12; 5:3-7; and 9:1-4).

Amos 9:7-15: The Promises

The fourth block in Amos stands in stark contrast to the remainder of Amos. Prior to 9:7, the oracles, the sayings, and the visions all stress that unavoidable judgment will devastate Israel. By contrast, Amos 9:7-15 offers a series of composite promises with a Judean slant, expressing increasingly optimistic long-term hope for restoration once judgment has occurred. First, Amos 9:7-10 presents two diametrically opposing views that effectively create a debate regarding whether or not a remnant will survive YHWH's judgment against Israel. The first part (9:7-8a) denies that Israel holds any special status for YHWH by relativizing Israel's claim that YHWH's deliverance from slavery in Egypt was unique to Israel. Using a series of rhetorical questions, Amos 9:7 implies that YHWH also acted redemptively on behalf of the Philistines and the Aramaeans. Then, 9:8a announces that YHWH will completely annihilate Israel, only to reverse course and claim that YHWH will leave a remnant (9:8b) using exactly the same verbal root:

The eyes of the Lord GOD are upon the sinful kingdom,
   and *I will destroy* it from the face of the earth (9:8a, NRSV; emphasis added) –
except that *I will not completely destroy* the house of Jacob, says YHWH (9:8b, NRSV; emphasis added).

117

The second half of the argument (9:9-10) proceeds from 9:8b using the metaphor of a sieve shaken among the nations to argue that YHWH will punish the sinners, yet some will survive.

The second and third promises (9:11-12, 13-15) have experienced editorial expansion, so in their current form they articulate three distinct (though interrelated) restoration promises, all of which presuppose the destruction of Jerusalem (i.e., the fallen booth of David). These promises can be categorized as physical, geographic, and utopian restoration.

Amos 9:11, 14-15 articulates restoration as the rebuilding of Jerusalem ("the fallen booth of David") and the cities so that they can be reinhabited and agricultural normalcy can return. These promises likely reflect a second stage of editing for the Book of the Four, which added hopeful endings to Amos and Zephaniah.[40] These promises display a pro-Judean perspective of hope, since it is the booth of David that will be restored, but the emphasis lies upon rebuilding.

The remaining two verses reflect broader literary horizons that extend beyond the Book of the Four. Amos 9:12 offers a rationale for 9:11 beyond simply rebuilding. It anticipates the repossession of Edom and other territories claimed by YHWH, thus envisioning the restitution of the Davidic kingdom boundaries. This same theme reappears in Obadiah, the book that follows Amos. By contrast, 9:13 expands the imagery of refertilization already present in 9:14 by adding a utopian eschatological perspective that supersedes the portrait of normalcy in 9:14. This promise describes restoration as a harvest so grand that it will be ongoing when the time comes to replant the next crop. Furthermore, this promise also draws upon the language of Joel 3:18 (Heb. 4:18): "The mountains shall drip with sweet wine, and all the hills shall flow with it."[41] Thus, Amos 9:12, 13 reflect knowledge of the books that precede and follow Amos in the Twelve.

Composition of Amos and Its Contexts

Compositional models assume that the core of the OAN, the sayings, and the vision cycle reflect early recollections of the prophet's ideas, the wording of which was fixed close to his lifetime. Many of the oracles presuppose a period of economic prosperity for the elite in Israel, which aligns with what is known of the latter half of the reign of Jeroboam II and contrasts with the more chaotic setting of Hosea that scholars place closer to the time of the Syro-Ephraimite War (734 BCE) and the fall of Samaria (722 BCE). That being said, most compositional models of Amos suggest that these blocks circulated independently for a considerable time before they were joined together after the fall of the Northern Kingdom (but likely not until the late seventh or early sixth century BCE).[42] Critical scholarship often links the editorial processes combining these early collections to the aftermath of Judah's destruction in 587 BCE.

When first combined, the three main blocks culminated in the pronouncement of judgment against Israel. The final vision evokes the events of 722 BCE, so that the last word of Amos refers to the overthrow of Israel by the Assyrians. The book of Micah then begins where this early form of Amos ends, making explicit reference to the fall of Samaria.[43] Hence, Amos anticipates the fall of the Northern Kingdom as YHWH's judgment which threatens Jerusalem (6:1), while Micah begins with references to Samaria's destruction as a means to challenge Judah to take seriously the implications of those events for its own relationship to YHWH.

The promises in Amos 9:7-15 develop in three or four stages, but they all appear to react to the lack of hope in the early edition of Amos that joined the three main sections. The first of these expanded endings (9:7-10) reflects an ongoing debate regarding whether or not YHWH would destroy Israel or leave a remnant. The second promise deals explicitly with the reconstruction of Jerusalem and Judah in the aftermath of 587 BCE (9:11 + 14-15).

The third (9:12) and fourth (9:13) promises reflect grander visions of restoration. Verse 12 reinterprets the rebuilding of the booth of David as restoration of the boundaries of the Davidic kingdom. This concept of restoration reflects a later setting in the Persian period because it assumes that the "remnant of Edom" has begun to experience loss.[44] Verse 13 uses hyperbole to promise agricultural fertility that extends beyond the hope for normalcy in 9:14b-15. Verse 13 draws its imagery from Joel 3:18 (Heb. 4:18). Further, the promise of the conquest of Edom as part of restoring the boundaries of the Davidic kingdom foreshadows the same themes at the end of Obadiah. Hence, these third and fourth promises reflect eschatological views more fully articulated in the writings on either side of Amos (Joel and Obadiah). Both of these promises thus reflect the inclusion of other writings beyond the Book of the Four.

Amos has a long and complex history as a book, but its literary function remains relatively consistent through this process. The early core of the three sections of Amos consistently announces the coming destruction of Israel. The decision to combine these three sections likely took place with an eye toward the larger multibook collection known as the Book of the Four (Hosea, Amos, Micah, and Zephaniah). As a key part of this collection, Amos maintained its focus on the destruction of Israel, though the addition of the Judah oracle (2:4-5) and the warning to "those at ease in Zion" (6:1) foreshadow the idea that Judah will ultimately not escape judgment, because they abandoned Torah and behaved like Israel. Hosea also experienced updating for a Judean context even though its primary focus concentrates on Israel. The books of Micah and Zephaniah

119

develop the message of judgment against Judah more fully. Each of these four books accuses Israel, Judah, or both of ethical violations against those in need and improper cultic practices. At this stage, Amos concludes with the fifth vision report and the subsequent doxology (9:1-6), in which the prophet watches in silence while YHWH destroys the northern temple. Micah 1 picks up where 9:1-4 leaves off.

The end of Amos expanded twice while still part of the Book of the Four, first with a debate regarding the role of the remnant of Israel in the aftermath of its destruction (9:7-10) and then with a foundational promise to rebuild Judah in the aftermath of Jerusalem's destruction (9:11, 14-15). Similar promises to rebuild Zion appear in expansions to Micah and Zephaniah.

The Book of the Four thus forms the chronological and theological foundation of what would become the Book of the Twelve. In its early iterations, it recounts YHWH's prophetic message first to Israel in Hosea and Amos and then to Judah in Micah and Zephaniah. The kings mentioned in the superscriptions link these four writings and provide a chronological and theological progression that moves from the eighth century to the time of Josiah. It draws a parallel between Israel's misdeeds and those of Judah. It conveys the message explicitly and implicitly that YHWH's painful decision to punish the Northern Kingdom should have been understood as a warning to Judah that the same fate awaited it if it continued to act in ways that resembled Israel. Hosea and Amos adumbrate those accusations and pronounce judgment against Israel. Micah and Zephaniah will do the same for Judah.

As the Book of the Four expanded, Amos received only slight modifications, most notably in the short insertions of Amos 9:12 and 9:13 that respectively link forward thematically to Obadiah and link backward lexically to Joel 3:18 (MT 4:18).[45] Joel interrupts the lengthy focus upon Israel with its warning to Judah and Jerusalem, and the editing of Obadiah goes to considerable lengths to structure the short book so that its judgment against Edom mirrors the structural and thematic elements of the judgment against Israel in Amos 9.

Micah

The Prophet and the Book

The only explicit biographical elements in Micah appear in 1:1 with the mention of his hometown (Moresheth) and the names of the three kings whom the reader should associate with Micah's preaching (Jotham, Ahaz, and Hezekiah). Unlike Amos and Hosea, Micah contains no narratives about events from the prophet's life. Instead, the book consists primarily of oracular materials spoken in the voice of the prophet or the deity. The hometown of the prophet, Moresheth (1:1) or Moresheth-Gath (1:14), is almost universally located in the Judean Shephelah a little over twenty miles southwest of Jerusalem. The tradition behind the claim reflects knowledge about the prophet because 2:1–3:12 demonstrates a negative attitude toward the leadership in Judah (by implication, King Hezekiah). Micah, whose oracles support the landowners of the Shephelah, condemns policies centralizing power in Jerusalem and the annexing of land from the Shephelah.[46]

Most Micah scholars conclude that only portions of chapters 1–3 actually reflect an eighth-century setting that relates to the reigns of the kings mentioned in 1:1. Chapters 4–7 represent later material from the sixth century and beyond that was appended in stages to chapters 1–3. Further, it has become increasingly clear that none of the material in chapters 1–3 can readily be dated to the time of Jotham (756–741 BCE) or Ahaz (742–725 BCE). Rather, the early material in chapters 1–3 seems to reflect the time of Hezekiah (725–696 BCE), which also fits with the tradition in Jeremiah 26:18-19 associating Micah with Hezekiah. As with most of the prophetic books, so especially with Micah: one has to look beyond biographical questions to ask how the book of Micah functions literarily and canonically. To do so, it is important to have a good grasp of the structure and contents of Micah.

The Structure and Contents of Micah

Micah 1–3: Jerusalem's Impending Destruction

These chapters contain the earliest material in Micah, but they also show signs of editing that anticipates passages in chapters 4–7, which were later incorporated into the early collection of chapters 1–3. Synchronically, the rhetorical units in these chapters include the superscription (1:1), the introduction to Micah (1:2-7), a lament over Jerusalem's impending devastation (1:8-16), confrontation with Jerusalem's leaders who are seizing land (2:1-11), a brief word of hope (2:12-13), and pronouncements of judgment because of ethical lapses in the city (3:1-12). *Micah 1:1.* The superscription serves as the title of the book and provides the only explicit biographical information about the prophet: his hometown and the names of three kings of Judah. Nevertheless, the superscription was edited after the lifetime of the prophet, likely in more than one stage. Micah 1:1b also announces that the prophetic material to follow addresses Samaria and Jerusalem. Only 1:5-7 refers to Samaria in Micah, so one can safely presume that 1:1b knows 1:2-7. The inclusion of Jotham and Ahaz were likely added with the initial formation of the Book of the Four to link with Hosea 1:1, while mention of Micah prophesying during the reign of Hezekiah is cited by Jeremiah 26:18-19 and may have been present earlier. Micah 1:5-7 presumes Samaria has fallen, thus presupposing the events of 722 BCE when Hezekiah was already king of Judah. None of the other material in Micah 1–3 can be dated to the time of Jotham or Ahaz with any degree of probability.

Micah 1:2-7. The first significant rhetorical unit (1:2-7) sets the book in the last quarter of the eighth century by combining a call to attention (1:2) and a theophany report (1:3-4) with accusations that the same behaviors that caused the destruction of Samaria now threaten Jerusalem as well (1:5, 6-7). While debate continues over when this rhetorical unit was created, widespread agreement exists that it serves as an introduction to the book.[47] This literary function becomes particularly clear when one notes that 1:5-7 draws a parallel between the destruction of Samaria and the destruction of Jerusalem (3:12) as heaps of rubble.

Micah 1:8-16. The remainder of Micah 1 also demonstrates a distinct rhetorical purpose. At its core, this unit reflects on the Assyrian capture of the Shephelah on the way to Jerusalem by warning a number of villages (including the prophet's hometown in 1:14) of the impending judgment. These pronouncements utilize names of villages as well as word plays to refer to the towns. Additionally, several parenthetical comments warn about the danger posed by the loss of the Shephelah for Jerusalem (1:9, 12b, 13b). These parenthetical comments align with the rhetorical purpose of 1:5-7, suggesting an editorial agenda imposed upon Micah 1 wherein the loss of Samaria and the Shephelah represents an imminent threat to Jerusalem as punishment for the same sins that destroyed Samaria (1:5, 9, 13b). The core of 1:8-16 elicits echoes of Sennacherib's military campaign at the end of the eighth century in the reign of Hezekiah.[48] Micah 1 devotes most of its space to announcing the impending destruction of Jerusalem, but two events take center stage: Samaria's destruction in 722 BCE and the siege of Sennacherib in 701 BCE. In other words, the "impending" destruction of Jerusalem announced in Micah 1 conveys the threat of two events that occur a full two decades apart. Both events occurred in the reign of Hezekiah, but this threat encroaching upon the "gate of Jerusalem" because of the sins of Samaria displays a theological perspective gained over time. Chapters 2–3 focus more concretely upon accusations against Jerusalem's leaders as the reason for divine judgment.

Micah 2:1–3:12. These two chapters contain seven small units: 2:1-3, 4-5, 6-11, 12-13; 3:1-4, 5-8, 9-12. Like the anthologies of Hosea (4–10; 12–13) and Amos (3–6), Micah 2–3 relies on repetition. These small units have been selected and arranged to document repeatedly the depth of the depravity of Jerusalem's political and religious leadership.

Formal unit markers give the impression that new sayings begin and end every few verses.[49] The drumbeat of judgment pronounced in 2:1–3:12 contains a series of embedded accusations against specific behaviors. Accusations include land grabbing by a powerful group (2:2, 4, 9), attempts to silence the prophet (2:6, 11), and robbery (2:8). These chapters also condemn leaders who take bribes (3:11) and who ignore justice (3:1) while metaphorically cannibalizing their own people (3:2-3). Accusations also confront religious leaders, priests, and prophets who show interest only in the money they can make (3:5, 11). The portrait conveyed by these accusations paints a dour picture of Judean society in the late eighth century.

The final oracle (3:9-12) likely ended the early collection of Micah, and it plays an important literary and canonical role. First, 3:12 serves as a literary *inclusio* to Micah 1:6, creating a heightened parallel between Jerusalem's impending destruction and Samaria's destruction, where both will become heaps of rubble. Second, Micah 3:12 plays an important role in the trial scene of Jeremiah (26:18-19) where the "elders of the land" successfully cite it in Jeremiah's defense. Third, in the final form of the Book of the Twelve, Micah 3:12 represents the exact midpoint of the scroll by the number of verses as it warns Jerusalem that the city and the temple will be destroyed.

Micah 6–7: Pleading the Case for Judgment and Hope

By most reckonings, Micah 4–7 does not stem from the eighth-century prophet but represents later material appended to chapters 1–3. The process remains debated, but compelling arguments suggest the addition of chapters 6–7 predates the addition of chapters 4–5.[50] Three units comprise these chapters: Micah 6; 7:1-7; and 7:8-20.

Two characteristics provide coherence to Micah 6: its genre as a trial drama and its reliance upon narrative traditions connecting Exodus, Hosea, Amos, and Kings. The admonition to "plead your case" (Heb. *rîb*) in Micah 6:1 begins a legal drama that will unfold across these chapters. Alternating voices combined with contentious speeches make sense against the backdrop of a courtroom setting.[51] Rhetorical questions by the three speakers convey the essential logic of the legal drama. YHWH asks in 6:3, "How have I wearied you?" He accuses the people of failing to remember YHWH's salvific acts from Exodus. The voice of the accused then offers a satirical set of rhetorical questions that critique the cultic expectations of YHWH (6:6-7). The questions become increasingly hyperbolic: Shall I bring burnt offerings, thousands of rams, ten thousand rivers of oil? Shall I sacrifice my own child? The questions challenge YHWH's expectations as too demanding. In response, the prophetic voice also raises a rhetorical question

Chapter 4

(6:8), formulated to deny the premise of their complaint that cultic obligations are too high. Instead, the prophet affirms that YHWH has told them what he expects: to do justice, love kindness, and walk humbly with your God. The claim of 6:8 that YHWH has told the accused what he expects, picks up commands that echo the message of Hosea 12:6 (MT 12:7): "But as for you, return to your God, hold fast to love (ḥesed) and justice (mišpāṭ), and wait continually for your God." This allusion becomes more noticeable when one also finds links to texts in Amos 8:5 in Micah 6:10.

YHWH responds in 6:9-16. Following a brief word from the narrator, the summons to hear hearkens back to 6:2 and more rhetorical questions suggest that readers understand these verses as a continuation of the trial scene. The rhetorical questions in 6:10-12 function as accusations that Judah and Jerusalem have broken faith with YHWH's ethical expectations expressed in 6:8. Verses 13-16 pronounce the verdict. The accusations and verdict summarize the accusations of Micah 2–3 and recall language of Hosea and Amos.[52]

The verdict (6:13-16) also evokes Deuteronomic curse language from Hosea and Amos while evoking Micah 1. The covenant curse in Micah 6:14-15 directed against Judah echoes the curse language in Amos 5:11 and Hosea 4:10 directed against the Northern Kingdom.[53] The opening pronouncement (6:13) refers to YHWH's "wounding" (nākâ) Judah because of its sin. This pronouncement uses language similar to Micah 1:9, which connects Samaria's "wound" (mākâ) that has reached Judah and Jerusalem. Further, 7:16 compares Judah's situation to that of Israel's worst kings (Omri and his son Ahab; see 1 Kgs 16:25, 30; 21:25). The combination of these parallel expressions evoking the language of Hosea, Amos, Kings, and Deuteronomy to express both accusations and judgments do more than merely share similar linguistic expression. They draw a parallel between the fate of Israel and the fate of Judah similar to the parenthetical comments of Micah 1.

Micah 6 reflects knowledge of canonical traditions: YHWH's liberation of Israel from Egypt, the wilderness wanderings, the journey up the Transjordan, the crossing of the Jordan, and Israel's idolatry during the reigns of Omri and Ahab.[54] The logic of these references evokes the salvific acts of YHWH (6:3-5) and accuses Judah of the same idolatry that led to Israel's demise (6:16). These canonical allusions thus use traditions from the Enneateuch to pronounce judgment on Judah and to draw a comparison between Judah and Israel.

Micah 7:1-7 functions as a prophetic response to the verdict of 6:9-16. A lament by form, the prophet speaks about himself at the beginning and end (7:1, 7). The intervening verses describe social chaos that essentially repeats the charges levied against Judah in chapters 2–3 and the verdict announced in Micah 6. Specifically, the prophet condemns the bribery of leaders (cf. 7:3; 3:11), mis-

124

treatment of the upright (cf. 3:9; 2:7), and bloodshed instituted by leaders (7:2; 3:10). The prophetic self-descriptions that frame the description of the land use images of famine (7:1) to open the lament by portraying the isolation and hunger he faces. Yet, as with many laments, the prophet pronounces confidence that YHWH will change the situation (7:7).

Micah 7:8-20 offers hope, seen from the end of the eighth century (but addressing the postexilic community). The text unfolds as a dramatic dialogue, though one has to analyze the speakers carefully to follow the conversation.[55] This final unit constitutes five interrelated speeches that function as a dialogical response to the prophetic lament. These dialogues include: an affirmation of justice by Lady Zion to Lady Nineveh (7:8-10), a complex promise of a reprieve (7:11-13), a prophetic intercession with a brief response from YHWH (7:14-15), a prophetic response to the people (7:16-17), and a hymnic prayer from the people (7:18-20).

Micah 7:8-10 exhibits Hebrew rhetorical markers that are unclear in English translations. Second feminine singular verbs and pronouns signal one feminine entity speaks to and about another. The constellation of possible speakers and the context identify the two entities as personified cities, Lady Zion and Lady Nineveh.[56] Lady Nineveh currently has the upper hand, but Lady Zion expresses confidence that her punishment will pass. Lady Zion acknowledges her situation as punishment from YHWH (7:9a), and then turns her enemy's taunt against her. Lady Nineveh will be defeated and Lady Zion restored (7:9b-10). Read against the backdrop of the siege of Sennacherib in the reign of Hezekiah when Assyria surrounded Jerusalem before quickly withdrawing, Lady Zion's speech takes on poignant significance.[57]

Micah 7:11-13 offers a complex response to Lady Zion, wherein second feminine singular forms address her with words of promise and judgment. Micah 7:11 announces a reprieve for Lady Zion to extend her walls. Micah 7:12 can be read as a promise of a return from the diaspora set in the Persian period.[58] The phrasing of the verse is ambiguous, however, and can also be read as a reference to the coming threat. When read with its intertextual similarities to Isaiah 9–12 and Hezekiah traditions (see 2 Kgs 18:35 [= Isa 36:30]; 2 Chr 32:5) in mind, the statement that "he will *come to you* from Assyria and the cities of Egypt and from Egypt to the Euphrates" is no promise. It anticipates hostile powers controlling the political fate of Judah for the entirety of the seventh century.[59] This understanding of 7:11-13 also explains the dramatic switch to the judgment in 7:13 that is otherwise ignored as a parenthetical (and nonsensical) gloss. The arrival of Assyria and Egypt and Babylon (7:12) leads to the land's desolation (7:13).

In Micah 7:14-17 the prophet intercedes by accepting the punishment but imploring YHWH to restore the inhabitants of Bashan and Gilead (7:14) and to replicate the exodus (7:15a). YHWH responds with a promise "I will show him marvelous things" (7:15b), referring to the liberation from Egypt (7:15a). This intercession and response leads to the prophet's response in 7:16-17 which continues allusions to the Exodus and conquest narratives. It draws upon the motif of the fear of the nations that plays a prominent role in describing the Transjordan before entering the land (Numbers 10–Joshua).[60] In a sense, Micah 7:14-17 foreshadows the message of the OAN in Zephaniah 2:5-15 that pronounce divine judgment against Assyria and the nations that supported its policies. YHWH's response (7:15b) does not remove the coming judgment: the people recognize the degradation of the nations (7:16-17), and their response (7:18-20) articulates a hope that the anger of YHWH will not be permanent (though it assumes it will happen).

Micah 7:18-20 offers a fitting end to Micah. The hymn opens with a pun upon the name of the prophet. Its opening rhetorical question ("Who is a God like you?") evokes the name "Micah," which means: "Who is like YHWH?" This hymn also draws upon Exodus 34:6-7, emphasizing YHWH's covenant fidelity (*ḥesed*) from 34:6.[61] Verse 20 reaches back behind the exodus narrative to allude to Jacob and Abraham (note the reverse order) as the ancestral paradigm of receiving YHWH's *ḥesed*.

Micah 4–5: The Distant Future

Several structural and literary markers suggest that Micah 4–5 has been artfully arranged for its current location, though the component parts derive from different hands. Jeremias demonstrates that Micah 6–7 and Micah 4–5 both respond primarily to chapters 1–3, but neither 4–5 nor 6–7 draw upon one another.[62] Two issues suggest that the chapters function together. First, the two blocks exhibit a structural cohesion while displaying thematic development. Second, chronological markers make sense of these chapters contextually.

Structural cohesion and thematic development lead the reader to understand chapters 4–5 as a compilation of four texts that have been arranged and edited together to affirm YHWH's decision both to punish and restore Judah and Jerusalem. The first unit (4:1-7) speaks of a future time of peace with the nations (4:1-5) and a regathering of the remnant in Zion (4:6-7). The second unit (4:8–5:4 [Heb. 4:8–5:3]) coheres around the repetition of two different Hebrew words that sound the same, though they begin with different letters: the second masculine singular pronoun "you" begins with alef (*'atāh* in 4:8; 5:2) and the adverb "now" begins with ayin (*'atāh* in 4:9, 11; 5:1). This second unit consequently shifts from the future to the "present," yet the "present" anticipates both Jerusalem's exile to Babylon and attacks from many nations (4:11) as punishment for Zion (4:10) and YHWH's redemption of Zion from that punishment (4:10b, 12-13; 5:4). Its message, therefore, addresses the postexilic community. The third unit (5:5-10) again emphasizes the future by its fourfold repetition of the Hebrew word *wehāyāh* ("and it will be" in 5:5, 7, 8, 10 [Heb. 5:4, 6, 7, 9]) addressing the "remnant of Jacob in the midst of many peoples (5:7-8 [Heb. 5:6-7]). The fourth group four times repeats the verb *wehikratî* ("and I will cut off . . .") to convey future destruction in 5:10-13 (Heb. 5:9-12).

The implicit chronological functions of these structural markers force the attentive reader to treat the anthology of chapters 4–5 as a message to the remnant community. The units address those having returned to Jerusalem from the perspective of the prophet who speaks for YHWH at the end of the eighth century. Critical scholars recognize chapters 4–5 as a late addition to Micah. Its address to the remnant community (4:6-7; 5:7-8 [Heb. 5:5-7]), its borrowing from Isaiah 2:2-4, and its specific mention of Babylon (4:10) all confirm that these chapters represent a late theological reflection presupposing the destruction of Jerusalem. The structural markers in these chapters also communicate their message dialectically between the distant future and the immediate present. The first and last units begin with eschatological formulas anticipating coming days of YHWH's intervention ("in the latter days" in 4:1 and "on that day" in 4:6; 5:10). The third group (5:5-10 [Heb. 5:4-9]) accentuates its message for the future with the quadruple use of "and it will be." In between, the second group of sayings addresses Zion (4:8) and Bethlehem of Judah (5:2 [Heb. 5:1]) with the pronoun "you" (*'atāh*) while accenting the present using "now" (*'atāh*) three times (4:9, 11; 5:1 [Heb. 4:9, 11; 14]).

Rhetorically, these chapters address the community of Judah's future remnant with a hope tempered by the somber knowledge that Judah and Jerusalem will experience punishment from both the Babylonians (4:10-12) and the Assyrians (cf. 5:5-6 [Heb. 5:4-5]). Though written later, these words convey the prophet speaking to the remnant with knowledge of the time from Hezekiah to 587.[63] Placement of chapters 4–5 immediately after 3:12 brings a jarring rhetorical shift for the readers of Micah. To jump from the pronouncement of Jerusalem's destruction in 3:9-12 to the utopian vision of universal peace centered in Zion in 4:1-4 represents a dramatic shift in the message that would be hard to miss for anyone reading the book. The two units share catchwords in 3:12 and 4:1 that accentuate Jerusalem's coming judgment and future peace by the unusual phrase, "the mountain of the house (of YHWH)."[64] Micah 3:12 anticipates "the mountain of the house" will become "a bump in the forest," while 4:1 states "the mountain of the house of YHWH" will be established as the highest mountain.

The fact that Micah 4:1-4 parallels Isaiah 2:2-4 has long suggested that Micah 4:1-4 represents a later addition.[65] Also, the difference in the two messages concerns the dramatic change of time introduced in 4:1, which addresses its message to the distant future ("And it will happen in the latter days"). Micah 4–5 thus displays for its readers the long-term plans of YHWH that include YHWH's judgment against Judah, administered by the nations, and the punishment of the nations. It also imagines Zion's ultimate role as YHWH's home and the center of instruction and justice that the nations will seek. The fact that Micah 4–5 appears right at the beginning of the second half of the Twelve makes this depiction of the "long-term" goal particularly appropriate for the readers of the Book of the Twelve. One should also note the strong link between Micah 4:6-7 and Zephaniah 3:18-20, which updates the promise of Micah to reflect the time of Zephaniah.[66]

Micah within the Book of the Twelve

The book of Micah reached its final form as the result of four major stages: (1) an early eighth-century collection (1–3); (2) an exilic update that reflects on the reasons for Jerusalem's destruction and connects Micah with Hosea, Amos, and Zephaniah (6:1–7:7); (3) a Persian-period salvific ending (7:8-20); and (4) a late Persian-period summation of the more distant future (4–5).

The early collection contained much of chapters 1–3 that delivered words of judgment against Judah and Jerusalem. This collection challenged Hezekiah's policies and warned that Jerusalem's political and religious leaders had failed. This collection was likely known by the "elders of the land" according to Jeremiah 26:18-19.

Exilic editors added material to Micah 1 (1:1b, 5, 9, 12b, 13b) that bemoans Judah and Jerusalem's fate because they did not change following the destruction of Samaria. Micah 6:1–7:7 shows similar concerns and served as the new conclusion to the book. It anticipates a time when Assyrian ascendancy will serve as punishment for Judah because of Judah's idolatry and unethical behavior. Its concluding verses pronounce the prophet's dependency upon YHWH and hope that God will act salvifically. The additions display knowledge of Hosea, Amos, and Kings.

The third phase (7:8-20) comforts Zion and its people with the message that Assyria will not always be the dominant power. It depicts a complicated reprieve for Zion (7:11-13), which anticipates the events from Hezekiah to the destruction of Jerusalem as a delay of punishment (7:11-12), without, however, removing the foreboding devastation to punish Judah's inhabitants (7:13). Next, the prophet petitions YHWH who responds positively (7:14-15), and the people rejoice that YHWH will also punish the nations who have attacked Judah (7:16-

17). The salvific ending (7:18-20) draws noticeably upon traditions from Exodus, the conquest, and the ancestral stories.

The late Persian-period summation displays a carefully crafted structure that suggests it functions like a themed anthology. The structural elements suggest that chapters 4–5 assume a *literary setting* at the end of the eighth century, but deliver a word of hope for the postexilic community. In this sense, it shares functional characteristics with Micah 6–7. Micah 4–5, however, shapes its message for those in the distant future while chapters 6–7 address the more immediate future in the aftermath of Sennacherib's siege. Some of the units in chapters 4–5 may have already existed as part of the collection, but their final form begs that they be read together. Micah 4, in particular, contains texts that have relationships to other texts (e.g., Mic 4:1-4 = Isa 2:2-4; Mic 4:5 reflects the Deuteronomic blessing; and Mic 4:6-7 anticipates the return of the remnant in Zephaniah 3:18-20; see on Zephaniah below). Thus, the three main sections of Micah reflect on the events of the eighth century (chapters 1–3), then offer lengthy discourses on the distant future (chapters 4–5) and the more immediate future (chapters 6–7).

Zephaniah

The Prophet and the Book

Only the superscription (1:1) provides explicit biographical information concerning the prophet, yet that data raises questions about the time of Zephaniah's active ministry and the ancestral information it lists. The superscription includes a five-generation genealogy depicting Zephaniah as the descendant of Hezekiah, the king of Judah (726–696 BCE) last mentioned in Micah 1:1, while dating Zephaniah to the reign of Josiah (639–609 BCE), just prior to the time of Jeremiah.[67]

The genealogical information is unusual on two fronts: the foreign name of Zephaniah's father and its length. The name of Zephaniah's father, Cushi, means "Cushite," and Cush refers to one of two different places in biblical texts: the country Ethiopia, whose political fortunes were ascendant through significant portions of the seventh century BCE, or the Arabian Desert region, whose population is distinct from the Israelites.[68]

The length of the genealogy has no parallel among prophetic superscriptions.[69] The genealogy traces the prophet's ancestry back through his father (Cushi), his grandfather (Gedaliah), his great-grandfather (Amariah), to his great-great-grandfather (Hezekiah). Scholars have suggested three possible reasons for the length. Some propose that the length of the superscription results from the desire to highlight the relationship to Judah's king, thereby providing additional weight to Zephaniah's message. Others suggest that the lengthy genealogy undercuts any suggestion that Zephaniah's ethnic heritage was not Jewish.[70] Finally, linking the superscription to the prophet's relationship to Hezekiah with the time of Josiah helps connect Zephaniah to the Book of the Four.[71]

Indirect information concerning Zephaniah comes from inferences in the speeches. Given the biological connections to Hezekiah, criticisms directed toward the royal household appear surprising (see 1:8). The concern for the marginalized emphasizes social justice (1:11-13, 18a; 2:3), not unlike concerns in Amos and Micah 2. Like Amos, as well, these texts illustrate that such actions are closely related to righteous living (2:3; cf. Amos 5:7, 12, 24). Cultic accusations like those in Hosea appear in Zephaniah 1:4: the idolatrous priests (cf. Hos 10:5) and the remnant of Baal (cf. Hos 2:8, 13, 16-17; 9:10; 11:2; 13:1).

Zephaniah's setting recalls the reign of Josiah (1:1), yet recent studies argue that significant portions of Zephaniah postdate 587 BCE and the return from exile.[72] Two issues help explain Zephaniah's shape: the date assigned by the superscription and the functions it plays in the developing corpora. In both the Book of the Four and the Twelve, Zephaniah's location plays a climactic role. In the former, Zephaniah ended the collection, while in the latter Zephaniah is the last book with a date preceding Jerusalem's destruction. The fact that Zephaniah is set in Josiah's reign means the book anticipates Jerusalem's *future* destruction and its restoration.

Thus, the final form involves three developmental stages, heuristic categories that highlight functions of the developing corpus: (1) a sixth-century collection announcing judgment against Jerusalem, (2) a postexilic update that treats Jerusalem's destruction *and* restoration, and (3) scribal reflections that connect Zephaniah to a variety of other texts.

All three stages anticipate Jerusalem's destruction literarily, and the final stages express hope for those who endure the destruction. The first stage likely contains material from the seventh century, but this early material probably existed as independent traditions until combined with material written after 587 (the year of Jerusalem's destruction) to form a structured collection. In so doing, even this first stage of compilation aimed its message at those who survived those events. The second stage updates the existing message of judgment with words of hope by promising a remnant to Zion and YHWH's return. The final (probably composite) stage correlates Jerusalem's destruction and restoration with cosmic consequences: the undoing of creation, the destruction of the line of Ham, and a concept of restoration that reverses the alienation of the tower of Babel. This final stage anticipates Jerusalem's restoration as a fulfillment of Micah 4:6-7, and anticipates the beginning of Haggai (though this last could be a separate, final addition).

Each of these stages adds new dimensions to the structure and message of Zephaniah. Since the final stages presuppose a kind of scribal prophecy demonstrating reflective use of postexilic texts from Genesis, Micah, and Haggai, it appears quite likely that the final stages stem from no earlier than the mid-fifth century BCE.[73]

The Structure and Contents of Zephaniah

The Early Core of Zephaniah

The early core of Zephaniah combines two smaller collections: judgment oracles against Judah and Jerusalem (1:4-18a; 2:1-3; 3:1-8bα) and the OAN condemning Assyria and its regional allies (2:4-15*).[74] These two collections recall Zephaniah's message, but they were joined as the initial conclusion to the Book of the Four with the addition of 3:1-8bα.[75] The judgment oracles begin by condemning syncretistic worship practices, and they share vocabulary with the accounts of Josiah's reforms (2 Kgs 22–23).[76] The superscription (1:1) merely places the prophet's message in the time of Josiah (640–609 BCE), but the reader should assume that Josiah's reforms have already begun since 1:4 refers to "the remnant of Baal," a phrase that makes sense after actions had been taken to restrict the worship of Baal and the host of heaven (2 Kgs 23:4-5). By most reckonings, 1:4 implies that the judgment oracles postdate 622 BCE.

The core of the OAN (2:4-15) makes the most sense after Assyria's destruction in 612 BCE. At that point, the handwriting would have been on the wall for those nations and groups whose fortunes were closely associated with Assyria. The same could be said about the king's family who adopted Assyrian customs (such as the style of dress and cultic practices mentioned in Zeph 1:8).

The early core ended with the composition of 3:1-8bα, a passage that condemns Jerusalem as a violent, oppressive city (3:1) that failed to heed YHWH's instruction (3:2, 7). This passage takes the form of a woe oracle that begins and ends with a pronouncement of doom against Jerusalem, spoken first in the voice of the prophet (3:1-2) and concluding with the voice of YHWH (3:7-8bα). The *inclusio* between 3:2 and 3:7 repeats the same general statements about Jerusalem: it did not trust or fear YHWH and it accepted no correction. Consequently, it would not avoid the punishment. The central section contains two parts (3:3-4, 5-6). The first part expounds the accusations against the leadership of the city—its princes, judges, prophets, and priests (3:3-4). These verses accuse each group of violating their duties. Jerusalem's officials (*śar*, a term that can refer to the royal family or to appointed officials) are condemned as roaring lions. Its judges take bribes. Its prophets are reckless and commit treachery. Its priests profane the holy and do violence to Torah. The second part (3:5-6) focuses upon

YHWH's character and his actions. These verses contain a pronouncement of doom (3:5) expanded by a statement that draws upon the theme of the OAN (3:6). The same thematic expansion (judgment against the nations and the earth) appears in 3:8bα, and cites 1:18 (changing only the pronoun):

Zeph 1:18	Zeph 3:8
¹:¹⁸ᵃᵃ Neither their silver nor their gold will be able to save them on the day of the LORD's wrath;	³:⁸ᵃ Therefore wait for me, says the Lord, for the day when I arise as a witness.
¹:¹⁸ᵃᵝ⁻ᵞ *in the fire of <u>his</u> jealousy all the earth shall be consumed;*	³:⁸ᵇᵃ For my decision is to *gather nations*, to collect kingdoms, to pour out upon them my indignation, all the heat of my anger;
¹:¹⁸ᵇ for a full, a terrible end he will make of all the inhabitants of the earth.	³:⁸ᵇᵝ *for in the fire of <u>my</u> jealousy all the earth shall be consumed.*

Consequently, 3:8bα picks up the theme of 2:4-15 while 3:8bβ cites 1:18aβ-γ, which essentially summarizes the message of chapter 1 once the larger cosmic connections have been made. This repetition of the themes of the two main blocks of Zephaniah makes 3:8a-bα understandable as the conclusion of the book once the pronouncement against Judah (1:4–2:3*) and the OAN (2:4-15) were joined, but before the allusions to Genesis 1–11 (see below) were added that portrayed these actions on a more cosmic scale. The fact that 3:8bβ offers a second rationale for the coming judgment, one that includes the universalizing language of judgment, suggests that it entered the corpus as part of the second stage.

Hence, the early core ended with 3:1-8bα. It combines the themes of judgment against Jerusalem and the nations, but it did not yet contain the cosmic language reversing Genesis 1–11. This early version attempts to come to terms with Jerusalem's destruction, along with judgment against other nations who pitted themselves against YHWH. The fact that these other nations were also the ones that benefitted from their arrangements with Assyria suggests that the combination of these oracles and the judgment against Jerusalem would most likely reflect a time of Babylonian ascendancy. Babylonian control of the Levant in the late seventh or early sixth century accounts for much of the material within these two blocks (1:4–2:3 and 2:4-15*), but 3:1-8a (which assumes the two parts are combined) reflects back on Jerusalem's destruction. Following the events of 612 BCE (Nineveh's destruction), the exile of 597, and the destruction of Jerusalem in 587 BCE, the combination of the two main anthologies—in their earliest form— would have served to affirm the message of the memory of Zephaniah's speeches.

Hope for Restoration

The restoration material adds a new dimension to Zephaniah by anticipating YHWH's return to Zion and the removal of YHWH's punishment. The theme of Zephaniah changes from judgment to restoration beginning with 3:9, but 3:9-20 contains five units (3:9-10, 11-13, 14-17, 18-19, and 20). Each unit contains a number of characteristics that signal something new is beginning. Consequently, while the theme of restoration appears in each of the five units, the material appears to be more of a thematic anthology than a clearly structured composition. That being said, most scholars recognize that these units did not all enter Zephaniah 3 at the same time, and 3:9-10 will be discussed below with other scribal prophecy texts.

A new unit appears in 3:11-13 with the introductory formula "on that day." It focuses upon the promise of a remnant that will remain in Jerusalem after the rebellious and haughty have been removed. This remnant will be characterized by its humility and lowliness and by its desire to seek YHWH.[77] While scholars often recognize the opening phrase ("on that day") as the introduction to a redactional addition, they often ignore the syntactical and rhetorical function of this formula.[78] In Zephaniah 3:11, the antecedent to "that day" refers back to 3:8a and the "day when I rise as a witness." Verses 11-13 add a new element to the anticipated events of that day. "The day" in 3:8a is a day of judgment against Jerusalem (and the nations in 3:8bα), but 3:11-13 shifts the focus to a group of survivors who are neither the "haughty ones" of Jerusalem nor the nations who have taken advantage of Judah. Rather, 3:11-13 promises safety for the remnant in Jerusalem, even though the unit still anticipates a coming judgment for Jerusalem.

Zephaniah 3:14-17 exhibits a very tight thematic chiasm that repeats four main points:

A (v. 14) Sing (רנן), shout (חרש), be glad (שמח), exult (עלז) Lady Zion
  B (v. 15) YHWH has removed judgments, turned away enemies
    C King (YHWH) is in your midst;
      D You shall fear no more
      D´ (v. 16) Do not fear, or let your hands grow weak
    C´(v. 17) YHWH, your God, is in your midst;
  B´ Warrior YHWH gives victory;
A´   He will rejoice (שוש) over you with gladness (שמחה)
    He will renew (חרש) you in his love
    He will exult (גיל) over you with singing (רנה)

A number of scholars have noted similar vocabulary in this verse and portions of Isaiah 40–55, suggesting that this material did not enter Zephaniah prior to the return of the exiles to Jerusalem that began after the rise of Cyrus (539–529 BCE) in the second half of the sixth century.[79]

Rhetorically, Zephaniah 3:14-17 exhorts Jerusalem, as the personified city, by consistently addressing Lady Zion directly ("you" here reflects feminine singular pronouns and verbs). The outer portions of the chiasm (A) provide these verses with a sense of joy, first as a command to Lady Zion and then as a statement of YHWH's pleasure in her. The inside of the chiasm (D) repeats the exhortation not to fear. The other two sections (B, C) provide the rationale for this exhortation: YHWH has returned to Zion and has removed Zion's enemies. It is important to put this exhortation in context. The literary setting of the book in the time of Josiah (Zeph 1:1) has not changed in terms of how the reader conceptualizes the voice of the prophet. The collection of prophetic sayings and oracles anticipates *both* the destruction of Jerusalem *and* its restoration as events that lie in the future. The restoration described in 3:14-17 does not eliminate the coming judgment; rather, it moves beyond the judgment to provide hope that YHWH will not abandon Zion even though he will punish her. Verses 14-17 presuppose 3:11-13 in that they continue to address Zion and presume that its inhabitants are now prepared to live as YHWH's people (which in turn assumes that the haughty and rebellious who led the city astray are no longer in the picture). Verses 14-17 depict the end of Judah's punishment that included the presence of enemies, foreign armies, in Zion (3:15, 17). These exhortations anticipate future events that come about after the judgment of Jerusalem described in 3:1-8a. Also, verses 14-17 (especially when combined with the language of 3:18) subtly but clearly anticipate a path for the reconstruction of the temple since these verses twice refer to YHWH dwelling in the midst of Zion (3:15, 17).

Scribal Prophecy with Other Texts

The final group affecting the composition of Zephaniah includes the last three verses of the book as a composite promise (3:18-20) and a series of three texts (1:2-3; 2:11b-15; 3:9-10) that draw upon Genesis 1–11. Thematically, 3:18-20 returns to the fate of the remnant, but the syntactical disruptions and repetitions strongly suggest that more than one hand has shaped this final unit.[80] The thematic development of 3:1-18, essentially proclaims Jerusalem's destruction (3:1-8a), recounts a message of deliverance for the humble remnant (3:11-13), announces YHWH's return to Zion to remove the enemies (3:14-17), and then turns its attention to those suffering in and around Zion (3:18).

Zephaniah 3:19 offers a second message of restoration, but one that expands the literary horizon beyond Zephaniah to the Book of the Four. The verse essentially reformulates the salvific message of 3:11-18, but it also takes up the language of a previous passage in the Book of the Four (Mic 4:6-7) and promises a time of renown when YHWH will deal with "all" Zion's "oppressors," will return the remnant of the people, and will restore their possessions. Zephaniah 3:19 takes up the promise of Micah 4:6-7, but formulates that promise in terms of a more imminent event, essentially assuming a time closer to the destruction of Jerusalem (as assumed by Zeph 1:1 compared to Mic 1:1).[81] Thus, 3:18-19 could have concluded the corpus when the initial restoration layer of Zephaniah was added, in all likelihood as part of the Book of the Four.

Zephaniah 3:20 changes the addressee from Lady Zion (second feminine singular) to the people (second masculine plural) and in so doing helps set the stage for Haggai.[82] Other lexical and thematic changes accentuate this change of addressee. In essence, 3:20 merely repeats elements from 3:18-19, but addresses the people instead of Zion personified. In so doing, it reflects awareness of a larger multivolume corpus than just the Book of the Four Prophets. The humility of the remnant prized in Zephaniah 3:11-13 gives way to the remnant's renown when its fortunes are restored in 3:20.[83] The final verses also conclude with two promises that the remnant (the lame and the outcast) will become famous among "all the peoples of the earth," a phrase that aligns with the universal perspective of the reversal of the allusions to Genesis 1–11. Thus, the context and language suggest that Zephaniah 3:20 broadens the role of Zephaniah as the Book of the Twelve expands.

In addition to 3:18-20, three short passages (1:2-3; 2:11b-15; 3:9-10) allude to texts in Genesis 1–11. These texts appear at key points in the redactional structure of Zephaniah, and each text reverses the message of its Genesis source material. Moreover, these three texts fall under the category of scribal prophecy, wherein texts from other biblical books become embedded into the growing prophetic books. The presence of Genesis allusions in Zephaniah reflects a subtle but sophisticated means of accenting the message of Zephaniah. Since an article by Michael DeRoche, scholars have noted that Zephaniah 1:2-3 uses language from Genesis 1 (the Priestly creation story) to evoke a reversal of creation itself as a means of accentuating the impact of the destruction of Jerusalem that follows in 1:4–2:3.[84] Zephaniah 1:2-3 pronounces judgment on the elements of creation that inhabit the earth, but in a completely reverse order from Genesis 1: humanity and beasts, the birds of the air, and the fish of the sea. In so doing, 1:2-3 depicts the coming judgment as the undoing of creation. Adele Berlin demonstrates that Zephaniah 2:11b, 12-15 alludes to the Table of Nations material in Genesis 10.[85] Genesis 10 contains both Priestly and non-Priestly materials, suggesting that the allusions in Zephaniah again assume awareness of Priestly Torah texts. Zephaniah 3:9-10 offers hope that also reverses the judgment of the Tower of Babel story in Genesis 11. As such, these verses likely entered with the

135

other material in Zephaniah 1–2 that reverses the imagery of Genesis 1–11, and this material almost certainly presupposes the combined Pentateuch that contained Priestly and non-Priestly materials somewhere between the late sixth and mid-fifth century BCE.[86] The English translation masks the use of paronomasia in the Hebrew, but quite a number of scholars have noted that the promise that YHWH will change the speech of the nations to "pure" (*brr*) speech plays off the judgment against humanity in Genesis 11:9 which claims YHWH "confused" (*bll*) the speech on earth. Zephaniah, by contrast, depicts YHWH's restoration of Zion as the reunification of speech. The book of Zephaniah thus begins with an announcement of judgment against Judah and Jerusalem that portrays the judgment on par with the reversal of creation while the final salvific message begins with a reversal of the judgment narrated in the tower of Babel story.

Hence the three allusions represent a literary thread running through Zephaniah that places Zephaniah's message into a universal context of creation and recreation. Cumulatively, the allusions span Genesis 1–11, but their placement at key locations also demonstrates a keen awareness of the structural flow of Zephaniah. The first (1:2-3) offers a message at the beginning of the judgment against Judah and Jerusalem, which does nothing less than portray that judgment as the undoing of creation. The second (2:11-15) offers a word of hope for Jerusalem in that it reverses the message of the birth of the line of Ham and Japheth in Genesis 10. The third allusion assumes YHWH's judgment against the nations (3:8b) has now forced the nations to recognize YHWH's power and caused them to bring tribute to Jerusalem (3:9-10).

Zephaniah within the Book of the Four and the Book of the Twelve

Zephaniah plays a pivotal role in the Book of the Twelve and its precursor known as the Book of the Four Prophets (consisting of the early collections and editions of Hosea, Amos, Micah, and Zephaniah). The brevity of Zephaniah and its units continues to fuel debates about how the pieces came together. What seems clear, however, is that Zephaniah displays a remarkably flexible ability to serve a climactic role for both multivolume collections.

Zephaniah's early core consisted of two independent collections that were first fused together as part of the Book of the Four Prophets. The reasons for this claim derive, in part, from Zephaniah's parallel to the role of Amos. Zephaniah has a recognizable form that functions in many ways within the Book of the Four as the Judean counterpart to the book of Amos, whose message of judgment focuses heavily on Israel. The early core of Zephaniah 1–2 brings an unrelenting message of judgment against Jerusalem because of its illicit religious practices and beliefs (1:4-6, 9, 12), the involvement of Judah's leaders in non-Yahwistic worship and adoration of all things foreign (1:5, 8), the trust in wealth (1:11-13), and general accusations of sin (1:17).

The conclusion of this early stage of Zephaniah ended with 3:1-8a. Its message of judgment against Judah, set in the time of Josiah, serves well as the first conclusion to the Book of the Four, a corpus originally designed to explain the destruction of Jerusalem as a result of ongoing problems with its leadership, its people, and its inability to learn from the destruction of the Northern Kingdom as recounted in the books of Hosea, Amos, and Micah. Zephaniah 3:1-8a expresses this judgment in a manner quite similar to the message of judgment against Judah and Israel with which the book of Amos begins. Amos 2:4-5, 6-16 surprisingly concludes the OAN that begins the book (1:3–2:3). For its part, Zephaniah 3:1-8a also appears without warning at the end of the Zephaniah OAN, but directs its message of judgment against Judah and Jerusalem.

Scholars working on the Twelve have noted the extent to which the "day of YHWH" language permeates the Twelve in comparison to the other three prophetic scrolls.[87] Often unobserved, or only noted in passing with respect to the Book of the Four, is the fact that both Amos and Zephaniah also include references to the day of YHWH in the early core of those respective writings. Significantly, the day of YHWH anticipated the day of judgment against YHWH's own people in these two books, against Israel in Amos and against Judah in Zephaniah (1:7-9, 14-18a; cf. "on that day" in 1:10 as well). In Zephaniah, ancient and modern readers alike can hardly fail to understand the implications of this coming day of judgment against YHWH's people as relating specifically to the events surrounding Jerusalem's destruction. In the subsequent developmental phases of Zephaniah, the day of YHWH language expands its focus to include a day of judgment against all the inhabitants of the earth (1:18b). In all likelihood, this dual pronouncement of the day of YHWH coming against YHWH's own people in Amos and Zephaniah already functions within the Book of the Four as one of a number of parallels connecting the punishment of the north with the punishment of the south. As the Book of the Four expanded, the day of YHWH sayings took up this language but also conceptualized it as a time of judgment against foreign nations, both near and far.

Like Amos, Zephaniah receives a series of restoration promises directed toward Judah and Jerusalem. These promises begin with a message concerning the remnant (3:11-13), then continue with a tightly constructed promise of restoration in which YHWH returns to Jerusalem to rule as warrior-king, restores his relationship with Zion, and expels Zion's enemies (3:14-17). The last verses of Zephaniah (3:18-20) conclude the book with two perspectives on the remnant. The first message continues the direct address to Lady Zion but also promises help for "those mourning the appointed feasts" (3:18a). This message extends

YHWH's promise to the remnant (3:19) that reformulates Micah 4:6-7 to convey a more imminent fulfillment of the promise. Second, these verses reinterpret the fate of the remnant from a humble and lowly group who survive Jerusalem's destruction (3:12) to a group who will be known throughout the earth because of YHWH's salvific acts (3:19). The last verse of Zephaniah addresses the remnant directly (second masculine plural) to reiterate that their fame will cause them to be praised throughout the earth when their fortunes are restored (3:20).

Those reading Zephaniah must remember that these promises of restoration and renown all take place in the distant future (when read from the perspective of the date of the prophet according to Zeph 1:1). These promises represent words of hope for those who returned to Jerusalem after its punishment. These words of hope were written by those later scribal prophets who transmitted the collections, even though the messages appear in a prophetic collection dated prior to Jerusalem's destruction. They serve a dual purpose: first, to frame Jerusalem's "coming destruction" (literally speaking) and the more distant return of the people of Jerusalem as part of YHWH's grand plan, and second, to affirm that YHWH's ongoing relationship with Judah will soon manifest itself in the restoration of Jerusalem's former glory.

A significant shift in the hermeneutical role of Zephaniah occurs when the multivolume corpus expands to include Haggai, Zechariah 1–8, and Malachi. At this point, Zephaniah no longer concludes the scroll, but it still plays a climactic role as the last prophetic voice to be heard prior to Jerusalem's destruction, and indeed prior to the point when Haggai begins to exhort those living near Jerusalem to rebuild the temple. In fact, the allusions to Genesis 1–11 created by the latter stages of editing Zephaniah function in part to attribute an even grander significance to Jerusalem's destruction by drawing upon texts with cosmic overtones. Probably concurrent with the second restoration layer, these Genesis allusions appear at key thematic junctures in Zephaniah. At the very beginning of Zephaniah, 1:2-3 frames the coming destruction of Jerusalem as nothing short of the undoing of creation. At the end of the OAN, the wording reverses the Table of Nations material from Genesis 10. Genesis 10 speaks of the birth of the line of Ham while Zephaniah's OAN document the death of this genealogical line. Finally, Zephaniah 3:9-10 utilizes a word play that reverses the message of Genesis 11. Whereas Genesis 11 narrated YHWH's decision to destroy the tower of Babel and scatter the nations through "confused speech," Zephaniah 3:9-10 anticipates a time that will see the "pure speech" of the nations calling upon YHWH. These three texts also share a more universal perspective that appears in both the judgment and salvific sections elsewhere in Zephaniah (1:18b; 3:8b, 20). To be sure, the early core of Zephaniah joined the OAN material in 2:4-15, but this collection concerned the nations who benefitted by working with Assyria, and as such was not truly focused upon a universal perspective as presumed in the Genesis allusions (1:2-3; 2:12-15; and 3:9-10), the day of YHWH against the nations material (1:18b), and the promise of fame and prosperity for the remnant (3:20).

Discussion Questions

1. Why do we speak about the Book of the Twelve or the Twelve Prophets rather than the Minor Prophets? What differences could be communicated with these titles?

2. Explain the structural, chronological, and literary agendas of the four books that have given rise to the idea of the Book of the Four as a collection that preceded the Book of the Twelve.

3. Explain the role of Micah 4–5 and 6–7, which most scholars date well after the time the prophet Micah lived.

Chapter 5
The End of the Twelve

Introduction

The three books treated in this chapter, Haggai, Zechariah, and Malachi, appear as the last three books in the Twelve. They have a complex history in that each book has its own distinct literary profile, but they have also come together in stages and ultimately now function as the conclusion to the Twelve. According to most scholarly models, Haggai and Zechariah 1–8 were edited and published together to commemorate the role of the two prophets in helping to complete the temple sometime in the late sixth or the first half of the fifth century BCE. The next steps are more debated. Zechariah 9–14 represents a later addition to Zechariah 1–8 because its message differs dramatically from those chapters. Malachi was compiled after the temple was reconstructed and was added as the final book when the larger scroll was created, though when that happened remains debated. For some, Malachi was first added to the end of Zechariah 8, and Zechariah 9–14 was added later. For others, Malachi was added after Zechariah 9–14 was added to Zechariah 8. These three books function as the Persian-period books at the end of the Twelve, so treating them together helps illuminate the function of each book and their role in the Twelve. Consequently, the four parts will be presented separately (Haggai, Zechariah 1–8, Zechariah 9–14, and Malachi) following a discussion of the historical backdrop for Haggai and Zechariah 1–8.

Historical Backdrop to
Haggai and Zechariah 1–8

Darius I, king of Persia, came to power in 522 BCE under somewhat mysterious circumstances following the death of Artaxerxes (465–424 BCE) and two of his sons over a period of several months. Not surprisingly, the transition created an opportunity for a number of countries to test the new king by attempting to revolt. It took a couple of years to put down these rebellions, but Darius I proved to be an effective leader, administrator, and military strategist. The small territory of Judah, by contrast, appears to have remained on relatively good terms with Darius, though judging from the scenario presumed in Haggai, life in and around Jerusalem remained difficult.

Jerusalem in the late sixth century remained a shadow of its former self. The exuberance of the return of groups of exiles in the time of Cyrus (see the discussion of Isaiah 40–55) had given way to the reality of the hardships faced by refugees returning to find that life in their former homeland would not be easy. For nearly twenty years, groups had returned to Judah. It would become a Persian province known as Yehud and remain relatively stable politically throughout the Persian period, though economically it remained poor. The backstory for the book of Haggai reflects ongoing difficulties created by drought (1:5-6; 2:15-19). According to traditions in Ezra 3, early attempts to rebuild the temple failed when the first wave of returnees arrived in the region, due to resistance from regional interests, so only an outdoor altar existed.[1]

Theological debates added to the pressure, and the dilapidated state of the temple complex represented a focal point of those debates. Some thought the temple should be built immediately to spur restoration, while others argued that the temple should not be rebuilt until YHWH's punishment was fully complete.[2] These dynamics help to explain why the prophet confronts, in the opening unit of the book, those who have resisted rebuilding the temple (1:2). Haggai also confronts those who tended to their own extravagant housing needs (1:4) without drawing a connection between the temple lying in ruins and the economic reality (1:5-6).

Haggai

The Prophet and the Book

The book of Haggai displays characteristic features: five dated introductions that appear in sequential order covering roughly four months of the year 520

BCE (1:1, 15; 2:1, 10, 20) and a report style that refers to the prophet in the third person. These stylistic characteristics cause scholars to label the compiler as the Haggai chronicler or the chronicler of Haggai and Zechariah 1–8. The selection of the speeches and the rhetoric about the prophet demonstrate that this chronicler holds Haggai in high regard as the prophet who inspired the leadership and the community to rebuild YHWH's temple. The governor, the high priest, and the people unite to begin the project within a single month (1:14-15). Along the way, the prophet also must exhort these same three entities not to give up on the project (2:3-4), and he does so by describing past works of YHWH in the exodus (2:5) and the future implications of their project when the nations will bring wealth and prosperity to the temple (2:7-9). At the end of the four months, the cornerstone of the temple has been laid, and the reader assumes that progress will continue. The book ends by conveying great hope that Zerubbabel will have a key political role in the transformation of Jerusalem (2:20-23). Zerubbabel was the grandson of Jehoiachin, the king of Judah exiled to Babylon in 597, and the great-grandson of Josiah (2 Kgs 23:25). This speech expects that Zerubbabel will restore the link to the Davidic dynasty by reversing Jeremiah's denunciation of Jehoiachin. The signet ring that YHWH cast off (Jer 22:24) becomes a sign of promise for Jehoiachin's grandson. Zerubbabel never became king and in fact disappears from the scene very quickly and quietly, leading many scholars to speculate that hopes for a restoration of Davidic kingship through Zerubbabel may have actually caused Darius to remove him as governor.[3]

Most scholars accept the dates in Haggai as reliable historical data for the beginning of the rebuilding of the temple and concomitantly for the time of the prophet. Debate exists about when the Haggai chronicler added these introductions to the speeches.[4] The hope for an uprising among the nations that will elevate Zerubbabel to king in 2:20-23 convinces most scholars to assume that the book was produced in relatively close proximity to the dates in the book. In either case, the core material of the speeches would have taken shape in the late sixth or early fifth century BCE. The Haggai chronicler drew together existing accounts of the prophet and published these together with the first version of Zechariah (see Zechariah 1–8 below).

The Structure and Contents of Haggai

As already noted, the introductions not only provide a chronological flow to the book, but they also denote the literary parameters of at least five prophetic speeches.[5] The speeches of Haggai, viewed synchronically, progress from words of admonishment, to words of encouragement, to words of hope, as the prospects of rebuilding the temple become increasingly realized.

143

This opening unit creates confusion because the chronicler (1:1) names Zerubbabel and Joshua as the addressees, but most commentators interpret the people as the addressees.[6] The rhetorical structure of 1:2-11 helps resolve this confusion. The speech combines the formal elements of a disputation and two judgment oracles with the rhetorical aim of convincing the governor (Zerubbabel) and the high priest (Joshua) that the time has come to rebuild the temple.

The speech account (1:2-11) functions thematically as a single rhetorical unit, but it combines two different oracles. The unit begins like a disputation, laying out the thesis it will challenge: "This people says that the time has not come, the time to rebuild YHWH's house" (1:2). The larger rhetorical unit continues with a word-event formula (1:3) and two messenger formulas (1:5, 7), which often introduce oracles. Both oracles contain a climactic rhetorical element. Nevertheless, the two parts (1:3-6, 7-11) serve the larger rhetorical agenda laid out in 1:2, namely, to refute the argument that the time for rebuilding the temple has not yet come.

The first oracular report (1:3-6) opens with a word-event formula but immediately puts forward a rhetorical question designed to challenge the status quo: "Is it time for you [mp] to dwell in your fine paneled houses when YHWH's house lies in ruins?" (1:4). Rhetorical questions rarely need a response. By asking his hearers to consider the contrast between their houses and YHWH's house, the prophet accuses them of negligence. The climax of this first oracular report drives home the point by contrasting the paneled houses with the difficulty of survival. Verses 5-6 admonish the addressees to look around and see that the situation can barely be called subsistence living. No one has enough to eat or drink. Clothing is insufficient against the elements, and wages are too low. The rhetorical question of 1:4 hangs in the air, essentially asking, "Is it time . . ." "Is it time for you to live in fine houses while you face a losing battle to survive?" Who is this group that lives in such fine houses? Recent archaeological excavations tend to confirm the lack of major housing developments in Jerusalem in the sixth century BCE, so who would be living in these paneled houses to which 1:4 refers? According to 1:1 the word of YHWH was delivered to Zerubbabel and Joshua. If so, then perhaps Haggai has not been given enough credit for working as an agent of change who speaks truth to power. These words are designed to open the eyes of those with means to the suffering of the community.

The second oracle report (1:7-11) continues to connect the current difficulties with the state of YHWH's temple (1:7-9). The unit begins by demanding action, and the climax comes with the pronouncement of judgment following the word "therefore" (1:10), which plays such a prominent role in judgment oracles. In 1:10-11, YHWH announces a drought wherein the lack of rain stops the land

144

from producing. The point is clear. The oracle argues that the fate of those living in the area will not change unless and until the temple is rebuilt.

The second dated unit in the book (1:12-15) narrates the response of Zerubbabel and Joshua to Haggai's first speech, but it is the only speech in which the chronological element (1:15) appears at the conclusion of the unit rather than the beginning.[7] At any rate, 1:12-14 narrates the positive response of Zerubbabel and Joshua to the speech recounted in 1:2-11. The report credits Zerubbabel and Joshua with obedience and the remnant of the people with the fear of YHWH (1:12). It ends by stating that work on the temple began just three weeks after Haggai delivered his speech (1:14-15).[8]

The third unit (2:1-9) opens roughly one month later on the twenty-first day of the seventh month (2:1), this time offering words of encouragement more than admonition. The encouragement mirrors a setting similar to that described in the account of the temple's reconstruction in Ezra 3.[9] The vignette in Haggai 2:1-9 exhorts Zerubbabel and Joshua not to be disappointed in the current size of the temple (2:2-4) because greater things await (2:6-9). This speech claims that YHWH has great plans for Jerusalem as a place to which all the nations will turn and that the nations will bring great wealth to the temple.

The last two accounts (2:10-19, 20-23) occur on the same day, the twenty-fourth day of the ninth month of 520 BCE. The first of these accounts concerns the purification of the new building. It recounts a conversation between Haggai, the people, and the priests, to remind the people that what is unholy can profane what is holy (2:12-13). The passage applies the priestly ruling to the people (2:14) before narrating the laying of the foundation stone, depicting the event as the turning point for Judah's fate (2:15-19). Three things stand out for understanding this passage. First, a number of studies demonstrate that the passage presupposes the need for a purification ritual.[10] Hence, this date may well mark a significant event in preparing for rebuilding the temple. Second, for Haggai's theology, this date also marks a turning point in the economic situation of the land. Haggai expects that the rebuilding will change the economic situation. Twice, the text refers to what will happen "from this day forward" (2:15, 19). Reconstructing the temple was not just another building project. Rather, it required ritual purity from all those involved.

Third, evidence suggests that 2:17, 19 have been updated to reflect an editorial thread that runs through the Book of the Twelve, not just the book of Haggai alone. Haggai 2:17 cites the refrain of Amos 4:6-11 after recounting a series of punishments that include blight, mildew, and hail: "Yet you did not return to me, says the LORD" (Amos 4:6, 8, 9, 10, 11). Two of these punishments, blight and mildew, also appear in Amos 4:9. The citation of these particular elements, however, more likely reflects the hand of a later scribal prophet linking Haggai with Amos. The situation presumed in Haggai 1 specifically anticipates a drought (1:11) as the cause of the current suffering, and while drought could account for the blight in Haggai 2:17, the mildew and hail reflect damage to crops that results when water is present in greater quantities. The litany of punishments in Amos 4:6-11 represents past actions taken by YHWH against Israel, while Haggai focuses upon the threat to the land's productivity that is ongoing.

A phrase has been added to Haggai 2:19 that draws upon the drought imagery of Joel 1 in a way that is syntactically awkward and conceptually confounding. English translations smooth over the difficulties, but a literal translation of Haggai 2:19 illustrates the problem:

1. Is the seed still in the grain pit?
2. Or the vine, or the fig tree, or the pomegranate?
3. Or has the olive tree not borne fruit?
4. From this day I will bless.

This verse contains four syntactical lines, three of which (lines 1, 3, and 4) flow together seamlessly to make the same rhetorical point: the agricultural situation is changing for the better. Line 2, however, though it seeks to fit the rhetorical point of the unit, creates real difficulties. One of these difficulties is masked by the tendency of the English translations to use misleading English words like *granary* or *barn* when the Hebrew word in line 1 refers to an underground pit for storing seed to keep it dry until it can be planted. The rhetorical question of line 1 makes perfect sense. It implies that the seed is no longer being stored but is being planted. The rhetorical point of line 3 is similar: it implies that the olive tree has begun to bear fruit. The problem comes with line 2. No one would store a vine, the fig tree, or pomegranate in an underground grain pit. Line 2 makes sense as an extension of line 3, which in all likelihood suggests line 2 was added as a marginal gloss and later mistakenly copied before the line on which it commented. But why would a reader have extended line 3 with the vine, the fig tree, and the pomegranate? Those who read Haggai in isolation explain this triad as symbols of fertility. In fact, these three plants appear together twice in the Torah to describe the fertility of the land into which Israel shall enter (Num 20:5; Deut 8:8). Those who read Haggai within the Twelve, however, recognize the symbols of fertility as part of an ongoing literary thread running through the scroll. In fact, the only other place these three plants appear together in a single verse is Joel 1:12, where they also appear in precisely this order (vine, fig tree, and pomegranate). The significance of this fertility claim should not be lost on the reader of the Twelve or Haggai. Joel 1:12 laments the withering of these three plants as signs of the curse that has unfolded for covenant disobedience.[11] Only with the purified rebuilding of the temple will the land begin to recover. When one understands this line of Haggai 2:19 as an allusion back to Joel, one begins to understand Joel's dual significance in the Book of the Twelve. It functions locally, showing YHWH's confrontation with Judah and Jerusalem in a manner that depicts YHWH's willingness to respond to YHWH's people when they cry out and to reverse the punishment (Joel 2:12-14, 23-25). Yet, Joel also functions globally as the book through which virtually every recurring theme of the Book of the Twelve runs.[12] The paradigm that plays out in Joel essentially repeats itself across the Twelve, and Haggai 2:19 plays a significant role in evoking Joel's paradigm. The message is already present in 2:19, but the reader who added the clause in line 2 connected this promise of fertility to the larger pattern.

The chronicler places the final dated unit (2:20-23) on the same date as 2:10-19, concluding the book of Haggai with a message of hope that reverses the punishment of Jehoiachin described in Jeremiah 22:4. Haggai 2:20-23 presupposes the message of 2:10-19 since the chronicler specifically refers to the verses as the second time that the word of YHWH came to Haggai on that day (2:20). That day was important because 2:10-19 presupposes the temple's foundation stone was placed at that time. The content of Haggai's final speech begins (2:21) by citing 2:6, marking the date as a significant turning point on which the nations of the world are about to be upended. The next verse recounts a battle scene in which the army representing the "throne of the kingdoms" and the "kingdoms of the nations" will be annihilated. Consequently, YHWH's final promise anticipates Zerubbabel will be installed as political leader (2:23).

This last verse is remarkable for three reasons. First, it promises something that never comes true. While unusual, recording unfulfilled prophecy is not unique in the Hebrew Bible.[13] Zerubbabel plays a role in Haggai and Zechariah, but by the end of that book, he is nowhere to be found. It has often been suggested, given the context in the early years of Darius's reign when he put down a number of revolts, that Haggai's hopes for Zerubbabel here and Zechariah 4:6-10 would have made Darius nervous and resulted in him calling Zerubbabel back to Persia (or worse). Whatever the reason, a Davidic king never retook the throne in Jerusalem.

Second, Haggai 2:23 frames its promise as a reversal of the judgment against Jehoiachin in Jeremiah 22:24-27. The Jeremiah text announces the removal of Jehoiachin by YHWH as though removing a signet ring from his finger. The signet ring (a symbol of royal power) is torn off, sent to Babylon (22:26), never to return to the land. By contrast, Haggai 2:23 compares Jehoiachin's grandson, now governor in Jerusalem, to a signet ring whom YHWH has "chosen," a verb

147

that appears in the context of YHWH's selection of David as king (Ps 78:20). While Hag 2:23 does not specifically claim that Zerubbabel will become king, the significance and the subtlety of this allusion should not be missed. In formulating the promise this way, Haggai not only makes a claim about the future (the royal imagery used to describe Zerubbabel), he also signals an important theological affirmation for the present (for Haggai's audience). It signals an end to the time of punishment.

Third, for Haggai and those who included these verses in the book, Zerubbabel's obedience in rebuilding the temple signaled the expectation of a changing world order (2:21-22), one that would see a scion of David returned to power in the aftermath of the overthrow of the nations. The fact that this promise results from his role in laying the foundation stone connects the temple with political aspirations. The prominent role given to this oracle as the final saying in Haggai suggests that these hopes for a restoration of the Davidic monarchy retained an enduring appeal for those transmitting Haggai. This hope becomes tempered for those reading the Book of the Twelve, especially in the material found in Zechariah 9–14.

Haggai within the Book of the Twelve

Haggai's role in the Book of the Twelve stands out for its chronological framework, its use of earlier texts, and its position in the Twelve. The chronological framework in Haggai creates a sense of progression wherein the individual speeches become increasingly more positive. The five dated reports highlight three events in the life of Yehud in the early Persian period: an initial speech that credits Haggai with inspiring the rebuilding of the temple (1:2-11); the actual beginning of the work three weeks later (1:14); and the day when the cornerstone was laid (2:10, 15, 20). These events unfold in a span of less than four months according to the chronicler's superscriptions and thus create an impression of rapid change.

Alongside these events, Haggai's role changes. Initially confrontational, Haggai becomes exhorter-in-chief, and finally articulates hope for a new political dynamic. While 1:2-11 recounts the means by which Haggai confronted the people, the governor, and the chief priest to get them to begin work on the temple, the next two vignettes presuppose a message of encouragement in the face of resistance. One line of resistance came from those who were disheartened that this temple would begin as a much smaller version of the previous temple. Haggai exhorts Zerubbabel, Joshua, and the people to think about the long-term implications (2:3-9). Haggai involves the priests to make sure that purity expectations were taken into account as the temple was built (2:10-15), and Haggai commends Zerubbabel as a sign of political restoration (2:20-23).

148

Haggai 2:10-19 and 2:20-23 exhibit an interpretive style that draws upon other texts to frame their message. Specifically, 2:17, 19, and 23 take up Amos, Joel, and Jeremiah. These allusions help accentuate the sense of imminent change. Haggai 2:17 and 2:19 utilize Amos 4 and Joel 1 to evoke threats to the fertility of the land that were about to change. Haggai 2:23 alludes to and reverses the sign of judgment in Jeremiah 22:24 by claiming that Zerubbabel is like a signet ring that YHWH has chosen. Haggai thus communicates that Jeremiah's time of punishment has ended. This promise aligns well with the opening call to repentance in Zechariah 1:2-6 and Zechariah's first vision account (1:12-13) that also interpret the present time as the end of punishment announced in Jeremiah. Importantly, the opening speech of Zechariah (1:1) overlaps with Haggai so that Zechariah's account of repentance helps explain changes before the last two speeches of Haggai.

Finally, the location of Haggai in the Twelve plays an important role in the structure of the Twelve, particularly in comparison to the scroll of Isaiah. As noted in the chapter on Isaiah, Isaiah exhibits a clear change of setting even as it continues to display a certain chronological progression. Isaiah 36–39 focuses upon the aftermath of the siege of Jerusalem by Sennacherib (701 BCE), whereas chapter 40 presumes a series of speeches delivered to a group of exiles in Babylon in the immediate aftermath of Cyrus's defeat of Babylon (539 BCE). Chronologically, this gap covers approximately one hundred and sixty years. The Book of the Twelve exhibits a similar chronological gap, though it is not quite as long. The superscription in Zephaniah (1:1) places Zephaniah in the time of Josiah, sometime before Josiah's death and after the beginning of his reforms (622–609 BCE). The chronological introductions in Haggai, which appears right after Zephaniah, begin quite specifically in the year 520, or roughly ninety to one hundred years after the time of Zephaniah's superscription. These gaps are significant for both scrolls since the content presupposes a dramatic pivot from prophetic material that primarily expects the reader to presume a setting prior to Jerusalem's destruction (Isa 1–39; Hosea–Zephaniah) before jumping to a crucial moment for the early postexilic period (the rise of Cyrus and the Persians that enabled groups of exiles to return to Judah in Isaiah, and the reconstruction of the temple in the time of Darius I in the Book of the Twelve). Neither Isaiah nor the Twelve, therefore, devotes any space to the actual experience of Jerusalem's destruction and the removal of a significant portion of its elite population. By contrast, Jeremiah and Ezekiel focus heavily on events surrounding Jerusalem's destruction and the exile of part of Judah's population.[14]

Evaluated from a canonical perspective, both the beginning and end of the chronological gap in the two scrolls highlight important elements. The gap in Isaiah begins with Hezekiah, while Zephaniah is set in the reign of Josiah. The book of Kings presents every king of Judah and Israel as flawed. Apart from David and Solomon, only Hezekiah and Josiah receive credit for instituting reforms that attempted to save Jerusalem from itself. In other words, in the pantheon of the kings of Judah, Hezekiah and Josiah stand tall. The other end of the gap in both Isaiah and the Twelve highlights significant moments for Judah in the early Persian period. Isaiah 40 begins after Cyrus has defeated Babylon.[15] Isaiah credits Cyrus with allowing Judean exiles from Babylon to return to Judah and Jerusalem. The Twelve opens its Persian-period section (Haggai, Zechariah, and Malachi) with accounts that document the rebuilding of the temple nearly twenty years after the first refugees made their way back to Judah. Finally, while both scrolls begin by portraying the Persian period rather optimistically, neither Isaiah nor the Twelve describes a utopian change. Both the Twelve and Isaiah attest to conflicts that arise from debates within the community as well as from external threats. Thus, the thematic trajectory of both scrolls, in a certain sense, displays a theological tendency to circle back to where the scroll began. More will be said about this topic when dealing with Zechariah 9–14 and Malachi.

Zechariah 1–8

The Prophet and the Book

Scholars have long recognized that Zechariah 9–14 comes from a much later time and underwent a considerably different compositional history than chapters 1–8. For this reason, Zechariah will be treated in two parts. Zechariah 1–8 shares a historical setting with Haggai since dating formulas (1:1, 7; 7:1) situate 1–8 in the second and fourth years of Darius (520 and 518 BCE). The three dates in Zechariah 1–8 also represent a key part of the evidence that Zechariah 1–8 was published together with Haggai (1:1, 15; 2:1, 10, 20). The date of Zechariah's first speech precedes Haggai's last two speeches by about a month, and fits well with the progression in Haggai (see discussion of 1:1-6). Both prophets are also associated with the temple reconstruction in later writings (Ezra 3–6; 1 Esd 6:1-3; 7:1-6).

Regarding the question of the authorship of Zechariah 1–8, it is important to recognize that each of the three main sections of 1–8 begins with a chronological note (1:1, 7; 7:1) introducing a new composition. The three introductions are often associated with the editor who combined Haggai and Zechariah 1–8 into a single, chronologically-oriented collection.[16]

While some assume that the first unit (1:2-6) comes from the prophet for whom the book is named, a number of scholars now attribute 1:2-6 to the editor who combined Haggai and Zechariah.[17] These scholars note stylistic similarities in 1:2-6 to sermonic recitations and to portions of chapters 7–8 (e.g., 7:7-14; 8:14-17, 19b). They also point out that the vision cycle presupposes the theme of repentance that dominates 1:2-6. Zechariah 1:1 dates the speech to the eighth month (but provides no specific day), so Zechariah 1:2-6 precedes Haggai's last two speeches since Haggai 2:10, 20 refer to the twenty-fourth day of the ninth month. Importantly, 1:2-6 conveys a very important theological turning point by recounting the people's repentance in response to the prophet's sermon (1:6). This change of the people overlaps with Haggai's concern for purity and a new royal figure, helping to explain the inclusion of Zechariah 1:2-6 in its current location, whether or not it was composed as part of the process that connected Zechariah 1–8 and Haggai.

The largest section of Zechariah 1–8 (1:7–6:15) contains eight vision reports. It begins with the superscription of 1:7, setting the visions two to three months later than the opening unit. This superscription comes from the editor who joined the vision cycle to the introductory materials of 1:1-7. The vision cycle probably circulated on its own before it was joined with the other two compositional blocks of Zechariah 1–8 (1:1-6; 7:1–8:23). The eight-vision cycle has a high degree of first-person speech, stylized vision reports, and editorial commentary on the visions themselves. The promises to Joshua (3:1-10) and Zerubbabel (4:6-10) portray them as the chief priest and the political head for the new temple. Most scholars attribute the early collection of the visions to the prophet for whom the book was named, or someone close to him.

The final compositional block appears in 7:1–8:23, and is best classified as an optimistic anthology of sayings attributed to the prophet Zechariah. The short sayings differ stylistically from the vision reports. A compiler has arranged the sayings thematically to challenge the prophet's audience to reflect upon the past (7:1-14), to hear promises about Jerusalem's future (8:1-13), and to exhort the current generation to behave differently than their ancestors (8:14-23). In one instance (8:9), the material refers back to events mentioned in Haggai (2:17) and the vision reports (4:9). One cannot definitively know that the sayings actually come from the prophet, but the introductory formulas convey that impression given that several refer to Zechariah by name (7:1, 8) or to "me" (7:4; 8:1, 18, see the discussion of structure and composition below). One should also note that this anthology presents itself as a message to the community two years into the temple construction project (7:1). Chapters 7–8 essentially encourage the community to continue rebuilding the temple and reestablishing obedience to YHWH's ethical instruction.

151

The Structure and Composition of Zechariah

Zechariah 1:1-6: The People Repent

The first compositional unit in Zechariah contains the first of three super-scriptions that appear in chronological order (1:1, 7; 7:1), followed by a sermon report and response (1:2-6). The three superscriptions provide a chronological framework to Zechariah 1–8 that overlaps with similarly styled chronological introductions in Haggai. The two prophets were contemporaries, and the two books have likely been edited together.

Zechariah 1:2-6 recounts a call to repentance (1:2-6a) and the people's positive response (1:6b). The sermon report begins with a statement that the people's ancestors had angered YHWH (1:2), causing the current situation. YHWH invites the current generation to return (1:3), an invitation continued through the *via negativa* in 1:4-6a by recalling the fate of the ancestors who rejected a similar call. The call assumes the current situation is bad, but does not say why (suggesting the reader should fill in the gap based on Haggai). Finally, 1:6b explicitly recounts that the current generation responded positively. The explicit positive response is unusual with calls to repent in prophetic literature, most notably in the Book of the Twelve.[18]

Zechariah 1:7–6:14: The Vision Cyle

This vision cycle, also called the night visions of Zechariah, poses questions concerning its composition, its relationship to the chronological structure, and its original setting(s). The vision cycle contains eight reports unfolding as conversations between the prophet and a mediating messenger. These reports repeat four elements: a description of the image, one or more questions from the prophet, an explanation of the image, and a prophetic oracle. The images which the prophet sees in these eight visions include a man on a horse speaking to those patrolling the earth (1:8-10), four horns (1:18), four craftsmen (1:20), a man with a measuring line (2:1), the high priest Joshua (3:1), a lampstand with seven bowls (4:2), a flying scroll (5:1-2), a basket (*ephah*) with a woman inside (5:5-7), two women who fly away with the basket (5:9), and four chariots and horses who patrol the earth (6:1-3).[19]

The Meaning of the Images

This array of images seems odd at first glance, but interpretive clues suggest these visions depict how Jerusalem should be inhabited and its polity structured.

The horses and riders in the first and last vision patrol the earth at YHWH's behest to keep him informed and carry out his directives.

The first vision (1:8-17) declares the world is at rest, and Jerusalem's punishment is over. The four horns and four craftsmen of the second vision (1:18-21 [Heb. 2:1-4]) symbolically relate to punishing the foreign nations that scattered Judah, Israel, and Jerusalem among the nations (1:19 [MT 2:2]) and the rebuilding that must now take place (1:21 [Heb. 2:4]). Recent discussions of horns and craftsmen in the second vision interpret the horns as political powers because they scatter YHWH's people among the nations. Relatedly, the word *craftsmen* is understood here because the Hebrew word (*ḥārāšîm*) refers to artisans working on wood (2 Sam 5:11; 2 Kgs 12:12; 22:6), stone (Exod 28:11; 2 Sam 5:11; 1 Chr 14:11), and various metals (1 Sam 13:19; 2 Chr 34:11).[20]

The prophet sees a measuring line in the third vision (2:1-4 [Heb. 2:5-8]), which symbolizes the need to rebuild Jerusalem. The vision promises that Jerusalem will be larger than before because of all the people who will return. The promises continue in the oracular material that follows (2:5-9 [Heb. 2:9-13]) when YHWH declares he will defend Jerusalem like a wall of fire and provide Jerusalem glory from within (2:5). It also anticipates that the nations be punished (2:8-9 [Heb. 2:12-13]) and that they will marvel at Jerusalem (2:11 [Heb. 2:15]). This oracular material relates thematically to both the second and third vision report.

The fourth vision report (3:1-10) deviates from the pattern for the visions discussed above. The prophet reports seeing Joshua, the high priest, not a symbolic item. The fourth vision also does not use a question-and-response style like the other visions. It describes a commissioning of Joshua as high priest.[21] The passage also expects a reappearance of the "branch," a term that draws upon Jeremiah 23:5 and 33:15 to refer to a Davidic descendant who will rule in Jerusalem. The image refers to Zerubbabel, Jehoiachin's grandson.[22] Consequently, the fourth vision anticipates a leadership role for both a civil and a religious authority, but the reinstitution of a Davidic descendant never materialized in the Second Temple period. The Persians continued to appoint governors, but after Zerubbabel, no Davidic descendant filled that role. To the contrary, biblical traditions present Ezra and Nehemiah as the civic leaders of the fifth century, but neither descended from David.[23]

The fifth vision report (4:1-14) resumes the pattern with the reappearance of the mediating messenger, a description of the items seen (a golden lampstand and two olive trees), and a question-and-response format as part of the formal vision report itself (4:1-5). The report precedes two oracles, one honoring Zerubbabel (4:6-7) and one claiming that he will see the temple completed (4:8-10a). It also contains an explanation of the meaning of the lampstand and the olive trees (4:10b-14). This fifth vision report and the oracle surrounding it connect closely to the fourth, which focused on the leadership of the high priest Joshua. Taken together, these two visions presuppose a civil and religious leadership for Jerusalem, one that highlights the role of the Zadokite priesthood and a Davidic descendant. Thus, the first three visions lay the groundwork for restoring the glory of Jerusalem, and visions four and five endorse a leadership model for Jerusalem that recognizes Zadokite priests and a representative of David's line. The next two vision reports deal with the expectations for society at large in this rebuilt Jerusalem.

In the sixth vision (5:1-4), the prophet sees a flying scroll that threatens a curse over the land for anyone who steals or bears false witness (5:3) or who swears falsely on YHWH's name (5:4). This vision threatens those disregarding YHWH's ethical expectations for the community.

The seventh vision report (5:5-11) concerns the removal of wickedness from the land. The prophet sees a basket (with the Hebrew word indicating a basket about the size of a bushel). He also sees a woman inside the basket covered with a metal lid (5:9), and two feminine, winged beings carry her away to Shinar (another name for Babylon; see Gen 10:10). According to the messenger's words to the prophet, she represents "wickedness" (5:8) who is banished from the land. The sixth and seventh visions thus work together to delineate proper behavior by threatening a curse upon the house of those who do not live up to YHWH's expectations and by removing wickedness from the land.

In the final vision (6:1-8), the four chariots and their horses representing the four winds of heaven (6:5) are sent forth again to patrol the earth even as the land in the north is described as being at rest in YHWH's spirit (6:8). The final oracle (6:9-15) that follows the vision depicts the crowning of the high priest Joshua. This investiture raises numerous questions because of text-critical problems (namely the MT has a plural word for crowns in 6:11) and the fact that Zerubbabel is not mentioned at all in these verses.

Some scholars argue that the individual visions were composed across a twenty-year period during the lifetime of the prophet.[24] Most, however, interpret the block as a series of visions that took place in a single night.[25] The latter option seems to be the most logical reading since 1:7 lists only one date (the twenty-fourth day of the eleventh month in the second year of Darius). Just as importantly, the thematic development and the reappearance of the horses and messengers patrolling the earth connect the eighth vision with the first vision and exhibit a general conceptual cohesion, even though oracles periodically expand the vision report. The first three visions recount YHWH's decision to rebuild Jerusalem and punish the nations who took advantage of it. Visions four and five depict Joshua and Zerubbabel as the priestly and civil leaders responsible for governing Judah and Jerusalem. Visions six and seven portray the cleansing of the people and the land. Finally, the eighth vision reiterates YHWH's control of the heavens and the earth. Setting these visions in the second year of Darius puts these portraits in close proximity to the building of the temple (the primary subject of Haggai), but only the fifth vision focuses on the temple foundation explicitly (4:9). The vision reports, instead, deal with the fate and polity of Jerusalem and Judah. They portray two leaders designated by YHWH: the chief priest Joshua who has been cleansed in a heavenly ceremony and a descendant of David in the person of Zerubbabel who serves as the governor appointed by Persia. These visions appear after the repentance of the people, roughly three months earlier (1:2-6), and about two years prior to the anthology of sayings dated to the fourth year of Darius that begins in 7:1.

Zechariah 7:1–8:23: An End to Fasting

The third compositional block consists of a series of short sayings arranged thematically as an anthology of prophetic speeches with a rhetorical purpose. A narrative that involves a question (7:3) and a response (7:4-5; 8:18-19) frames this collection. This question-and-answer format thus creates an envelope around a host of sayings, thereby presenting these verses as a single "event." This final block begins with the third superscription of Zechariah 1–8 (7:1), which dates the "event" roughly two years after the date beginning the vision cycle. Inside this frame, the units change topics, but as a group they summarize the prophet's message. The units often begin with a word-event formula ("the word of YHWH came to . . ." in 7:1, 8; 8:1, 18) or a messenger formula ("thus says YHWH," in 7:9; 8:2, 3, 4, 6, 7, 9, 14, 19, 20, 23). Chapters 7–8 thus present a collage of short sayings and speeches.

The collection's purpose derives not from a linear rhetorical argument but from two other factors: the frame that begins and ends the collection (7:1-3; 8:18-19) indicating that the time for fasting is over, and the emphasis that comes from thematic repetition. Most of the smaller units progress through interlocking thematic and/or lexical repetition:

7:1-3:   Is the time for fasting over?

7:4-7:   Why were you fasting?

7:8-14:   The reasons for punishment derived from the failure to judge
           with justice and truth or to act with kindness and mercy (7:9)
           and from disregarding the law and the words of YHWH (7:12).

8:1-2:   I am jealous for Zion.

8:3:   I will return to dwell in Zion/Jerusalem.

8:4-5:   The population of Jerusalem will have long lives.

8:6:   There will be benefits for the remnant of this people.

8:7-8:   The exiles will return from the East to Jerusalem.

8:9-13:   Positive changes in Jerusalem began with the laying of the cornerstone; consider the past, present, and future.

8:14-17:   Live in justice and truth, and YHWH will do good to Jerusalem.

8:18-19:   The times of fasting will be turned to rejoicing.

8:20-22:   Many nations will come to Jerusalem to seek the favor of YHWH.

8:23:   Ten foreigners will attach themselves to every Judean because of Judah's God.

These two chapters, marked by thirteen introductory formulas, display a certain logical development through keyword repetition and concatenation. Keywords play a critical role in framing 7:1–8:19. A delegation from Bethel asks the prophet whether the time for fasting in the fifth month is over or not (7:1-3), but the answer to this query is delayed until 8:19 when the prophet announces that fasting shall become rejoicing not only in the fifth month but also in the seventh and tenth months. In between this question and response, three thematic groups appear that clarify the reasons why the people are fasting (7:4-14), YHWH's decision to return to Jerusalem and its benefits for the remnant population (8:1-13), and the exhortation to live according to YHWH's expectations (8:14-17).

The content of chapters 7–8 also develops thematically. In the center section, YHWH's zeal for Zion (8:2) leads to YHWH's decision to return to Jerusalem (8:3), which in turn leads to a series of promises depicting how Jerusalem will benefit (8:4-7) and a reminiscence that things began to change for the better once the temple foundation was laid (8:9-13). The end of these chapters twice reaches back to the beginning for rhetorical effect. First, the opening historical reminiscence blamed YHWH's punishment upon the people's inability to judge justly and with truth (cf. 7:9), but after YHWH's decision to return (8:2-3), the prophet recounts YHWH's desire to do good to the house of Judah (8:14-15) and admonishes the people to do what their ancestors did not, namely to judge justly and with truth (8:16). Second, as already noted, 8:18-19 answers the question of fasting asked by the delegation from Bethel in 7:1-3.

The final two sayings (8:20-22, 23) at first appear less connected to the larger thematic development of 7:1–8:19. These two units anticipate a positive relationship with the peoples of the world. They offer a more distant promise for the glory of Jerusalem that presupposes the continuation of the good that YHWH does to Jerusalem. In this sense, they presuppose the reader's knowledge of 7:1–8:19 and expand the promises to include foreign nations coming to Jerusalem to learn the ways of YHWH, a topic that appeared following the fourth vision (2:11).

Zechariah 9–14

Authorship

The question of the authorship of Zechariah 9–14 has created debates since long before modern critical analysis took up these chapters in earnest. Earlier interpreters puzzled over the fact that Matthew 27:9-10 quotes Zechariah 11:12-13, but erroneously ascribes the quote to Jeremiah. This misplaced quote created some level of suspicion among early Christian exegetes that continued into the critical period.[26] Since then, a broad (but not uniform) consensus ascribes chapters 9–14 to a different, and later, author than chapters 1–8. Three recurring reasons are typically cited: the superscriptions in 9:1 and 12:1 (along with Mal 1:1) begin separate blocks; the increasingly pessimistic tone of 9–14 clashes with the optimistic message of 1–8; and the changed eschatological perspectives of 9–14 have their closest parallels in late texts.

The superscriptions of Zechariah 9:1; 12:1; and Malachi 1:1 signal new sections and correspond to major thematic shifts in the surrounding material. These superscriptions use a highly unusual phrase that only occurs in these three texts: *maśśāʾ debar yhwh* ("An oracle. The word of YHWH . . ."). To be sure, the heading functions differently in each of these blocks.[27] Nevertheless, these identical headings begin the last three sections of the Book of the Twelve and suggest that editorial deliberations created these headings. For a number of reasons, the Malachi heading likely existed first and was imitated by Zechariah 9:1 and 12:1 when they were inserted between Zechariah 1–8 and Malachi in the process of closing the Book of the Twelve.[28]

The increasingly pessimistic tone in Zechariah 9–14 makes it difficult to as-cribe these chapters to the same author, editor, or setting as those who transmit-ted chapters 1–8. In chapters 1–8, YHWH is in charge and threatens to punish the nations, but the land is at rest. When chapters 9–14 begin, YHWH takes a defensive position to protect the land like a shield (Zech 9), the Greeks attack Judah and Ephraim (9:12-13), and yet Judah and Ephraim split (11:4-17). In chapters 12–14, Judah's relationship to Jerusalem is problematized (12:5-8) and the leadership of Jerusalem must mourn, including the house of David, the prophet Nathan (12:12), and the Levites (12:13). These groups must undergo ritual cleansing beginning with the house of David (13:1-2) and (implicitly) the priests (13:2). The prophets will incur even stronger punishment as they will be removed from the land (13:3-6). Finally, unlike the peaceful setting of the night visions, peace is nowhere to be found. Rather, the nations attack Jerusalem and Judah (12; 14), and only some in Jerusalem will survive (14:2). Nevertheless, Jerusalem will be established as YHWH's city (14:8-9), and the nations will be punished (14:12-15; cf. 14:16-19). Jerusalem's elevation only happens after Jerusalem is taken and looted. Its women are raped and its citizens exiled on the day of YHWH (14:1-2). Thereafter, YHWH will intervene on Jerusalem's behalf (14:3-9), and Jerusalem and Judah will be purified (14:20-21).

From the description above, clearly the eschatological perspectives of 9–14 differ from those of 1–8. Chapters 1–8 see the current time as a pivotal point of change when YHWH will act to rebuild and repopulate Jerusalem and to punish the nations who have inflicted pain upon Jerusalem and Judah. YHWH takes charge of the moment because the world is at rest and the seventy years of pun-ishment have ended (1:12; 7:5). By contrast, chapters 9–14 presuppose that the current age is a time of danger from both internal and external enemies. These chapters anticipate that an impending day of YHWH will be required to purify Jerusalem and Judah.

Scholars in the nineteenth and twentieth centuries demonstrated the means by which 9–14 draws upon other written prophetic texts. Consequently, many scholars now classify Zechariah 9–14 as scribal prophecy. In other words, these chapters do not derive from oral settings, but represent literary texts that draw upon existing prophetic tradition in order to actualize the message for a new generation. Among the many works that articulate this assumption, four deserve special mention for their contributions or the questions they raise.

Rex Mason represents a turning point in the study of Zechariah 9–14 and its reuse of earlier materials.[29] Mason devotes considerable energy to document-ing both the places where earlier prophetic tradition has been utilized and the creative ways these traditions have been altered for their context in Zechariah 9–14.

Nicholas Tai offers a systematic tradition-historical analysis of Zechariah 9–14 that documents how the prophetic materials in chapters 9–13 draw heavily and distinctively from Jeremiah and Ezekiel.[30] Concurrently, Tai notes that the texts in 9–13 treat the two prophetic traditions differently. While drawing from both, the author tends to draw from Jeremiah without changing the content of the source text, while the author tends to change the content when drawing from Ezekiel.[31] Thus, some texts that draw from Ezekiel's imagery critique Ezekiel's message (as when Zech 11:4-16 reverses Ezek 34 and 37), yet one passage (Zech 12:9–13:6) draws conceptually from Ezekiel without changing the content. Unfortunately, Tai equates this tendency with the redactional agenda, and assigns Zechariah 12:9–13:6 to a different author. He does not seriously consider the possibility that an editor could disagree with the Ezekiel texts on two particular issues (the restoration of the Davidic line and the reunification of the northern territory with Judah) while leaving other aspects of the Ezekiel tradition (e.g., purity) unchanged, as with Jeremiah. Tai also argues that Zechariah 14 borrows neither from Jeremiah nor Ezekiel, and thus he assigns it to a later hand, the hand that connected Zechariah 9–13 + 14 to the book of Zechariah.

Recently, Mark Boda argues convincingly that both Zechariah 1–8 and 9–14 rely upon other texts.[32] Boda also correctly notes that the historical settings reflected in the various texts in 9–14 demonstrate a different audience than 1–8 and reflect later readings.[33] The two sections are too diverse to explain dependence on other texts as signs of one author for both 1–8 and 9–14.

Clear thematic groupings concerning the subject of the prophetic materials appear in Zechariah 9–14. These groupings include the nations (9; 12; and 14), Ephraim and Judah (9:12-13; 10–11), Jerusalem and Judah (12–14), and the day of YHWH (12 and 14). Paul Redditt has demonstrated how the shepherd materials in chapters 9–14 connect several of the larger compositional blocks within 9–14.[34] What makes the shepherd materials unusual is that the ideological movement of the individual blocks changes as one reads across the chapters. For example, Ephraim and Judah begin as allies (9:12-13), but by the end of chapter 11 they have split irreconcilably. The nations threaten YHWH's land in chapters 9 and 12, but by the end of chapter 14 they recognize YHWH's power. In a related way, the royal figure (i.e., the shepherd) first enters the land in peace (9:9-10), but in the final appearances (11:4-17; 13:7-9) the shepherd has become a hindrance to peace and prosperity.

159

Historical Backdrop to Zechariah 9–14

Zechariah 9–14 has proven very resistant to consensus regarding dating. In the last three decades, major commentaries have proposed a setting in the early, middle, or late Persian period, and since at least the 1950s, a significant percentage of scholars dates these chapters to the early Hellenistic period.[35] In part, these debates illustrate the difficulty of interpreting poetic imagery as a reflection of historical reality. The key decision depends upon how one interprets the role of the Greeks in 9:12-13. Those who interpret 9–14 as a Persian-period composition interpret these verses as reflecting longstanding animosity between the Greeks toward Persia and its allies (including Judah and Samaria), or they assume that the text refers to an eschatological battle. By contrast, those who interpret 9:12-13 as a text presuming the arrival of Alexander in 333–332 BCE understand Zechariah 9 as a response to an actual threat from Alexander's army. The early Hellenistic period makes better sense of the chapter for three significant reasons. First, while animosity between Persian and Greek forces existed throughout the Persian period, those arguing for a Persian-period date ignore the fact that Persia appears nowhere in the chapter. Zechariah 9:12-13 pits Judah and Ephraim, not Persia, against the Greeks. Second, the enemy's pathway assumed by 9:1-8 fits Alexander's campaign, not battles against Persia.[36] Third, while scholars find it difficult to reconstruct the deterioration of the relationship of Samaria and Yehud in the early Hellenistic period because so many of the sources for this period contain legendary elements, all of these sources portray events that created or sharpened a divide between the two regions after the Greeks arrived.

Dates of Composition and Point of Compilation

Recent models regarding Zechariah 9–14, while they vary on many issues, agree that it uses preexisting sources. One therefore must distinguish between the date of the original composition and the point at which it was incorporated into the current literary setting. For example, Boda interprets 11:4-17 as a commentary upon events surrounding Zerubbabel in the late sixth century, but does not think that chapters 9–14 were combined until the mid- to late fifth century.[37] The question of dating the final form, or at least the point at which the bulk of 9–14 was combined, is complicated, but the combination of the chapters likely did not happen until after Alexander's conquest in 332. To understand why someone brought these units together, one has to assess the rhetorical agenda indicated by the repetition and progression of the thematic groupings and the connective shepherd materials, as suggested by Redditt above.

The Structure and Contents of Zechariah 9–14

Zechariah 9–14 is a composite collection with rhetorical aims. Zechariah 9–11 highlights the deterioration of the relationship of Judah and Ephraim. Zechariah 12–14 conveys an eschatological focus since the three blocks use the eschatological phrase "on that day" seventeen times—seven in chapter 12, three in chapter 13, and seven more in chapter 14.[38]

Zechariah 9:1-17 contains five rhetorical sections (1-8, 9-10, 11-13, 14-15, 16-17) that cohere around the theme of YHWH's deliverance of the land by establishing a new power dynamic. YHWH traverses the western Levant from north to south (Syria, Phoenicia, and Philistia) in order to defend the temple (9:1-8). With the way to peace established, Zion's king enters the city (9:9-10), though interpreters disagree on whether this king is a human king or YHWH. YHWH then alludes to Zion's covenant of blood and promises Lady Zion the release of prisoners and a double portion in restoration (9:11-12)—motifs reminiscent of Deutero-Isaiah—before announcing YHWH's decision to use Judah and Ephraim to battle the Greeks (9:13). The last two sections describe YHWH's victorious battle (9:14-15) and the glorious aftermath (9:16-17).

Zechariah 10:1–11:3 divides into four sections (10:1-2, 3-6, 7-12; 11:1-3). These units probably represent compositionally independent but rhetorically interdependent units that a redactor has arranged to show a progression of thought. A thematic element from the end of one passage reappears at the beginning of the next. The previous passage ended with a promise of fertility for the grain and the new wine (9:17), while Zechariah 10:1 exhorts the people to pray for rain so that the vegetation may grow. Next, 10:2 implies the shortfall stems from idolatry and the fact that the people lack a shepherd, while 10:3-6 begins with judgment upon the shepherds and goats (metaphors for the leaders of the people). The majority of 10:3-6 anticipates the military resurgence of Judah, but 10:6 introduces the central focus of 10:7-12 with the topic of the deliverance of Joseph (a name used here for the northern territories). Zechariah 10:7-12 anticipates a return of exiles from "Egypt and Assyria" to populate the northern territories of Gilead and Lebanon (10:10), while 11:1-3 warns Lebanon and Bashan about a coming period of devastation. This shift to judgment continues in the renewed threat against the shepherds (11:3), which in turn anticipates the story of the two shepherds in 11:4-17 that results in the rejection of "unity" and "favor" for YHWH's people (specifically, both Judah and Israel in 11:14). These three chapters thus end with a sober note regarding a rejection of the former northern territories, a dissolution of the territorial expectations that framed the promise of land in the ancestral narratives, and expectations for a renewal of ideal boundaries of the former Davidic kingdom.

Chapter 12 coheres around the theme of nations attacking Jerusalem. It unfolds in three thematic sections: a hymnic introduction emphasizing YHWH's power over creation (12:1), a series of statements regarding an impending attack on Jerusalem (12:2-11), and a description of the future mourning of Jerusalem's leadership—the royal house, prophets, and Levites (12:12-14). As already noted, the chapter shifts to an eschatological message. Despite the chapter's general thematic groupings, it offers little in the way of a consistent rhetorical line of thought.

Zechariah 13 continues to focus upon the fate of Israel's leaders, but takes a decidedly negative turn as it deals with the purification and punishment of Jerusalem's leaders in three parts (13:1, 2-6, 7-9). These three parts expect cleansing from the Davidides (13:1), but the end of the chapter rejects the shepherd (13:7-9) and the text in between (13:2-6) announces the end of the prophets. The last unit (13:7-9) also links the themes of chapter 12 and 13 with Zechariah 14. Of these three groups, chapter 13 thus rejects all but the Levites.

The last two sections of Zechariah (13:7-9 and chapter 14) demonstrate an intertextual awareness of texts and have canonical implications. Significantly, 13:9 alludes to both Malachi 3:2-3 and Hosea 2:21-23 (Heb. 2:23-25), thereby citing the first and last book in the Twelve. Zechariah 14 links thematically and lexically with both the beginning and end of the Isaiah scroll.[39] Finally, many have noted that the end of Malachi (4:4-6 [Heb. 3:22-24]) takes up the vocabulary of Joshua 1 and refers to the major prophetic figure in the Torah (Moses) and Kings (Elijah). At the same time, much of Zechariah 9–13 is drawn from Jeremiah and Ezekiel. Thus, these three sections of the Book of the Twelve cross-reference three canonical units in reverse order—the beginning and end of the Twelve, the beginning and end of Isaiah (the first of the Latter Prophets), and Joshua 1 (the beginning of the Former Prophets and the Nebi'im)—even while evoking the most prominent prophet in the Torah and the Former Prophets. One should not view Zechariah 9–14 in isolation. It represents a text that reflects upon new historical paradigms created by cultural shifts in the Hellenistic period, while grounding that reflection in the texts of the developing canon.

Finally, Zechariah 14 contains four rhetorical units (14:1-5, 6-11, 12-15, 16-21) with an eschatological orientation on the day of YHWH's battle against the nations that will result in the purification of Jerusalem. Zechariah 14 shares conceptual similarities with Joel 3 (Heb. 4) and Isaiah 66 about the coming day of YHWH, but the links are especially pronounced with Isaiah 66:16-21. These texts assume that YHWH will fight against the nations directly, that the nations will be defeated, and that a remnant will recognize the importance of Jerusalem as the center of YHWH's kingdom. Scholars with a variety of presuppositions note these similarities.[40] The view of Bosshard and Kratz has much to commend it when they describe Zechariah 14:16-21 as an imitation and extension of the nations motif in Isaiah 66, while Zechariah 13:8-9 reflects upon the ideas concerning YHWH's people in Isaiah 66.[41]

Zechariah 14 focuses upon the concept of the day of YHWH, even though the phrase does not appear. Rather, the day of YHWH's intervention against the nations is first described as the point when YHWH will "fight as on a day of battle" (14:3). Thereafter, the formula "on that day" refers to the battle and its aftermath seven times in this concluding chapter of Zechariah (14:4, 6, 8, 9, 13, 20, 21), including the very last words of the book. While the day of YHWH's battle for Jerusalem serves as the primary theme, the chapter does not present a single coherent treatise. Rather, most see Zechariah 14 as an anthology of different portrayals. The first account describes a cataclysmic earthquake of historic proportions (14:4-5). The second "on that day" reference describes a day of continuous daylight (14:6-7), while the third (14:8) anticipates living water flowing from Jerusalem to the sea in the east and the west. The fourth "on that day" passage (14:9) proclaims the kingship of YHWH over all the earth and a leveling of the land to create an agricultural blessing (14:10-11), especially for Jerusalem. These first four "on that day" sayings describe positive changes in creation after YHWH's destructive intervention that will make life more hospitable for Jerusalem and its environs.

The thematic focus of Zechariah 14 shifts in 14:12 with a gruesome portrait of a plague that will afflict the nations who attack Jerusalem (14:12, 15). This portrait incorporates the fifth "on that day" saying (14:13) proclaiming that when the nations turn upon one another (14:13), Judah will fight against Jerusalem (14:14a), and the wealth of the nations will be gathered for YHWH's city (14:14b). Another thematic shift begins in 14:16: punishment inflicted upon the remnant who survive from the nations. They will be expected to come annually to the Festival of Booths in order to worship YHWH (14:16). Punishments are delineated for any of the nations who do not comply, with a special emphasis upon Egypt (14:17-19). Finally, the last two "on that day" formulas appear at the beginning and end of the final two verses (14:20-21), which depict the aftermath of the day of YHWH's battle as a time in which the city of Jerusalem has experienced purification. Its horses wear bells inscribed with the words "holy to YHWH" (a phrase reserved for priestly garments), and the cookware in Jerusalem shall be deemed as holy as the implements of the altar.

Zechariah and the Prophetic Corpus

Zechariah 1–8 displays intertextual links with Jeremiah's traditions concerning seventy years of punishment, with Haggai's dates, and with Joel's repentance

163

motifs. The end of Jeremiah's seventy years of punishment twice receives special notice: in the first vision report (1:12) and in the prophet's initial response to the delegation from Bethel (7:5). The former recounts a conversation between the messenger and YHWH. The messenger reminds YHWH that the world is at peace (1:11) and asks how long YHWH will maintain his anger, which has lasted seventy years (1:12). YHWH responds with "good words" and "comforting words" (1:13).

This question and response allude to the seventy-year tradition that appears across three texts in Jeremiah (25:11-13; 29:10-11; and 33:14). Jeremiah 25:11-13 announces a seventy-year period when the nations will serve the king of Babylon, after which YHWH will lay waste to Babylon. Then, Jeremiah 29:10-11 affirms that after the seventy years are complete and they call upon YHWH (cf. 29:12), then YHWH will return them to Jerusalem and institute his plans for good and not for evil. Finally, Jeremiah 33:10 alludes to the promise of Jeremiah 29:10-11 when it affirms the times are coming when YHWH will fulfill the "good word" which he made to Judah and Israel.

Zechariah 1:2-6 should be noted for its relationship to Haggai and its mention of "the former prophets." Zechariah 1:3-4 summarizes the message of the "former prophets" to the ancestors of the current generation as a call to repent: "Return to me, and I will return to you." Zechariah 1:2-6 portrays the ancestors as having refused to listen to this message (1:4), while the current generation repents (1:6). This repentance vignette helps to explain the change in Haggai's portrayal of the people. At the beginning of Haggai, the people are not committed to establishing the temple (1:2-11), and the prophet confronts the people in the sixth month of the second year of Darius (520 BCE). By the end of Haggai (in the ninth month), the people have begun working on the temple at the stirring of the Spirit (1:14), and when the foundation stone ritual has been laid the prophet expects change in the land's fertility (2:15-19). In between, according to Zechariah 1:2-6, the current generation repented in the eighth month (Zech 1:1). In other words, both Haggai 2:15-19 and Zechariah 1:2-6 report YHWH's punishment as due to the failure of earlier generations to repent, but Zechariah's repentance account (Zech 1:2-6) paves the way for the ritual cleansing in Haggai 2:15-19 to lay the foundation stone properly.[42]

Zechariah's use of repentance motifs from Joel can be detected in at least two places in ways that signal to the reader of the Twelve that Joel's prophetic promises are underway.[43] These passages appear in the first vision report (1:8-17) and the sayings (8:9-12). The first vision makes clear that Judah has reached a turning point since seventy years have essentially passed.[44] The horses and their riders (YHWH's messengers) who patrol the earth report that the world is at peace (1:11). The angel accompanying the prophet asks YHWH how long he will withhold mercy from Jerusalem and Judah's cities since he has been angry for seventy years (Jer 25:11-13 and 29:10-11). YHWH's response (Zech 1:14) echoes Joel 2:18. If the people repent (Joel 2:12-14), YHWH promises to "become zealous" for his land and his people (Joel 2:18) and will comfort Zion (cf. Joel 2:13). In Zechariah 1:14-16, after the people repented (1:6), YHWH announces he has "become zealous" for Zion. He will punish the nations and "comfort" his people.

Zechariah 8:9-12 also connects more than one book in the Twelve. This passage extends ideas from Haggai and Joel. The unit begins with a new messenger formula ("Thus says the YHWH of hosts"), and it references "the prophets who were present when the foundation was laid," which means Haggai and Zechariah. Since chapters 7–8 are formally set two years after the vision cycle (cf. 1:7 and 7:1), the admonition to take heart assumes that people are wavering.

The rhetorical logic of Zechariah 8:10-11 recalls what life was like "before those days" when there was no food, security, or wages (8:10). This period is contrasted with the current time ("but now," 8:11) when YHWH will deal with the remnant of this people as he had done before the time of punishment. Then, in the final stage, 8:12 presents a more expansive promise for the future by echoing the language of Haggai 1:10 and Joel 2:22:

Joel 2:22	Hag 1:10 (NRSV)	Zech 8:12
the tree bears **its fruit**, the fig tree and **vine give** their full yield.	←	the vine will give its fruit,
	The earth has withheld its produce;	the earth shall give its produce,
	the heavens above you have withheld the dew.	and the heavens shall give their dew.
	→	

In other words, Zechariah 8:9-12 hints at a level of discontent, and addresses those concerns by reminding the audience changes are happening by referring specifically to the events from Haggai (1:10, 12) and a promise of even more fertility for the land using the imagery of Joel.

Zechariah 9–14 addresses a different historical setting and, as a work of scribal prophecy, draws heavily upon the other three prophetic scrolls. One must distinguish between the use of other prophetic texts and the theological agenda behind them. Zechariah 9–13 shows deliberate use of Jeremiah and Ezekiel, even though its theological assertions are more closely aligned with the theology of the former than the latter. Zechariah 14 appears to have been formulated with an eye toward the end and the beginning of Isaiah to portray the future events as part of the coming day of YHWH. The connective link transitioning between major source blocks in Zechariah 9–14 appears in the shepherd imagery, the last passage of which (Zech 13:7-9) climactically alludes to Hosea and Malachi. For the redactor who combined the sources to compose Zechariah 9–14, the Torah and the Prophets had begun to take on a special status.

Malachi

The Prophet and the Book

Scholars date Malachi to the fifth century BCE for two reasons: the presence of a functioning temple and a Persian civil magistrate. Most of the book concerns a debate over how to conduct cultic sacrifices, which only makes sense if the temple is functioning. Malachi 1:8 charges that certain priests are accepting inferior sacrifices that they would not present to the "governor." The word "governor" (*peḥâh*) is used for the position occupied by Zerubbabel (Hag 1:1; 2:2) and Nehemiah (Neh 5:18). Beyond these two points, a consensus on dating the book precisely remains elusive, with scholars largely divided between the early, middle, and late fifth century.[45]

The form and content of Malachi reflect debates about the role of Israel among the nations and about cultic ritual in the fifth century BCE. At issue, some priests do not hold strictly to expectations for sacrifices. Scholars consistently identify the literary parameters of the compositions, but continue to debate the best term to label them: disputations, discussion words, or diatribes.[46] Finding a single classification remains difficult because the term "disputation" relies on a legal setting not present; "discussion words" highlights a question-and-response format that is not consistent across the units; and the term "diatribe" comes from later Hellenistic parallels. The terminology notwithstanding, the rhetorical agenda of the six units, individually, raises little question. The degree to which the editorial sequencing of these units reflects a deliberate design and the extent of editorial insertions into the core material remain points of considerable debate among scholars. One passage, 4:4-6 (Heb. 3:22-24), receives wide recognition as a late editorial supplement. Quite a number of scholars also recognize the positive attitude toward the nations in 1:11-14 as a later expansion.[47] Some recent works isolate a foundational layer of Malachi that has been expanded by one or more redactional supplements.[48]

Authorship

The author of Malachi remains anonymous. The name of the prophet means "my messenger," and likely stems from Malachi 3:1. Early Jewish traditions considered Ezra the author, but those are largely discounted by critical scholars for lack of evidence and differences in theological perspectives. Despite the anonymity of the author, certain characteristics of the book provide some insight. First, scholars have increasingly recognized Malachi as scribal prophecy, along with Joel, Zechariah 9–14, and Jonah, because of the extent to which it draws upon other texts.[49] This quality means that the author comes from a milieu in which scribes were trained in incorporating allusions to other texts for a variety of reasons. In Malachi, the sources of these allusions include texts from the Torah (Genesis, Exodus, Numbers) and the prophets (especially Ezekiel). Second, the rhetorical flow of 1:6–2:9 reflects a debate between at least two priestly groups, but the argumentation does not specifically align with Priestly or Deuteronomic laws.[50]

The Structure and Composition

The unity of Malachi has been challenged and defended. Little disagreement exists about the individual units: 1:1; 1:2-5; 1:6–2:9; 2:10-16; 2:17–3:5; 3:6-12; 3:13–4:3 (Heb. 3:16-21); 4:4-6 (Heb. 3:22-24). Most of the book (1:2–3:12) displays a rhetorical interest in literary accounts of cultic and theological disagreements. Form-critical observations play a major role in describing these units as disputations, discussion speeches, or diatribes.[51] Petersen notes that the stylized discourse, in which one party quotes the other, means that they do not technically record dialogues. Rather, they represent one speaker's version of a disagreement. Whether one calls this form a disputation, discussion, or diatribe, Petersen's observations highlight an important characteristic. Petersen, however, too quickly discounts the idea that the sequence of these units represents a redactional progression that intends to have an impact upon the reader. Several points of connection suggest that the editorial placement did provide some level of progression in terms of thematic intensity, lexical links, and literary horizons embedded in the collection.

Malachi 1:1: The Burden of the Word of YHWH

Malachi's superscription shares unusual characteristics with Zechariah 9–11 and 12–14, which many scholars conclude relate the three blocks to one another in some way. As already noted in the discussion of Zechariah 9–14, the phrase "the oracle of the word of YHWH" appears only in Zechariah 9:1, 12:1, and Malachi 1:1 in the entire Hebrew Bible. Additionally, one should also note that Malachi 1:1 has two distinct elements in comparison to the superscriptions in Zechariah 9:1 and 12:1: the inclusion of a name (Malachi) and the presence of the unusual preposition "through" (*beyad*). The name offers the identity of the prophet, and most scholars consider it an eponym created to provide a prophetic identity for the book. The presence of the phrase "speak through" (literally, "by the hand of") appears only seven times in prophetic literature.[52] The fact that four of the seven appear in superscriptions of the Book of the Twelve suggests that they could be related. Since Malachi assumes a functioning temple and Haggai concerns the building of the temple, Haggai would be the earlier of the two collections.

Malachi 1:2-5: I Love Jacob

Malachi 1:2-5 presents the first disputation. The issue under dispute concerns the rhetorical question, "How have you loved us?" (1:2). The argumentation draws on the theme of YHWH's election of Jacob over Esau in Genesis to announce that YHWH has punished Esau. The allusion to the Genesis story does not, however, focus on the characters Esau and Jacob in that story. Rather, Malachi 1:2-5 focuses upon the political entities of Edom and Israel. Edom's downfall (and Israel's ongoing existence) proves YHWH loves Jacob more than Esau. Two important points should be noted. First, Edom's punishment and its recent destruction play an important role in the bridge texts of Isaiah 34:6-9 and 63:1-6. Second, the same is true for the Book of the Twelve, where Edom's future destruction appears in Joel 3:19 (Heb. 4:19), Amos 1:9-10, and especially Obadiah 1–15 (see particularly the discussion of Obad 11–14). By contrast, Malachi 1:2-5 assumes (with Isa 63:1-6) that Edom's punishment has begun. This thematic link is heightened by the phrase "I have made his [i.e., Esau's] mountains a desolation." The only other reference to the "mountain(s) of Esau" is Obadiah.[53] The theme of Edom's punishment likely gained prominence in the Persian period because Edom aided the Babylonians, at least in the aftermath of Jerusalem's destruction. This theme thus appears in Isaiah and the Twelve in terms of promise and fulfillment.

Malachi 1:6–2:9: Contesting Sacrifices

This second disputation centers upon the theme of improper sacrifice. The rhetorical flow of this passage condemns "the priests" and those who bring improper sacrifices. In contrast to 1:2-5, those outside the land model proper worship (1:11-14), a contrast so dramatic that quite a number of commentators argue these verses were inserted later. Finally, the literary character of 1:6–2:9 includes allusions to a wide variety of texts across the canon.[54] The phrasing often suggests that the author(s) knew an interpretive tradition of the developing canon. As a result, Malachi has become increasingly recognized as a scriptural interpreter, not unlike the portrayal of the Levites as teachers depicted in Ezra and Nehemiah.[55] The end of Malachi 1:6–2:9 highlights the importance of the "covenant of Levi" (2:4, 8) which suggests that the author(s) of this passage was no outsider. The author was deeply concerned with the proper attitudes and functioning of temple processes.

The subunits of the passage are clear: 1:6-10; 1:11-14; 2:1-3; 2:4-9. Malachi 1:6-10 offers a direct challenge to those priests who have neglected their duties by accepting inferior animals. The opening verse introduces keywords of the extended unit: "glory" (1:6; 2:2); "fear" (1:6; 2:5); "name" (1:6, 11, 14; 2:2, 5); and "despise" (1:6, 7, 12; 2:9). This introduction ends with a rhetorical question (how have we despised your name?) that sets up the theme of the extended passage: the ways their sacrificial practices dishonor YHWH. Verses 7-10 explicitly condemn bringing inferior animals and even more blatantly challenge those who accept these offerings, namely the priests addressed in 1:6.

Surprisingly, Malachi 1:11-14 contrasts the negative behavior of those who despise YHWH's name in Judah with those outside of the country honoring the greatness of YHWH's name. This contrast, however, implicitly targets the priests (1:12-13) who violate ritual expectations by accepting stolen, maimed, or sickly animals to offer to YHWH. By contrast, those "among the nations" reverence YHWH's name (1:11, 14b). This section has its own cohesive structure, but referring to those among the nations in such positive terms stands out thematically (especially after highlighting YHWH's love of Jacob and hatred of Esau in 1:2-5).[56]

Malachi 2:1-3 confronts the priests with a challenge to change their behavior or be prepared to suffer the curse of YHWH's rejection. The form of this curse conveys poetic justice against the priests because YHWH promises to spread the feces of the animal sacrifices on the priests' faces, making them ritually impure, so they will no longer qualify to serve in YHWH's temple. Such highly charged rhetoric betrays the speaker's radical disagreement with how laxly the priests are treating YHWH's expectations for sacrifice.

Malachi 2:4-9 climaxes with a negative comparison of the current priests to the qualities of Levi. Verse 4 refers to "this command" articulated in 2:2, the command to glorify YHWH's name and preserve the "covenant of Levi" (2:4, 8). Verses 5-7 manifest a tight structure that delineates the virtues of Levi (2:5-6, by drawing from Deut 33:8-11 and Num 25:10-13).[57] These virtues made Levi the ideal priest, a trusted instructor, and YHWH's messenger (2:7). Yet, these virtues in 2:5-6 contrast directly with the current priests in 2:8-9: Levi revered YHWH (2:5), while the priests' behavior corrupts YHWH's covenant with Levi (2:8); Levi spoke true instruction (2:6) whereas the current priests cause many to stumble (2:8); Levi walked with integrity and uprightness (2:6), while the priests in Malachi's time have turned aside from the path (2:8); Levi's integrity and uprightness turned many from iniquity (2:6) while the teaching of the priests causes many to stumble (2:8). These contrasts, juxtaposed against the ideal qualities of Levi, function as accusations against the priests and lay the foundation for the judgment that is pronounced in 2:9: the priests will be despised and humiliated.

Malachi 2:10-16: Covenant Fidelity and Marriage

The third disputation (2:10-16) changes topics from ritual impurity to the worship of other deities, while the addressee expands to the entire community (as with 1:2-5) rather than the priests. Treacherous behavior lies at the heart of the unit since the word for "to act treacherously" (Heb. *bagad*) appears five times in these seven verses (2:10, 11, 14, 15, 16). Scholars debate whether the passage explores the issue of divorce from foreign wives or whether these verses utilize divorce as a metaphor to limn the worship of foreign deities.[58] Petersen's analysis of the phraseology compellingly demonstrates that this diatribe primarily (though not exclusively) condemns worship of foreign deities. Additionally, those with an eye toward the Book of the Twelve recall that this scroll began with a focus upon marriage as a metaphor for fidelity to YHWH, so it is hardly surprising to find the theme returning near the end of the scroll. This looping back to the beginning of the Twelve coincides with a number of Hoseanic themes revisited in Malachi.[59] In essence, this disputation confronts the people with the issue of covenant obligations, not unlike the priests charged with breaking covenant in 1:6–2:9.

Malachi 2:17–3:5: The Day of YHWH's Coming

The fourth disputation presumes the accusations leveled against the priests and the people in the previous disputations, especially the second. Scholars debate whether the final form represents the ideas of one, two, or several authors.[60] Even scholars who see a complex process behind the creation of these verses recognize that the later material (usually 3:1b-4) functions as a commentary upon the existing text. This commentary adds an eschatological dimension to 2:17-3:1a, 5. Thus, the "secondary" material is not an independent composition. This eschatological perspective reappears in Malachi 4:1-3 (Heb. 3:19-21) and represents the same presupposition that judgment from YHWH will be required to change the status quo (cf. 3:17; 4:1-3 [Heb. 3:19-21]). This perspective makes sense when one reads the verses as a verdict upon those who have refused to change. YHWH will not allow the current state to continue where the people and the priests disregard YHWH's instruction. The rhetoric of 2:17–3:5 as a whole makes sense in this respect. The accusation that the addressees weary YHWH implies that the problem continues and that nothing has changed as a result of the first three disputations. In this case, the language of 3:1 implies a judgment in the imminent future, not some distant eschatological expectation.

Malachi 3:6-12: Return to YHWH

The fifth disputation changes the theme, but subtle clues suggest that the passage should not be read in isolation. First, the conjunction "for" that begins 3:6 relates 3:6-12 to what precedes. Second, the reference in 3:6 to the "sons of Jacob" who have not perished is often seen as an allusion to the opening of the book in 1:2-5 where Jacob was chosen and Esau was destroyed. Third, Malachi 3:7 cites Zechariah 1:3, which suggests a wider literary horizon for interpreting Malachi 3:6-12. The phrase "return to me . . . and I will return to you" appears only in these two verses, though calls to return to YHWH play a recurring role in the Book of the Twelve.[61]

Fourth, Malachi 3:11-12 describes YHWH's curse with imagery of the land's infertility that echoes other texts. The infertility of the land as a sign of a curse appears prominently in Deuteronomy as punishment if Israel fails to keep the covenant. The blessings and curses in Deuteronomy 27–28 play a role in how Malachi conceptualizes the current state of affairs.[62] Particularly striking is the promise to rebuke the "one devouring" who is destroying the "produce of your soil" in 3:12, a reference to the locust (Deut 28:38).[63]

For these reasons, Malachi 3:6-12 should be treated as something like a programmatic text with a literary horizon that includes Deuteronomy, Haggai, and Zechariah 1–8, resolving a thematic thread of the infertility of the land that figures prominently in the end of the Twelve. In Haggai, this infertility began to change once the temple foundation was laid (Hag 2:15-19), an event preceded by the people's repentance (according to the dates of Hag 2:10 and Zech 1:1). Zechariah 8:9-12 shows concern that the land's fertility has not returned as quickly as some had hoped, but 8:12-13 promises that the land's fertility and its produce will return so that all the nations will take note. By contrast, Malachi 3:6-12 presupposes that returning to YHWH obligates the people to bring the tithe not just build the temple. Culminating the disputations, 3:6-12 assumes that nothing has changed for the people or the priests, so the curse remains in effect.

171

Malachi 3:13–4:3 (Heb. 3:16-21): Confronting the Arrogant and Rewarding Those Who Fear YHWH

Scholars often classify Malachi 3:13–4:3 (Heb. 3:16-21) as the book's final disputation, but labeling this entire unit as a disputation overlooks the fact that the disputation style does not appear in 3:16-18. The disputation material in 3:13-15 and 4:1-3 forms an envelope around 3:16-18, which narrates a positive response from "those fearing YHWH" (3:16). By contrast, the challenge to the speaker's opponents in 3:13-15 receives its direct response in 4:1-3.

The relationship between the disputation and the narrative requires that the reader supply some kind of connective logic. Verses 13-15 begin with the speaker quoting the antagonists, a group characterized as clueless: "You have spoken harsh words against me, says YHWH. Yet you say, 'How have we spoken against you?'" This quotation functions as a rhetorical device to set up the opponents. The speaker answers the opponents' question in 3:14 with another quote of his opponents. The opponents essentially raise a question: What is in it for me? According to 3:14-15, they doubt the efficacy of serving YHWH because they observe the prosperity of the evildoers who test YHWH and nothing happens.

In 4:1-3, YHWH finally answers the question raised in 3:14-15 by the opponents. YHWH affirms a traditional moral equation. A day of YHWH is near when YHWH will punish the evildoers and the arrogant (4:1), the very same terms used in 3:13-15 to refer to the speaker's opponents. Simultaneously, those fearing the name of YHWH will be healed by the sun of righteousness on that day (4:2).

The speaker states his opponents' charges in 3:13-15 and refutes their challenge in 4:1-3. In between (3:16-18), a narrative positively recounts the actions of another group, "those fearing YHWH." Their acceptance juxtaposes the improper response of the opponents with a proper response. The narrative is often incorrectly interpreted. Verse 16 recounts three actions: (1) those who feared YHWH spoke with one another, (2) YHWH took note of their response, and (3) a "scroll of remembrance" was written for them. This third action is often interpreted anachronistically by assuming that the "book of remembrance" be identified with the later Christian idea of the "book of life" that records the names of those who will be saved. Instead, both the syntax of 3:16 and the parallel terminology found elsewhere in the Old Testament depict this book of remembrance as a multigenerational account of the deeds of the king. The syntax of the Hebrew is often ignored in the English translations. The Hebrew phrasing very distinctly states, "a scroll of remembrance was written *before* YHWH *for* those fearing YHWH." In other words, the scroll was written in YHWH's presence

172

(thereby providing it with a divine imprimatur), but the scroll is to be given to the YHWH-fearers.[64]

Malachi 4:4-6 (Heb. 3:22-24): Remember the Torah

The last three verses of Malachi are classified as an epilogue with canonical implications. The form is an admonition to all Israel. Rhetorically, these verses admonish Israel that Torah obedience remains the only way to avoid YHWH's wrath. After confronting those who have strayed from Torah expectations, Malachi ends by showing how to avoid the coming judgment. Scholars increasingly note the canonical intertextuality that colors this passage, and treat Malachi 4:4-6 as a composition created to conclude the Torah and the Nebi'im.

The terminology in 4:4-6 evokes the transition from Deuteronomy to Joshua, the end of the Torah and beginning of the Nebi'im. The intertextual links present in 4:4-6 are impressive. First, labeling Moses as YHWH's servant is not common. Apart from Malachi 4:4, this phrasing appears only in Numbers 22:18, the end of Deuteronomy (34:5), and the beginning of Joshua (1:2, 7). Similarly, reference to the mountain of revelation during the time of Moses as *Horeb* represents the prominent term for that mountain in Deuteronomy (Deut 1:2, 6, 19; 4:10, 15; 5:2; 9:8; 18:16; 29:1) while the rest of the Torah prefers the term *Sinai*. Third, Elijah appears to avoid YHWH sending total destruction (*ḥerem*), which represents a major *leitmotif* in the book of Joshua where the term appears more than two dozen times. Fourth, the likelihood that Malachi 4:4-6 represents a deliberate conclusion to the Law and the Prophets increases when one recognizes the pairing of Moses and Elijah, the main character in the Pentateuch and the most significant prophet in the book of Kings (in terms of the amount of space devoted to Elijah in 1 Kgs 17–2 Kgs 3). Fifth, the language used to describe the coming day of YHWH does not pick up on the smelting imagery from Malachi 3:1-4. Instead, the phrase "the great and terrible day of YHWH" appears elsewhere only in Joel (2:31, but cf. Joel 2:11). By invoking Joel's terminology for the day of YHWH, Malachi 4:6 elicits the Twelve's first book dealing with the day of YHWH against Jerusalem and Judah.

Malachi within the Book of the Twelve

The last three verses of Malachi utilize canonical allusions to accentuate the need for Torah obedience to avoid judgment on the day of YHWH, but they also evoke the Former Prophets and Joel. Recent scholarship has tended to treat these verses in isolation from the remainder of Malachi and from larger literary endeavors, but the extent to which Zechariah 9–14 evokes traditions from the Latter

Prophets suggests these verses may have been added to Malachi when Zechariah 9–14 was inserted between Zechariah 8 and Malachi.[65] Zechariah 9–14 and Malachi 4:4-6 go to considerable lengths to combine language and concepts from the Latter Prophets, the Torah, and the Former Prophets. Whoever added Malachi 4:4-6 (and Zech 9–14) had a strong sense that the Law and the Prophets function together.

Hence, the end of the Twelve (Zech 9–14 and Mal 3:6-12; 4:4-6) draws extensively upon other portions of the canon. The interplay with Moses and Joshua raises an implicit threat. Most English translations conclude Malachi with the threat of a curse (see NRSV, NASB, KJV, CEB), but the word used is not the same word as in Malachi 2:2 and 3:9. Rather, 4:6 speaks of Elijah coming before YHWH sends total destruction (*ḥērem*) upon the land, a driving concept in Joshua. The day of YHWH in Malachi 4:6 has the potential to bring *ḥērem* to the entire land.

Discussion Questions

1. Explain the focus on the temple in Haggai, Zechariah 1–8, and Malachi.

2. What are the "night visions" of Zechariah? Describe their contents and their significance.

3. Explain the relationship of Zechariah 9–14 to the books of Jeremiah, Ezekiel, Isaiah, and the Twelve.

4. Describe the canonical awareness of Malachi 4:4–6. What implications do you draw from the allusions?

Chapter 6
The Remainder
of the Twelve

Introduction

The remaining five books of the Twelve, like Malachi, owe their location to thematic interests more than chronology, and yet chronology plays a role in the placement of Nahum, Habakkuk, and Jonah. Additionally, all five interact with their context in the Twelve in meaningful ways to enhance the corpus. Nahum and Habakkuk fill the chronological gap between Micah and Zephaniah. Joel links itself to Hosea and Amos in significant ways. Obadiah draws a parallel between the destruction of Edom and Israel. Jonah expands the theology of Joel and Nahum. In addition, all five show an increasing reliance on scribal prophecy to express their messages.

Nahum

The Prophet and the Book

The book of Nahum provides no biographical information about the prophet except the name of his hometown, Elkosh, whose location remains unknown. Other place names mentioned in Nahum include Judah (1:15 [Heb. 2:1]) and the foreign cities Nineveh (1:1) and Thebes (3:8). The direct address to Judah reflects a Judean background. Utilizing indirect information to speak about the prophet Nahum also proves difficult. Attempts to profile the prophet involve complex questions that produce minimal answers, since Nahum involved two developmental stages and even the earliest stage existed as an anthology of sayings directed against Nineveh and its king. When analyzing the provenance of these short sayings, one cannot assume that the sayings were composed at the same time or even by the same person. Additionally, the book does not refer explicitly to the prophet (except in 1:1), nor does the prophet speak autobiographically. Nahum could have written some of or all of the sayings or could have compiled the early anthology.

The Structure and Contents of Nahum

To understand the origins of Nahum, one must account for two distinct phenomena. First, part of the book demonstrates a thoughtful structure that conveys Assyria's imminent demise and does so by sequencing parallel pronouncements against Nineveh, the capital of Assyria. Second, the opening hymn (1:2-8) stands outside that structure with an acrostic poem covering the first half of the Hebrew alphabet.[1] This hymn takes the form of a theophanic hymn that anticipates YHWH's arrival to punish YHWH's enemies. Scholars working on the Book of the Twelve note that this theophanic hymn opening, Nahum mirrors the theophanic hymn ending Habakkuk (3:1-19).[2] Both hymns were added when Nahum and Habakkuk were incorporated into the larger corpus. To understand these competing structural elements, which function as thematic bookends for Nahum and Habakkuk, it will be helpful to discuss the final form of Nahum as the consequence of two stages of production: the initial anthology of anti-Assyrian poems and an expansion putting the rise and fall of Assyria into a broader historical and theological context.

The Anti-Assyria Anthology

The initial publication of Nahum appeared shortly after Nineveh's destruction in 612 BCE. This version consists of an inner core (2:1–3:15aβ) and an editorial frame (1:1, 11-12a, 14; 3:15aγ-19). The inner core and the outer frame parallel one another and emphasize Nineveh's destruction. The inner core contains three parts (2:1–13; 3:1–13; 3:14–15aβ), each of which begins with a pronouncement of Nineveh's destruction (2:1; 3:1, 14) and contains a battle account that ends with Nineveh's defeat (2:3-9; 3:1-3, 15). In addition, each part subsequently develops this image with several short pronouncements regarding the implications of Assyria's imminent demise (2:10-12, 13; 3:5-7, 8-9, 10-13, 16-17).

These battle scenes and brief pronouncements likewise share thematic emphases so that the bulk of Nahum 2–3 essentially repeats the same message three times: Nineveh is destroyed and her inhabitants scattered. The parallel motifs in Nahum 2–3 are striking even though they do not appear in precisely the same order:

Recurring Motifs in Nahum 2–3

Nah 2	Nah 3
2:1-5: Military attack by an army dressed in red with chariots and horses attacking the city wall	3:1-3: Military attack by an army of horses, chariots, and horsemen using swords and spears
2:4: Chariots dash through the streets	3:10: Children lying dead in the streets
2:6-9: Nineveh's location by the river used against it, leading to Nineveh's plunder	3:8-9: Nineveh compared to Thebes, whose use of water as a defense failed to protect it
2:7: Nineveh's population exiled	3:10: Nineveh's population exiled
2:10: Destruction of the city—Nineveh has lost the battle	3:3: Piles of corpses—Nineveh has lost the battle
2:11-12: Comparison of Nineveh's destruction to a lion's prey	3:12-13: Comparison of Nineveh's destruction to a fig tree ready to drop its fruit
2:13: "See, I am against you," says YHWH of hosts	3:5: "See, I am against you," says YHWH of hosts

The smaller units do not flow seamlessly.[3] They pile images of destruction one after the other. Three times the verses anticipate an imminent attack that ends with destruction: 3:14-15 calls Nineveh to prepare for battle, yet twice previously (2:7; 3:10) the exile and death of its inhabitants resulting from battle have been recounted. Repetition of Nineveh's destruction and the brevity of the units characterize these chapters as an anthology of sayings, artfully arranged.

The poetic imagery of Nahum is often noted for its graphic nature and its extreme vengeance. This emphasis makes Nahum difficult to interpret constructively. This difficulty is quite acute in Nahum 3:4-7, a passage O'Brien calls porno-prophetic because it depicts YHWH's defeat of Nineveh using brutal, explicitly sexual language to label Nineveh as a prostitute whom YHWH (the victorious warrior) strips and taunts before the nations.[4]

The outer frame of the early version of Nahum (1:1, 11-12a, 14; 3:15aγ-19) surrounds the inner core with two motifs: the futility of Assyria's superior numbers and the death of its king. Scholars increasingly recognize that major editorial revisions occurred at the front of Nahum. A number of observations suggest that the early corpus had an introduction (1:1a, 11-12a, 14; 2:2-3). Its function was subsumed, and its logic complicated by adding the hymn (1:2-8) and transitional material to connect the two parts (1:9-10, 12b-13, 15 [Heb. 1:9-10, 12b-13; 2:1]).[5] These additions add two new emphases: YHWH's retribution against all enemies (in the hymn) and exhortations for Judah after Assyria's demise (the transitional material).

The key to delineating this early introduction lies in recognizing the characters addressed in 1:9–2:1 (Heb. 1:9-15). Determining the characters in 1:9–2:1 requires one to pay attention to the changing pronouns in the Hebrew text (see table below). The foundational layer (the left-hand column of the table below) distinguishes itself from the later material in that the foundational layer addresses Lady Nineveh and talks to second masculine singular and about third masculine singular, the king of Assyria (who is identified as Belial, or the worthless one). This early material announces judgment against the king who goes forth from Nineveh (1:11). It challenges the idea that the numerical superiority of Assyria assures success (1:12a). And it announces three specific judgments against the king: removal of his name, destruction of his religious icons, and impending death (1:14). The same motifs reappear at the end of Nahum, creating a double thematic *inclusio* between the beginning (1:12a, 14) and end (3:15aγ-17, 18-19) of the early anthology of Nahum where the futility of numerical strength (1:12a; 3:15a–17) and the death of the king of Assyria (1:21a, 14; 3:18-19) appear in both parts.

178

Two Layers in Nah 1:11–2:2

Foundational Layer:

Lady Nineveh and Her King

¹ An oracle against Nineveh.

¹¹ From you (2fs) has gone forth one devising (2ms) evil against YHWH, one counseling worthlessness *(bly`l)*. ¹²ᵃ Though complete and numerous, they (3mp) will be cut off and he (3ms) will pass away.

Zion/Judah Application

¹²ᵇ I have afflicted you (2fs). I will not afflict you (2fs) any longer. ¹³ But now I will break his yoke from upon you (2fs) and I will tear apart your (2fs) chains.

¹⁴ And YHWH commanded concerning you (2ms): Your (2ms) name will not be sown any longer. I will cut off the idol and the cast image from the house of your (2ms) gods. I will make your (2ms) grave, for you are cursed.

¹⁵ Behold, on the mountains, the feet of the herald proclaiming peace. Celebrate (2fs) your festivals, Judah, and pay your vows, for never again will the worthless one *(bly`l)* pass through you (2fs). He has been completely cut off.

²:¹ A scatterer has come up against you (2fs). Guard the ramparts; watch (2ms) the road; gird (2ms) the loins; gather (2ms) strength exceedingly, ²:² for YHWH is restoring the pride of Jacob, like the pride of Israel, for plunderers have plundered (3cp) them (3mp) and ruined their (3mp) branches.

2fs = second feminine singular; 2ms = second masculine singular; 3cp = third common plural; 3mp = third masculine plural

The Theophanic Hymn (1:2-8) and the Transitional Material (1:9-10, 12b-13; 2:1 [Heb. 1:15])

The expansion of Nahum added two thematic foci that changed the nature of the collection. The hymn (1:2-8) adds a theological affirmation of YHWH's power over his enemies, while the transitional material (see table above) continues that theme (1:9-10) and offers encouragement directly to Jerusalem (1:12b-13) and Judah (1:15 [Heb. 2:1]). The direct addresses to Jerusalem and Judah appear nowhere else in Nahum, and they interrupt the speech to Lady Nineveh and her king. Nahum 1:15 quotes Isaiah 52:7 to parallel YHWH's destruction of Assyria and Babylon.[6]

The acrostic hymn extends halfway through the Hebrew alphabet, yet it shows signs that it has been disturbed, most likely when added to the early anthology.[7] The hymn was likely selected for thematic reasons. It describes YHWH's appearance to punish those who stand against him. This hymn develops three lines of thought: YHWH's vengeance (1:2-3); his effects on nature (1:4-5); and admonitions to take this message to heart (1:6-8). The hymn never names Assyria, and in fact it speaks of enemies (plural) at the beginning and end of the hymn (1:2, 8). The central part of the hymn draws upon divine-warrior traditions associated with creation, thus focusing on YHWH's power, justice, and protection.

The transition to the Nineveh-specific portion of the book occurs with a series of statements that take up the language of the hymn and anticipate the anti-Assyrian polemic of the early corpus.[8] At the same time, the Judah and Zion expansions (1:12b-13, 15 [Heb. 1:12b-13; 2:1]) emphasize the hopeful nature of YHWH's actions for the fate of Judah and Jerusalem.

Dating the Prophet and the Book

When trying to date of the book of Nahum, several points must be taken into account: the fall of Thebes in 663 BCE, the fall of Nineveh in 612 BCE, and the role of 1:15 (Heb 2:1). Nahum 3:8 refers to the fall of Thebes as a lesson from history, so the first stage of Nahum postdates that event. On the other hand, since the majority of small units in the early core of Nahum anticipate the fall of Nineveh, at least some of these units probably predate Assyria's demise (612 BCE).[9] These two starting points become more complicated, however, when one considers Nahum 1:15, because this verse contains a verbal parallel to Isaiah 52:7 (a late sixth-century text):

Nah 1:15	Isa 52:7
Look! *On the mountains the feet of one who brings good tidings, who proclaims peace!* Celebrate your festivals, O Judah, fulfill your vows, for never again shall the wicked invade you; they are utterly cut off.	*How beautiful upon the mountains are the feet of the messenger who announces peace, who brings good news*, who announces salvation, who says to Zion, "Your God reigns."

The similarities are too pronounced to assume independent origins, but Nahum 1:15 likely borrows from Isaiah.[10] Hence, Nahum 1:15 postdates the rise of Cyrus. Isaiah 52:7 celebrates Babylon's downfall while Nahum 1:15 celebrates the fall of Assyria, so the combined versions of this saying effectively create parallel calls to rejoice over the fall of the occupying power.

The first stage of Nahum was compiled shortly after Nineveh's destruction (612 BCE). This date simultaneously accounts for the future orientation of most of the preexisting units, while recognizing that publishing the anthology would be difficult with Assyria still in power.[11]

The second stage added Nahum to a growing corpus of prophetic writings that included the Book of the Four Prophets (Hosea, Amos, Micah, Zephaniah), Habakkuk, and perhaps Joel, Haggai, Zechariah 1–8, and Malachi. Dating the second stage presupposes conversations about Nahum and the Twelve below. Anticipating that discussion, two dates set the parameters. Some think Nahum and Habakkuk entered the Book of the Four before the inclusion of Joel, Haggai, Zechariah, and Malachi, and they typically date the expansion of Nahum and Habakkuk earlier, probably the second half of the fifth century. Others argue that the hymns include allusions to Joel and other books and thus tie their models to the date of Joel (which often means the first half of the fourth century). Links to Joel, Micah, Exodus, and Isaiah complicate attempts to assign absolute dates even when relative dating of the individual pieces seems less problematic.

Nahum within the Book of the Twelve

When Nahum and Habakkuk were added to the larger corpus remains debated, but significant agreement exists on their function as a pair within the Twelve. First, both Nahum and Habakkuk received redactional expansions that included a theophanic hymn (Nah 1:2-8; Hab 3:2-19). Further, these two books close the chronological gap between Micah and Zephaniah.[12] Thus, a number of scholars argue Nahum and Habakkuk entered a larger corpus together.[13]

The function of Nahum in the Twelve involves its location in the scroll, the theological impulses of its second stage, and the interplay between Nahum and other texts in the Twelve. Micah ends with allusions to Hezekiah's siege, so Nahum's concern with the downfall of Assyria fits thematically right afterward. Nahum and Habakkuk were adapted to fill the lacuna between Micah and Zephaniah. Nahum puts Assyria's fall into a larger theological context, one that claims YHWH exerts power over all enemies. Similar work in Habakkuk accentuates both the rise and the fall of Babylon as the work of YHWH. As a result, Nahum reflects theologically on Assyrian power. Nahum assumes the downfall of Assyria will happen at YHWH's instigation, as with Micah 6–7. Habakkuk claims that YHWH sends Babylon to punish Judah for its failures.

The theophanic hymn in Nahum (1:2-8), along with an exhortation to Judah (1:12b-13, 15 [Heb. 2:1]; 2:2 [Heb. 2:3]), adds new theological foci to the early collection. By contrast, the hymn's focus on YHWH's retribution against all enemies introduces a thematic element that works better as an introduction to Nahum's judgment against Assyria, to Habakkuk's judgment against Judah and Babylon, and to Zephaniah's oracles against those foreign nations that benefitted from Assyrian hegemony. Two recurring assumptions run through each of these prophetic books that point in opposite directions: a day of impending judgment against Jerusalem cannot be avoided, and Zion will be restored while those who attacked her will be brought down. On the one hand, these two emphases appear to be odd partners if one has a purely mechanical view of the redactional work that shaped prophetic literature. On the other hand, such redactional expansion makes good sense once one understands the nature of the larger scrolls as compendia of YHWH's prophetic message to Judah from the eighth century on.[14] Not only does the larger scroll exhibit a chronological structure in the Book of the Four, but Nahum and Habakkuk fit into this chronological structure. The primary focus of the Book of the Four recounts YHWH's message to Israel and Judah. Ongoing discussions in the Book of the Four incorporated affirmations that YHWH had not abandoned Judah and Jerusalem. In the end, these discussions could no longer ignore the fact that the relationship between Judah and YHWH was different. For most of the seventh century, the Assyrians served as suzerains to Judah, and by the end of that century, the last Judean kings had to demonstrate their fealty to Babylon. The scribal circles who preserved the prophetic books had to provide a theological explanation for these events. The books of Nahum and Habakkuk provide that message.

Nahum and Habakkuk continue the basic thrust of the prophetic message begun in the Book of the Four Prophets: prophets delivered words of warning and judgment against Israel and Judah before YHWH acted against his own people. Nahum and Habakkuk assume that judgment against Judah is coming and that YHWH will use foreign kings to punish it. Nevertheless, Nahum and Habakkuk also affirm those foreign powers are also subject to YHWH's power. This emphasis appears in the theophanic hymn that opens Nahum and in the word of hope addressed to Judah in 1:15 (Heb. 2:1). Yet, Nahum also connects thematically to other texts.

Nahum follows Micah 7 in the Masoretic order of the Twelve. Several observations from the discussion of Micah 7 suggest this placement was deliberate. Micah 7 draws upon the anti-Assyrian polemic of Isaiah 10. Micah 7:8-10 contains a dialogue between Lady Zion and Lady Nineveh, a dialogue that hints at Nineveh's taunting of Zion with the claim that YHWH has abandoned her (7:10). Zion, for her part, rejects the taunt. Rather, Zion affirms her own sin has caused her plight (7:9), which actually makes sense of YHWH's response to Jerusalem in Nahum 1:12b-13. The divine speech in Nahum 1:12b-13 (part of the expansion of Nahum; see table on page 179) also addresses both Lady Nineveh and Lady Zion, promising that Assyria will be punished and the yoke of its king removed from Zion.

In addition to this thematic continuation, several allusions in Nahum take the form of redactional parenthetical comments evoking texts in other books to help ground the assumption that YHWH has sent Assyria to judge Judah but will now punish Assyria for its arrogance and disobedience. For example, the theophany in Nahum 1:2-8 functions well as a thematic introduction to Nahum, but the breaks in the acrostic poem suggest editorial changes to its original form occurred, likely at the time it was incorporated at the front of Nahum because several of the disruptions to the hymn pick up vocabulary from Micah 7.[15] Further, both pairs of text (Joel 2 with Joel 4 and Micah 7 with Nahum 1) allude to Exodus 34:6-7. This intertextual relationship is created in Nahum 1 by an expansion between the *'alef* and the *bêt* lines of the acrostic. More telling, both Joel and Micah 7 and Nahum 1 make use of the thematic change from YHWH's compassion toward YHWH's people (Exod 34:6) and retribution toward YHWH's enemies (Exod 34:7). Joel 2:13 and Micah 7:18-20 draw more heavily upon Exodus 34:6 to elicit the theme of YHWH's compassion toward YHWH's people, while Joel 3:19-21 (Heb. 4:19-21) and Nahum 1:2b-3a use the language of Exodus 34:7 to assert YHWH's justice will by no means clear the guilty. As a result, both sets of allusions evoke Exodus 34:6 *and* 34:7 to reinforce the motifs of YHWH's compassion *and* YHWH's justice. This same theme appears in Joel and a corrective appears in Jonah where it is both problematized and affirmed.

The parallels to Isaiah texts in Nahum's transitional material, as has already been noted, are not random. For example, Nahum 1:15 (Heb. 2:1) recapitulates Isaiah 52:7 (a text that announces the coming release from Babylon), but the context in Nahum changes the message into a command to rejoice over the impending fall of Assyria. This parallel between the downfall of Assyria and the rise and fall of Babylon functions as a significant theme that develops across Micah–Nahum–Habakkuk.[16]

In addition to the allusion to Exodus 34:6-7, one should note the intertextual relationship between Nahum 3 and Joel 1–2 created when Nahum 3:15-16* incorporates references to the *yelek* locust representing the foreign power that comes to attack:

> [15aα] There, fire will devour you (second feminine singular).
> [15aβ] (The) sword will cut you (second feminine singular) down.
> > [15aγ] It will devour (third feminine singular) you (second feminine singular) like the hopping locust (*yeleq*).
> [15bα] Multiply yourself (second feminine singular) like the swarming locust (*'arbeh*).
> [15bβ] Multiply yourself (second masculine singular) like the hopping locust (*yeleq*).
> [16a] Increase your traders more than the stars of heaven.
> > [16b] The hopping locust (*yeleq*) spreads out and then flies away.
> [17] Your (second feminine singular) courtiers are like the swarming locust (*'arbeh*),
>
> and your (second feminine singular) scribes are like a swarm of locusts (*gōb gōbay*),
> > those encamped in the walls on a cold day.
> The sun rises, but the place where they are is not known.

In most of this passage, the locusts appear as a symbol of the ineffectual nature of Nineveh's superior numbers. Nineveh's size will not help it when YHWH acts. The two indented lines above (also underlined), however, assume the hopping locust (*yeleq*) attacks the Nineveh-locust. The *yeleq* will devour its prey (Nineveh) and move on to the next location. This image comes quite close to the portrait of Babylon in Habakkuk 1:9, but this final form of Nahum 3:15-17 also correlates precisely with the articulation of Joel 1:4, where the leftover from one locust (Assyria) is "devoured" by another (Babylon). Given the early documentation of traditions associating Joel's locusts with the attack of enemy nations, these redactional comments facilitate such a reading and probably reflect a scribal hermeneutic when Nahum and Habakkuk were inserted between Micah and Zephaniah.[17]

When reading from Nahum 3 to Habakkuk 1, one will be struck by the number of shared words. Such lexical clusters appear regularly between the end of one book and the start of the next in the Twelve. Not every recurring word deliberately evokes its counterpart, yet one can see a trend in Nahum 3 and Habakkuk 1. The recurring words represent an escalation of fear and power when comparing the Babylonians (Hab 1) to the Assyrians (Nah 3).[18]

Finally, Nahum also reflects Joel's use of Exodus 34:6–7 when read with Micah 7:18–19. YHWH will punish Judah with Assyria (Nahum) and Babylon (Habakkuk), and yet Judah will remain YHWH's people after those empires have faded from the scene.

Habakkuk

The Prophet and the Book

As is typical for the Twelve, Habakkuk contains virtually no biographical information about the prophet for whom the book is named. The only biographical datum recorded about Habakkuk is that he was a prophet (1:1; 3:1). Two superscriptions both introduce independently transmitted compositions, one labeled an oracle (1:1) and the other labeled a prayer (3:1).

The dual reference to Habakkuk as a prophet, combined with the genre classifications (oracle and prayer) and actions, provides insight into the prophet's social location. The actions assumed in the early core of Habakkuk suggest the prophet lodges a complaint to YHWH concerning the fate of the wicked and the righteous (1:2-4, 13-14) and then proceeds to the rampart to wait for a divine response (2:1). This dramatic account presumes that the figure at its center takes it upon himself to confront YHWH because the righteous suffer and the wicked prosper. This prophet assumes the authority to act on behalf of the righteous and recounts public acts, requesting a response from YHWH and posting himself to await this response.

An autobiographical style provides the prophetic character a more prominent role in Habakkuk than most of the other prophetic writings in the Book of the Twelve.[19] For example, in Nahum the prophet never speaks of himself. Habakkuk's autobiographical style provides some stylistic consistency for the book, but other observations suggest the final form of Habakkuk derives from two stages. One must pay close attention to the prophetic character as speaker and actor, but the content of core speeches provides few clues to the date or to a specific historical setting that gave rise to these prophetic speeches.

The Structure and Contents

Understanding Habakkuk requires one to account for four compositions and the work of a compiler who arranged these compositions and inserted comments

185

at key points in the book. The four compositions represent existing sources: a prophetic complaint that challenges YHWH to respond to questions regarding the prosperity of the wicked (1:2-4, 12-14; 2:1-4); an oracle of divine punishment at the hands of the Babylonians spoken by YHWH to a group (1:5-11), alongside comments about the Babylonians (1:15-17); a collection of five woe oracles against the wicked (2:5-20), also updated with a series of comments about the Babylonians (2:5b, 8, 10, 17); and a preexisting theophanic hymn regarding YHWH's defeat of the enemy (3:1-19).

The prophet's complaint begins immediately after the superscription of the book (1:1). In all likelihood, the original complaint consisted of 1:2-4, 12-14 and a report of the prophet's decision to wait for a response from YHWH (2:1-4). The original complaint takes the form of a prayer in which the prophet speaks directly to YHWH, laying out an enduring problem wherein violence, strife, and contention fill the land while instruction (*torah*) is deemed ineffectual and justice is perverted (1:2-4). This prayer continues in 1:12-14, where the prophet reaffirms his sense that YHWH must act to restore justice because of YHWH's own character. The unit ends with a narrative (2:1-3) recounting the prophet's decision to await a response, and YHWH's command to record a vision on a tablet that the end is coming.[20] The original complaint regarding the fate of the wicked and the righteous ends with a response exhorting the righteous to remain faithful despite the current situation (2:4).

In its current location, the divine oracle (1:5-11) interrupts the individual complaint of 1:2-4 and 1:12-14. One should distinguish between the original form of the oracle and the rhetorical function it plays in its current location. The style of address, the presumptions of the second complaint (1:12-14), and the military rhetoric set 1:5-11 apart from the complaint material on either side. The complaint delivers a prayer between an individual and YHWH, while the divine oracle in 1:5-11 warns a group that YHWH is sending the Babylonians and describes the insurmountable brutality of this force.

Hence, the oracle stands apart from its surrounding context and seems to be deliberately inserted to *function* as the divine response to the prophet's complaint, even though the oracle was composed independently. Without this reference to the Babylonians as punishment sent from YHWH, the prophet's complaint is largely devoid of anything tying it to the seventh century. The complaint language (1:2-4, 12-14) only utilizes nonspecific terminology (e.g., the righteous, wicked, treacherous), but the oracle's reference to the impending arrival of the Babylonians creates a late seventh-century setting for the reader, after Assyria's destruction but prior to Jerusalem's punishment in 597 or 587 BCE.

The woe oracles (2:5-20) constitute a third preexisting source. Like the foundational complaint in 1:2-4, 12-14, these five woes denounce those who conspire to increase their own wealth. These five sayings begin with the particle "woe"

(2:6, 9, 12, 15, 19) and then condemn the following practices: spending funds that were left as collateral while not paying one's own financial obligations (2:6-7), building large houses using stolen resources (2:9, 11), relying on bloodshed to build a city (2:12-14), getting neighbors so drunk that they abase themselves (2:15-16), and practicing idolatry (2:18-19). These oracles thus condemn un-ethical behavior and cultic misdeeds, but they also contain parenthetical com-ments (2:5b, 8, 10, 17) that connect punishment to a political entity, largely recognized as the Chaldeans who were the subject of the oracle in 1:5-11. These comments, together with the oracle, emphasize the degree to which the power of the Babylonians would be directed against the wealthy in Judah. They do not celebrate the idea that the Babylonians will come. Rather, in light of the issues raised by the prophetic complaint, they imply that the situation will get worse before it gets better.

At least four lines of evidence argue that the final source block (3:1-19) is a composite text originating independently of chapters 1–2: the changing tar-get of the theophany in 3:3-7 and 3:8-15, the presence of both a superscription (3:1) and a subscription (3:19b), the threefold use of *selah* (3:3, 9, 13), and the first-person speech (3:2, 16-19a).[21] The material in 3:3-7 reports a theophany in which YHWH punishes Cushan and Midian (regions in the Sinai desert). By con-trast, 3:8-15 uses ancient motifs of the divine-warrior creation account, in which YHWH battles against the enemy led by the Sea (*Yam*) and the River (*Nahar*).

Habakkuk 3 has both a superscription and a subscription, each containing cultic notations that elsewhere appear only in the Psalter. No psalm, however, has both a superscription and a subscription, which raises suspicions that these cultic notes were retained when the two parts of the theophany joined, probably before the attachment to Habakkuk.

The enigmatic appearance of *selah* further suggests Habakkuk 3 derives origi-nally from a cultic context. The word *selah* appears elsewhere only in Psalms, and overwhelmingly in books 1–3 (Pss 1–89).[22] These cultic notations provided clues to the musicians either to pause or to repeat a line. These directions were under-stood when added to the individual psalms, but their function was eventually forgotten. Dating individual psalms is notoriously difficult, but the overwhelm-ing presence of *selah* in books 1–3 suggests a date in the Persian period.[23] If the two parts of the theophany were originally separate, the *selah* notes suggest they were combined in a cultic context before being incorporated into Habakkuk.[24]

Fourth, the manuscript evidence from early texts found in the Judean desert creates some level of ambiguity regarding Habakkuk 3. Two items in particular stand out. The Habakkuk Pesher stops after Habakkuk 2, while the Old Greek and the Barberini text differ from the MT in places.[25] Most scholars argue that these variations are explainable without resorting to the assumption that Habakkuk 3 was added after the Habakkuk Pesher was written in the second century BCE, but a few have raised questions. Relatedly, many variations in the Greek traditions are generally treated as arising from very obscure Hebrew terms and phrases that the translators felt the need to modify in order to make sense of the text for their own audiences. In all likelihood, these variations attest to the difficult style exhibited by Habakkuk 3, not a different version.

Fifth, the first-person speech structures the theophany as a prayer. The composite theophany begins with a first-person petition to YHWH (3:2). Habakkuk 3:7 concludes the first portion of the theophany with the speaker describing his own fear for Cushan and Midian at the sight of YHWH's appearance. The first-person speech dominates 3:16-19 as well. The "I" language thus frames the two theophany reports rhetorically. The first-person speaker becomes identified with the prophet, not only because of the explicit identification in 3:1, but because 3:2 (along with 3:16-19) assumes a response of both humble submission and the fear of what lies ahead for YHWH's people. The speaker acknowledges the coming wrath of YHWH, yet implores YHWH for mercy as well. This call for mercy hopes for the survival of the faithful.

The same motifs appear at the end of the theophany when the prophet speaks, as in 3:2. The prophet fears the enemy (3:16a) and anticipates its punishment (3:16b). The reference to those who will attack responds to the climactic announcement that YHWH defeats the enemy in 3:13-15. It assumes that an enemy will attack Judah and that the enemy will ultimately be defeated. At the same time, 3:16-19 knows that the enemy will inflict damage upon Judah on the day of distress. The speaker also anticipates the infertility of the land, a motif appearing often in the Twelve.[26] The speaker proclaims that even though infertility will come upon the land, "I will rejoice in YHWH" and "exult in the God of my salvation" (3:18). This last phrase echoes one of the last prophetic speeches of Micah (7:7), the only two times outside the Psalter where the phrase "God of my salvation" appears.[27] Whether one can say Habakkuk 3:18 was written with Micah 7:7 in view remains a difficult decision, but the two verses can function in tandem. Implicitly, the logic of Habakkuk assumes that Assyria is gone from the scene (which Nahum has demonstrated), but that the situation in Judah remains unchanged from the time of Micah (cf. Hab 1:2–4 and Mic 7:1–7).

Dating the Prophet and the Book

The question of how to date Habakkuk is inextricably bound to the question of how the book came to be. Three starting points should be stated, two assumptions and a deduction concerning the relevant evidence. First, one should assume that a prophet named Habakkuk existed, despite the book providing no biographical data.[28] Second, one should assume that the prophet's name implies a literary composition existed that was associated with the prophet. Third, one may deduce from the literary characteristics of Habakkuk 3 discussed above that it represents a preexisting composition with its own literary history prior to being affixed to Habakkuk. In much the same way that Nahum 1:2-8 was affixed to the front of Nahum and a thanksgiving song inserted into Jonah, Habakkuk 3 was added to the end of Habakkuk. As a result, one must consider whether Habakkuk 3 comes from the same author (Habakkuk the prophet) as the core material of chapters 1–2. The evidence suggests that Habakkuk 3 likely does not stem from the same author as the core of chapters 1–2, and that instead, the name Habakkuk was probably affixed secondarily to 3:1 (perhaps in place of a name that was already there). All three of these starting points affect how one describes the development of Habakkuk in the form we now have it.

Dating the book of Habakkuk has also become increasingly complex in the last forty years as the number of scholars arguing for a multistaged compositional process has grown. In most models, the most concrete historical reference (the oracle about the Babylonians) interrupts an existing complaint (1:2-4, 12-14), but the preexisting complaint uses only very general terms so any attempt to date the complaint becomes more subjective.[29] Consequently, dates suggested for the composition of Habakkuk now range from the seventh century to the Hellenistic period, though most of the models have the majority of the book in place by the late sixth to mid-fifth century BCE.[30] These dates also have implications for how one understands Habakkuk's relationship with other texts within the Book of the Twelve.[31]

Even a quick assessment of these redactional models creates two impressions relative to the isolation and sequencing of the material. On the one hand, most investigations recognize similar functional units, but on the other hand, the order in which the pieces come together differs considerably.[32] By recognizing that four existing literary compositions have been joined together to create a portrait of a prophetic complaint, a divine response, and an affirmation of YHWH's eventual punishment of *both* the injustice of the Judeans *and* the brutality of the Babylonians, one can actually account for the vast majority of the book as a redacted whole rather than a series of developmental stages. The biggest difference between this model and some others is that these elements would not have been combined in the seventh century BCE. Rather, the redactors who created Habakkuk from these four sources likely did so well into the Persian period. Habakkuk could plausibly have been named as the source for the complaint and narrative response, but it could have been composed in the seventh or fourth century.[33] The same holds true for the woe oracles before the anti-Babylonian commentary reinterprets their original focus. The cultic elements that existed with the hymn have Persian-period counterparts, especially *selah* in Habakkuk 3 and the first three books of Psalms.

Like Nahum, the book of Habakkuk works with a periodization of history. Rather than Assyria, Habakkuk testifies to YHWH's decision to continue punishing Judah by sending Babylon. Habakkuk opens by describing the ethical situation of Judah as essentially the same as the situation of Micah 7:1-7, except that Assyria is gone from the scene (as the reader of Nahum would know), but Judah will now face an even greater enemy (as Habakkuk leads the reader to see).

Habakkuk within the Book of the Twelve

Reading Habakkuk within the Book of the Twelve assumes other contexts. The decision to begin Habakkuk with a complaint illustrates quite effectively what happens when one reads the individual books within the Twelve as completely independent compilations of prophetic material or as part of a larger literary context. As an isolated book, scholars generally treat Habakkuk's opening question ("How long, YHWH?") as little more than a genre marker if they mention it at all. By contrast, those reading the Twelve as a collection (whose pieces beg to be read in light of one another) hear this opening question differently. The question presumes that the problems of violence and injustice existed before the prophet speaks in Habakkuk. In fact, while the book of Nahum promised Assyria's destruction would bring joy to Judah, Nahum never mentions the actions of YHWH's people. When one asks, however, what the people were doing the last time a prophet addressed them, the reader of the Book of the Twelve is drawn to the prophet's confrontation with people in Micah 7:1-7. This passage recounts a remarkably similar situation to that of the opening of Habakkuk.[34] Both Habakkuk 1:2-4 and Micah 7:1-6 describe a social situation in which there are no upright people, where violence abounds, and where justice is perverted. Also, Micah 7:7 concludes with a verbal parallel to Habakkuk 3:18. The close verbal parallel also conveys the sense that something has changed since the time of Hezekiah (assumed at the end of Micah). In Micah 7:8-10, Lady Zion addresses Lady Nineveh with an affirmation that YHWH will come to her aid. In Habakkuk, Assyria and Lady Nineveh have disappeared from the scene, yet the behavior of Judah's elite has not changed, so YHWH announces the sending of the Babylonians, an even greater danger.

The language describing the Babylonians in Habakkuk 1:5-11 contains a number of verbal similarities to the descriptions of Assyria in Nahum 3. These lexical clusters are likely not deliberate allusions, but the repetition of so many terms certainly invites comparison. The repetition leads the attentive reader to see that the dramatic fear created by Assyria in Nahum 3 either becomes superseded by the even more powerful force of Babylon or points to Assyria's destruction (by the Babylonians, even though they are not named in Nah 3). This dual threat of Assyria followed by Babylon comports with the historical epochs of the eighth–seventh centuries, when these two political entities became the regional superpowers that dominated the landscape. The Book of the Twelve reflects these epochs by including prophetic messages explaining the downfall of Assyria (Nahum) and the rise and fall of Babylon (Habakkuk) as imminent events. This sense of imminence forces the reader to walk through these epochs, so to speak, and to wrestle with the theological claims that YHWH's anger at Judah resulted in his commissioning first Assyria and then Babylon as instruments of justice who would also have to be punished.

Habakkuk 3:16-17 also ties into a number of texts in the Twelve which evoke the motifs of the land's infertility (or potential fertility) using some combination of vine, wine, grain, oil, and fig tree. These texts begin in Hosea and Amos, where they relate primarily to the Northern Kingdom (e.g., Hos 2:8, 22 [Heb. 2:10, 24]; 7:14; 14:7 [Heb. 14:8]; Amos 4:9). The majority of these texts, however, beginning with Joel, relate to Judah's infertility or potential fertility (e.g., Joel 1:7-14; 2:22-24; Hab 3:17; Hag 1:11; Zech 8:12; Mal 3:11). These agricultural threads have an effect upon the reader even though not all of them should be tied to a single redactor.

Joel

Historical Backdrop to Joel

In its final form, Joel represents one of the latest books in the prophetic canon.[35] Joel displays a highly refined awareness of other biblical texts, a number of which involve citations of postexilic texts. The breadth of literary texts to which Joel alludes must factor into the question of dating.[36] Joel presupposes a functioning temple (1:9, 13-16; 2:12, 17), which was completed in 515 BCE. It refers to city walls in ways that assume they should be capable of withstanding attacks, but these walls offer no obstacle to YHWH's army (2:7, 9). Assuming some kernel of authenticity to the tradition that Nehemiah did not restore Jerusalem's walls until 445 BCE, Joel 2 should not be dated until sometime after that point. Relatedly, Joel never mentions the king or the king's family. Further, the relationship of the political entities in Joel 3:4-8, 19 (Heb. 4:4-8, 19) is best explained by a date in the early fourth century.[37]

Dating the book of Joel depends heavily upon how one interprets several phenomena. On the one hand, a virtual consensus exists that Joel stems from the

Persian period for reasons stated above. On the other hand, serious differences exist among the compositional models concerning how to explain the radical shifts in perspective found within the book. For some, including this author, these differences resulted because Joel was compiled by combining a number of preexisting sources. For others, Joel developed in stages as later readers updated Joel with their own perspectives concerning the day of YHWH. In other words, Joel probably reflects a mid to late Persian-period setting, but since Joel is a composite work, the question remains complicated.

The Prophet and the Book

The book of Joel provides virtually no biographical data concerning the prophet, except the name of the prophet's father, Pethuel (1:1). Four characteristics, however, imply something about the prophet's context. First, the setting of the book is Jerusalem because of the references to the temple (1:9, 13-16; 2:12, 17) and Zion (2:1, 15, 23, 32; 3:16, 17, 21). Second, the extended call to repentance comprising chapters 1–2 challenges the population and the cultic personnel to return to YHWH, but does not contain accusations of misdeeds.[38] Third, Joel knows other biblical texts, suggesting that the prophet was trained as a scribal exegete who echoes other texts to make his own prophetic message relevant.[39] Fourth, Joel's language and themes reappear in key places within the Book of the Twelve, making Joel a pivotal book in the discussion of that scroll. These allusions have a clear purpose. They foreshadow a history of Judah in paradigmatic terms. Multiple threats to Judah lead to repentance. YHWH continually shows grace to YHWH's people when they return to him, but will hold those accountable who do not (both those inside and outside Judah).

The Structure and Contents of Joel

The book of Joel has a rhetorical purpose and a clear structure, but it also has several points of disjuncture that suggest the book has been compiled from a number of sources.[40] After the undated superscription (1:1), the larger rhetorical blocks stand out clearly: a prophetic challenge to recognize the serious problems facing the community (1:2-20); a poem warning of the coming day of YHWH (2:1-11); an explicit call to communal repentance (2:12-17); the first promise for the immediate future should the people repent (2:18-27); a second promise regarding the distant future (2:28-32 [Heb. 3:1-5]); and a third promise (also for the distant future) to punish the nations who have taken advantage of Judah (3:1-21 [Heb. 4:1-21]).

In Joel 1:2-20, the prophet confronts a series of groups within the population with the implications of a threat of unprecedented proportions facing the land. This confrontational style is characterized by a use of imperatives, a demand for attention, and a clear sense of urgency. Yet, when one looks closely at the details of this threat, one recognizes that the passages are not uniform since the threats include a series of locust plagues (plural, not singular) or rely upon locust imagery (1:4, 8), an enemy attack (1:6-7), a drought (1:10-12, 17-18), and wildfire (1:19-20). Some of these images may overlap, but cumulatively they suggest a composite literary piece designed to convey an extremely dire situation (1:4).[41] In addition, Joel 1 offers several linguistic and thematic connections to Hosea, suggesting that the compilation of Joel was completed with an eye toward its location between Hosea and Amos.[42]

The opening confrontation of 1:2-20 breaks down into a number of rhetorical segments, including an introductory call to attention (1:2-4); a series of rhetorically barbed challenges to the people as drunkards (1:5-10), to the farmers and vintners (1:11-12), and to the priests (1:13-14); the prophet's lamentation about the day of YHWH (1:15-18); and the prophet's petitionary prayer (1:19-20). As noted above, the careful reader cannot help but notice a great diversity of threats presupposed by these confrontations. Joel 1:2-4 anticipates a series of locust plagues unlike anything that the people have experienced previously.[43]

By contrast, 1:5-10 shows a different set of problems threatening Judah's agricultural output. These problems include an enemy attack from a foreign nation that strips the land of its vegetation (1:6-7) and a drought in which the land withers, making it impossible for offerings to be brought to temple personnel (1:8-10). Complicating the picture still further, 1:6 describes the attacking nation as a lioness whose teeth and fangs destroy the grapevines and fig trees (1:7).[44] All the threats mentioned in Joel 1 appear in the curses section of Deuteronomy as punishments set to befall YHWH's people if they abandon the covenant.[45] The fact that these curses appear in Joel's description of the current state of the land plays into the rhetorical agenda of Joel, since it began with the claim that the current situation is unprecedented in Judah's memory (1:2-3). The multiplication of curse manifestations should raise alarms for priests and people alike since, in the presupposition of the rhetorical logic of Joel, with so many curses confronting the land, one has to assume that covenant stipulations have been violated.

The devastation of the land continues to be a topic in 1:11-12, in which the prophet calls the farmers and vine dressers to lament because all crops are affected by a drought. A longer list of produce appears: grain, barley, grapevine, fig tree, pomegranate, palm tree (from which dates are harvested), and "all the trees of the field." Joel 1:13-14 calls upon the priests to proclaim a fast at the temple in order to restore the people's ability to make sacrifices of grain offerings and libations. As with the preceding units, the call for the priests to lament assumes that they have done something wrong in the eyes of YHWH.[46]

Joel 1:15-20 builds off the preceding threats but introduces a theme that will come to dominate the book, a theme recognized as distinctive for the Book of the Twelve, namely, the impending day of YHWH.[47] The concept of the day of YHWH refers to instances of YHWH's direct intervention (normally for judgment, but it can refer to deliverance as well).[48] The concept of the day of YHWH that appears in 1:15 and 2:1 will leave the land desolate, but it also presumes an enemy attack when it calls upon the people in Zion to raise the alarm (2:1) and when it describes the attacking army acting on YHWH's behalf (2:2-11).

Three qualities illuminate the rhetorical function of 2:1-11, the second major section of the book. First, these verses have been called a day-of-YHWH poem, because they describe YHWH's army (2:2-10) sandwiched between admonitions about the nearness and ferocity of the day of YHWH (2:1, 11).[49] Second, the poem's literary qualities demonstrate the use of dynamic parallelism to create a kind of storyline running through these poetic lines.[50] Third, intertextual citations in 2:1-11 highlight day-of-YHWH terminology from elsewhere in the Book of the Twelve that describes the impending day of YHWH directed against Jerusalem.[51]

Joel 2:12-17 plays a pivotal role in the structure and rhetoric of the book. These verses present a communal call to repentance. As with 1:4-15, these verses go to considerable lengths to show that the call to repent is intended for the entire population.[52] As with the previous units, 2:12-17 draws upon another text to strengthen the argument, specifically Exodus 34:6-7.[53] Exodus 34:6-7 not only plays a role in Joel, it also plays a significant part in the first half of the Twelve.[54] In Joel, the call to repent that begins in 2:12 cites Exodus 34:6 as its expression of hope that YHWH will not destroy Judah and Jerusalem. Joel presents this repentance as a last-ditch effort to avoid destruction, also articulating the assumption that the act of repentance alone does not guarantee YHWH will forego punishing Jerusalem (see 2:14). While Exodus 34:6-7 plays a pivotal role in the call to repentance of Joel 2:12-17, the end of Joel also alludes back to Exodus 34, but in so doing it picks up the elements related to the second portion (34:7b) by affirming that YHWH will by no means clear the guilty (Joel 3:21 [Heb. 4:21]).[55]

The next unit (2:18-27) functions in some way as YHWH's response to Judah's repentance. The crux of the problem concerns whether to understand the promises articulated in 2:18-27 as YHWH's past or future response.[56] In either case, YHWH's actions introduce a series of promises related to the health of the land that structures the rest of Joel. Nevertheless, one should not overlook the fact that the promises of 2:18-27 represent the reversal of the threats experienced by Judah and Jerusalem in chapter 1. The attacking army, the drought, and the locust plagues will all be removed according to 2:18-27 if the people repent. The language of 2:21-27 represents exhortation. These verses call for courage in the face of uncertainty, while at the same time articulating a hopeful portrait of YHWH's response.

Joel 2:28-32 (Heb. 3:1-5) changes the focus both chronologically and materially.[57] Chronologically, 2:18-27 presents its promises as related to the near future, but 2:28 articulates a promise for the more distant future ("And it will happen afterwards . . ."). The promises in 2:18-27 will unfold over time, but the changes in the verse 2:28 anticipate an even more distant period. Materially, these verses anticipate a future in which the outpouring of YHWH's spirit will be manifest to all: males and females, the elderly and the young, and male and female slaves. This radically inclusive portrait of the distant future is rare in the Old Testament.[58] These verses also anticipate a coming day of YHWH but not the same day of YHWH anticipated in 1:15 and 2:1. The previous actions anticipated a day of YHWH that threatened Jerusalem imminently. The day of YHWH in 2:28-32 represents a day of judgment presaged by cosmic upheaval (2:30-31), but the unit culminates in the pronouncement that those who call on the name of YHWH in Zion and Jerusalem will be delivered. Here, the day of YHWH is not used to explain drought, locust plagues, or an enemy attack.

Joel 3 (Heb. 4) closes the book with yet another thematic shift. These verses do not focus on Judah or on how to survive. Rather, they focus on the impending judgment against foreign nations who have taken advantage of Judah and Jerusalem. Whether Joel 3 represents part of a later addition to the book or was compiled later than the bulk of chapters 1–2, little doubt exists that Joel 3 was deliberately compiled as a conclusion to the book as we now have it. Its focus on the day of YHWH as a point of judgment against the nations fills out the third variation of the day explored in Joel. Its deliberate structure rhetorically foreshadows its message and reverses the destruction of chapter 1. Joel 3 presents itself in four parts: a thematic introduction (3:1-3 [Heb. 4:1-3]), a promissory conclusion (3:18-21 [Heb. 4:18-21]), an oracle against specific enemies (3:4-8 [Heb. 4:4-8]), and a generic oracle against all the surrounding nations (3:9-17 [Heb. 4:9-17]) who will face YHWH's judgment on the day of his choosing.

The framing elements often get overlooked in discussions of the rhetorical function of the book's final chapter. The opening verses (3:1-3 [Heb. 4:1-3]) introduce the themes of the remainder of Joel as a thematic chiasm:

A Restoration of Judah and Jerusalem (3:1)
 B Judgment in the Valley of Jehoshaphat (3:2)
  C Punishment for Selling God's People into Slavery (3:3)
  C′ Punishment for Selling God's People into Slavery (3:4-8)
 B′ Judgment in the Valley of Jehoshaphat (3:9-17)
A′ Restoration of Judah and Jerusalem (3:18-21)

Joel 3:1-3 thus sets the stage thematically, yet the chapter as a whole does not function as an independent unit since the end (3:18-21) reverses the desolation of chapters 1–2 and functions as a conclusion to the book.[59] Just as significantly, however, Joel 3:9-21 integrates allusions to other prophetic texts, including Micah 4:3 (= Isa 2:4), Amos 1:2, and 9:13.[60]

Joel 3:4-8 (Heb. 4:4-8) has often been interpreted as an independent text inserted secondarily into the chapter.[61] These verses have the makings of an independent composition, but so does the bulk of 3:9-17. Given the thematic structure of the chapter introduced by 3:1-3 (see C, C′), it seems unwise to separate 3:4-8 from the compilation of the rest of Joel 3.[62]

A second composition follows immediately in 3:9-17 with a call to judgment against the nations in the valley of Jehoshaphat. This unit does not name specific nations (as in 3:4-8 or 3:19) but issues a call to battle to "all the surrounding nations" (3:11) in the valley of Jehoshaphat (3:12; cf. 3:2 which creates B and B′). Both the genre and the location of the battle signify its outcome. Rhetorically, the nations are called to battle against YHWH and YHWH's army, a fight they cannot expect to win. Likewise, the name of the battle site, Jehoshaphat, means "Yahweh will judge." The center section of this call to battle (3:14-16, 18) connects intertextually to Joel and other texts, which likely reflects editorial adaptation of the preexisting call to battle for the context of Joel.[63] Joel 3:9-17 thus describes the day of Yahweh as a day of judgment against the nations that leads to security in Zion and Jerusalem.

Joel within the Book of the Twelve

Joel has been called the literary anchor to the Book of the Twelve, and its prophet has been called a scriptural interpreter who created an example of scribal prophecy.[64] These terms point to the way in which Joel draws upon biblical imagery and phraseology to make its case, and the extent to which this happens suggests that the final form of Joel is quite cognizant of its location between Hosea and Amos and its role in the Book of the Twelve.

When one recognizes the extent of Joel's use of other texts, from Exodus, Deuteronomy, and several prophetic writings, one can hardly be unimpressed

196

with the extent of this phenomenon. Yet, three particular features should be noted to show the extent to which Joel presupposes its location in the Twelve: its overlapping genres, its allusions to Hosea and Amos at the beginning and end of Joel, and the use of Joel in other writings. All three of these add texture and substance to the idea that Joel presupposes its literary context between Hosea and Amos and raises the question of how one should interpret the book with this knowledge.

In the early collection of the Four, Amos followed Hosea, and both focused on the Northern Kingdom. Whereas Hosea concludes with an open-ended call to repentance, leaving open the possibility that Israel might return to YHWH, the book of Amos allows no such ambiguity. Its message consistently announces Israel's destruction. By adding Joel, the redactors of the Twelve used genres at the beginning and end of Joel that dovetail with Hosea and Amos. Joel 1:2–2:17 now follows the call to repentance in Hosea 14 with its own extended, open-ended call to repentance, except Joel's call addresses Judah and Jerusalem, not the Northern Kingdom. The last chapter of Joel functions as a series of eschatological oracles against the nations that will result in Jerusalem's deliverance, while Amos 1–2 functions as a collection of oracles against the nations that results in Israel's destruction. This pairing of the fate of Israel with that of Judah deliberately interrupts the thematic focus on Israel's destruction that dominates Hosea and Amos. With the insertion of Joel, the Twelve more quickly signals its concern with the fate of Judah and Jerusalem.

Joel's thematic parallels between the fate of Israel and Judah also appear by evoking the language of Hosea and Amos. Joel's use of Hosea includes allusions, citations, and imitations.[65] Allusions, citations, and thematic contrast also link Joel and Amos. As already noted, Joel 3:16, 18 (Heb. 4:16, 18) effectively encompasses the book of Amos by citing Amos 1:2 and 9:13 respectively. At least one interpreter has noted that these citations attempt to reframe the oracles against nations and Amos in general into an eschatological composition.[66] These parallels certainly heighten the future orientation of Joel itself. Finally, Joel combines the themes of the repentance of YHWH's people from Hosea 14 with the theme of the day of YHWH. These two themes dominate Joel, but both play a significant role in Amos as well (4:6-12 and 5:18-24).[67]

The language of Joel also becomes embedded in other books within the Twelve (see below), subtly reminding readers that Joel's paradigm of history unfolds across the Book of the Twelve in the form of threats and promises. As mentioned above, the reader of the Twelve encounters the language of Joel periodically in other books. Not all these parallels were redactionally implanted into those settings, but in a number of instances, such is the case. When they do appear, these Joel-related images tend to cluster around two motifs: (1) the arrival of the locusts as punishment, and (2) the infertility or fertility of the land as a sign of curses for covenant infidelity.

From an early point in Jewish interpretation, a stream of reading has interpreted the locusts as attacking nations, though the powerful images of one locust plague followed by another and another has also created interpretations involving actual locusts.[68] In actuality, judging by how locusts appear in the Twelve, both may be intended for the final form of Joel.[69]

The land's fertility as a sign of YHWH's beneficence plays a prominent role in the recurring motifs of the Twelve by using some version of grain, wine, and (olive) oil. This triad utilizes common words, but using the cluster to symbolize the fertility and infertility of the land represents one of the distinctive motifs running across the Twelve in ways that do not appear in the other three prophetic scrolls.[70] Beyond this fixed phrase, variations of this imagery appear in Hosea 14:7 (Heb. 14:8); Amos 5:11; Habakkuk 3:17; Zechariah 3:10; 8:12; and Malachi 3:11. To be sure, one cannot classify all these passages as creations of a single redactor, but they are distinctive to the Twelve. In several ways, they intertwine with the day of YHWH motifs across the Twelve. The fate of the land as a sign of YHWH's pleasure or displeasure represents a recurring motif running through the Twelve, and this motif, as with others, appears prominently in Joel.

So, how should one conceptualize Joel's role in the Book of the Twelve? It focuses the reader's attention upon Judah and Jerusalem as opposed to the Northern Kingdom of Israel. Its motifs transcend the chronological structure created by other superscriptions that mention kings within the Book of the Twelve. Its imagery has sparked polyvalent interpretations of the book: from one prophet's reaction to a localized locust plague to a proto-apocalyptic treatise that anticipates the "history" of Judah unfolding through the Book of the Twelve. Steck describes the reading of a prophetic scroll within the metahistorical narrative with which it interacts.[71] In this sense, Joel becomes paradigmatic for the Book of the Twelve as a whole. YHWH seeks to punish Judah and Jerusalem for abandoning their covenant loyalty to YHWH, and the prophet calls out to the people to return to their God. The reader of the Twelve slowly learns that the people as a whole do not return to YHWH until the narrated response in Zechariah 1:6 (especially in conjunction with Haggai). Instead, Micah, Habakkuk, and Zephaniah make increasingly clear that judgment against Jerusalem cannot be avoided. At the same time, that judgment is not the end of the story. Those nations that attack Judah will themselves be taken down. Nahum and Habakkuk document the downfall of Assyria and Babylon respectively. Texts embedded within the books of the Twelve, in both its predestruction (Hosea–Zephaniah) and postmonarchic (Haggai–Malachi) sections, anticipate Judah's restoration and the ultimate conquest of the nations. The reader of Joel encounters these changes, and they are repeated across the Book of the Twelve. In this respect, Joel functions as the literary anchor to the Twelve and as the Book of the Twelve in miniature.

Joel also provokes theological discussions, two of the most important of which are the various concepts of the day of YHWH and how to respond to YHWH's justice and compassion. Joel presents at least three different conceptualizations of the day of YHWH: a day of judgment directed against YHWH's own people for unnamed wrongdoing; potential deliverance of YHWH's people should they repent; and eschatological judgment against those nations who have taken advantage of Judah.

Joel draws upon YHWH's self-presentation in Exodus 34:6-7 where YHWH describes himself as both a God of patient compassion and a God who punishes the guilty. These verses form the rationale in Joel and Micah 7 for hope that YHWH's patience with YHWH's people has not been exhausted and in Joel and Nahum 1 that YHWH will punish those who take advantage of Judah. These same verses also elicit discussion in Jonah 4 about whether YHWH should show the same compassion on foreign nations that he has demonstrated for YHWH's own people.

Obadiah

The Prophet and the Book

No biographical data appears in this short book. The superscription conveys no reference to the prophet's family or his hometown, and it provides no reference to a ruling monarch.[72] One can only infer a limited amount of data regarding the prophet, and much of that depends upon decisions made about the composition of the book. By most recent scholarly accounts, Obadiah shows considerable awareness of the content of other anti-Edom material and traditions in the Hebrew Bible. This knowledge presupposes scribal training in these texts. Relatedly, the promises in Obadiah have a distinctly Jerusalemite focus that anticipates Jerusalem as a place of safety for a remnant population. Almost certainly, both the knowledge of these texts and the concern for Jerusalem suggest that city as the location in which the prophet worked in the Persian period.

The name Obadiah is quite common in the Old Testament, with at least twelve different persons carrying the moniker.[73] Early Jewish tradition (Sanhedrin 39b) associates the book with the Obadiah who plays a role in the Elijah narratives. Critical scholarship, however, has largely discounted this tradition as historically inaccurate, but some argue that the editor who added the name to the book was trying to make the association.[74] A few have suggested that the name itself is an eponym, much like Malachi. Unlike the case for Malachi (as borrowing the name from Mal 3:1), however, nothing in Obadiah plays on the meaning of the name. Most, therefore, assume that Obadiah was the name associated with the composition of Obadiah 1-15 (or 1-21), but that we simply lack further biographic data.

Historical Backdrop to Obadiah

Virtual unanimity exists that the book of Obadiah stems from a period following the destruction of Jerusalem because verses 10-14 make explicit reference to Jerusalem's downfall by a foreign enemy. Yet, this consensus breaks down quickly, both historically and literarily, when one tries to narrow that time frame. The history of Edom after 587 BCE has been much debated. Conflicting reconstructions exist. Until recently, scholars tended to describe Edom as a nation-state that ceased to exist following an invasion by the Nabateans sometime in the sixth, fifth, or fourth century BCE. Increasingly, however, archaeological excavations have created problems for the theory of the Nabateans invading the country on a massive scale.[75] On the literary level, attempts to refine the date of the book become complicated by a series of decisions that individual scholars must make in terms of how the final form of Obadiah came to be. Respect for the coherence of the book has grown in recent decades, but a great many scholars still see Obadiah as a composite literary work, with the first fifteen verses stemming from one or more sources pronouncing Edom's downfall while the last six verses only mention Edom as one example of the fate awaiting all the nations who take action against Judah and Jerusalem.

References to political events point in different directions. Whereas the content of verses 11-14 presupposes knowledge of Jerusalem's destruction in 587 BCE, the language of the negative commands (*vetitives*) assumes that the author is warning Edom prior to 587. Further, a significant contingent of scholars understands the political situation described in Obadiah 19-21 to align more closely to expectations from the late Persian period than from the early Persian period. The implications of these different clues play out in the ways that scholars explain the composition of the book (see "Dating the Prophet and the Book" below).

The Structure and Contents of Obadiah

For all its brevity and clarity of message, Obadiah poses difficulties for determining how to understand its structure, date, and purpose. The primary difficulties have to do with structural models and Obadiah's use of preexisting material, especially its relationship to Jeremiah 49 and Amos 9 (the passage that precedes Obadiah in the Book of the Twelve).

Structural Models for Obadiah

Scholars have little difficulty noting transition points in the rhetorical flow of Obadiah, but this ease of recognition also complicates the question of how to understand the changes. The problem derives from the fact that Obadiah contains numerous examples of stylistic dissonance and formulaic expressions that scholars frequently treat as markers for the beginnings or endings of new prophetic units. The book contains a superscription (v. 1), the phrase "utterance of YHWH" that can mark the end of the unit (v. 4), the phrase "on that day" that often introduces a new unit (v. 8), a dramatic shift in theme from judgment against Edom to judgment against the nations (v. 15), followed by an equally obvious change of addressee from singular to plural (v. 16), and yet another concluding formula: "for YHWH has spoken" (v. 18). Relying upon these formal criteria exclusively, one could argue that Obadiah represents a collection of no fewer than six sayings that have been collected as an anthology of prophetic utterances (1-4, 5-7, 8-14, 15, 16-18, 19-21).

Nevertheless, most scholars do not divide the units this way because the rhetorical flow suggests more coherence of thought than these markers explain by themselves. For instance, Obadiah 1-4 parallels Jeremiah 49:14-16, but Obadiah 5 has direct parallels to Jeremiah 49:9, suggesting that one would be hard-pressed to disassociate Obadiah 1-4 from v. 5.[76] Yet, a significant number of scholars see signs of later theological paradigms in Obadiah 19-20, but they recognize that these verses comment on the immediate context and thus cannot be classified as independent sayings.[77] Hence, despite its brevity, Obadiah poses a host of difficulties in determining its literary parameters.

For three reasons it appears that the primary point of disjuncture is in Obadiah 15. First, material before and after Obadiah 15 deals with two distinct themes. Verses 1-14 deal consistently with Edom's punishment for its actions against Jerusalem. Verses 16-21 have their own logic depicting the coming judgment as a day of YHWH against all nations who will be forced to drink YHWH's cup of wrath (v. 16) while Zion (= Jerusalem) and the house of Jacob (= Judah) will not only be spared (v. 17), but will launch aggressive campaigns against Edom (v. 18) and other regions surrounding Jerusalem with the goal of reestablishing the boundaries of the ideal kingdom (vv. 19-20) as proof of Zion's centrality and the kingship of YHWH (v. 21).

Second, the change in theme corresponds with the distinct change in addressee. Verses 1-14 consistently address Edom directly using second masculine singular verbs and pronouns. Verses 16-21, by contrast, address a different group using second masculine plural pronouns and referring to Edom in the third person.

Third, suppositions regarding what will happen on the day of YHWH presuppose three distinct conceptualizations. Both 1-14 and 16-21 anticipate an impending day of YHWH, but like Joel, Obadiah does not portray a uniform view of what will happen on that day. Obadiah 1-14 assumes two different targets for two distinct but interrelated days of YHWH. Obadiah 1-14, 15b anticipates a "day" of intervention against Edom (v. 8) because it took action against Jacob on Jacob's "day" (vv. 10, 12). Verses 11-14 *anticipate* judgment against Edom, but they presume that Judah has already experienced its own day of disaster. Judah's day of punishment lies in the past and the threat of punishment for Edom lies ahead because of Edom's role in that past day of YHWH against Judah. Yet, verses 11-14 are formulated as negative commands (*vetitives*). Syntactically, they tell Edom what it *should not do* when Jerusalem is punished ("Do not . . .").[78] This confusion over whether the judgment against Jerusalem has already occurred is resolved by English translations with pluperfect formulations ("You should not have . . ."), but vetitives do not function this way logically or syntactically. Instead, one should treat these commands as warnings to Edom not to do in the future what everyone knows they did already.[79]

The concept of the day of YHWH in 15a, 16-21 is much more diffuse. Verse 15a and 16-17 anticipate a future day of YHWH against "all the nations" for what they have (also) done to Zion. Verse 18 anticipates action by a unified force from Jacob (= Judah) and Joseph (= the northern territory of Israel) sanctioned by YHWH against Esau (= Edom), while verses 19-20 articulate a series of resettlements (i.e., repossessions) by returning refugees who will repopulate the land with Jerusalem at its center, including repopulating the territory of Ephraim and Samaria, whose inhabitants are presumed to be participating with Judah in v. 18.[80] The most likely explanation of the diversity of these concepts in 15a, 16-21 is that the compiler of Obadiah borrowed from an existing speech (much like the way verses 1-5 begin with Jer 49:14-16, 9) but adapted this source in light of Amos 9:11-12 (see below).[81]

Parallels with Jeremiah 49:7-22 and Amos 9

A second key to understanding the rhetorical function of Obadiah appears in the degree to which Obadiah borrows from other texts. Two texts in particular play a structuring role, Jeremiah 49:7-22 and Amos 9. The relationship between Jeremiah 49:14-16 and 49:9 and Obadiah 1-5 has long been observed and represents one of the longest examples of nearly verbatim parallel texts in the entire prophetic canon. Debates have tended to focus on the question of which text borrowed from which. What has become increasingly difficult to ignore, however, is the extent to which the parallels between Jeremiah 49:9, 14-16 and Obadiah extend well beyond the nearly verbatim citation and include parallel phrases from the rest of Jeremiah 49:7-22. Consequently, a shift in the conversation has begun that recognizes Obadiah, in its entirety, as a pastiche of anti-Edom material heavily influenced by other prophetic texts, but also composed with a rather elaborate knowledge of anti-Edomite teaching. Jeremias is undoubtedly correct that Obadiah should be treated as scribal prophecy.[82] The composition of Obadiah exhibits an allusive style that has to be taken into account in order to appreciate fully the message of the book.

The nearly verbatim parallels between Obadiah 1-5 and Jeremiah 49:14-16, 9 are well documented and need not be recounted here since those comparisons would require careful analysis of the Hebrew.[83] A majority of scholars consider Obadiah as the borrower and not the source (though disagreement continues over whether Obadiah borrows specifically from Jeremiah or from a common source).[84] Despite arguments to the contrary, the majority position that Obadiah draws from Jeremiah (and not some putative common source) remains the best explanation of this citation. This borrowing, especially after v. 5, should be classified as allusive texture (not quotation) adding to the broader argument of Obadiah.

A number of scholars now recognize that connections between Obadiah and Jeremiah's oracles extend throughout Jeremiah 49:7-22.[85] Jeremias, in fact, offers a compelling portrait of these parallels and how they fit within a three-part structure (Obad 1-7, 8-14, and 15-21).[86]

Verses	Obad	
1-7	1aα	quotes Jer 49:7aα, the introduction to the Edom collection (in reverse order)
	1aβ-4	quotes Jer 49:14-16 nearly verbatim
	5	quotes Jer 49:9 nearly verbatim, but reverses 49:9b and 49:9a
	6	alludes more freely to Jer 49:10a
8-14	8	alludes to Jer 49:7aβ (the wisdom of Teman)
	9	alludes to Jer 49:10b
	9	picks up the image of the warriors of Teman from Jer 49:22.[87]
15-21	15-21 exegetes Jer 49:12 (the cup of YHWH's wrath must pass to Edom)	

Just as significantly for Jeremias, the three sections of Obadiah each begin with clear allusions to or quotations from Jeremiah 49:7-22.[88]

In addition to the close parallels between Obadiah and the anti-Edom oracles of Jeremiah and Ezekiel, Obadiah displays several linguistic, structural, and thematic parallels with Amos 9. When one looks at the number of unusual phrases, formulaic elements, and themes, the quality and quantity of these parallels are striking:

Linguistic, Structural, and Thematic Parallels	Amos	Obad
Vision	9:1	1
Five "if/though" clauses (using *ky*)	9:2-4	4-5
No escape from YHWH: "from there I will bring them/you down"	9:2	4
Destruction and remnant motifs (using agricultural imagery)	9:7-10	5
Thematic shifts/text markers with "Is it not"	9:7	8
"on that day"	9:11	8
"utterance of YHWH"	9:7,8,13	8
Introduction with eschatological "day" saying	9:11	15
Allusion to destruction of Jerusalem	9:11	16
Restoration of Davidic kingdom boundaries	9:11	19-20
"Possession" of Edom and other nations	9:12	17-20
Eschatological/agricultural abundance	9:13	—
Restoration of captivity/exiles	9:14	19-20
Restoration/reclamation of cities	9:14	20
Concluding promise for the restoration of the land/kingdom	9:15	21

These parallels demand explanation. The fact that they appear so closely to one another in the Book of the Twelve has been noted by a number of scholars, but the implications of this parallel are seldom explored.[89] At the end of the day, however, the transition from Amos to Obadiah in the Book of the Twelve presents a scenario that describes the downfall of the Northern Kingdom and the future overthrow of Edom. The fates of these two entities appear closely together, a fact which (along with their structural and thematic parallels) suggests a logical connection. Some scholars go to considerable lengths to interpret Edom in Obadiah purely as a cipher for all nations, but the answer is far simpler. Edom is Edom. Israel and Edom are Judah's two neighboring kingdoms that share deep ethnic and familial ties to Judah in its traditional literature. Esau is the twin brother of Jacob (Israel), and Obadiah highlights those ties. The Northern Kingdom of Israel broke away from Judah and its Davidic king, and they are destroyed in Amos 9 while Obadiah puts them back together to retaliate against Edom (Obad 18). The Twelve does not take a neutral stance on these two kingdoms, but repeatedly emphasizes the ascendancy of the Zion tradition, the centrality of Jerusalem, and the hope for reunification.

Dating the Prophet and the Book

As noted already, a significant group of scholars emphasizes the coherence of Obadiah over against signs of a composite origin. Definitions of this coherence usually involve taking the focus on Edom in 1-14 as a specific illustration of the author's larger agenda of the day of YHWH as a day of judgment against all nations (16-21).

Scholars usually take one of three paths to narrowing the time frame for Obadiah: (1) some harmonize the evidence in ways that could possibly explain the divergent settings as the work of a single author in the sixth or fifth century;[90] (2) most see the final form of Obadiah as the product of more than one author,[91] even though it is only twenty-one verses long (and debate continues about which verses were added later[92]); or (3) some see the book as the work of a single compiler adapting two or more sources, which receive additional insertions that comment on the existing text.[93] These models are closely associated with different understandings of how Obadiah reached the form in which it currently appears.[94] Here, it suffices to acknowledge that scholars still debate among several different contexts ranging from shortly after the time of Jerusalem's destruction in 587 BCE down to the sacking of Jerusalem by Ptolemy I in 302 BCE. A decided shift has occurred in that fewer scholars are willing to claim Obadiah 1-5 as the source of Jeremiah 49:14-16 + 9 or claim that Obadiah represents an eyewitness to the events of 587 BCE. In the end, though complete consensus has not yet been reached regarding Obadiah's absolute date, an increasing number see Obadiah's final form as the product of a middle to late Persian-period scribal prophet working with preexisting traditions to create an anthology of anti-Edomite sayings. The anthology has a purpose: to warn Edom as Judah and Israel had been warned before YHWH executed judgment on them.

Obadiah, the Book of the Twelve, and the Rest of the Latter Prophets

The structure and themes of Obadiah mirror those of Amos 9, thereby creating a book in which Edom joins Samaria and the Northern Kingdom as the recipient of YHWH's wrath. These two entities represent the countries with the closest ties to Judah. Both should have been part of the ideal kingdom promised to Abraham and realized ever so briefly in the time of David and Solomon, at least as remembered through the literary repository of the Deuteronomistic History and the Torah. Critical scholars in the last century rightly point out that this recollection of the grand kingdoms of David and Solomon represents an idealized past, but that conclusion does not change the fact that those producing prophetic writings like Obadiah would have accepted these traditions not only as the way things used to be but also as the way they should be in the future. Hence, both Amos 9 and Obadiah end with promises of restoration and unification, though restoration has a decidedly Judean perspective. The promises assume that Jerusalem, the Northern Kingdom, and Edom have been punished. The promises of unification, however, present a hope for a new kingdom with Jerusalem at the center and that includes the territory of the former Northern Kingdom (Amos 9:11-15) and the territory of Esau or Edom (Obad 19-20).

The warnings in Obadiah 11-14 not to do to Jacob what every informed reader knows they did function as a literary warning, not a narrative of past sin. This warning is paired with the assumption in Malachi 1:2-5 of Edom's downfall as proof not only of YHWH's punishment of Edom but also of YHWH's love of Jacob. This pairing of the warning to Edom of YHWH's impending judgment that presages Edom's fall at YHWH's initiative with the assumption of Edom's downfall in Malachi 1:2-5 offers a striking parallel to the same dynamic in the book of Isaiah, where the warnings of Edom's punishment in chapter 34 anticipate the description of the warrior YHWH who has defeated Edom in chapter 63.

Obadiah draws extensively from other anti-Edom sayings, but most extensively from Jeremiah 49. Yet, Obadiah's reworking of this material highlights Obadiah's distinctives in comparison to Jeremiah and Ezekiel. Obadiah condemns Edom, but does so with a much more prominent focus upon Zion as the center of YHWH's eschatological kingdom.

In a related way, Joel's citation (2:32 [Heb. 3:5]) of Obadiah 17 links these two books on either side of Amos, and it also emphasizes a similar eschatological perspective that accentuates the role of Zion and Jerusalem as a place of safety for those who call on the name of YHWH. On the one hand, this emphasis is not surprising since the Zion tradition has a long history and features prominently in Isaiah, Jeremiah, and the Twelve (though the name is assiduously avoided in Ezekiel). On the other hand, because it is expected, these connected motifs can often be ignored or overlooked when talking about the cohesion of the Twelve as a compendium of YHWH's prophetic word to Judah from the eighth century to the Persian period.

Jonah

The Prophet and the Book

As a prophet, Jonah is both an abject failure and a tremendous success. Jonah fails every test as a prophet. When called to proclaim YHWH's message by heading east across the desert, Jonah heads west across the ocean. Instead of recognizing communication with YHWH as a great honor, Jonah seeks to escape YHWH's presence. We as readers learn these character traits in the first three verses of the book. Thereafter, the story's narrator never misses a chance to satirize this prophet. While the storm rages and the sailors pray, Jonah lies fast asleep. While the sailors try to save his life, Jonah tells them to throw him into the ocean. When given a second chance to address the Ninevites, Jonah utters only five words. When YHWH shows grace to the Ninevites, Jonah asks YHWH to take his life so he does not have to see it. At every turn, Jonah becomes the example of how not to behave. If one misses this element of the book, and the humorous way it develops, one misses much of the point. The way of Jonah is the wrong way to follow YHWH.

Yet Jonah's message succeeds, much to his chagrin. His five-word sermon causes the people of Nineveh and then its king to repent. The king even makes the cattle fast and put on sackcloth. The city and its people, described as evil at the beginning of the book, become paradigms of a radical change of life. Their change moves YHWH to change his decision to destroy them, and instead YHWH responds to their penitent response and allows them to live. Only Jonah is unhappy with the outcome.

Literary and Historical Settings for Jonah

When considering Jonah's setting, one must distinguish between the literary setting in which the action takes place and the time of Jonah's composition by an author who lived roughly 400 years after the time of the prophet. Jonah represents one of the few prophets named in the book of Kings who have a book about them in the canon. As for its literary setting, the selection of Jonah, son of Amittai, as the central character around whom to compose a story already seems an unlikely choice. Jonah appears during the reign of Jeroboam II, king of Israel (786–746 BCE). The mention of Jonah in Kings stands out for its brevity, its

207

content, and the irony it poses for the prophetic character who appears in the book of Jonah. Jonah appears in part of one verse (2 Kgs 14:25) and tells Jeroboam YHWH will restore the territory from Lebo-hamath in the north to the Sea of Arabah in the south. The content of YHWH's decision to expand Israel's territory (14:25) is at odds with the condemnation of Jeroboam for not removing the sanctuaries at Bethel and Dan in the previous verse (14:24). Consequently, Jonah in Kings has often been interpreted as a court prophet hired by the king to provide counsel. Such prophets often appear as negative characters in Kings, but ironically such is not the case with Jonah, whose message comes true.

Consider the irony involved in the selection and portrayal of Jonah. The book of Jonah portrays him as the anti-prophet through the use of satire. The prophet in the book admonishes the Ninevites with a message of imminent destruction, but it never happens because YHWH changes his mind when all of Nineveh repents, which Jonah knew would happen all along (4:2). Adding insult to injury, Jonah's sermon leads to Nineveh's deliverance, and those who know Israel's history know that within two decades of Jeroboam's death, Israel fell prey to the military expansion of the Assyrians. Hence, the prophet who pronounces the expansion of Israel's territory also delivers the sermon that enables Assyria to subjugate Israel. Hence, the literary backdrop of 2 Kings 14:25 is not incidental to the poignancy of the Jonah story.

That being said, critical scholarship does not treat Jonah as a historical narrative, but as a satire or novella that is one of the latest prophetic books. The author was not a contemporary of the eighth-century prophet. Most investigations think the book was written sometime in the latter half of the fourth century BCE, toward the end of the Persian period or in the early Hellenistic period. Evidence for this late date is widely recognized and includes linguistic factors, the history of thought, and the book's genre.[95] Exact dates are difficult to determine with Jonah because the characters reflect the author's attempt to put the action in the literary setting of eighth-century Israel and Assyria. The hyperbole involved in these descriptions, however, does not correspond well with the historical realia of Nineveh in the eighth century.[96] All this evidence suggests Jonah, in all likelihood, represents the latest complete book to enter the prophetic canon.[97]

The Structure and Contents

The structure and contents of Jonah are driven by its plot. The plot of Jonah unfolds essentially as a satire consisting of five scenes: Jonah's commission and flight (1:1-3), Jonah and the sailors onboard the ship (1:4-16), Jonah's prayer of thanksgiving (1:17–2:10), Jonah's sermon to the Assyrians (3:1-10), Jonah's confrontation with YHWH over YHWH's compassion (4:1-11).

Jonah's commission and flight (1:1-3) set the tone for the whole book when it begins with the narrative account of Jonah's commission from YHWH to head east and deliver a message of judgment against Nineveh, the grand, evil city of Assyria. Yet Jonah's response sends him in precisely the opposite direction as he finds a boat going to Tarshish, probably a city in Spain at the far edges of the Mediterranean. The humor begins to unfold almost immediately. Not only does the prophet head in the opposite direction YHWH told him to go, but he does so hoping to escape "from the presence of YHWH" as we are told twice in 1:3. Anyone hearing the story of Jonah has to laugh at the thought of a prophet who not only disobeys YHWH but does so thinking he can escape from YHWH's presence. Additionally, twice 1:3 states that Jonah is heading in the direction of Tarshish, but when describing the boat, the verse says that the *boat* is going to Tarshish. Thus, the narrator slyly tips his hand. Though Jonah has "gone down" to Joppa and found a boat going to Tarshish, Jonah himself will never get there.

The scene describing Jonah and the sailors onboard the ship (1:4-16) continues the artful humor by describing YHWH's decision to send a dreadful storm against a personified boat (which considers breaking into pieces) and by describing the sailors' frightened response. First, the sailors pray to their own gods, and then they begin throwing cargo overboard in an effort to lighten the load of the boat. The humor does not diminish the danger, but it presents a story that runs against type. Israel, as a landlocked country, did not produce sailors. The sailors are foreigners, as is evident when the narrator indicates that each prays to his own god (1:5). Further, sailors are not known as a pious lot in any culture, yet the very first thing they do when faced with YHWH's storm is pray. Meanwhile Jonah had "gone down" into the belly of the ship and fallen fast asleep (1:5). In desperation, the captain of the sailors pleads with Jonah to pray as well (1:6). Thus, in response to the storm, it is not YHWH's prophet who responds in prayer but the foreign sailors.

After the sailors had prayed and thrown the cargo overboard, the storm still raged, so they cast lots to determine who on the ship had angered a deity (1:7). Not surprisingly, the lot falls on Jonah, but surprisingly, these foreign sailors do not rush to take care of the problem. They ask a series of questions (1:8): "Tell us *why* this calamity has come upon us. What is your occupation? Where do you come from? What is your country? What people do you belong to?" Jonah's response—that he worships the God who created heaven and earth—creates even more fear for the sailors, and yet they still do not try to kill Jonah (1:9-10). Instead, after repeated failures to row the boat out of the storm, Jonah tells them to cast him into the sea (1:11-13). As a result, the sailors pray to Jonah's God, throw him overboard, and offer sacrifices to YHWH, Jonah's God, because the sea stopped raging. Thus, Jonah's flight converts the foreign sailors into YHWH-fearers who offer sacrifice to the creator of heaven and earth (1:14-16). This conversion not only runs against type, but becomes even more comical when Jonah later confesses (4:2) that he disobeyed YHWH because he did not like the fact that he knew YHWH would end up showing compassion to the Assyrians. The satire is biting. Jonah wants to reserve YHWH's mercy for Israel, and yet Jonah's actions not once but twice bring light to the nations.

Meanwhile, Jonah's prayer of thanksgiving and account of deliverance (1:17–2:10) continues both the humor toward the prophet and the seriousness of the narrator's agenda. Jonah has descended once again, this time into the belly of a fish provided by YHWH, where after three days he finally offers a prayer (1:17 [Heb. 2:1]) whose content humorously unfolds as a thanksgiving song (2:2-9 [Heb. 2:3-10]). The psalmist recounts Jonah's deliverance, but Jonah remains in the belly of the fish at the bottom of the ocean. Scholars rightly note that the song does not fit the setting of the narrative despite the overlap of some of its vocabulary (see the discussion of the unity of Jonah below). In all likelihood, this preexisting song was inserted into the narrative.

Jonah's sermon to the Assyrians and their response (3:1-10) begins with the second command to Jonah to go and speak to them (3:1-2). This time, Jonah obeys, but barely. He walks into the city and utters the Bible's shortest and most effective sermon, consisting of only five words that do not even make a complete sentence: "Yet forty days—Nineveh overturned" (3:4). Jonah does not tell them why, nor does he tell them how to avoid the judgment. Yet, miraculously, they know. The people of Nineveh believe God, proclaim a fast, and put on sackcloth (a sign of mourning). For the second time in the book, Jonah's words and deeds set the stage for God's grace to foreigners. After the people repent, even the king of Nineveh gets in on the act. Upon hearing the report of the people's response, the king rises from his throne, puts on sackcloth, and then sits in ashes while he cartoonishly articulates an official proclamation to call a fast for all the people of Nineveh (3:7-8), which the people had already done (3:6). Yet the king does not stop with a simple, redundant proclamation. He raises the ante by inflicting the fast upon the animals as well as the people. He requires that all the animals shall also be covered with sackcloth and that all of them shall cry to God with great force (3:8). The king then commands all the people to repent of their ways and their violence (3:9). And then the king of Assyria displays his own Bible knowledge by quoting Joel 2:14: "Who knows? God may relent and change his mind . . ." The king adapts the quote for Nineveh's context: ". . . and he will turn from his fierce anger so that we do not perish" (3:9). Not surprisingly, YHWH did precisely this (3:10).

Jonah's confrontation with YHWH over YHWH's compassion (4:1-11) forms the climax of the book. It begins when Jonah petulantly complains that YHWH had extended mercy to Nineveh (4:1). Jonah utters a prayer of confrontation with all the righteous indignation he can muster. Jonah finally reveals why he disobeyed YHWH at the start of his journey. Jonah tells YHWH that he is too soft and compassionate, and that his reasoning (like the king of Nineveh's) mirrors the reasoning of Joel (2:12-13). Joel called YHWH's people to fast and repent in order to avoid destruction on the day of YHWH before citing Exodus 34:6 to remind YHWH that YHWH is gracious, compassionate, and slow to anger. Jonah uses the same words to complain. He vehemently disagrees with YHWH's decision and asks YHWH to kill him because death would be preferable to living in this situation (4:3). YHWH responds with a rhetorical question, asking Jonah what right he has to be so angry (4:4). Instead of responding, Jonah goes outside the city where he builds a hut to protect himself from the sun while he waits to see what happens (4:5). YHWH sends a plant to grow over the hut and provide shade for Jonah, for which Jonah is quite happy (4:6). His happiness disappears, however, when YHWH sends a worm to devour the plant providing the shade, which causes Jonah to ask YHWH to kill him a second time (4:7-8) using the same words he had used in 4:3. At this point, Jonah's request appears petty and small. God gives Jonah one last chance to learn by asking him a pointed question: "Is it right for you to be angry about the bush?" The depth of Jonah's obstinance becomes clear to all in his response (4:9): "Yes, angry enough to die." God, however, has the final word in the book, turning Jonah's response into a parable by asking another rhetorical question that puts Jonah in his place by pointing out the narrowness of his world. The loss of a plant triggered Jonah's anger, but YHWH's question hangs in the air as the book closes: "And should I not be concerned about Nineveh, that great city, in which there are more than 120,000 persons who do not know their right hand from their left, and also many animals?" (4:11).

Jonah's bigotry causes him to go to great lengths to keep from being God's messenger to the foreigners. It costs him dearly and gains him nothing. He cannot escape YHWH's presence and cannot change God's merciful character. In fact, Jonah's righteous indignation accomplished the dramatic conversion of foreigners not once but twice, first with the sailors who learned to recognize the power of the creator of heaven and earth and then with the utter repentance of the people and the king of Nineveh. No prophet accomplished more than Jonah, and Jonah despises the fact that he has been the medium through which YHWH's grace could flow.

The story of Jonah certainly stands out dramatically in the prophetic corpus, not only because Jonah is portrayed as a petulant prophet but also because the story cuts against the grain of how many experience the reading of prophetic books which repeatedly anticipate Israel's deliverance and the subjugation of the nations. Apart from Jonah, every book in the Twelve essentially ends with hope for the restoration of YHWH's people, for punishment against the nations, or

both. So, the book of Jonah is distinctive. The fact that the book of Jonah sati-
rizes the prophet Jonah and values YHWH's mercy over God's wrath represents
an important theological tenet and ethical corrective. As a single piece of literature, Jonah could be viewed as the isolated protest of a single artist who saw the
hypocrisy of worshiping a universal God who was *only* interested in showing
mercy to a single people. Yet, this biting satire exposes the prophet's piosity and
pomposity as the narrow-minded bigotry clothed in religiosity that it is, and it
was recognized as an important theological corrective that had to be included
among the Twelve.

Questions of Unity

Debates about the unity of Jonah have arisen through the years, with particular emphasis on whether Jonah 1 is a separate story, whether Jonah's thanksgiving song represents a later insertion (2:2-9 [Heb. 2:3-10]), and how to explain the narrative tensions created by 4:5. The work of Jonathan Magonet and
others demonstrates to many that Jonah 1 represents an extremely artistically
constructed narrative structure with an observably chiastic form.[98] This type of
artistic structure does not present itself in the other three chapters of Jonah,
causing some to question how to explain this quality of chapter 1 only.[99] While
a minority position, several scholars claim that the original narrative of Jonah
did not involve a flight across the ocean.[100] Their theories suggest it is possible to
conceptualize Jonah 1 as a later introduction, which would at least account for
the chapter's tight artistic structure as the work of a later author whose literary
embellishments added to the satire of Jonah.

Questions also exist about the thanksgiving hymn as the insertion of a preexisting hymn to provide the content of Jonah's prayer that gives him something of
a public-relations make over.[101] The most notable problem with the thanksgiving
song in comparison to the narrative derives from the fact that the thanksgiving
song presupposes that the psalmist has already been delivered, while the narrative presumes Jonah is crying out for deliverance from the belly of the fish. Some
unconvincingly try to explain away this difference by interpreting this jarring
discrepancy as part of the author's satire of the character Jonah.[102] Some interpret
the insertion of the song as an attempt to provide Jonah with some level of pious
respectability.[103] Some recognize the discrepancy and the resulting complications,
but opt to focus on the rhetorical function.[104] The questions of the motivation
for inserting the psalm remain harder to evaluate than does the evidence that it
was incorporated into an already existing narrative. In addition to the disjuncture of whether or not Jonah has been delivered already, the narrative reads more
smoothly if the song is removed.

Questions about the integrity of Jonah 4 surface periodically because 4:1-4 portrays Jonah as responding angrily to the repentance of the Ninevites, while 4:5 states that Jonah heads east of the city to wait to see what happens. Three models for explaining this discrepancy can be found in the secondary literature.

First, some argued in the twentieth century that 4:5 was accidentally transposed from earlier in the narrative. The discovery of the Dead Sea Scrolls and other biblical texts in the Judean desert has done much to dispel this image of scribal sloppiness.[105] As a result, the explanation of scribal error has largely disappeared in the last fifty years and has been replaced with the idea that 4:5 functions deliberately as a flashback.[106] A third model suggests that the tensions are best explained by the assumption that more than one hand created the narrative. They argue that Jonah was revised over time, undergoing literary changes from two or more layers of redactional activity.[107] In most cases 4:5 functions as the earliest response. One can also observe that 4:2-3 presents the content of Jonah's prayer (much like the insertion of 2:2-9 provided the content of Jonah's prayer in the belly of the fish). Significantly, 4:2-3 reflects upon the story of Jonah in light of other texts. In 4:2, Jonah explains why he fled at the beginning of the book, and that explanation is based upon YHWH's character as quoted from Exodus 34:6. Yet, this citation evokes Joel's citation of Exodus 34:6 (Joel 2:13) rather than citing Exodus 34:6 directly.

Exod 34:6 (NRSV)	Joel 2:13 (NRSV)	Jonah 4:2 (NRSV)
The LORD passed before him, and proclaimed, "The LORD, the LORD, a God *merciful and gracious*, slow to anger, and abounding in steadfast love and faithfulness."	Rend your hearts and not your clothing. Return to the LORD, your God, for he is *gracious and merciful*, slow to anger, and abounding in steadfast love, and *relents from punishing*.	He prayed to the LORD and said, "O LORD! Is not this what I said while I was still in my own country? That is why I fled to Tarshish at the beginning; for I knew that you are a *gracious* God *and merciful*, slow to anger, and abounding in steadfast love, and ready to *relent from punishing*."

Not once but twice the variations in Jonah and Joel agree with one another in comparison to Exodus 34:6.[108] A number of explanations have been suggested to explain these variations, but most likely, Jonah is not really quoting Exodus. Jonah quotes Joel quoting Exodus. This explanation fits the wider context and the theological agenda of Jonah, and it correlates with the widely held view that Jonah is later then Joel.

So then why does Jonah cite Joel citing Exodus 34:6? Thomas Dozeman argues that the key to answering this question lies in the way that the two books function.[109] For him, each author takes up Exodus 34:6 to emphasize YHWH's compassion, but they do so from different perspectives. Joel emphasizes YHWH's compassion upon YHWH's people while Jonah uses the same verse to emphasize YHWH's compassion upon all peoples. While this basic observation about how the books function thematically is correct, to say that Jonah and Joel each take up Exodus 34:6 independently does not do justice to Jonah's role as a theological corrective. Joel, as noted in this volume, plays a key role in the Book of the Twelve since virtually every recurring motif in the Twelve runs through Joel, including the use of Exodus 34:6-7. The fact that the *character* Jonah cites Joel citing Exodus 34:6 cannot be divorced from Jonah's role as a satirical figure. The character Jonah cites Exodus 34:6 for precisely the same reason as Joel, namely, to emphasize YHWH's compassion upon YHWH's people. Joel also underscores this image of protective compassion by drawing upon Exodus 34:7 near the end of the book to convey the idea that God's justice means judgment against the nations on the day of YHWH (see the discussion of Exod 34:7 in Joel 3:19-21). Left by itself, the message of Joel could be interpreted as an example of xenophobic nationalism that limits YHWH's salvific actions to YHWH's own people. By putting this theological perspective into the satirical lens of Jonah, such theology is lampooned and its inadequacy dramatically brought to light. The character Jonah justifies his flight at the beginning of the book as his attempt to stop YHWH from showing grace and compassion to the nations. The narrator of Jonah does this to show the absurdity of Jonah's (and also Joel's) theology when taken to this extreme. For the narrator of Jonah, YHWH is the creator of heaven and earth, not merely the God of Judah. For the narrator, Jonah correctly identifies YHWH's compassion as a core component of YHWH's identity when dealing with all peoples of the world; yet while the character Jonah thinks YHWH is wrong, the narrator of Jonah sees the bigger picture.

Jonah within the Book of the Twelve

Why was Jonah incorporated into the Twelve? One reason should already be clear. Jonah offers a humorous but powerful theological corrective to the dominant theological voices in the Twelve. To be clear, Jonah does not repudiate the message of Joel so much as it expands upon it. Jonah does not deny YHWH's compassion upon Israel; it presupposes that compassion. YHWH delivers Jonah from the belly of the fish, and YHWH uses the plant and the worm to show that YHWH continues to provide graciously for Jonah. The narrator of Jonah does not poke fun at the prophet to denounce Israel's role, but to expand it. Not once but twice Jonah serves as the instrument who leads foreigners to YHWH. The narrator's theology does not argue that Israel should be subjugated to the nations or that YHWH's compassion toward Israel has been superseded. Rather, the theology of the book of Jonah denies that YHWH's compassion and justice is limited to a concern for the well-being of Israel only. The book of Jonah adds its voice to a chorus of texts in the Prophets that explicitly articulate YHWH's salvific desire for the nations. Within the Book of the Twelve, this perspective is not dominant, but it is by no means lacking. Even Joel (2:28-32 [Heb. 3:1-5]) anticipates a day of YHWH when the spirit will be poured out upon "all flesh." Amos 9:7 challenges theological myopia by reminding Israel that while YHWH brought Israel out of Egypt, he was also at work among the Philistines and the Syrians to plant them in lands where they could flourish. Micah 4:1-4 anticipates a time when the nations will travel to Jerusalem to study YHWH's Torah. Zephaniah 3:9-10 depicts the salvific future as a reversal of the curse of Babel so that all the nations will offer "pure speech" and "call upon the name of YHWH." Zechariah 8:22-23 envisions a salvific future when foreigners ask, "May we go with you, for we have heard that God is with you." Zechariah 14:16 expresses a similar sentiment in that all the nations will worship YHWH as king in Jerusalem. Malachi 1:11-14 portrays the ideal future as a time when the nations will bring pure offerings to YHWH "from the rising of the sun to its setting" (1:11) and in so doing will make sure that YHWH's "name is reverenced among the nations" (1:14). Jonah provides the highest profile expression of this theology. It shows how deficient a portrait of God would be that limits God to working on behalf of one nation only.

Literarily, one cannot forget the book of Nahum when reading Jonah. Nahum depicts the downfall of Assyria as the regional superpower, and it portrays this downfall as part of YHWH's justice. In all likelihood, Nahum was already included in the Twelve when Jonah was integrated. Nahum entered the corpus with Habakkuk to document the theological assertion that YHWH controls the rise and fall of the kingdoms. It has long been noted that Jonah deliberately serves as a theological counterweight to Nahum.[110] Both books focus upon the fate of Nineveh, which Jonah portrays as the object of YHWH's grace and Nahum portrays as the object of YHWH's wrath. Of all the biblical books, only Jonah and Nahum end with a question. Both Jonah and Nahum draw on Exodus 34, though Jonah focuses on 34:6, while Nahum focuses upon 34:7. To understand why Jonah balances Nahum, one need only contemplate what was lacking theologically before Jonah was incorporated. Without the theological perspective of Jonah, the Twelve lacks a textual center depicting YHWH's salvific actions among the nations. Without Jonah, one could claim YHWH acts arbitrarily pronouncing Assyria's destruction. Jonah shows, however, that—theologically speaking—Assyria has experienced YHWH's grace, and Nineveh's repentance (in the time of Jeroboam II) shows that Assyria had denounced violence for the sake of YHWH. Thus, for the reader of the Twelve, when Assyria demolishes Samaria, their violent actions mean they have rejected the path of YHWH and brought YHWH's justice upon themselves. Not insignificantly, this surety of YHWH's justice upon the guilty is precisely the point of Exodus 34:7.

Finally, if one thinks of Jonah in its late Persian or early Hellenistic context, the theology of Jonah interacts with more than just Joel within the Book of the Twelve. The story of Ezra and Nehemiah continued the narrative of YHWH's people into the postmonarchic period. Ezra returns to Judah with a large contingent of exiles, goods, and political support. Nehemiah is credited with rebuilding the wall of Jerusalem in 445 BCE. Yet, both of these books contain a strong expectation for purity both ethnic and religious. In both books, one must prove one's ethnic lineage in order to participate fully in the life of Judah. Both Ezra (9:1-3; 10:3-19) and Nehemiah (10:30) articulate prohibitions against Judeans marrying foreigners. Ezra and Nehemiah articulate and assume a theology of purity with a strong insular quality. The theology of the book of Jonah challenges this limited understanding of YHWH. It reminds its readers that YHWH works beyond the borders of their own country. The book of Jonah challenges the theological myopia that can afflict all people of faith.

Discussion Questions

1. What role does each of the five books discussed in this chapter play in the thematic and historical structure of the Twelve?

2. What causes the differences in English translations of Joel 2:18, and what difference does it make for reading Joel as an individual book and as part of the Book of the Twelve?

3. These five books show an increasing tendency to draw upon other prophetic writings. Describe three places where one prophetic writing in this chapter draws significantly upon another prophet and discuss how these citations function within the rhetoric of the borrowing prophet.

Glossary

Compiled by Will Briggs

—This symbol appears in redaction-historical studies as a shorthand way to indicate that only part of a verse or a passage belongs to a particular redactional layer. It means "portions of," so 35:7 means portions of 35:7. Isaiah 60–62* means portions of Isa 60–62. One has to read the details of the author's argument to know which verses, half verses, or words are covered by the symbol.

allusive—The quality of a text characterized by repeated references to other works or traditions through the use of allusions, quotations, word plays, etc.

Book of the Four—The name used for a hypothetical scroll containing portions Hosea, Amos, Micah, and Zephaniah. The books in this scroll were likely edited and transmitted together from the early exilic period to explain the destruction of Jerusalem in light of the prophetic message to Israel (Hosea and Amos) and Judah (Micah and Zephaniah) as the result of their repeated turning away from YHWH. In this sense, it served as a precursor to the Book of the Twelve and provided the chronological framework to the larger corpus that was created in the Persian period.

casuistic law—Also called case law, casuistic law is a type of law or instruction containing conditional statements and mandating a certain punishment should the law be violated (if X happens . . . then Y should be done . . .). Casuistic law contrasts with apodictic law, which formulates a law simply as divine fiat (e.g., "Do not kill").

chiasm—A sandwich-like literary structure wherein a sequence of words, images, phrases, or ideas is repeated in reverse order (e.g., ABCC'B'A'). Genesis 9:6 contains an example of a chiasm: Anyone shedding (A) the blood (B) of a human (C) by a human (C') their blood (B') will be shed (A').

217

concatenation—A literary technique whereby clauses, lines, or sections of text are connected through the repetition of a certain word, words, or imagery.

Davidides—Dynastic successors to King David who ruled the kingdom of Judah in Jerusalem until Jerusalem's destruction in 587 BCE. The term is also used of successors of those kings (e.g., Zerubbabel) who were still identified as David's descendants in the Persian period even though no further kings from the line of David ever ruled Judah again.

diachronic—Models of research and interpretation that are concerned with the way in which biblical texts developed *through time*, taking into account issues such as historical background, sources, and editorial processes.

diaspora—A group of people from the same homeland who are scattered or dispersed beyond their original home.

didactic—Designed for teaching or instructional purposes.

Deuteronomistic—Influenced by the language, themes, and theology of Deuteronomy, particularly with respect to its emphasis on a conditional covenant between God and Israel and polemics against idolatrous worship practices.

Deuteronomistic History—The name given to the posited unified work spanning Joshua to 2 Kings (excluding Ruth, see Enneateuch below) that uses the language and theological emphases of Deuteronomy and was completed following the fall of Jerusalem in 587 BCE for the purpose of explaining the exile.

Enneateuch—Literally, the phrase means "nine containers," but in canonical discussions, the term refers to the first nine books of the Hebrew Bible in the Hebrew canonical order, comprised of Genesis-2 Kings. Prior to the medieval period, Hebrew manuscripts included Samuel and Kings on one scroll each, so the nine scrolls of the Enneateuch included the Pentateuch (Genesis, Exodus, Leviticus, Numbers, and Deuteronomy) and the four Former Prophets (Joshua, Judges, Samuel, and Kings). The book of Ruth was included in the Writings section of the Hebrew canon and thus was not included in the Enneateuch.

eschatological—Relating to the future climactic events in history or the ultimate fate of humanity and the earth.

form criticism—A method of study that classifies biblical texts into groups according to their literary patterns and seeks to uncover the life-setting that lies behind these literary patterns within the text.

Fortschreibung (plural: *Fortschreibungen*)—A redactional technique whereby an editor takes an older text and updates or expands it in order to adapt its message for a contemporary audience.

golah—The Hebrew word for "exile," referring to the exile of a number of Judeans after the fall of Jerusalem in 587 BCE.

Holiness Code—The name given to the collection of laws in Leviticus 17–26 due to its repetition of the word *holy* and that many scholars believe to have a different compositional history than the Priestly laws of Leviticus 1–16.

inclusio—Also known as an "envelope," a literary technique in which the same or similar language brackets a text at its beginning and end.

Isaiah Memoir—The name given to Isaiah 6–8 due to its concern with the life of the prophet Isaiah, which prompted early scholarship to attribute this textual unit to the prophet himself.

leitmotif—A recurring image, theme, or idea that appears throughout a given text and that the writer(s) wish to emphasize or develop.

Levant—The geographical area around the eastern Mediterranean Sea, including land in modern-day Israel, Palestine, Jordan, Lebanon, and Syria.

Masoretic Text (MT)—The earliest extant, complete Hebrew (and Aramaic) manuscripts of the Hebrew Bible, dating to the medieval period and copied, edited, and annotated by a group of Jewish scribes known as the Masoretes.

paranomasia—Also known as "soundplay" or a "pun," paranomasia is a literary device where words with similar sounds are placed in close proximity for rhetorical effect.

realia—Concrete historical or material data, including physical structures or objects from everyday life, as opposed to literary depictions or accounts.

redaction—The process of editing the biblical text in which editors arrange, correct, and add to the text.

retrovert—Used in the process of text criticism, the term refers to attempts to retranslate a translated text back into the language from which it was translated. For example, retroversion is used to translate a Greek translation back to Hebrew in order to compare the Hebrew text used by the translator to the Masoretic Text.

Septuagint (LXX)—The name of the Greek translation of the Hebrew Bible made during the 3rd-2nd centuries BCE.

Shephelah—The Judean hill country in south-central Palestine between the Judean mountains and the coastal plain.

subscription—A brief, formal note at the end of a text that marks the end of the text and provides additional information. Subscriptions serve the same function as superscriptions, but superscriptions appear at the beginning of a text.

superscription—A heading written above a text or a section of text, usually a verse or shorter in length, providing the reader with a context for the subsequent material while separating it from what came before. Superscriptions appear most commonly in Psalms and the Latter Prophets.

Syro-Ephraimite War—The invasion of Judah by the allied forces of Syria and Israel around 734–732 BCE in an effort to force Judah to join a military coalition against Assyria.

Table of Nations—The genealogy of the children of Noah in Genesis 10, including their spread into many different lands following the Flood.

Theophany—An appearance of a deity to humans, frequently accompanied in the Hebrew Bible by a number of natural phenomena (e.g., language of thunder, earthquake, etc.).

topos (plural: topoi)—A common motif, theme, or formula used in a text that forms a part of the text's argument or exhortation.

tradent—Someone who is responsible for maintaining and transmitting traditions, whether oral or written, to subsequent generations.

vetitive—A linguistic term referring to a negative command or a wish that something would not happen.

via negativa—Literally translated from Latin, "negative way," a way of describing something by saying what that thing is not.

Vorlage—The version or edition of a text in one language that a translator uses as the source for his or her translation into another language.

220

For Further Reading

Books on Prophets and Prophetic Literature

Blenkinsopp, Joseph. *A History of Prophecy in Israel, Revised and Enlarged.* Louisville: Westminster John Knox, 1996.

Kratz, Reinhard Gregor. *The Prophets of Israel.* Critical Studies of the Hebrew Bible 2. Winona Lake: Eisenbrauns, 2015.

Nissinen, Martti, ed. *Prophets and Prophecy in the Ancient Near East.* Writings from the Ancient World 12. Atlanta: Society of Biblical Literature, 2003.

Nogalski, James D. *Interpreting Prophetic Literature: Historical and Exegetical Tools for Reading the Prophets.* Louisville: Westminster John Knox, 2015.

Petersen, David. *The Prophetic Literature: An Introduction.* Louisville: Westminster John Knox, 2002.

Redditt, Paul. *Introduction to the Prophets.* Grand Rapids: Eerdmans, 2008.

Sharp, Carolyn J., ed. *The Oxford Handbook of the Prophets.* Oxford: Oxford University Press, 2016.

Steck, Odil Hannes. *The Theological Witness of Prophetic Books.* James D. Nogalski, trans. St. Louis: Chalice Press, 2000.

Sweeney, Marvin A. *The Prophetic Literature.* Interpreting Biblical Texts Series. Nashville: Abingdon, 2005.

Books on Scribes, Scrolls, and Literary History

Carr, David. *Writing on the Tablet of the Heart: Origins of Scripture and Literature.* Oxford: Oxford University Press, 2005.

Schmid, Konrad. *The Old Testament: A Literary History.* Linda M. Maloney, trans. Minneapolis: Fortress, 2012.

Van der Toorn, Karel. *Scribal Culture and the Making of the Hebrew Bible.* Cambridge, MA: Harvard University Press, 2007.

Notes

Preface

1. See Mark McEntire, *A Chorus of Prophetic Voices: Introducing the Prophetic Literature of Ancient Israel* (Louisville: Westminster John Knox, 2015) and Mark E. Biddle, *Polyphony and Symphony in Prophetic Literature: Rereading Jeremiah 7–20*, Studies in OT Interpretation 2 (Macon, GA: Mercer University Press, 1996).

1. Isaiah

1. Joseph Blenkinsopp, *Isaiah 1–39: A New Translation with Introduction and Commentary*, AB 19 (New York: Doubleday, 2000), 223–45, is fairly typical in labeling 6:1–8:22 as the Isaiah memoir, though he recognizes several places in these chapters that reflect later hands.

2. See also Blenkinsopp, *Isaiah 1–39*, 89–90.

3. The names most widely associated with this position are Hermann Barth and Ronald E. Clements. See Barth, *Die Jesaja-Worte in der Josiazeit: Israel und Assur als Thema einer produktiven Neuinterpretation der Jesajaüberlieferung*, WMANT 48 (Neukirchen-Vluyn: Neukirchener Verlag, 1977); and Clements, *Isaiah 1–39*, New Century Bible Commentary (Grand Rapids: Eerdmans, 1980), 5-6.

4. See Blenkinsopp, *Isaiah 1–39*, 91–92.

5. Hugh G. M. Williamson, *The Book Called Isaiah: Deutero-Isaiah's Role in Composition and Redaction* (Oxford: Clarendon, 1994).

6. Odil Hannes Steck, *Bereitete Heimkehr: Jesaja 35 als redaktionelle Brücke zwischen dem Ersten und dem Zweiten Jesaja*, Stuttgarter Bibelstudien 121 (Stuttgart: Katholisches Bibelwerk, 1985).

7. *Heaven and earth* witness YHWH's acts against those who rebel (1:2, 4) and they experience a new form at the end of Isaiah (66:22) after YHWH has destroyed the rebels (66:24). The *sinful cult* of chapter 1 gives way to a purified cult at the end of the book (66:22-23). The condemnation of offerings presented by the unrepentant makes a mockery of the cult (1:10-21). The cleansing of the cult represents a theme that reappears in the latest stages of Isaiah, where the cult will be purified in 63–66 (as well as 56:1-8). The *remnant of Zion* is already called to respond at the beginning of Isaiah (1:8-9) and at the end, where YHWH will restore Zion with her children and with the wealth of *the nations* who *trek to Jerusalem* (66:7-14). Isa 2:2-4 anticipates *nations worshiping in Zion* using an almost verbatim parallel to Mic 4:1-3. Most scholars agree that Isa 2:2-4 reflects prophetic theological perspectives of the late Persian period, but they have not yet conclusively settled which prophetic text is the source of the other's citation. The respective texts (Mic 4:1-4 and Isa 2:2-4) end with distinct variations of this theology. See discussions in James D. Nogalski, *The Book of the Twelve: Micah–Malachi*, SHBC (Macon, GA: Smyth and Helwys, 2011), 898–99; and Jakob Wöhrle, *Die frühen Sammlungen des Zwölfprophetenbuches: Untersuchungen zu ihrer Entstehung und Komposition*, BZAW 360 (Berlin: de Gruyter, 2006), 156–59.

8. This recurring motif does not likely stem from a single redactional stage because it lacks consistent vocabulary and because the perspectives in which it appears vary considerably. Nevertheless, the repetitive drumbeat of the idea of the lack of knowledge is certainly distinctive in Isaiah. See especially 5:13; 6:9-13; 33:15; 44:18; 45:3-6; 48:3-8; 52:6; 55:10; 59:12; 60:16; 61:16.

9. Even though the phrase "day of YHWH" does not appear, the context is clear since it describes a time of terror when the haughty will be brought low while YHWH will be "exalted on that day" (2:11-12).

10. See Ulrich F. Berges, *The Book of Isaiah: Its Composition and Final Form*, trans. Millard C. Lind, Hebrew Bible Monographs 16 (Sheffield: Sheffield Phoenix, 2012), 70. Berges agrees with Wolfgang Werner that 4:2-6 displays a tendency to cite phrases from elsewhere in the book (Wolfgang Werner, *Eschatologische Texte im Jesaja 1–39: Messias, Heiliger Rest, Völker*, FB 46 [Würzburg: Echter, 1982], 92). Williamson agrees, but notes that the citations do not link it to chapters 40–55, so it must reflect a postexilic (not exilic) summation (Williamson, *The Book Called Isaiah*, 143, 183).

11. Berges, *The Book of Isaiah*, 74; Gerald T. Sheppard, "The Anti-Assyrian Redaction and the Canonical Context of Isaiah 1–39," *JBL* 104 (1985): 193–216, especially 196. Sheppard relies upon Barth's description of the anti-Assyrian redaction of the late seventh century (in the time of Josiah), which reinterpreted Assyria from the instrument of YHWH's wrath into an enemy whom YHWH would destroy, but Sheppard argues for a double inclusion around the Isaiah memoir as one of the goals of the relocation of Isa 25–30 and the final woe oracle of 10:1-4. See Barth, *Die Jesaja-Worte*, 110–17, 203–7).

12. A smaller number of scholars have suggested that the seventh woe oracle originally appeared in 5:23, but that it was lost or deliberately changed and that the seventh and final woe oracle was created with 10:1-4 to form the frame. See the discussion in Berges, *The Book of Isaiah*, 74; Uwe Becker, *Jesaja: Von der Botschaft zum Buch*, FRLANT 178 (Göttingen: Vandenhoeck and Ruprecht, 1997), 142; and Erhard Blum, "Jesaja und der דבר des Amos: Unzeitgemässe Überlegungen zu Jes 5,25; 9,7–20; 10,1–4," *Dielheimer Blätter zur Archäologie und Textüberlieferung der Antike und Spätantike* 28 (1992–1993): 75–95, especially 82.

13. Since early in the critical period, this memoir was thought to have been composed by Isaiah shortly after the events to which it alludes. Barth and Steck argue that the majority of 6–8 comes from the prophet, with only a few verses added later (Barth, *Die Jesaja-Worte*, 278–79; Odil Hannes Steck, "Bemerkungen zu Jesaja 6," *Biblische Zeitschrift* 16 [1972]: 188–206). More recently, the discussion of the origin of this collection has shifted to the time of Manasseh (697–643) or Josiah (640–609) or even a time after 587 BCE. See the discussion in Hermann Spieckermann, *Juda unter Assur in der Sargonidenzeit*, 129 (Göttingen: Vandenhoeck and Ruprecht, 1982), 376. Becker, for example, sees only a small core that goes back to the time of the prophet (Becker, *Jesaja: Von der Botschaft zum Buch*, 121). Even this view, however, has been challenged in recent decades, since it has become increasingly clear that these chapters have a literary character that puts the reader in the events of the Syro-Ephraimite War (734–732 BCE) while at the same time expects the reader to know that those events began a lengthy period of decline, leading to Jerusalem's destruction in 587 BCE. See especially Becker, *Jesaja: Von der Botschaft zum Buch*, 35. Questions about the historical plausibility of these events portrayed in the biblical accounts have been directly or indirectly raised by historians, e.g., Henning Graf Reventlow, "Das Ende der sog. 'Denkschrift' Jesajas," *BN* 38/39 (1987), 62–67; J. Maxwell Miller and John H. Hayes, *A History of Ancient Israel and Judah*, 2nd ed. (Louisville: Westminster John Knox, 2006), 380–83. The question of verifiability is not germane to the portraits of Isaiah that presuppose the events because these traditions

became the Judean version of these events relatively early, but probably not in the lifetime of the prophet. See Berges, *The Book of Isaiah*, 77–79. Whatever the reality behind the textual traditions, the Old Testament biblical accounts presuppose knowledge of traditions about this war.

14. The place names mentioned explicitly in Isa 9 represent regions of the Northern Kingdom (Naphtali, Zebulun, Galilee, Ephraim, Samaria, Manasseh) or nations who will be punished because they have attacked Israel (the Arameans and the Philistines; 9:12).

15. A similar perspective appears in the hopeful ending of Amos. See especially Amos 9:11-12.

16. This song responds to the promises of Isa 11. Isa 12:2b quotes Exod 15:2, the victory song that appears immediately after the crossing of the Sea of Reeds. Since Exod 15 celebrates YHWH's deliverance of Israel from Egypt, the quote in Isa 12:2 forms a reference back to the motif with which Isa 11 ended, namely equating a return from Assyria with YHWH's deliverance of Israel from bondage in Egypt (see 11:15-16).

17. See Williamson, *The Book Called Isaiah*, 156–83; Blenkinsopp, *Isaiah 1–39*, 271–73; Berges, *The Book of Isaiah*, 123–80.

18. Among others, Berges (*The Book of Isaiah*, 130–31) interprets the broken rod that struck the Philistines as a reference to the death of Tiglath-pileser III.

19. Isa 17:1-3 makes sense following the death of Tiglath-pileser III (727 BCE) who died before defeating Damascus and Samaria. His successor, Shalmaneser V (726–722 BCE), completed the overthrow of Damascus and began the siege against Samaria that his successor Sargon II (722–705 BCE) finished.

20. Assyria crushed the Ashdod rebellion in 713–711 BCE and the resistance in Egypt and Ethiopia receded in the face of the Assyrian campaign. The allusions to these events were intended to warn Hezekiah against becoming embroiled in their machinations against Assyria.

21. These verses report the downfall of the Ashdod king who led the rebellion of 713–711. He fled to Egypt to find safety, but he was taken by the Ethiopian king and delivered over to Assyria.

22. Isa 23 comprises several anti-Phoenician oracles, but they demonstrate knowledge of Babylon's punishment of Tyre. Note especially 23:13.

23. Compare the theories in Steck, "Bemerkungen zu Jesaja 6," 188–206; idem, "Beiträge zum Verständnis von Jesaja 7,10–17 und 8,1–4," *TZ* 29 (1973), 161–78; Marvin A. Sweeney, *Isaiah 1–4 and the Post-exilic Understanding of the Isaiah Tradition*, BZAW 171 (Berlin: de Gruyter, 1988); Jacques Vermeylen, "L'unité du livre d'Isaïe," in *The Book of Isaiah/Le livre d'Isaïe: les oracles et leurs relectures unité et complexité de l'ouvrage*, ed. Jacques Vermeylen; BETL 81 (Leuven: Leuven University Press, 1989); Williamson, *The Book Called Isaiah*, 156–83; Blenkinsopp, *Isaiah 1–39*, 273; and Berges, *The Book of Isaiah*, 135–36.

24. Whether the entire block was updated prior to 539 BCE (Williamson) or an editor added preexisting material concerning Babylon after 482 BCE (Berges) in the end rests upon decisions regarding other compositional blocks in the book, so a healthy dose of caution (Blenkinsopp) should be maintained. That being said, the arguments of Berges generally make the most sense of the widest varieties of texts within these chapters.

25. Up to six texts within 13–23 exhibit some aspect of this theological expectation: 13:2; 14:1-2; 16:1, 3-5; 18:7; 19:16-25; and 23:17-18 (though 13:2 remains debated). See Berges, *The Book of Isaiah*, 143–54; and Williamson, *The Book Called Isaiah*, 165–68.

26. Berges, *The Book of Isaiah*, 163.

27. This unnamed city appears in 24:10, 12; 25:2; 26:5 and stands in the background as a contrast to the restored city in 26:1. This universalizing perspective dominates the opening portion of 24–27, where *earth* appears some sixteen times in chapter 24 alone.

28. Debate continues regarding how much of chapters 28–31 reflects early sources from the eighth century BCE and which texts represent later updates. For example, Becker argues that very little of chapters 28–31 could be classified as texts from the eighth century BCE. For him, only 28:1*, 3 and 28:7b-10 could possibly stem from such an early date, while the rest exhibits signs of three redactional phases (Becker, *Jesaja: Von der Botschaft zum Buch*, 263–68). By contrast, Berges assigns considerably more of 28–31 to the foundational core, including the five woe oracles that begin with the Hebrew word *hoy* (28:1-6; 29:1-8, 15-24; 30:1-5; 31:1-3) and early portions of three judgment oracles containing "prophetic indictment and threat" (28:7-18*; 29:9-14*; 30:6-8, 12-14; Berges, *The Book of Isaiah*, 189–91). For Berges, this last group of texts aligns with the political situation at the end of the eighth century. These oracles follow the classic

pattern in which the threat is introduced by the word "therefore" at the beginning of the description of YHWH's impending action.

29. A very similar dynamic is at play in the message of the early portions of Mic 1–3. See the discussion of Micah in the chapter "The Beginning of the Twelve."

30. These verses tend to be understood as references to an attempt to send a delegation to meet Egyptians in 701 BCE that was unable to reach them because the Assyrians had defeated the Egyptians in a battle near Eltekeh, which forced Egypt's army to retreat back to its own territory. See Berges, *The Book of Isaiah*, 195.

31. For example, see Berges, *The Book of Isaiah*, 214. Berges speaks of a Zion redaction in the second half of the fifth century that updates the core texts in 28–31 for the returned community to promote Zion as the place of rest.

32. Some commentators understand the king as YHWH (as is more clearly the case in 33:17, 22), while others interpret the king as a human king. Berges, who sees Isa 32 as a Persian-period composition, interprets the king as YHWH (Berges, *The Book of Isaiah*, 215). Becker thinks Isa 32 is composite, though 32:9-14 may be part of an older unit that now leads into 32:15-20 (Becker, *Jesaja: Von der Botschaft zum Buch*, 268). Barth sees a core unit in 32:1-8 + 15-20 interrupted by an existing unit (Barth, *Die Jesaja-Worte*, 212–13). Williamson thinks Isa 32 refers to a Davidic king, while chapter 33 connects to Deutero-Isaiah (Williamson, *The Book Called Isaiah*, 226). Blenkinsopp considers 32–33 to be a "cohesive compilation unified by the theme announced at the beginning and end" as well as "many echoes of the preceding discourses" (Blenkinsopp, *Isaiah 1–39*, 383).

33. Each woe oracle in 27–33 has been directed against a different entity: Ephraim (28:1), Ariel (29:1), those hiding counsel (29:15), rebellious children (30:1), and those relying on Egypt (31:1), so it makes a certain sense that the final woe would turn its attention to the entity threatening Zion and the land, labeled here as the destroyer (33:1).

34. Berges labels Isa 33 as the first bridge text uniting Isa 1–32* with 40:1-2 and 52:7-8. For him, in the second half of the fifth century BCE, the scroll already contained the bulk of chapters 1–32; 33; 40–52. Chapter 33 builds upon and corrects chapter 32 by anticipating YHWH's return to Zion in 52:7-10 (and 40:1-2). What distinguishes Becker and Berges from Steck is the conviction that chapter 35 (also a bridge text) is *not* the first bridge text connecting the earlier

collection with material in 40–66. In other words, the more recent treatments of the growth of the book tend to see a clear bridging function as the key to understanding 33–35, with 34 responding to 33 and 35 responding to 34. The goal of the initial bridge (Isa 33) is to proclaim the *restoration* of Zion through the punishment of an unspecified "destroyer" by YHWH, the king of all the earth.

35. Following the woe against the destroyer (33:1), verses 2-6 petition YHWH to show grace on behalf of "us" (2), affirm hymnically YHWH's power over the nations (3-4), and exalt YHWH's care for Zion that rests upon justice and righteousness (5-6). Verses 7-9, however, shift the focus to the current state of Zion and the land which has been devastated, while 10-13 announces YHWH's decision to act and his confrontation of the enemy.

36. Verses 14-24 announce YHWH's return to Zion as king on behalf of those in Zion and in a foreign land. Verses 14-17 refer to the sinners in Zion who wonder who will survive (14), while verses 15-17 answer this rhetorical question by affirming that the righteous and upright will see the king return in his beauty return. Verses 18-21, however, describe the terrors of those living in a foreign land who will no longer have to endure life among a people whose language they cannot understand (18-19). Rather, they will look to Zion (20), where they will see the king in his majesty (21). Verses 22-24 announce YHWH is judge, ruler, and king (22) and affirm the sins of those living in Jerusalem (24).

37. Steck, *Bereitete Heimkehr*; Berges, *The Book of Isaiah*, 228–42.

38. The Kings account and the Isaiah account share too much identical wording and structural flow to be explained as independent traditions. Since Gesenius wrote on the topic early in the nineteenth century, the primacy of the Kings account went largely unchallenged until the end of the twentieth century, but also uninvestigated. For an extensive summary of the arguments of Gesenius, see Berges, *The Book of Isaiah*, 246–47.

39. These authors downplay the very different portrait of Hezekiah in 36–39 and the early core of material in the Isaiah scroll. Instead, they argue that Isa 36–39 manifests wording and themes that fit better in the context of Isaiah than they do in the context of Kings. Representatives include Klaas A. D. Smelik, "Distortion of Old Testament Prophecy: Purpose of Isaiah XXXVI and XXXVII," in *Crises and Perspectives: Studies in Ancient Near Eastern Polytheism, Biblical Theology, Palestinian Archaeology, and Intertestamental Literature*, ed. Johannes C. de Moor, OTS 24 (Leiden: Brill, 1986): 70–93; Edgar W. Conrad, "Second Isaiah and the Priestly Oracle of Salvation," *ZAW* 93 (1981): 234–46; Christopher

R. Seitz, *Zion's Final Destiny: The Development of the Book of Isaiah; A Reassessment of Isaiah 36–39* (Minneapolis: Fortress, 1991); and Barry G. Webb, "Zion in Transformation: A Literary Approach to Isaiah," in *The Bible in Three Dimensions: Essays in Celebration of Forty Years of Biblical Studies in the University of Sheffield*, ed. David J. A. Clines, Stephen E. Fowl, and Stanley E. Porter, JSOTS 87 (Sheffield: Sheffield Academic, 1990), 65–84.

40. See the summaries of Williamson and Berges, both of whom carefully survey and analyze these challenges to the priority of the Kings account (Williamson, *The Book Called Isaiah*, 189–209; and Berges, *The Book of Isaiah*, 253–56).

41. According to Blenkinsopp, chapters 36–39 presuppose a positive relationship between Hezekiah and Isaiah, while the early poetry in Isa 28–31 differs markedly because it assumes that the prophet's message is not accepted (Blenkinsopp, *Isaiah 1–39*, 381–82).

42. Debate will likely continue on these issues. Among those scholars arguing for a bridging function, see the analyses in Berges, *The Book of Isaiah*, 253–56; and Williamson, *The Book Called Isaiah*, 188–211. They both conclude that 2 Kgs 18–20 arose independently of Kings and that 2 Kings 18–20 was already influenced by knowledge of the Isaiah collection that was available at that point, though both allow that some of the similarities to Isaiah result from the creative redactor who incorporated these chapters as Isa 36–39, pointing both backward to parts of 1–35 and forward to parts of 40–66. Blenkinsopp exemplifies scholars who still think that 36–39 was simply appended to some form of 1–35 in much the same manner as Jer 52 adds 2 Kgs 25 to the end of the Jeremiah scroll to provide historical context and complete the narrative of Jerusalem's destruction (Blenkinsopp, *Isaiah 1–39*, 458–61).

43. This idea has gained recognition since it was first developed in the seventies. See the seminal studies of Peter R. Ackroyd, "An Interpretation of the Babylonian Exile: A Study of 2 Kings 20, Isaiah 38–39," *SJT* 27 (1974): 329–52; idem, "Isaiah 36–39: Structure and Function," in *Von Kanaan bis Kerala: Festschrift für Prof. Mag. Dr. J.P.M. van der Ploeg zur Vollendung des siebzigsten Lebensjahres am 4. Juli 1979*, ed. W. C. Delsman et al., AAOT 211 (Neukirchen-Vluyn: Neukirchener Verlag, 1982), 3–21.

44. Bernhard Duhm, *Das Buch Jesaja übersetzt und erklärt*, 4th ed., vol. 1, HK (Göttingen: Vandenhoeck and Ruprecht, 1922). Though Duhm was by no means the first to make this observation, his work solidified the idea that 40–55 represents the work of a late exilic prophet living in Babylon.

45. Berges, *The Book of Isaiah*, 344–50. The recent treatment by Williamson both confirms the significance of the term *Jacob* in 40–48 and warns against a simple assignation of sources based upon changes in this terminology: H. G. M. Williamson, "Jacob in Isaiah 40–66," in *Continuity and Discontinuity: Chronological and Thematic Development in Isaiah 40–66*, ed. Lena-Sofia Tiemeyer and Hans M. Barstad, FRLANT 255 (Göttingen: Vandenhoeck and Ruprecht, 2014), 219–29.

46. Isa 2:8, 18, 20; 10:10-11; 19:1, 3; 21:9; 30:22; 31:7; 40:19-20; 41:29; 42:8, 17; 44:9-10, 15, 17; 45:16, 20; 46:1; 48:5; 57:13; 66:3.

47. Earlier objections to dating chapters 40–55 to the time of Cyrus tended to take one of two tracks, neither of which withstands critical scrutiny. First, fundamentalists have long argued that Isaiah simply predicted the rise of Cyrus because of Isaiah's status as a canonical prophet. Aside from the improbability of an eighth-century Judean prophet anticipating the name of a Persian king from the sixth century, and the equally problematic misunderstanding of the nature of prophetic literature such explanations presume, the biggest obstacle to such an explanation remains the text itself. The texts referring to Cyrus, when read for the plain sense of their meaning, do not use predictive language. Rather, they presume the existence of such a king: it is YHWH "who says of Cyrus, 'he is my shepherd'" (44:28) and "thus says the Lord to his anointed, to Cyrus" (45:1). Second, some suggest that the specific references to Cyrus represent later glosses that interpreted Cyrus as the realization of earlier prophetic pronouncements. No good rationale can be found, however, for striking the name Cyrus from the original version of these texts. Such attempts to attribute at least the bulk of chapters 40–55 to the historical prophet Isaiah have long since been abandoned by critical scholars as they attempt to understand the dynamics of the text against the early Persian-period background in the time of Cyrus and beyond.

48. For example, see the discussions in Joseph Blenkinsopp, *Isaiah 40–55: A New Translation with Introduction and Commentary*, AB 19A (New York: Doubleday, 2002), 292–94; Berges, *The Book of Isaiah*, 303. In addition to the explicit mention of Cyrus by name and 48:14-16, other texts are also cited as containing references to Cyrus whose role of overthrowing Babylon makes him YHWH's servant. These texts include 41:1-5, 25; 43:14; 46:11, and some (e.g., Blenkinsopp) would include the original identity of the servant in the first Servant Song in 42:1-6.

49. So especially the royal tenor of the commission and 42:1-9; see the discussion in Blenkinsopp, *Isaiah 40–55*, 209–12.

50. The end of 48:22 also manifests a precise parallel with 57:21 that, as a number of commentators have noted, functions as a structural divide for all of 40–66: "There is no peace, says the Lord, for the wicked." See Blenkinsopp, *Isaiah 40–55*, 296; Berges, *The Book of Isaiah*, 256–57, 310–11. The divisions created by 48:22 and 57:21 divide 40–66 into three sections of nine chapters (40–48; 49–57; 58–66) and the content of these verses align with the emphasis of the final chapters that the wicked will not find peace (both those inside and outside Judah). According to Berges and others, this motif connects 39:8 and 66:24.

51. This emphasis does not appear in chapters 49–55, though some would claim it reappears in modified form in the latest editorial additions to 56–66 (specifically in the language of the new heavens and new earth that appears in 65:17 and 66:22). The imagery of a new heaven and new earth does not, however, share the same imagery of the return from Babylon or the references to the impotence of idolatry that also appear in the texts in 40–48.

52. A number of commentators interpret these verses as a reversal of lament songs in general, e.g., Claus Westermann, *Isaiah 40–66*, OTL (Philadelphia: Westminster, 1969), 218–21; Blenkinsopp, *Isaiah 40–55*, 310; Berges, *The Book of Isaiah*, 348–49. See also their arguments that Isa 49:14-21 resonates with a number of other texts in Isaiah and beyond. For the parallels and the implications, see Williamson, *The Book Called Isaiah*, 53–54 (who focuses on parallels with Isa 5–6); and Berges, *The Book of Isaiah*, 348–50 (who draws attention to the dual claims of abandonment by Lady Zion in 49:14 and Jacob in 40:27).

53. So Berges, *The Book of Isaiah*, 335–44, 385–87. Berges sees 49–52, the fourth Servant Song (52:13–53:14), and 54–55 as separate compositions added at different times.

54. For example, see Williamson, *The Book of Isaiah*, 150–52.

55. See the more extensive surveys in Berges, who builds off the work of Vermeylen (Berges, *The Book of Isaiah*, 388–93; and Williamson, *The Book Called Isaiah*, 3–18).

56. For example, Oswald T. Allis, *The Unity of Isaiah* (Philadelphia: Presbyterian and Reformed Publishing, 1950); Edward J. Young, *Studies in Isaiah* (Grand Rapids: Eerdmans, 1954).

57. See Edgar W. Conrad, *Reading Isaiah*, OBT 27 (Minneapolis: Fortress, 1991).

58. For example, Julian Morgenstern, "Isaiah 49–55," *HUCA* 36 (1965): 1–35.

59. Proponents of this model largely build off the work of Elliger in the 1920s and 1930s, such as Karl Elliger, *Die Einheit Tritojesajas (Jes. 56–66)*, BWANT 45 (Stuttgart: Kohlhammer, 1933).

60. This view was already argued early in the twentieth century by Karl Marti, *Das Buch Jesaja* (Tübingen: Mohr Siebeck, 1900).

61. Wolfgang Lau, *Schriftgelehrte Prophetie in Jes 56–66: Eine Untersuchung zu den literarischen Bezügen in den letzten elf Kapiteln des Jesajabuches*, BZAW 225 (Berlin: de Gruyter, 1994).

62. Westermann, *Isaiah 40–66*, 296–308.

63. Jacques Vermeylen, *Du prophète Isaïe à l'apocalyptique: Isaïe, I-XXXV, miroir d'un demi-millénaire d'expérience religieuse en Israël* (Paris: J. Gabalda, 1977–1978), 2:503.

64. See Odil Hannes Steck, *Der Abschluss der Prophetie: Ein Versuch zur Frage der Vorgeschichte des Kanons* (Neukirchen-Vluyn: Neukirchener Verlag, 1991).

65. Otto Plöger, *Theocracy and Eschatology*, trans. S. Rudman (Richmond: John Knox, 1968); Paul Hanson, *The Dawn of Apocalyptic* (Philadelphia: Fortress, 1975).

66. Brooks Schramm, *Opponents of Third Isaiah*, JSOTSup 193 (New York: T & T Clark), 81–111.

67. Schramm, *Opponents of Third Isaiah*, 108–9.

68. Schramm, *Opponents of Third Isaiah*, 111.

69. Willem A. M. Beuken, "The Main Theme of Trito-Isaiah: The 'Servants of Yhwh,'" *JSOT* 47 (1990): 81.

70. Willem Beuken, "Isaiah Chapters LXV–LXVI: Trito-Isaiah and the Closure of the Book of Isaiah," in *Congress Volume: Leuven, 1989*, ed. John A. Emerton, VTSup 43 (Leiden: Brill, 1991), 204–21.

71. Rainer Albertz, *A History of Israelite Religion in the Old Testament Period*, vol. 2, *From the Exile to the Maccabees*, trans. John Bowden, OTL (Louisville: Westminster John Knox, 1994).

72. Albertz, *A History of Israelite Religion*, 2:442, 454–58.

73. Albertz illustrates the first of these elements in Haggai-Zechariah and the last two with Isa 60–62. For him, a layer of redaction was added in Haggai and Zechariah (Hag 2:5a; Zech 1:1-6; 6:15b; 7:1–8:19) that used Deuteronomistic language and language from JerD to change the unconditional promises of Haggai and Zechariah to promises that were contingent on obedience to the Torah.

74. See Berges, *The Book of Isaiah*, 401–34.

75. The NRSV, CEB, and NIV assume textual corruption for 57:9 and incorrectly translate *lammelek* ("to the king") in the MT as "Molech." See NAS, NET, and KJV, which follow MT. This decision is influenced by the reference to child sacrifice in 57:5. Blenkinsopp tends to follow the NRSV as well, but also notes this word is one of a number of (likely deliberate) double entendres in the passage. See Joseph Blenkinsopp, *Isaiah 56–66: A New Translation with Introduction and Commentary*, AB 19B (New York: Doubleday, 2003), 160–63.

76. See Blenkinsopp, *Isaiah 56–66*, 159, 164.

77. See "Diagram IV" in Berges, *The Book of Isaiah*, 520; and Steck, *Abschluss der Prophetie*, 196–98. For Berges, the final stage of Isaiah comes at the beginning of the fourth century. For Steck, it extends into the latter portions of the third century BCE.

78. Judith Gärtner, *Jesaja 66 und Sacharja 14 als Summe der Prophetie: Eine traditions- und redaktionsgeschichtliche Untersuchung zum Abschluss des Jesaja-und des Zwölfprophetenbuches*, WMANT 114 (Neukirchen-Vluyn: Neukirchener Verlag, 2006), 1–7, 10–11.

79. While scholars largely agree on the relative dating of these chapters as arising later than 40–55, no consensus yet exists regarding their absolute date. A number of recent studies have suggested the possibility that the more inclusive group responsible for the latest material has in view as the opponents those associated with the reforms initiated by Ezra and Nehemiah, or at least that these chapters presuppose the setting of the mid-fifth century in Judah. Other studies have concluded that these chapters belong in the later Persian or Hellenistic period. See Berges, *The Book of Isaiah*, 452–53; Blenkinsopp, *Isaiah 56–66*, 51–54; Lena-Sofia Tiemeyer, *Priestly Rites and Prophetic Rage: Post-exilic Critique of the Priesthood*, FAT 2/19 (Tübingen: Mohr Siebeck, 2006), 274–86, all of whom recognize a complicated relationship between such groups. See also Odil Hannes Steck, "Zu jüngsten Untersuchungen von Jes 56,1–8; 63:7-24," in *Studien zu*

Tritojesaja, BZAW 203 (Berlin: de Gruyter, 1993), 233–42; Gärtner, *Jesaja 66 und Sacharja 14, passim*; Konrad Schmid, *The Old Testament: A Literary History*, trans. Linda M. Maloney (Minneapolis: Fortress, 2012), 207–8.

80. Berges has a different take on this passage, arguing that YHWH is continuing on to Jerusalem in order to battle the foes of the servants of YHWH in the postexilic Judean community. See Berges, *The Book of Isaiah*, 199–202, 399–400, 453–54. While his reading certainly exhibits considerable coherence, he must base the argumentation upon the claim that 63:6 represents a later addition to 63:1-5.

81. Commentators have, at times, misleadingly referred to the entire unit as a confession of sins. In reality, however, the genre is more complicated rhetorically since the people *petition* YHWH. They refer to the events in the past, ask where YHWH is now (63:15), question why YHWH has strayed from them (63:17), and petition YHWH to return to deliver his people from their adversaries (63:17b–64:11). To be sure, 64:5 offers a short profession of sins, but the remainder of this unit either describes the desperate situation or asks YHWH to cease the punishment.

82. For example, Blenkinsopp is skeptical that the "psalm-like composition" was written for its context (Blenkinsopp, *Isaiah 56–66*, 257). By contrast, others see 63:7–64:11 as a response to the preceding anti-Edom material. This view has been expressed regularly since the time of Duhm (*Das Buch Jesaja*, 469). See also the work of Bautch, who argues that a preexisting lament was adapted for this context (Richard J. Bautch, "Lament Regained in Trito-Isaiah's Penitential Prayer," in *The Origins of Penitential Prayer in Second Temple Judaism*, vol. 1, *Seeking the Favor of God*, ed. Mark J. Boda, Daniel K. Falk, and Rodney Werline, *Early Judaism and Its Literature* 21 [Atlanta: SBL, 2006], 83–99).

83. See the summary in Blenkinsopp, *Isaiah 56–66*, 257–58.

84. See also the phrase of those who "rebelled against me" (1:2; 66:24) in the opening verse after the superscription and the last verse of the book describing the destruction of the rebels and sinners while leaving a remnant in Zion (cf. 1:27-28).

85. Steck, *Der Abschluß der Prophetie*, 29–30, 43–46; Gärtner, *Jesaja 66 und Sacharja 14*; James D. Nogalski, "Intertextuality in the Twelve," in *Forming Prophetic Literature: Essays on Isaiah and the Twelve in Honor of John D. W. Watts*, ed.

James W. Watts and Paul House, JSOTSupp 235 (Sheffield: JSOT Press, 1996), 123–24; Schmid, *The Old Testament: A Literary History*, 208.

2. Jeremiah

1. For a more extensive reconstruction of these events, see Rainer Albertz, *A History of Israelite Religion in the Old Testament Period*, vol. 1, *From the Beginnings to the End of the Monarchy*, trans. John Bowden, OTL (Louisville: Westminster John Knox), 198–231.

2. See Albertz, *A History of Israelite Religion*, 1:207–9. Albertz discusses the privileges that benefitted the Jerusalem priesthood in the context of larger societal systems, especially in the collection of the tithe.

3. The works of Thiel represent a major voice in noting these differences, e.g., Winfried Thiel, *Die deuteronomistische Redaktion von Jeremia 1–25*, WMANT 41 (Neukirchen-Vluyn: Neukirchener Verlag, 1973); idem, *Die deuteronomistische Redaktion von Jeremia 26–45*, WMANT 52 (Neukirchen-Vluyn: Neukirchener Verlag, 1981). See the recent summary in Mark Leuchter, "Jeremiah: Structure, Themes, and Contested Issues," in *The Oxford Handbook of the Prophets*, ed. Carolyn J. Sharp (Oxford: Oxford University Press, 2016), 179–81.

4. Jer 29 represents the most extensive treatment of this group. They are told to plant roots in Babylon and work for its welfare (29:5-7) because they will remain there for seventy years (29:10; cf. 25:11) before YHWH will bring them back to Jerusalem where they will implement YHWH's plans to restore Jerusalem (29:11). The fact, however, that "this place" refers to Judah and Jerusalem indicates that this chapter reflects an interest in the late sixth-century reintegration of Judah's exiles once they are back in the land. This group returned to Judah and brought resources with them to help resettle Jerusalem and rebuild the temple. See also the discussion of Pohlmann's *golah*-oriented redaction model below. See also Ezekiel's pro-*golah* stance in the next chapter.

5. For Samaria, see Gary N. Knoppers, *Jews and Samaritans: The Origins and History of their Early Relations* (Oxford: Oxford University Press, 2013), 103–9; concerning Mizpah, see Albertz, *A History of Israelite Religion*, 1:241–42, 2:371–73; and concerning Ramat Raḥel, see Oded Lipschits et al., "Palace and Village, Paradise and Oblivion: Unraveling the Riddles of Ramat Raḥel," *Near Eastern Archaeology* 74 (2011): 2–3, 5–13, 15, 19–21, 23–25, 30–49.

6. In addition to the narrative of the two scrolls in the time of Jehoiakim (chapter 36), Jer 45:1 refers to that first scroll, and Jer 49:59-64 refers to a scroll containing all the anticipated judgment pronouncements against Babylon that was intended to be taken to Babylon and thrown in the Euphrates to symbolize Babylon's fall. Two other texts (25:13 and 30:2) also refer to a collection of materials as a scroll/book that marks particular sections. The former occurs just prior to the original location of the oracles against the nations, while the latter opens the book of consolation, the collection of hopeful sayings that appear in chapters 30–33. Also, Jer 51:64 ends with the statement "Thus far are the words of Jeremiah" immediately preceding chapter 52 (with its parallel account of 2 Kgs 25).

7. Estimates for the time of Gedaliah's control and death range from two months to five years, based in part on the reference to a third deportation in 582 BCE that appears in Jer 52:30 some five years after the destruction of the city. See Miller and Hayes, *A History of Ancient Israel and Judah*, 480–81, 485–87.

8. Emanuel Tov, *Textual Criticism of the Hebrew Bible*, 3rd ed. (Minneapolis: Fortress, 2012), 286–94.

9. For an appreciation of the way these differences function in the two texts, see the English translation in the commentary by Leslie Allen, who uses italics to highlight places he considers expansions in the MT compared to the Hebrew *Vorlage* of the LXX (Leslie C. Allen, *Jeremiah*, OTL [Louisville: Westminster John Knox, 2008]).

10. See Moon Kwon Chae, "Redactional Intentions of MT Jeremiah Concerning the Oracles Against the Nations," *JBL* 134 (2015): 577–93. See also the discussion of 46–51 later in this chapter.

11. Jer 26:1; 27:1; 28:1; 29:1; 32:1; 33:1; 34:1; 35:1; 36:1; 37:1; 39:1; 40:1; 41:1.

12. Bernhard Duhm, *Das Buch Jeremia* (Tübingen: Mohr Siebeck, 1901); Sigmund Mowinckel, *Zur Komposition des Buches Jeremia* (Kristiania: Dybwad, 1914).

13. The grouping of these (mostly poetic) materials often displays a loose connection by theme, and some of the groups of sayings show signs they existed as a smaller collection (e.g., the groupings of materials about kings in chapters 21:1–23:8, followed by another group that begins with the heading "concerning the prophets" at the beginning of 23:9, which introduces the remainder of that chapter's focus).

14. These texts focus upon the people's guilt and disobedience, prophetic admonitions, and pronouncements of punishment. Texts in this source remain debated, but generally include 7:1–8:3; 11:1-14; 18:1-12; 21:1-10; 22:1-5; 25:1-11; 34:8-22; and 35.

15. Scholarship has qualified Mowinckel's arguments for a number of reasons. First, his "sources" omit several significant sections of the book, including the second half of the so-called book of consolation (32–33). Second, these "sources" function better as descriptions of text forms (poetic sayings, autobiographical accounts, biographical accounts, sermons, etc.). Third, the four sources by themselves do not account for the differences in the Hebrew and Greek traditions of Jeremiah. The differences suggest that the corpus continued to develop.

16. Karl-Friedrich Pohlmann, *Studien zum Jeremiabuch: Ein Beitrag zur Frage nach der Enstehung des Jeremiabuches*, FRLANT 118 (Göttingen: Vandenhoeck and Ruprecht, 1978). Pohlmann builds off the work of Rudolph and Thiel, who argue that the Deuteronomistic character of Source C material actually extends much further into the corpus, making it likely that the redactor incorporating this material should be considered the main redactor of the book, active sometime in the middle of the sixth century BCE. Pohlmann, however, objects that making this claim overlooks a significant redactional agenda that can be tied to specific texts with a recognizable purpose.

17. Major texts exhibiting this pro-*golah* perspective include Jer 21:1-10; 24; 38:1-6; 39:1–40:6*; 40:7-10*; 41:4-7; and chapter 42.

18. Pohlmann claims, for instance, that this agenda represents the final stages of the debates regarding the privileged status of the Babylonian exiles, which he thinks represent the time close to the Chronicler (Pohlmann, *Studien zum Jeremiabuch*, 183–91). A case can also be made for the time of Zerubbabel and Ezra, when the influx of new resources brought by members of the Babylonian *golah* and Persian administrators enhanced the influence of returnees in ways that would have increased their political and economic power in Judah.

19. Werner H. Schmidt, *Das Buch Jeremia. Kapitel 1–20*, ATD 20 (Göttingen: Vandenhoeck and Ruprecht, 2011), 28–41.

20. For example, Schmidt argues that 2–6 contains the core contents of the first scroll mentioned in Jer 27, which was rewritten after Jehoiakim burned the first scroll Jeremiah dictated. By contrast, for Schmidt, the third person narratives

that dominate 26–45 cannot have been an entirely independent source. Third person accounts like those in 26–45 already appear in 1–20.

21. Schmidt, *Jeremia 1–20*, 37. He refers specifically to the "word event superscriptions" that appear in 1:2; 7:1; 11:1; 18:1; and 21:1, but he seems to imply as well the superscriptions that appear in the second half of the book that draw upon the same phrasing to present new scenes or the word of YHWH within those narratives: 27:1; 29:30; 30:1; 32:1, 26; 33:1, 19, 23; 34:1, 8, 12; 35:1, 12; 36:1, 27; 37:6; 39:15; 40:1; 42:7; 43:8; and 44:1.

22. E.g., Jer 17:5-9; 9:22-23.

23. E.g., the people's confession of guilt in 3:25; 8:14b-15; 14:19-20, and elements from lament ceremonies in 3:21–4:2 that include the prayer of the people in 10:23-25, the call to praise in 20:13, and perhaps the promise to the nations in 16:19-21.

24. E.g., the idolatry polemic in chapter 10 and the salvific sayings that draw upon language from Deutero-Isaiah (31:35-37, 38-40).

25. Allen, *Jeremiah*, 7.

26. Ibid., 8.

27. Ibid., 11.

28. See Schmidt, *Das Buch Jeremia*, 33. The difficulty of establishing this claim as plausible concerns the polyphonous character of the material. It hardly reads like a single composition. See Mark E. Biddle, *A Redaction History of Jeremiah 2:1–4:2*, ATANT 77 (Zurich: TVZ, 1990), 30–32. Biddle demonstrates the complexity of backgrounds that comprise the final form of 2:1–4:2, which ultimately functions as a theological paradigm for sin and repentance that shows clear signs of postexilic temple forms. Biddle argues that the final form demonstrates at least three different redactional agendas.

29. The MT version is roughly 15 percent longer than the LXX when it is retroverted back into Hebrew. At some point, a copy of this shorter Hebrew form was separated from the official copy in Jerusalem, and both Hebrew versions were revised independently, though the shorter version was less dramatically altered.

30. See Biddle, *Polyphony and Symphony in Prophetic Literature*.

31. See, for example, Exod 32:14; Judg 2:18; 2 Sam 24:16; Joel 2:13-14; Amos 7:3, 6. The most important of these texts is likely Amos 7:3, 6 where YHWH responds to prophetic intercession. There, YHWH twice relents concerning his decision to destroy Israel because the prophet has intervened for them. In Jer 15:6, YHWH tells Zion that he has tired of relenting, which simultaneously recognizes that YHWH has a history of doing so, but that he has reached the limit of his patience.

32. See Allen, *Jeremiah*, 237. Allen correctly notes that 25:1 begins with another "word of YHWH" superscription that marks a new unit, so he limits the longer unit to chapters 21–24. Nevertheless, Allen overlooks the two different thematic foci reflected in the chapter. He isolates Jer 25 as a separate composition, but its focus as a summation of the prophet's work for the past twenty-three years (see 25:3), along with the reference in 25:13 to "this book," suggests that the chapter served two connective functions. It originally served as an editorial conclusion to chapters 1–24 with a summation of the prophet's work (25:1-13) and a thematic summary of the coming judgment on the nations (25:15-38). Verse 14 was added by those who moved the oracles against the nations. These two portions of the chapter were originally separated by six chapters of material, so the chapter was not a single composition from the outset. In its current form, it belongs better with 21–24. The expansions in MT should generally be interpreted as additions to the earlier form represented by the Greek tradition.

33. Note the number of times a member of the Shaphan family is mentioned in Jer 26–45: 26:24; 29:3; 36:10-12; 39:14; 40:5, 9, 11; 41:2; 43:6.

34. See the assessment of Mark Roncase, *Jeremiah, Zedekiah, and the Fall of Jerusalem*, LHBOTS 423 (New York: T & T Clark, 2005).

35. See Deut 18:22: "If a prophet speaks in the name of the Lord but the thing does not take place or prove true, it is a word that the Lord has not spoken. The prophet has spoken it presumptuously; do not be frightened by it" (NRSV).

36. See the discussion below regarding how this theology advanced the agenda of those returning from Babylon in the early Persian period.

37. These formulas include the messenger formulas (30:2, 5, 12, 18; 31:2, 7, 15, 16, 23, 35, 37; 32:3, 14, 15, 28, 36, 42; 33:2, 4, 10, 12, 17, 20, 25), "at that time" sayings (31:1; 32:2; 33:15), various "word" formulas (30:1, 2, 4; 31:10, 23; 32:1, 6, 8, 26; 33:1, 19, 23), and others. One cannot always be sure these formu-

las introduce completely independent sayings because some depend syntactically upon their literary context.

38. The OAN were moved, but originally appeared in the middle of 25:13, between 25:13bα and 25:13bβ (the underlined portion): "I will bring upon that land all the words that I have uttered against it, everything written in this book, <u>which Jeremiah prophesied against all the nations</u>" (Jer 25:13 NRSV). The underlined dependent clause of 25:13bβ was originally a full sentence and functioned as a concluding statement to the OAN in the shorter Greek version. Jer 25:13bβ still appears at the end of the OAN in the Greek version in 32:13: "These are what Jeremiah prophesied against all the nations."

39. Compare the following: Jer 48:5 with Isa 15:5; Jer 48:29-39 with Isa 15–16; Jer 48:43-44 with Isa 24:17-18; and Jer 48:45-46 with Num 21:28-29.

40. See Terence E. Fretheim, *Jeremiah*, SHBC (Macon, GA: Smyth and Helwys, 2002), 576.

41. Schmid, *The Old Testament: A Literary History*, 170.

3. Ezekiel

1. Ezek 1:1 creates confusion as it begins "in the thirtieth year" without further clarification, and 1:2 refers to the fifth year of Jehoiachin's exile. The majority understand this date as a reference to the prophet's own birth. For many, the fact that Ezekiel was a priest (1:3) provides significant context since a male from the priestly line can only begin to serve as priest after turning thirty (Num 4:3, 23, 30, 39). A second group postulates that a missing phrase has dropped out, associating that phrase with the thirtieth year since the finding of the Book of the Law (which occurred in 622 during the eighteenth year of Josiah's reign). Others have suggested that the thirtieth year refers to the thirtieth year of Jehoiachin's exile, since all the other dated superscriptions are tied to that event. For these scholars, then, this date would be the latest dated superscription (around the year 569) and would represent a brief note of the date that the book of Ezekiel was first published; see the discussion and rejection of this point in Karl-Friedrich Pohlmann, *Der Prophet Hesekiel/Ezechiel Kapitel 1–19*, ATD 22, pt. 1 (Göttingen: Vandenhoeck and Ruprecht, 1996), 47–48; and Moshe Greenberg, *Ezekiel 1–20: A New Translation with Introduction and Commentary*, AB 22 (New Haven: Yale University Press, 1983), 39–40.

2. John Ahn, "Ezekiel 15: A מָשָׁל," in *The Prophets Speak on Forced Migration*, ed. Mark J. Boda et al., Ancient Israel and Its Literature 21 (Atlanta: Society of Biblical Literature, 2015), 103–4; Andrew Mein, "Ezekiel: Structure, Themes, and Contested Issues," in *The Oxford Handbook of the Prophets*, 194.

3. See David Vanderhooft, *The Neo-Babylonian Empire and Babylon in the Latter Prophets*, HSM 59 (Atlanta: Scholars Press, 1999), 110; and David L. Petersen, "Prophetic Rhetoric and Exile," in *The Prophets Speak on Forced Migration*, 12.

4. See Petersen, "Prophetic Rhetoric and Exile," 12.

5. See Ezek 40:46; 43:19; 44:15; 48:11; Steven Tuell, *Ezekiel*, NIBC (Grand Rapids: Hendrickson, 2009), 288–89.

6. See the rehearsal of scholarship in Walther Zimmerli, *Ezekiel 1: A Commentary on the Book of the Prophet Ezekiel, Chapters 1–24*, trans. Ronald E. Clements, Hermeneia (Philadelphia: Fortress, 1979), 3–8.

7. Similar expectations appear in the eschatological promises in Amos (9:11-12) and Hos (1:11 [Heb. 2:2]) that likely date to a time roughly contemporaneous with Ezekiel. See Paul Redditt, "The King in Haggai-Zechariah 1-8 and the Book of the Twelve," in *Tradition in Transition: Haggai and Zechariah 1–8 in the Trajectory of Hebrew Theology* (New York: T & T Clark, 2008), 56–82.

8. See the discussion of the location of 37:22-23 in the rhetorical flow of the larger speech in the section The Structure and Contents in Ezekiel below.

9. A third, much smaller, group argues that while a few passages may go back to the prophet, a far larger percentage of the book presupposes later redactional processes. Hence, for this group the book essentially represents a pseudepigraphic work from the fifth century BCE or later. See Gustav Hölscher, *Hesekiel, der Dichter und das Buch: Eine literarkritische Untersuchung* (Giessen: Töpelmann, 1924); Volkmar Herntrich, *Ezechielprobleme* (Giessen: Töpelmann, 1932); Jörg Garscha, *Studien zum Ezechielbuch: Eine redaktionskritische Untersuchung von 1-39* (Bern: Lang, 1974). Few have followed their lead.

10. For example, see Walther Eichrodt, *Ezekiel*, trans. Coslett Quinn, OTL (Philadelphia: Westminster, 1970), 18–22; Zimmerli, *Ezekiel 1*, 68–74; and Pohlmann, *Ezekiel 1–19*, 22–39.

11. So Greenberg, *Ezekiel 1–20*, 14–15, 18–27.

12. Compare Pohlmann, *Ezekiel 1–19*, 53–54; Zimmerli, *Ezekiel 1*, 106–7; and Greenberg, *Ezekiel 1–20*, 73. A brief look at the arguments of these three illustrates how the different redactional models account for the underlying material. Both Pohlmann and Zimmerli note the duplications present in the two texts and the difficulty of removing either account from the larger composition of chapters 1–3. Concerning 2:3-7, Pohlmann recognizes the two passages do not come from the same hand. Rather, he argues (1) that 2:3-7 gives a strong impression of being supplemental, (2) that the motif of ancestral apostasy reflects the ideas of a later author influenced by Deuteronomistic ideas about prophets, and (3) that 2:3-7 was inserted along with 3:4-9 because of the interconnected material in those two passages. Zimmerli argues that 3:4-9 represents an addition that develops ideas from 2:3, 5 by drawing connections to the call narratives from Isa 6 and Jer 1. It seems implausible that the prophet Ezekiel would have had access to a Jeremiah scroll hundreds of miles from Jerusalem, so one can understand how Zimmerli could treat this material as a later reflection on 2:3-7. By contrast, Greenberg does not treat 3:4-9 as a duplication but classifies it as "a renewed charge" that proceeds by taking up the themes from the preceding material and "in every case heightening them." Given that 3:4 begins with its own introductory formula, and thus gives the impression of a new unit, the idea that 3:4-9 merely represents a renewal of the charge seems less likely than that it represents a separate transmission piece. Greenberg, however, correctly highlights the effect that the sequence of the two versions communicates to the reader. The second unit is decidedly more pessimistic than the first, but Zimmerli's point should not be ignored. Someone has framed 3:4-9 so that it looks and sounds more like the words of Isaiah and Jeremiah, both of whose call narratives foreshadow the failure of the people to hear YHWH's word (Isa 6:9-13 and Jer 1:16-19).

13. Note that the prophet is commanded to speak more than twenty times in Ezekiel and the majority of these references appear between the command to be silent (3:22-27) and the lifting of the command (33:21-22): Ezek 6:11; 11:5, 16, 17; 12:10, 11, 23, 28; 13:11; 14:6; 17:9, 12; 20:30; 21:14; 22:24; 24:21; 28:2; 31:2; 33:10, 11, 12, 25; 36:22; 39:17.

14. Three examples illustrate the variety of explanations: Pohlmann, *Ezechiel 1–19*, 69–70; Zimmerli, *Ezekiel 2*, 183, 191; and Tuell, *Ezekiel*, 17–18. Pohlmann argues convincingly that the double appearance of the command to be a sentry followed closely by the motif of the prophet's silence cannot be accidental. The motifs appear as part of the opening commission to the prophet (3:16-21, 22-27) and at the end of the oracles against the nations, just before the oracles begin focusing upon Israel's restoration (33:1-20, 21-22). The fact that

the lifting of the suspension of the prophet's ability to speak on the very night he learns of Jerusalem's destruction further solidifies the importance of connecting these two motifs at key junctures in the book. Pohlmann therefore limits the silence motif to the concept of the sentinel. The reader should understand the silence regarding the prophet's role as sentinel. In other words, Ezekiel could only play the role of sentinel once Jerusalem had already fallen because YHWH had already determined to destroy Judah.

Zimmerli sees the watchman motif in both 3:17-21 and 33:2-9 as insertions into existing contexts. He treats the recurrence of the watchman motif in 33:2-9 as having "something of the weight of a second call to the prophet for the phase of proclamation at and after the fall of Jerusalem." He thinks that 33:21-22, by contrast, originally ended a version of the scroll before the addition of the oracles against the nations was inserted. In other words, Zimmerli argues that 33:21-22 immediately followed 24:25-27. Certainly, 24:25-27 anticipates 33:20-21 since it refers both to the messenger who will arrive in the night with word of Jerusalem's destruction and to the return of the prophet's ability to speak. That means, however, that 33:21-22 connects to the beginning and the end of chapters 1–24 and transitions from the oracles against the nations into the third part of the book of Ezekiel where the material begins to deal with the process of restoration.

Tuell prefers to see YHWH's command to be silent as YHWH placing limits upon the prophet's role to intercede for the people. Tuell may be correct that the editor of the book who created these links could not have intended the command to be silent to be taken literally, since chapter 4 immediately begins recounting the prophet's actions and speech. The idea that the editor conceptualized this command in terms of delimiting intercession from the prophet seems problematic, however, since the book records several instances of such intercession between chapters 4 and 33.

15. See also the condemnation of idols (Ezek 8:10; 14:3-7; 16:36; 18:6, 12, 15; 20:7-8, 16, 18, 24, 31, 39; 22:3-4; 23:7, 30, 37, 39, 49; 30:13; 33:25; 36:18, 25; 37:23; 43:9; 44:10, 12) and the high places (6:3, 6; 20:29).

16. Contrast this view with Amos 9:8-10, where those punished are removed from the land.

17. Pohlmann correctly identifies this pro-*golah* theology as part of the book's glue (Pohlmann, *Ezekiel 1–19*, 20–21).

18. See Tuell, *Ezekiel*, 128.

244

19. Ezek 22:25 in the MT condemns "her prophets" while the Greek tradition has "her princes." The difference in the two words is only one letter in Hebrew.

20. See Amos 9:11-12.

21. Only with the arrival of Alexander the Great over two hundred years later was Tyre conquered.

22. See Tuell, *Ezekiel*, 229.

23. Such are essentially the arguments, for example, of Zimmerli, *Ezekiel 1*, 218; Allen, *Ezekiel 20–48*, 159.

24. Commentators struggle to explain these verses. Greenberg indicates only that they are out of context but then says the issue is "elaborated" in 37:15-22, 24 (Greenberg, *Ezekiel 21–37*, 702). Zimmerli explores the problems of several attempted explanations (Zimmerli, *Ezekiel 2*, 218–20), including the uniqueness of the "one" shepherd, the avoidance of the word *king* by referring to David as a "prince," and the idea of a David *redivivus*.

25. Ezekiel tends to avoid the term *king* in favor of the word *prince* when talking about royal leadership from the house of David or the kings of the Northern Kingdom. See Tuell, *Ezekiel*, 240, and the rejection of this idea in Zimmerli, *Ezekiel 2*, 218.

26. This interpretation emphasizes that Ezekiel could favor Jehoiachin based on the fact that the dated superscriptions in Ezekiel align with the reign of Jehoiachin, not Zedekiah and not Nebuchadnezzar. Contrast Ezekiel's superscriptions with those of Haggai and Zechariah, which date the material to the reign of the Persian king Darius.

27. See the discussion of Obadiah in the last chapter of this book. One can see, for example, a similar dynamic at play in the placement of Obadiah following Amos within the Book of the Twelve. Edom is warned and its destruction anticipated immediately after the final vision of Amos recounts the destruction of Samaria. The structural and thematic parallels between Obadiah and Amos 9 clearly want the readers to see the similarities.

28. These last two units, along with the end of 36:23, do not appear in Vaticanus or in the Greek manuscript P967, which represents the earliest physical copy of significant portions of Ezekiel. Recent study has largely confirmed

MT as the later version, although both Vaticanus and P967 also show signs of development as well. See Ingrid E. Lilly, *Two Books of Ezekiel: Papyrus 967 and the Masoretic Text as Burial Literary Additions*, VTSup 150 (Leiden: Brill, 2012); and Ashley Crane, *Israel's Restoration: A Textural Comparative Exploration of Ezekiel 36–39*, VTSup 122 (Leiden: Brill, 2008).

29. See Tuell, *Ezekiel*, 263.

30. The Old Greek and P967 indicate that the bulk of 38–39 originally preceded chapter 37 with its installation of a Davidic monarch to rule the united kingdom. Pohlmann argues that 39:25-29 originally belonged with 36:16-23bα before the addition of the rest of 38–39 (Pohlmann, *Ezekiel 20–48*, 525). The proto-MT tradition at some point moved chapters 38–39 after chapter 37 and added 36:23c-38.

31. The programmatic nature of the description belies the fact that Ezekiel's plan bears little, if any, resemblance to the temple that was actually rebuilt. It should be noted, of course, that the text presumes that the prophet remains in Babylon during this vision. The prophet is transported to the temple by the "hand of YHWH" (40:1).

32. Each section will measure 25,000 cubits long and 10,000 cubits wide (45:3, 5). Additional land is set aside for each of the twelve tribes and for the prince, though each of these sections is smaller (25,000 x 5000 cubits; 45:6, 7). Given that a cubit generally represents approximately eighteen to twenty inches, the land allotted to the priests and Levites would have been approximately seven to eight miles long by three miles wide. The length of a cubit varied by time and location, so one can only speak in approximate terms, but these would have been massive dimensions for a city the size of Jerusalem. This holy district also factors into the allotment of land according to Ezek 48:8-21.

33. See "the city" (4:3; 5:2; 7:15, 23; 9:1, 4, 5, 7, 9; 10:2; 11:23; 30:18; 33:21; 40:1; 43:3; 45:6, 7; 48:15, 17, 18, 19, 20, 21, 22, 30, 31, 35) or "this city" (11:2, 3, 6, 7, 11).

34. See the discussion in Zimmerli, *Ezekiel 2*, 345, 356–58. He pays particular attention to why this vision cannot be treated as a recollection of the Solomonic temple. Further, the description of the building cannot be a blueprint since the directions are two dimensional (length and width only). Zimmerli typifies those who attribute the core of the vision to Ezekiel himself, with periodic expansions from the priestly school which transmitted the scroll of Ezekiel.

35. Stephen L. Cook, "Second Isaiah and the Aaronide Response to Judah's Forced Migrations," in *The Prophets Speak on Forced Migration*, 48–49.

36. Cook, "Second Isaiah and Aaronide Response," 48.

37. Tuell, *Ezekiel*, 288. Tuell speaks only of two lines of priestly tradition, the Levites and the Zadokites. Cook bases his threefold distinction on the works of Israel Knohl (Knohl, *The Sanctuary of Silence: The Priestly Torah and the Holiness School* [Minneapolis: Fortress, 1995]; idem, *The Divine Symphony: The Bible's Many Voices* [Philadelphia: Jewish Publication Society, 2003]).

4. The Beginnings of the Twelve

1. "Incipit prologus duodecim prophetarum," *Biblica Sacra Vulgata*, vol. 2, 1374

2. See Steven Tuell, *Reading Nahum–Malachi: A Literary and Theological Commentary* (Macon, GA: Smyth and Helwys, 2016), 2–5.

3. Karl Budde, "Eine folgenschwere Redaktion des Zwölfprophetenbuchs," *ZAW* 39 (1921): 218–29; Rolland Emerson Wolfe, "The Editing of the Book of the Twelve," *ZAW* 53 (1935): 90–129.

4. Umberto Cassuto, "The Sequence and Arrangement of the Biblical Sections," in *Biblical and Oriental Studies*, trans. Israel Abrams (Jerusalem: Magnes, 1973), 1:5-6.

5. Dale Allen Schneider, "The Unity of the Book of the Twelve" (PhD Diss., Yale University, 1979); Andrew Yueking Lee, "The Canonical Unity of the Scroll of the Minor Prophets" (PhD Diss., Baylor University, 1985).

6. James D. Nogalski, *Literary Precursors to the Book of the Twelve*, BZAW 217 (Berlin: de Gruyter, 1993); idem, *Redactional Process in the Book of the Twelve*, BZAW 218 (Berlin: de Gruyter, 1993).

7. For example, Schart argues Hosea and Amos formed a book of two prophets that circulated together and that Nahum and Habakkuk entered soon after the Book of the Four.

8. Aaron Schart, *Die Entstehung des Zwölfprophetenbuchs: Neubearbeitungen von Amos im Rahmen schriftenübergreifender Redaktionsprozesse*, BZAW 260 (Berlin: de Gruyter, 1998).

9. Burkard M. Zapff, *Redaktionsgeschichtliche Studien zum Michabuch im Kontext des Dodekapropheton*, BZAW 260 (Berlin: de Gruyter, 1997); idem, "The Book of Micah—The Theological Center of the Book of the Twelve?" in *Perspectives on the Formation of the Book of the Twelve: Methodological Foundations—Redactional Processes—Historical Insights*, ed. Rainer Albertz, James D. Nogalski, and Jakob Wöhrle, BZAW 433 (Berlin: de Gruyter, 2012), 129–46.

10. Boshhard's first article documents these parallels; see Erich Bosshard, "Beobachtungen zum Zwölfprophetenbuch," *BN* 40 (1987): 30–62. His dissertation explores the parallels with Isaiah further (Erich Bosshard-Nepustil, *Rezeptionen von Jesaia 1–39 im Zwölfprophetenbuch: Untersuchungen zur literarischen Verbindung von Prophetenbüchern in babylonischer und persischer Zeit*, Orbis Biblicus et Orientalis 154 [Freiburg, Switzerland: Universitätsverlag, 1997]).

11. Jakob Wöhrle, *Die frühen Sammlungen des Zwölfprophetenbuches: Entstehung und Komposition*, BZAW 360 (Berlin: de Gruyter, 2006); idem, *Der Abschluss des Zwölfprophetenbuches: Buchübergreifende Redaktionsprozesse in den späten Sammlungen*, BZAW 389 (Berlin: de Gruyter, 2008).

12. See Hag 1:1, 15; 2:1, 10, 18, 20; Zech 1:1, 7; 7:1.

13. Note the different messages for Judah and Israel in 1:7 and the pro-David ideology of 1:11 and 3:5. Not every reference to Judah requires a later hand, but many of these references stand out from their context.

14. For example, see Peggy L. Day, "A Prostitute unlike Women: Whoring as Metaphoric Vehicle for Foreign Alliances," in *Israel's Prophets and Israel's Past: Essays on the Relationship of Prophetic Texts and Israelite History in Honor of John H. Hayes*, LHBOTS 446 (New York: T & T Clark, 2006), 167–73; and Renita J. Weems, *Battered Love: Marriage, Sex, and Violence in the Hebrew Prophets*, OBT (Minneapolis: Fortress, 1995).

15. The Hebrew term *zônâ* is often misleadingly translated as *prostitute*. A *zônâ* refers to any unregulated and illicit sexual act, although the word is only used to refer to women. See J. Kühlewein, "znh," *Theological Lexicon of the Old Testament* 1:389.

16. These promises containing a distinctively Judean perspective appear elsewhere in Hosea (e.g., 4:15; 11:12) as well as at the end of Amos (9:11). Judah is also castigated in Hosea for following the lead of Ephraim (5:5, 10, 12-14; 6:4, 11; 8:14; 12:2).

17. YHWH's promise that he will "sow her" (i.e., the earth) for himself plays off the name "Jezreel," which means "God sows." Of course, the word *sow* also carries connotations of fertility. The names of the other two children are reversed. The names mean "not pitied" (Lo-ruhamah) and "not my people" (Lo-Ammi). YHWH promises to show pity upon Lo-ruhamah and to call Lo-Ammi "my people" instead.

18. Weiser already demonstrates this view (Artur Weiser, *Die Propheten Hosea, Joel, Amos, Obadja, Jona, Micha*, ATD 24 [Göttingen: Vandenhoeck and Ruprecht, 1955], 22–23). Despite the disclaimers of a number of synchronic studies in the late twentieth century, this opinion remains the majority opinion today among diachronic scholars, yet until recently, a surprising number of diachronic scholars treated 2:16-23 (Heb. 18–25) as added by disciples of Hosea in the latter third of the eighth century. So, for example, Weiser, ibid.; and Hans Walter Wolff, *Hosea*, trans. Gary Stansell, Hermeneia (Philadelphia: Fortress, 1974), 48. Both date 2:16-23 shortly after 733. Recent studies see the editing of the chapter as a more complex process, e.g., Roman Vielhauer, *Das Werden des Buches Hosea: Eine redaktionsgeschichtliche Untersuchung*, BZAW 349 (Berlin: de Gruyter, 2007).

19. For example, Fretheim summarizes three possible approaches to the question suggested by scholars: (1) continuing the story of Hosea and Gomer from Hos 1, (2) another version of the story of Hos 1 that presents different details, and (3) the story of a second woman and the prophet. See Terence E. Fretheim, *Reading Hosea–Micah: A Literary and Theological Commentary* (Macon, GA: Smyth and Helwys, 2013), 33–37. Fretheim opts for the chapter as a continuation of both Hos 1 and 2.

20. The verb appears more than twenty times throughout Hosea: 2:9, 11; 3:5; 4:9; 5:4, 15; 6:1, 11; 7:10, 16; 8:13; 9:3; 11:5, 9; 12:3, 7, 15; 14:2, 3, 5, 8.

21. Hos 9 begins with the final use of the harlot metaphor (9:1) and then threatens the land with a loss of fertility (9:1-2) and exile to Egypt and Assyria (9:3). They will lose the ability to offer sacrifices and celebrate festivals (9:4-6). "Days of punishment" will come for the prophets who have shown themselves corrupt and sinful (9:7-9). Israel's families will also experience infertility (9:14), and Ephraim will be punished for not listening to God (9:16-17). Hos 10 announces the coming punishment in terms of Assyria's overthrow of Israel's cult and king (10:1-9). These verses announce the death of the king and the destruction of Israel's altars, pillars, and the calf at Bethel along with the priests who run them.

22. The indictment includes in a call to "return to God" (12:1-6 [Heb. 12:2-7]). Immediately thereafter, the prophet recounts Ephraim's denial of guilt (12:7-8 [Heb. 12:8-9]) after which YHWH recounts his deliverance of Israel from Egypt and his sending of the prophets (12:9-10, 13 [Heb. 12:10-11, 14]), whose efforts were unsuccessful in keeping Ephraim from improper sacrifice on multiple altars (12:11 [Heb. 12:12]). In 13:1-3, one finds a brief judgment oracle that is heavy on the accusation against Ephraim for worshiping Baal, making idols, and worshiping them (13:1-2), followed by a short verdict that these worshipers will be wiped away (13:3). YHWH speaks about himself in 13:4-8. The remainder of the chapter continues with a series of judgment pronouncements in which YHWH announces he has removed Israel's kings (13:9-11), will withhold his compassion (13:12-14), and destroy Samaria and its people (13:15-16 [Heb. 13:15–14:1]).

23. Jörg Jeremias, *Der Prophet Hosea*, ATD 24, pt. 1 (Göttingen: Vandenhoeck and Ruprecht, 1983), 169.

24. For example, see James L. Mays, *Hosea*, OTL (London: SCM, 1969), 4; and Wolff, *Hosea*, xxi. Wolff and Mays associate Hos 5:8-11 with the Syro-Ephraimite War.

25. See, for example, Mays, *Hosea*, 4. Mays notes that 7:7 and 8:4 allude to the concluding period of Israel when a number of kings were murdered.

26. See Wolff, *Hosea*, xxi; Mays, *Hosea*, 4–5.

27. The vast majority of epithets are directed specifically at Ephraim, Israel, Bethel, or Samaria as the target of YHWH's anger. In fact, these Judean references contain at least two different ideas. The words of judgment imply a certain level of fear that the sins of Israel will find their way to Judah (4:15; 5:5, 12-14) or that Judah will be punished as well (6:11; 8:14; 12:2). Conversely, the words of promise that reflect a Judean outlook hold that Israel will find its true restoration only when reunited with Judah (e.g., 1:7, 11; 11:12).

28. Hos 2:21; 4:1; 5:1, 11; 6:4-6; 10:4, 12; 12:7; Amos 5:7, 15, 24; 6:12; Mic 3:1, 8-9; 6:8; 7:9, 18, 20; Zeph 2:3; 3:5, 8, 15.

29. Scholars explain the variations differently. Some consider all eight to be original, e.g., Francis Andersen and David Noel Freedman, *Amos: A New Translation with Introduction and Commentary*, AB 24A (New York: Doubleday, 1989), 26–30. Others differentiate two groups, e.g., Hans Walter Wolff, *Joel and Amos:*

A Commentary on the Books of the Prophets Joel and Amos, trans. Waldemar Janzen et al., Hermeneia (Philadelphia: Fortress, 1977), 139–40.

30. For example, see the discussion in Wolff, *Joel and Amos*, 139–40; and the chart in James D. Nogalski, *The Book of the Twelve: Hosea–Jonah*, SHBC (Macon, GA: Smyth and Helwys, 2011), 276–77.

31. Hos 4:15; 5:5, 10, 12-14; 6:4, 11; 8:14; 10:11; 12:2; Amos 2:4-5; 6:1.

32. James L. Mays, *Amos*, OTL (Philadelphia: Westminster, 1969), 114; Jörg Jeremias, *Der Prophet Amos*, ATD 24, pt. 2 (Göttingen: Vandenhoeck and Ruprecht, 1995), 85.

33. See especially the discussion of Mic 1:2-7.

34. Arguments against originality highlight the very different structure and the likelihood that it reflects Samaria's destruction (722 BCE). Compare the opposing views of Wöhrle, *Die frühen Sammlungen*, 114–17 and Marvin A. Sweeney, *The Twelve Prophets*, Berit Olam (Collegeville, MN: Liturgical Press, 2000), 268–70.

35. For example, see Werner H. Schmidt, "Die deuteronomistische Redaktion des Amosbuches: Zu den theologischen Unterschieden zwischen dem Prophetenwort und seinem Sammler," ZAW 77 (1965): 168–93; and J. D. W. Watts, "The Origin of the Book of Amos," *Expository Times* 66 (1954–1955): 109–12.

36. Debate exists regarding the origin of this narrative. Many posit that it circulated with the visions, since 7:10 assumes the reader knows Amos. Others suggest that such narratives were transmitted for a lengthy time among the prophet's followers. Others point to a similar vignette about Jeremiah, and suggest that Deuteronomistic circles collected stories about the prophets. Some studies suggest that the narrative was composed for this context because of the reference to the sword of Jeroboam that appears at the end of the third vision (7:9) and in the narrative (7:11). See Wolff, *Joel and Amos*, 119–21, 308–10; Jeremias, *Der Prophet Amos*, 106–12; and Helmut Utzschneider, "Die Amazjaerzählung (Am 7:10-17) zwischen Literatur und Historie," *BN* 41 (1988): 76–101.

37. See the chart in James D. Nogalski, *The Book of the Twelve: Hosea–Jonah*, SHBC (Macon, GA: Smyth and Helwys, 2011), 344.

38. See the discussion in Nogalski, *Literary Precursors*, 81.

39. Rick W. Byargeon, "The Doxologies of Amos: A Study of Their Structure and Theology," *Theological Educator* 52 (1995): 47–56.

40. See the discussion of the composition of Amos below.

41. The second half of this promise differs slightly from Joel, which says that the hills will flow with milk. Nevertheless, there is little doubt that the quote is intentional. The motto of Amos (1:2) begins with a parallel to Joel 3:16 (Heb. 4:16), and Amos 9:13 draws upon Joel 3:18 (Heb. 4:18).

42. Some maintain that early collections of Amos and Hosea were linked to one another editorially from the time of Hosea onward. See especially Schart, *Die Entstehung des Zwölfprophetenbuchs*, 185–90, 201–4; Jörg Jeremias, "Die Anfänge des Dodekapropheton: Hosea und Amos," in *Hosea und Amos: Studien zu den Anfängen des Dodekapropheton*, FAT 13 (Tübingen: Mohr Siebeck, 1996), 34–54. Other scholars reject the early combination of Hosea and Amos and argue the two books were joined after Jerusalem's destruction with the creation of the early form of the Book of the Four. See Wöhrle, *Die frühen Sammlungen*, 241–44.

43. See discussion of Mic 1:5-7 as a transitional introduction to the Four Prophets below.

44. See the history of Edom after Babylon's destruction in Joel S. Burnett, "Transjordan: The Ammonites, Moabites, and Edomites," in *The World around the Old Testament: The People and Places of the Ancient Near East*, ed. Bill T. Arnold and Brent A. Strawn (Grand Rapids: Baker, 2016), 337–39.

45. Debates continue regarding whether the insertions linking Amos 9:12 to Obadiah and Amos 9:13 to Joel occurred simultaneously or in two stages. The majority of scholars working on the Book of the Twelve suggest that Obadiah entered the multivolume corpus prior to Joel. See Schart, *Die Entstehung des Zwölfprophetenbuchs*, 272–74; Wöhrle, *Der Abschluss des Zwölfprophetenbuches*, 212–18; and Nogalski, *Redactional Processes*, 89–92.

46. Jer 26:18-19 reinforces the image of Micah as an opponent of Hezekiah. The "elders of the land" come to Jeremiah's defense by quoting Mic 3:12, a verse that uncategorically pronounces Jerusalem's destruction. These elders stress that Hezekiah did not kill Micah when he pronounced this judgment.

47. Scholars note that the nations as the recipient of YHWH's judgment only comes into play in chapters 4–7. Wolff and Mays, for example, see Mic 1:3-5 (Wolff) or 1:5b, 6-7 (Mays) as Deuteronomistic additions from the time

of the exile (Hans Walter Wolff, *Micah*, trans. Gary Stansell, Continental Commentaries [Minneapolis: Augsburg, 1990], 51–53; and James L. Mays, *Micah*, OTL [Philadelphia: Westminster, 1976], 24–26). Utzschneider argues that 1:2-7 comes from the late sixth or early fifth century (Helmut Utzschneider, *Micha*, Zürcher Bibelkommentar 24, pt. 1 (Zurich: TVZ, 2005), 26.

48. Utzschneider, *Micha*, 25–26; Mays, *Micah*, 23; Wolff, *Micah*, 53.

49. Several introductory markers often open new units: "Woe" (2:1), "on that day" (2:4), "thus says YHWH" (3:5), and "hear this" (3:1, 9). Relatedly, several climactic uses of "therefore" typically mark the end of judgment oracles when YHWH pronounces the verdict (2:3, 5; 3:6, 12). This verdict serves to bring the oracle to a close.

50. Nogalski, *Literary Precursors*, 141–44; Wolff, *Micah*, xxvii; and Mays, *Micah*, 21–33.

51. Some question whether a legal setting should frame our understanding of the speeches. See Utzschneider, *Micha*, 131–32. Nevertheless, the legal drama begins with a call to attention as the opening of the legal case (*rîb* in 6:1-2).

52. The wealthy who practice violence in 6:12aα coincide with the property owners who forcibly evict people from their homes (2:1-5) and leaders who commit violence against their own people (3:1-3). The verbal and ethical deceit of the people (6:2aβ-b) parallels the accusations in Zeph 2:6-11. The charge of shortchanging customers by using false weights and baskets (Mic 6:10b-11) echoes Amos 8:5. The "house of wickedness" (*bêth-reš'a*) refers to Jerusalem (Mic 6:10) and parallels the "house of injustice" as Bethel (*bêth-'āven* in Hos 4:15; 5:8; 10:5).

53. See Schart, *Die Entstehung des Zwölfprophetenbuchs*, 199–200. Schart connects these passages to the curse material in Deut 28:30-31, 38-41.

54. These traditions appear within the legal rhetoric of the trial speech in 6:1-16 as they call to mind liberation from slavery, and name Moses, Aaron, and Miriam (6:4). YHWH refers to the battles in the Transjordan (recalling Balak and Balaam) and the crossing of the Jordan (6:5) by mentioning Shittim (the last camp beyond the river) and Gilgal (the major base of operations within Israel in Joshua). Mic 6:16 accuses Judah of idolatry by mentioning the statutes of the wicked kings Omri and his son Ahab, whose story covers large swaths of the book of Kings (6:16).

55. Gunkel classified 7:8-20 as an independent, postexilic, prophetic liturgy appended to Micah to provide a hopeful ending to the book, and his explanation dominated the interpretation for much of the twentieth century. This liturgical interpretation furnished a framework to account for the changing speakers and addressees, but treating Mic 7:8-20 as a preexisting source created difficulties identifying the unnamed enemy in 7:8-10. Babylon and Edom were frequently named in these discussions. In the last two decades, the literary context of Micah has increasingly received attention as the context from which to interpret the changing speakers, even though most scholars still see the text as a Persian-period composition. The discussion here interprets Mic 7:8-20 as a Persian-period dialogical composition composed as a response to Mic 1–3 and 6, with particular attention to the ways 7:8-20 assumes the siege of Sennacherib and its aftermath as it looks to the "future" from the perspective of Micah's eighth-century setting. See Hermann Gunkel, "Der Micha-Schluss: Zur Einführung in die literaturgeschichtliche Arbeit am AT," *Zeitschrift für Semitistik* 2 (1924): 145–78. Mays (*Micah*, 158–59) follows Gunkel in assuming Edom as the enemy. Theodor Lescow argues for Babylon ("Redaktionsgeschichtliche Analyse von Micha 6–7," *ZAW* 84 [1972]: 205). Nogalski argues for Lady Nineveh (James D. Nogalski, "Micah 7:8-20: A Re-evaluation of the Identity of the Enemy," in *The Bible as a Witness to Divine Revelation: Hearing the Word of God through Historically Dissimilar Traditions*, ed. Randall Heskett and Brian Irwin, LHBOTS 469 [New York: T and T Clark, 2010], 125–44).

56. For a discussion of the background of Lady Zion and other personified cities in the context of Western Semitic texts and traditions, see Nogalski, "Micah 7:8-20," 125–44.

57. This late text has been interpreted in one of two ways: as an independent liturgy promising to rebuild the walls of Jerusalem in the aftermath of Jerusalem's destruction and as a promise to Jerusalem from the time of Hezekiah. Those interpreting 7:8-20 as an independent "liturgy" stress the postexilic audience, while those treating it as a redactional composition tend to read these verses against the literary backdrop of Sennacherib's siege during the reign of Hezekiah, who is credited with the foresight of extending the walls of Jerusalem to help stave off Sennacherib's army (2 Chr 32:1-5; 2 Kgs 20:20). The biblical accounts in 2 Kgs 18–20; 2 Chr 29–32; and Isa 36–38 attribute Sennacherib's withdrawal to YHWH's intervention, while the annals of Sennacherib record that Hezekiah paid tribute to Sennacherib (*ANET*, 288). Two lines of evidence are significant. First, the superscription (1:1) associating Micah with Hezekiah would have existed, and second, 7:8-20 repeatedly evokes key words and phrases found in Isa-

iah 9–10, a text that refers to the events of 701 BCE. The allusive character of Mic 7:8-20 assumes that the speeches are intended to address Lady Zion (= Jerusalem personified) and the people at the end of the eighth century. See James D. Nogalski, *Literary Precursors*, 155–58; idem, "Micah 7:8-20," 129–30; and idem., *Micah–Malachi*, 587–88.

58. Nogalski, *Micah–Malachi*, 587–89.

59. The phrase "come to" (*bw'* + *'ad*) can imply military attacks (Judg 7:13; 9:52; 11:33; Judg 15:14; 1 Sam 17:52).

60. The fear of the nations appears prominently in passages such as Num 22:3; Deut 2:25; 11:25; Josh 2:9, 24; 9:24.

61. Van Leeuwen demonstrates that texts in Joel–Nahum allude to Exod 34:6-7, and Book of the Twelve scholars have subsequently incorporated these allusions into their models for the development of the Twelve. The allusions use key terms, but the theme of YHWH's *hesed* toward YHWH's people that appears in Mic 7:18-19 draws upon Exod 34:6, while the theme of judgment against YHWH's enemies emphasized in Nah 1:2b-3 draws more upon Exod 34:7. The two themes appear in Joel with 2:13b-14a drawing upon YHWH's compassion using Exod 34:6, as in Mic 7:18-19, and Joel 3:19-21 drawing upon Exod 34:7, like Nah 1:2b-3a. See Raymond C. Van Leeuwen, "Scribal Wisdom and Theodicy in the Book of the Twelve," in *In Search of Wisdom: Essays in Memory of John G. Gammie*, ed. Leo G. Perdue, Bernard Scott, and William Wiseman (Louisville: Westminster John Knox, 1993), 31–49; and Nogalski, *Hosea–Jonah*, 14–15.

62. Jörg Jeremias, *Die Propheten Joel, Obadja, Jona, Micha*, ATD 24, pt. 3 (Göttingen: Vandenhoeck and Ruprecht, 2007), 118–20. As Jeremias (ibid., 124) notes, chapters 4–5 focus thematically upon the future plans of God for Jerusalem after its destruction, while chapters 6–7 focus upon how the experience of exile changes Israel.

63. Mic 5:5 anticipates "seven . . . and eight" shepherds who fight against the enemies. This formula likely reflects knowledge that eight Judean kings reigned from the time of Sennacherib's siege to the removal of Zedekiah from the throne (Hezekiah, Manasseh, Amon, Josiah, Jehoahaz, Jehoiakim, Jehoiachin, Zedekiah).

64. The phrase "the mountain of the house" or "the mountain of the Lord's house" appears only five times in the Old Testament, with four of them related to either Mic 4:1 (= Isa 2:2) or Mic 3:12 (cited in Jer 26:18).

65. Critical scholars and ancient traditions often assume that Micah (the younger contemporary of Isaiah) borrowed the passage. Redactional investigations in recent decades demonstrate that the passage enters both Isaiah and Micah at a relatively late stage, complicating analysis of the borrower. See Burkard M. Zapff, *Redaktionsgeschichtliche Studien zum Michabuch im Kontext des Dodekapropheton*, BZAW 256 (Berlin: de Gruyter, 1997), 64–77. By focusing on the function in Micah, one need not resolve this question. Still, arguments that Mic 4:1-4 quotes Isa 2:2-4 are more compelling for two reasons: first, appending Mic 4:5 to the quote modifies the promise toward the nations since it qualifies the more radical expression in Isa 2:2-4; and second, in most redactional models, Isa 2:1-4 enters Isaiah before most of chapter 1, while the carefully constructed version of Mic 4–5 represents the latest additions to Micah.

66. See Nogalski, *Literary Precursors*, 209–11.

67. Scholars continue to debate specific times in Josiah's reign that might explain the setting of these oracles. Most situate the early material between the beginning of Josiah's reforms in 622 BCE and his death in 609 BCE at the hands of Pharaoh Neco II (610–595 BCE). References to the "remnant of Baal" and the "idolatrous priests" in 1:4 make more sense after Josiah's reforms had begun, since eliminating the worship of Baal and Assyrian astral deities formed a central plank in those reforms. Second, scholars increasingly explain the OAN in Zeph 2:4-15 as a collection against those nations who benefitted most from collusion with Assyria. Assyria's political control declined relatively rapidly, beginning in the 620s, and ended when the Babylonians destroyed Nineveh in 612 BCE.

68. For example, Gen 10 assigns Cush to the line of Ham, along with Nimrod, his son (10:8) who became the founder of Babylon, Accadia, and Assyria (10:10-11). Debates exist about the relationship between Cush and the Arabian Desert.

69. See Robert R. Wilson, *Genealogy and History in the Biblical World* (New Haven: Yale University Press, 1981), 59–62.

70. See J. Heller, "Zephanjas Ahnenreihe," *VT* 21 (1971): 21–31; Gene Rice, "The African Roots of the Prophet Zephaniah," *Journal of Religious Thought* 36 (1979–1980): 102–4.

71. See the discussion of the Book of the Four in Hosea, Amos, and Micah above. For specifics regarding Zeph 1:1, see Nogalski, *Literary Precursors*, 181–87.

72. Debates continue regarding the number of stages involved before Zephaniah reached its final form. A few read the whole book as a seventh-century composition, e.g., Marvin Sweeney, *Zephaniah*, Hermeneia (Minneapolis: Fortress Press, 2003), 14–15. Others treat Zephaniah as entirely postmonarchic, e.g., Ehud Ben Zvi, *A Historical-Critical Study of the Book of Zephaniah*, BZAW 198 (Berlin: de Gruyter, 1991), 271, 298–306. Wöhrle argues that a small foundational layer grew with a series of four redactional layers and a few isolated additions (Wöhrle, *Die frühen Sammlungen*, 198–228).

73. The redactional seams of Zephaniah (1:2-3; 2:11b-15; and 3:9-10) allude to texts in Gen 1–11 containing both Priestly and non-Priestly materials. The penultimate unit at the end of Zephaniah (3:18-19) presupposes a late text in Micah (4:6-7), and Zeph 3:20 anticipates a transition to Haggai, after it had been joined with Zech 1–8. See James D. Nogalski, "Zephaniah's Use of Genesis 1–11," *HeBAI* 2 (2013): 1–23.

74. Portions of 2:11-15 were likely edited to reflect knowledge of Gen 10. See discussion below.

75. Scholars still debate how these compositions entered the book. Several characteristics suggest the early core combines short compositions that exhibit three rhetorical purposes. The announcement of judgment and accusations against those who have turned their back on YHWH begins the early collection (1:4-6), followed by descriptions of the coming day of YHWH (1:7-18), and a concluding exhortation to seek YHWH (2:1-3). These compositions read like summaries of speeches that are joined editorially. They frequently use new introductory formulas or new commands. The second thematic unit appears even more disjointed since it has no fewer than three separate introductory formulas: "on that day" (1:9, 10) and "at that time" (1:12). This section announces the coming day of YHWH (1:7; also called the "day of the Lord's sacrifice" in 1:8) and condemns the royal household who dress like their foreign overlords. Zeph 1:14-18 reads like an extended composition with an ongoing refrain referring to "the day" ten times. Thematically, each unit deals with images of a coming day of judgment against Jerusalem. It may be composite, but rhetorically the unit focuses on the coming judgment against Jerusalem as the day of YHWH.

76. See the extensive list in Wöhrle, *Die frühen Sammlungen*, 201–3.

77. This remnant motif gives way to a promise to restore YHWH's kingdom in Zion (3:14-17). Compare the promise in Zeph 3:14-17 with Amos 9:11, 14-15. Following a brief introduction of a remnant (Amos 9:8b-10), YHWH

promises to raise the fallen booth of David, to rebuild the cities, and to restore the fortunes of Judah. Zeph 3:11-13 deals briefly with the remnant while 3:14-17 exhorts Lady Zion to rejoice over YHWH's defeat of the enemies, his return to Jerusalem, and his restoration of her fortunes (cf. 3:20).

78. James D. Nogalski, "The Day(s) of YHWH in the Book of the Twelve," in *Thematic Threads in the Book of the Twelve*, ed. Paul L. Redditt and Aaron Schart, BZAW 325 (Berlin: de Gruyter, 2003), 193–95.

79. For example, Günter Krinetzki, *Zefanjastudien: Motiv- und Traditionskritik und Kompositions- und Redaktionskritik*, Regensburger Studien zur Theologie 7 (Frankfurt: Lang, 1977), 157–66; and even more concretely, Erich Bosshard, "Beobachtungen," 34–35, 56–62.

80. These verses stand apart from the tightly constructed unit of 3:14-17, but they also presuppose that YHWH has returned to Jerusalem from 3:14-17. Zeph 3:18a promises to gather "those among you (feminine singular) mourning the appointed times," thus continuing the second feminine address of Zion from 3:14-17 but introducing a cultic focus. A change of address appears in 3:18b (from 2fs to 3fs pronouns) that acknowledges these mourners "have been a burden for her (Zion), a reproach." As such 3:18b speaks about (not to) Zion but reintroduces the salvific message for the remnant linked thematically to 3:1-8a, 3:11-13, and 3:14-17, 18a.

81. The reformulation of Mic 4:6-7 in Zeph 3:19-20 expresses the promise of the "gathering" and "salvation" of "the lame" (*ndḥ*) and "the outcast" (*ṣl'*) using the construction *hinēh* plus a participle that demonstrates imminent future, whereas the time frame of Mic 4:6-7 attaches itself to the message that is placed in the "days to come" (Mic 4:1). See Nogalski, *Literary Precursors*, 209–11. The fact that these two verses also use the word *time* three times in rapid succession to refer to the period when Jerusalem will be restored offers an inviting parallel to the beginning of Haggai, whose opening speech begins with the prophet confronting the people who are not sure that the "time" has come for temple reconstruction to begin. The prophetic challenge to the people also uses the word *time* three times (Hag 1:2 twice, 4). The triple use of *time* in such close proximity does not occur elsewhere in the Old Testament.

82. Haggai begins with a series of speeches that challenge "this people" to rebuild the temple if they wish to improve their economic plight, among other reasons. The juxtaposition of the salvific expectations for the people in Zephaniah contrasted with the current situation of the people's suffering in Haggai

happens elsewhere in the Book of the Twelve, and probably represents deliberate decisions on the part of the compilers of the scroll. See Nogalski, *Redactional Processes*, 212–15 (and see ibid, 219–21, for the narrower horizon of Haggai).

83. The restoration of the fortunes of Judah articulated in 3:20 concludes a thread that appears in Hosea (6:1), Amos (9:14), and (Joel 4:1). The substance of this expectation fits Joel better than Hosea and Amos. Hos 6:1 contrasts the restoration of Judah with the punishment of Israel. Amos 9:14 anticipates a restoration that involves the rebuilding of the ruined cities and the return to agricultural normalcy. By contrast, the language of Joel 4:1 anticipates that restoration "in those days and *at that time*" (as with Zeph 3:20) will include judgment on the surrounding nations, who have taken advantage of Judah and Jerusalem, and exhibits a much grander expectation for YHWH's return.

84. Michael DeRoche, "Zephaniah 1:2-3: The 'Sweeping' of Creation," *VT* 30 (1980): 104–9.

85. Adele Berlin, *Zephaniah: A New Translation with Introduction and Commentary*, AB 25 (New York: Doubleday, 1994), 111–13, 120–24. See also Nogalski, *Micah–Malachi*, 704–6, and idem, "Zephaniah's Use of Genesis 1–11," 8. Berlin's evidence includes a series of six lexical and logical arguments: (1) Only Zeph 2:11b and Gen 10:5 use the phrase "islands of the nations," (2) the combination of Cush and Assyria is also rare (Zeph 2:13; Gen 10:11), (3) the line of Ham includes Assyria according to Gen 10:11, (4) the line of Ham also includes Canaan according to Gen 10:15 (cf. Zeph 2:5), (5) the material in Zeph 2:4-15 condemns two of the three genealogical lines of Noah's sons (Japheth and Ham), (6) the omission of Edom from Zeph 2:4-15 makes sense because Edom does not appear in Gen 10.

86. James D. Nogalski, *Micah–Malachi*, 702, 704–5.

87. For example, see Rolf Rendtorff, "Alas for the Day! The Day of the Lord in the Book of the Twelve," in *God in the Fray: A Tribute to Walter Brueggemann*, ed. Tod Linafelt and Timothy K. Beal (Minneapolis: Fortress, 1998), 186–92.

5. The End of the Twelve

1. Ezra 3–4 describes a scenario in which Joshua and Zerubbabel rebuilt the altar and laid the foundation for the temple before resistance from nonreturnees, Benjaminites, and Samarians thwarted those attempts. Historical details in Ezra 3–4 raise many questions, but the portrait of groups with conflicting agendas

would almost certainly have been part of the communal reality. See Knoppers, *Jews and Samaritans*, 135–68.

2. For explanations of the backgrounds of these debates, see Odil Hannes Steck, "Zu Haggai 1:2-11," *ZAW* 83 (1971): 355–79; Rainer Albertz, *A History of Israelite Religion*, 2:451–56; and Miller and Hayes, *A History of Ancient Israel and Judah*, 512–13. Albertz suggests that Zerubbabel, Haggai, and Zechariah were gone before the temple was completed and that prophetic hopes for Zerubbabel created a rift among Judean elites, who toned down prophecy's political aspirations and socially marginalized those groups. A prophetic backlash advocated a renewed kingdom that became more "eschatologized" and dehistoricized. Miller and Hayes recognize three different versions in Ezra 1–6 that credit temple restoration to alternating combinations of Sheshbazzar, Zerubbabel, Joshua, Haggai, and Zechariah.

3. Albertz, *A History of Israelite Religion*, 2:453–54; Miller and Hayes, *A History of Ancient Israel and Judah*, 512–13.

4. A few argue the combined version of Haggai and Zechariah 1–8 was published together near the time of the completion of the temple in 515 BCE, e.g., Eric M. Meyers and Carol L. Meyers, *Zechariah 9-14: A New Translation with Introduction and Commentary*, AB 25C (New York: Doubleday, 1993), xlvii; Mark J. Boda, *The Book of Zechariah*, NICOT (Grand Rapids: Eerdmans, 2016), 33. Others, however, point to evidence that the introductions ascribed to the Haggai chronicler in several cases represent secondary introductory elements inserted into speech reports that already had introductions. See Steck, "Zu Haggai," 355–57, 372–73; and Albertz, *A History of Israelite Religion*, 2:454–55. The dates in these models could be a century after Haggai.

5. All but one of the chronological notes functions as an introduction to what follows: Hag 1:1 → 1:2-11; 2:1 → 2:2-9; 2:10 → 2:11-19; and 2:20 → (2:21-23). Hag 2:20 lists the same day as 2:10. Unusually, 1:15 concludes the narrative response to Haggai's first speech in 1:12-14.

6. Eric M. Meyers and Carol L. Meyers, *Haggai, Zechariah 1–8: A New Translation with Introduction and Commentary*, AB 25B (New York: Doubleday, 1987), 23; Hans Walter Wolff, *Haggai*, trans. Margaret Kohl (Minneapolis: Augsburg, 1988), 31–33; Martin Leuenberger, *Haggai*, HThKAT (Freiburg im Breisgau: Herder, 2015), 100–105. The problem of three different introductory formulas that appear in 1:1, 2, 3 is frequently resolved diachronically, but few take note that the people are addressed in the third person in 1:2. The second per-

son plural forms in 1:4 (and the question of the paneled houses) could actually intend to refer only to Zerubbabel and Joshua. The result of this reading is that 1:2 accuses the people of resisting the rebuilding of the temple, and that 1:3-4 would be challenging Zerubbabel and Joshua to recognize that their own living in comfortable homes adds to the problem. This reading would explain why "paneled houses" are referred to when only a small percentage of people would have lived in such houses.

7. For years, scholars explained this chronological element as an introduction to a speech that had been lost or moved. In recent years, such speculation has given way to treating the date formula in 1:15 as the conclusion to 1:12-14 (Nogalski, *Micah–Malachi*, 778).

8. The date in 1:1 refers to the first day of the sixth month while 1:15 refers to the twenty-fourth day of that month.

9. Ezra 3:10-13 describes two very different responses to the initial rebuilding of the temple. One group rejoiced as the work began, while another group of elderly inhabitants and cultic leaders wailed in lamentation.

10. The space, and the people working upon it, have to be ritually purified in order for the work to continue. Building temples in the ancient Near East often involved ritual purification ceremonies at key points along the way, probably including at the point when the foundation stone was laid. See David L. Petersen, *Haggai and Zechariah 1–8*, OTL (London: SCM, 1984), 33, 71–85.

11. James D. Nogalski, "Presumptions of Covenant in Joel," in *Covenant in the Persian Period: From Genesis to Chronicles*, ed. Richard J. Bautch and Gary N. Knoppers (Winona Lake: Eisenbrauns, 2015), 211–28.

12. See James D. Nogalski, "Joel as Literary Anchor in the Book of the Twelve," in *Reading and Hearing the Book of the Twelve*, ed. James D. Nogalski and Marvin A. Sweeney, Symposium Series 15 (Atlanta: Society of Biblical Literature, 2000), 91–109. Joel imagery reappears in several places across the Twelve. A series of "locusts" attacks play out across the Twelve in the form of foreign armies who devour what other locusts had left (Joel 1:4; cf. Nah 3:15; Hab 1:9; Mal 3:11). Images of infertility involving the signs of covenant curse through lists of items that are threatened and restored (wine, vine, and grain or the vine, fig tree, and pomegranate) ultimately give way to the hope that fertility is returning to the land using similar images (Joel 2:19-20; Hab 3:17-18; Hag 2:19; Zech 8:12; Mal 3:10-12).

13. For discussion of the various ways that prophetic statements about the future can be classified, see J. J. M. Roberts, "A Christian Perspective on Prophetic Prediction," *Interpretation* 33 (1979): 240–53. Similar expectations for the future leadership of Zerubbabel appear in Zech 4:6-10, though that passage focuses more explicitly on Zerubbabel's completion of the building of the temple after laying the temple cornerstone.

14. Jeremiah recounts a series of events leading to Jerusalem's destruction in great detail including confrontations with Jehoiakim (Jer 25; 35–36) and Zedekiah (Jer 37–38), parallel narratives of Jerusalem's fall (Jer 39; 52), as well as a series of narratives regarding the aftermath of Jerusalem's destruction for the people left behind (Jer 40–44). Ezekiel records events from the perspective of the exile. The beginning of the book records the prophet's vision five years into the first deportation following 597 BCE (Ezek 1:2), and Ezekiel is living among the exiles in Babylon. Thus, the four prophetic scrolls of the Latter Prophets can be grouped into two pairs, with each pair providing a slightly different historical perspective. The scrolls of Isaiah and the Twelve cover the eighth century to the Persian period. The scroll of Isaiah speaks with the voice of one named prophet, while the Twelve moves its readers through the same time frame using twelve different prophetic voices. Both Isaiah and the Twelve omit any narrative of Jerusalem's destruction or the exile of its leaders. To be sure, both scrolls contain numerous passages that either anticipate Jerusalem's impending destruction or that look back upon those events after the fall of Babylon. By contrast, Jeremiah and Ezekiel devote a great deal of time to the events surrounding Jerusalem's destruction and the deportation of its people. Jeremiah looks at these events primarily through the lens of those who remained in the land, while Ezekiel reports from outside the land as one of the deportees.

15. Isa 40 opens with YHWH's decision to end Jerusalem's punishment and to create a pathway for the exiles to return. Cyrus is presented as YHWH's new servant king carrying out YHWH's orders to rebuild Jerusalem (Isa 44:28; 45:1-6).

16. See Petersen, *Haggai and Zechariah 1–8*, 110–25. Petersen refers to these three sections of the book as the "prologue," "the visions," and "the oracles."

17. See Petersen, *Haggai and Zechariah 1–8*, 110; Martin Hallaschka, *Haggai und Sacharja 1–8*, BZAW 411 (Berlin: de Gruyter, 2010), 150.

18. Hos 14 and Joel 1–2 present extended calls first to Israel and then to Judah in the Book of the Twelve, but neither narrates an explicit response. By contrast, Amos 4:6-11 lists a number of opportunities for Israel to return to

YHWH in which they failed to do so. In Mal 3:7, a call to "return" is met with a claim of ignorance. The response in Zech 1:6 raises expectations for a positive outcome, and this hope largely continues throughout Zech 1–8.

19. For the relationship of these vision reports to those of Amos, Jeremiah, and Ezekiel, see Boda, *Zechariah*, 90–100.

20. A few scholars interpret the four horns in the context of a cultic setting because of texts outside Zechariah that refer to the horns of the altar, but this reasoning creates other problems because altars do not scatter nations. Boda basically agrees that the horns represent political powers, but interprets the four horns as two oxen and the *ḥārāšîm* as farmers (plowers). His suggestion is creative, but since he has to repoint the *ḥārāšîm* to *ḥōrešîm* to translate the word as *farmers*, caution should be advised. See Boda, *Zechariah*, 163–64. Boda's suggestion demonstrates a possible double entendre in that the consonantal text could be read either way. It does not account for the fact that the community responsible for the MT pointing did not read the text in this way.

21. The scene involves a court setting where YHWH rebukes the accuser (3:2) and the heavenly council re-clothes Joshua in priestly garments (3:3-5), followed by an admonishment to Joshua that his access to the heavenly realm remains contingent upon following YHWH's commands (3:6-7). See Boda, *Zechariah*, 226–62.

22. See the discussion of Hag 2:20-23 above and Boda, *Zechariah*, 253–55, 382–86.

23. Davidic descendants continued to exist as a recognizable group. See Meyers and Meyers, *Haggai, Zechariah 1–8*, 13–18 (especially the chart on p. 14).

24. Most notably, Kurt Galling, "Die Exilswende in der Sicht des Propheten Sacharja," *VT* 2 (1952): 18–36. Galling finds three settings for the visions: the time of Babylon's downfall, the time shortly before the temple construction, and the time mentioned in 1:7, just a few months after the foundation stone had been set (according to Hag 2:10-23). Galling also notes a progression in the sequence of the visions that is more thematic than chronological.

25. Petersen, *Haggai and Zechariah 1–8*, 111–12.

26. See Andrew E. Hill, "Dating Second Zechariah: A Linguistic Reexamination," *Hebrew Annual Review* 6 (1982): 105–34; and Boda, *Zechariah*, 33–34.

27. In 9:1, many scholars and translators separate *maśśā'* and treat "the word of YHWH" as the syntactical beginning of the first oracle. By contrast, in 12:1 neither *maśśā'* nor "word of YHWH" are syntactically connected to what follows but truly function as a title. Mal 1:1 also functions as a title, but adds a name and a topic to the heading: "An oracle. The word of YHWH concerning Israel by the hand of Malachi." The Hebrew name *Malachi* means "my messenger" and is often considered a name derived from 3:1: "Behold, I am sending you my messenger . . ."

28. See the discussion of compositional models below.

29. Mason's 1972 dissertation was published belatedly, with essays evaluating its importance. See Rex Mason, "The Use of Earlier Biblical Material in Zechariah 9–14: A Study in Inner Biblical Exegesis," in *Bringing out the Treasure: Inner Biblical Allusion in Zechariah 9–14*, ed. Mark J. Boda, JSOTSup 370 (Sheffield: Sheffield Academic, 2003), 3–208.

30. Nicholas Ho Fai Tai, *Prophetie als Schriftauslegung in Sacharja 9–14: Traditions- und kompositionsgeschichtliche Studien*, Calwer Theologische Monographien 17 (Stuttgart: Calwer, 1996).

31. Tai, *Prophetie*, 280–84.

32. See Boda, *Zechariah*, 39–41. Boda notes that both sections draw upon texts and traditions from the Torah, the Former Prophets, and especially the Latter Prophets. The differences between the presumed settings and theological agendas of 1–8 and 9–14 argue against the early dates that Boda suggests (see ibid., 31–37).

33. Boda, *Zechariah*, 37. Less clear is Boda's contention that the theological perspectives of the various sections function in close proximity to the political agenda of Nehemiah.

34. Paul L. Redditt, "Israel's Shepherds: Hope and Pessimism in Zechariah 9–14," *CBQ* 51 (1989): 631–42; idem, "The Two Shepherds in Zechariah 11:4-17," *CBQ* 55 (1993): 676–86; idem, *Haggai, Zechariah, Malachi*, NCB (London: HarperCollins, 1995). For a summary of Redditt's arguments, see James D. Nogalski, "Zechariah 13:7-9 as a Transitional Text: An Appreciation and Reevaluation of the Work of Rex Mason," in *Bringing out the Treasure: Inner Biblical Allusion in Zechariah 9-14*, 295–97.

35. For Persian-period arguments see Petersen, *Zechariah 9–14 and Malachi*, OTL (Louisville: Westminster John Knox, 1995), 3–5; Eric Meyers and

Carol Meyers, *Zechariah 9–14*, 15–29; Paul L. Redditt, *Zechariah 9–14*, IECOT (Stuttgart: Kohlhammer, 2012), 26–29; and Boda, *Zechariah*, 26–29. The most extensive argument for the time of Alexander remains D. Karl Elliger, "Ein Zeugnis aus der jüdischen Gemeinde im Alexanderjahr 332 v. Chr.: Eine territoralgeschichtliche Studie zu Sach 9, 1–8," *ZAW* 62 (1949): 63–115.

36. The description of the threat in Zech 9 proceeds north to south and includes both an attack on Syria and Tyre. After the battle of Issus in 333 when Alexander defeated the Persians, Alexander attacked the Phoenician coast while he sent his general Parmenion to Damascus to track and defeat the Persian king Darius III (336–330 BCE). The fights between Persia and Greece prior to Alexander largely took place in Asia Minor, and during the period of the Diadochoi, battles along the coast involved aggression from the Ptolemies, meaning that the action moved from south to north—the opposite direction of the attacks described in Zech 9.

37. Boda, *Zechariah*, 648–55.

38. See Zech 12:3, 4, 6, 8 [2x], 9, 11; 13:1, 2, 4; 14:4, 6, 8, 9, 13, 20, 21.

39. See Nogalski, *Redactional Processes*, 241–44; Erich Bosshard and Reinhard Gregor Kratz, "Maleachi im Zwölfprophetenbuch," *BN* 52 (1990): 44–45.

40. See Nogalski, *Redactional Processes*, 241–44.

41. Bosshard and Kratz, "Maleachi im Zwölfprophetenbuch," 44.

42. See Petersen, *Haggai and Zechariah 1–8*, 93–95. Petersen interprets Hag 2:15-19 in light of the ancient Near Eastern *kalû* festival. A number of scholars see 2:17 (or 2:17b) as a later addition, e.g., Wolff, *Haggai*, 62, 65; Nogalski, *Micah–Malachi*, 790–93; and Martin Leuenberger, *Haggai*, HThKAT (Freiberg, Herder, 2015), 192–93. Even Petersen leaves open the possibility that 2:17 comes from the hand of a redactor (*Haggai and Zechariah 1–8*, 92). Nogalski sees Hag 2:17 (along with a parenthetical comment in 2:19) as the work of a redactor of the Book of the Twelve evoking the imagery of Amos and Joel as part of a series of allusions that reflect a fertility motif in the Book of the Twelve. See the discussion of Hag 2:15-19, 20-23 in the section on Haggai.

43. See the discussion of Joel's paradigm for "history" within the structure of the Book of the Twelve.

44. Seventy years is not a precise date, but it fits the general time of Jeremiah between the time of Jehoiachin's exile (597 BCE) and Jerusalem's destruction (587 BCE) since the first vision is set in the year 520 BCE (Zech 1:7).

45. For examples, compare Petersen, *Zechariah 9–14 and Malachi*, 5–6; Andrew E. Hill, *Malachi: A New Translation and Commentary*, Anchor Bible 25D (New Haven: Yale University Press, 2008), 80–84; Helmut Utzschneider, *Künder oder Schreiber: Eine These zum Problem der "Schriftprophetie" auf Grund von Maleachi 1, 6–2, 9*, BEATAJ 19 (Frankfort: Lang, 1989), 80–84; Wilhelm Rudolph, *Haggai, Sacharja 1–8, Sacharaja 9–14, Maleachi*, KAT 13, pt. 4 (Gütersloh: Gütersloher Verlagshaus, 1976), 248–49; and Pieter A. Verhoef, *The Books of Haggai and Malachi*, NICOT (Grand Rapids: Eerdmans, 1987), 156–60. Petersen and Hill argue for a late sixth- to early fifth-century composition, both giving considerable weight to a computer analysis of the linguistic style, but the comparative data represents a very small sample size and includes texts whose dates are debated, leaving those results unreliable. See the extensive critique of Julia M. O'Brien, *Priest and Levite in Malachi*, SBL Dissertation Series 121 (Atlanta: Scholars Press, 1990), 125–31. Rudolph argues from the lack of awareness of the P material that Malachi could precede the arrival of Ezra, but he counters that the events of Neh 13 indicate that debates about the relationships between Levites and Zadokites remained unsettled even after Ezra. He notes that after Ezra's arrival and the compilation of the Torah, Malachi's omission of P material makes less sense. Verhoef suggests that the book should be dated between the two terms of Nehemiah, probably around 433 BCE, because its themes are the same as those addressed in Nehemiah (*Haggai and Malachi*). Utzschneider situates the bulk of 1:6–2:9 with the remainder of the book, but thinks 1:11-14 comes from a Hellenistic scribe. He wrestles with the difficulties of pinning down a precise date and prefers to allow for a sixty-year time frame when the book could have been composed, though he also leans toward the time of Neh 13 when the priestly conflict was raging at its highest (*Künder oder Schreiber*, 84).

46. Petersen, *Zechariah 9–14 and Malachi*, 31–32.

47. See Petersen, *Zechariah 9–14 and Malachi*, 227–28, 232–33; and Hill, *Malachi*, 363–66. For a contrasting point of view, see Sweeney, *The Twelve Prophets*, 713–14; and Verhoef, *Haggai and Malachi*, 337–38.

48. See Bosshard and Kratz, "Maleachi im Zwölfprophetenbuch," 27–46; and Wöhrle, *Der Abschluss des Zwölfprophetenbuches*, 255–63. Bosshard and Kratz argue that the foundational composition of Malachi undergoes two expansions, first with the addition of two units (2:17–3:5; 3:13-21) and the second contain-

ing a number of smaller, but significant, insertions (1:1, 14a; 2:20-12; 3:22-24). Each layer offers a distinct perspective on Malachi as the conclusion of the Book of the Twelve. Wöhrle finds six redactional layers in Malachi. Wöhrle's foundational layer includes 1:2-3, 6 (minus the word "priests"); 7b-8a, 9b, 10b, 12-14 (minus two words in 1:12); 2:10, 14-17 (minus four words in 2:16); 3:1-2, 5-6, 8-15, 19. The second layer critiques the cult functionaries by adding the words "priests" in 1:6 and "it is despised" in 1:12 as well as the more extensive insertions in 1:7a, 10a; 2:1-9, 11-13 (minus one word in 2:11); 3:3a, 4. Wöhrle's third layer deals with the pious and wicked by adding 3:16-18, 20-21. The fourth and fifth layers, for Wöhrle, involve insertions that related to the Book of the Twelve. The fourth layer inserts material at the beginning to link Malachi with the Foreign Nations II layer of the Twelve (Mal 1:1, 4-5), while the fifth layer involves only the insertion of 1:9a with other texts involving the Twelve's "grace layer." Finally, the concluding verses (4:4-6 [Heb. 3:22-24]) transcend the Book of the Twelve to connect the Torah and the Nebi'im. Few have yet accepted Wöhrle's complicated dissolution of the priests from the foundational material in the book.

49. See Utzschneider, *Künder oder Schreiber* and Petersen, *Zechariah 9–14 and Malachi*, 32–34.

50. See Utzschneider, *Künder oder Schreiber*, 9–17, 75–87; Petersen, *Zechariah 9–14 and Malachi*, 33.

51. See Egon Pfeiffer, "Die Disputationsworte im Buche Maleachi: Ein Beitrag zur formgeschichtlichen Struktur," *Evangelische Theologie* 19 (1959): 546–68; Hans Jöcken Boecker, "Bemerkungen zur formgeschichtlichen Terminologie des Buches Maleachi," *ZAW* 78 (1966): 78–80; Petersen, *Zechariah 9–14 and Malachi*, 31–33. Petersen suggests that these accounts be called diatribes. While the term has not caught on, his careful analysis demonstrates why it remains inadequate to focus upon a simple tripartite structure associated with the disputation or upon the question-and-answer format associated with the discussion words.

52. Isa 20:2; Jer 37:2; 50:1; Hag. 1:1, 3; 2:1; Mal. 1:1. See also Nogalski, *Redactional Processes*, 187–89.

53. Obad 8, 9, 19, 21, though three texts refer to "Esau and the mountains of Seir" (Gen 36:8-9; Deut 2:5; Josh 24:4).

54. See especially Utzschneider, *Künder oder Schreiber*, 71–74.

55. See Utzschneider, *Künder oder Schreiber*, 20–22; Paul L. Redditt, *Haggai, Zechariah, and Malachi*, NCB (Grand Rapids: Eerdmans, 1995), 155. Redditt sees Malachi as a combination of written sources.

56. The dramatic change has caused several to treat 1:11-14 (or portions thereof) as a later commentary. For example, see Bosshard and Kratz, "Maleachi im Zwölfprophetenbuch," 45. They see 1:14a as an addition (along with 2:10-12 and 3:22-24).

57. Utzschneider, *Künder oder Schreiber*, 64–70.

58. Compare Rudolph, *Haggai, Sacharja 1–8, Sacharaja 9–14, Maleachi*, 271 and Petersen, *Zechariah 9–14 and Malachi*, 195, 204–5.

59. See John D. W. Watts, "A Frame for the Book of the Twelve: Hosea 1–3 and Malachi," in *Reading and Hearing the Book of the Twelve*, 209–17; and Laurie Braaten, "Hosea's Land Theme in the Book of the Twelve," in *Thematic Threads in the Book of the Twelve*, 104–32.

60. See this history in Rex Mason, *The Books of Haggai, Zechariah, and Malachi*, Cambridge Bible Commentary (London: Cambridge University Press, 1980), 152–53; and Petersen, *Zechariah 9–14 and Malachi*, 207–12.

61. See the exploration of this theme in Jason T. LeCureux, *The Thematic Unity of the Book of the Twelve*, Hebrew Bible Monographs 41 (Sheffield: Sheffield Phoenix, 2012), 218–21. While LeCureux overstates the degree to which the verb functions in nearly every writing of the Twelve, there can be little doubt that Mal 3:7 quotes Zech 1:3 and fits well thematically with Joel 2:12-17, which also calls for the repentance of those in Zion to avoid a curse from YHWH. This blessing and curse imagery also functions meaningfully in Hag 2:10-19 and Zech 8:3, 9-12.

62. A number of texts have been noted by scholars that may have influenced the formulation of Mal 3:11-12. Petersen points specifically to Deut 28:10-12 to account for the rain from the heavens that will be recognized by all the peoples of the earth (Petersen, *Zechariah 9–14 and Malachi*, 218).

63. This participle is even translated as "locust" in the NRSV. Petersen objects that "devourer" is not a normal term for locusts, and so should be understood as an interpretation rather than a translation. While correct, his suggestion that it indicates any insect seems forced to avoid associating Mal 3:11 specifically with Joel 1:4. Joel 1:4 refers to a series of locusts who arrive sequentially to devour

what remains and could also account for the formulation in Mal 3:11, since the singular could simply refer to the latest "locust" to "devour" the land.

64. English translations present a muddled picture that tries to allow room for the names of the YHWH-fearers as the content of the scroll: "a book of remembrance was written *before* him *of* those who revered the Lord (NRSV); "a scroll of remembrance was written *in his presence concerning* those who feared the Lord" (NIV); "a scroll of remembrance was written *before* the Lord *about* those revering the Lord" (CEB). By contrast, NASB translates the Hebrew accurately: "a book of remembrance was written *before* Him *for* those who fear the Lord." For an analysis of the parallel phrasing regarding the "scroll(s) of remembrance" in Hebrew and Aramaic, see James D. Nogalski, "How Does Malachi's 'Book of Remembrance' Function for the Cultic Elite?" in *Priests and Cult in the Book of the Twelve*, ed. Lena-Sofia Tiemeyer (Atlanta: SBL Press, 2016), 199–222.

65. See discussion above on Zech 9–14's use of Jeremiah, Ezekiel, and Isaiah and the citation of Hosea and Malachi in 13:9.

6. The Remainder of the Twelve

1. Nahum's acrostic is broken in four places where the first letter of the line no longer contains the correct consonant. The disruptions resulted from editing the hymn for the broader corpus. See Nogalski, *Redactional Processes*, 101–11; idem, "The Redactional Shaping of Nahum 1," in *Among the Prophets: Language, Image and Structure in the Prophetic Writings*, ed. Philip R. Davies and David J. A. Clines, JSOTSup 144 (Sheffield: JSOT Press, 1993), 193–202.

2. For examples, see the discussion of Nahum in the Book of the Twelve below.

3. These rhetorical units include a first battle description (2:1-9); an aphorism regarding Nineveh's destruction and fear (2:10); a parable comparing Nineveh's destruction to a lion (2:11-12); a short pronouncement of judgment concluding the parable, which could stand on its own (2:13); a second battle description in the form of a woe oracle (3:1-4); a sexually graphic description of YHWH's violent punishment of Lady Nineveh (3:5-7); a comparison of Nineveh to Thebes (3:8-11); a sexually laden comparison of Nineveh's fortresses and army to a fig tree (3:12-13); a call to prepare for battle (3:14-17*); and a death bed taunt to the mortally wounded king of Nineveh (3:18-19).

4. See Julia Myers O'Brien, *Nahum* (Sheffield: Sheffield Academic, 2002), 67–69 and 87–103.

5. See the similar models of Heinz-Josef Fabry, *Nahum*, HThKAT (Freiburg im Breisgau: Herder, 2006), 91–92; Walter Dietrich, *Nahum, Habakkuk, Zephaniah*, IECOT (Stuttgart: Kohlhammer, 2016), 29–34.

6. For the implications for dating the final form of Nahum, see "Dating the Prophet and the Book" below.

7. The disruptions to the acrostic form will be treated below (see "Nahum within the Book of the Twelve").

8. Nah 1:9, for example, takes up the image of YHWH "making an end" of the enemies (plural) from 1:8 and asks, Why do you (plural) plot against him? The verb *plot* appears in the opening lines of 1:11, which is the beginning of the early Nahum corpus. Thus, 1:9 creates a lexical bridge between the hymn and the early corpus.

9. The alternative to this assumption would be to suggest that Nahum represents sayings against Nineveh created after its destruction and after Jerusalem's destruction. Several authors have made this suggestion, but they represent a minority opinion. See Paul Humbert, "Essai d'analyse de Nahoum 1,2–2,3," *ZAW* 44 (1926): 266–80; Herman Schulz, *Das Buch Nahum*, BZAW 129 (Berlin: de Gruyter, 1973). For reasons why scholars have resisted these claims, see Dietrich, *Nahum, Habakkuk, Zephaniah*, 30–32.

10. Isa 52:7 fits within its immediate and extended context much more integrally than does Nah 1:15. Isa 52:7 falls within Isa 40–55, a text universally regarded as stemming from no earlier than the rise of Cyrus in 539 BCE. For an opposing view, see Heinz-Josef Fabry, *Nahum*, HThKAT (Freiburg im Breisgau: Herder, 2006), 151–52. For a critique of this view, see Dietrich, *Nahum, Habakkuk, Zephaniah*, 54.

11. This first stage involves the arrangement of preexisting compositions (2:1–3:15aβ) along with an introduction and conclusion composed for the collection, which served as the editorial frame highlighting two specific motifs (1:11-12a, 14; 3:15aγ-17, 18-19).

12. The last king mentioned in Micah's superscription is Hezekiah (726–696 BCE), while Zephaniah's superscription dates that prophet to the reign of Josiah, presumably after the instigation of the king's reforms in 622 BCE (based upon

reference to the "remnant of Baal" in Zeph 1:4). This gap covers roughly seventy-five years from the death of Hezekiah to the reforms of Josiah (622 BCE). During most of this period, Assyria held political and economic sway over Judah, but by the end of the seventh century, Assyria had been defeated by Babylon (612 BCE), and Babylon had also defeated Egypt at the battle of Carchemish (605 BCE) to establish its own political control over the Levant. Judah's resistance to Babylonian control ultimately led to two failed attempts by Judean kings (appointed by Babylon) to reestablish its own independence (597 and 587 BCE respectively).

13. Some of these suggestions precede the recent work on the Twelve. For example, see already Rolland Emerson Wolfe, "The Editing of the Book of the Twelve," *ZAW* 53 (1935): 90–129 (especially 95); Brevard Childs, *Introduction to the Old Testament as Scripture* (Philadelphia: Fortress, 1979), 454. Others see the combination as part of the editing of the developing multiprophet scroll, e.g., Dietrich, *Nahum, Habakkuk, Zephaniah*, 17–19; Schart, *Die Entstehung des Zwölfprophetenbuchs*, 242–51. See also Wöhrle, *Der Abschluss des Zwölfprophetenbuches*, 53–66, 311–23. Wöhrle reaches different conclusions, largely because he thinks the early core of Nahum was directed against Judah, not Nineveh. Similarly, he sees the bulk of Hab 3 entering with the earliest focus on the pious/wicked, prior to the inclusion of the Babylonian material.

14. Too often, even redactional studies presuppose that a redactor could only work with one theological agenda. See James D. Nogalski, "Teaching Prophetic Books," *PRS* 36 (2009): 251–54.

15. Note especially Nah 1:4 in what should be the *dalet* line that now begins with *alef*. The disrupted acrostic refers to the withering of Bashan and Carmel, two regions lost to the Assyrians but also mentioned explicitly in the prophet's petition in Mic 7:14. This rare combination of Carmel and Bashan appears elsewhere only twice, both in prophetic contexts that long for restoration of these lands from Assyrian control (Isa 33:9; Jer 50:19).

16. James D. Nogalski, "One Book and Twelve Books: The Nature of the Redactional Work and the Implications of Cultic Source Material in the Book of the Twelve," in *Two Sides of a Coin: Juxtaposing Views on Interpreting the Book of the Twelve/Twelve Prophetic Books*, ed. Ehud Ben Zvi and James D. Nogalski (Piscataway, NJ: Gorgias, 2009), 30–39.

17. Nogalski, *Micah–Malachi*, 606, 631–35.

18. Nogalski, *Redactional Processes*, 151–52.

19. See James D. Nogalski, "Where are the Prophets in the Book of the Twelve?" in *The Book of the Twelve and New Form Criticism*, ed. Mark J. Boda, Michael H. Floyd, and Colin M. Toffelmire, Ancient Near East Monographs (Atlanta: SBL Press, 2015), 163–82.

20. At least five different responses have been suggested regarding how to understand the content of the vision. See Dietrich, *Nahum, Habakkuk, Zephaniah*, 126–31. Most recognize the content of the vision as some part of 2:4-5, while others argue the vision is the entire book of Habakkuk, the woe oracles in 2:5-20, the prayer (Hab 3), or a riddle. The stronger argument lies with those who see the vision recounted in 2:4, because the command in 2:2 assumes that the vision is small enough to be written on a tablet yet large enough to be read while the prophet runs.

21. Dietrich, *Nahum, Habakkuk, Zephaniah*, 178–82; Nogalski, *Micah–Malachi*, 679–87.

22. The word *selah* appears around seventy times in books 1–3 of the Psalter, but only appears in two psalms in books 4–5 (Pss 140:4,6; 143:6).

23. Evidence suggests that books 1–3 of the Psalter were edited with a different set of techniques than those used in books 4–5. See Gerald Henry Wilson, *The Editing of the Hebrew Psalter*, SBLDS 76 (Chico, CA: Scholars Press, 1985), 155–58, 207–14.

24. Some scholars suggest that the cultic notations were added because of the popularity of the chapter, but it hardly seems likely that the chapter would have been singled out in this manner. Preexisting poems are inserted in a number of passages. Hab 3 connects to chapters 1–2 only on a loose thematic level, which allows one to ask why an editor chose the poem to place after 2:5-20.

25. See William H. Brownlee, *The Midrah Pesher of Habakkuk*, SBLMS 24 (Missoula, MT: Scholars Press, 1979); Dietrich, *Nahum, Habakkuk, Zephaniah*, 103–5; F. F. Bruce, "The Dead Sea Habakkuk Scroll," *The Annual of Leeds University Oriental Society* I (1958–1959): 5–24. The Barberini version represents a Greek translation of Hab 3 found in several medieval manuscripts that does not depend upon the LXX. The translation itself, however, propbably goes back to the second century CE. See Edwin M. Good, "The Barberini Greek Version of Habakkuk III," *VT* 9 (1959): 11–30.

26. See James D. Nogalski, "Recurring Themes in the Book of the Twelve: Creating Points of Contact for a Theological Reading," *Interpretation* 61 (2007): 228–30.

27. The phrase appears elsewhere only in Pss 18:46; 25:5; 27:9; 51:14; and 88:1.

28. If one were to invent a prophet from whole cloth, one would more likely create a character with a symbolic name (e.g., "Malachi" = "my messenger" or "Obadiah" = "servant of YHWH").

29. See the discussion of the recent history of these redactional studies in Dietrich, *Nahum, Habakkuk, Zephaniah*, 98–103. The summary includes works by Jeremias, Gunneweg, Lindström, Otto, Koenen, Bosshard-Nepustil, Seybold, and Dietrich himself.

30. Otto unnecessarily slices Habakkuk into six redactional stages that extend from the seventh century into the fifth (Eckart Otto, "Die Theologie des Buches Habakuks," *VT* 35 [1985]: 277–83). See also his extensive work in "Die Stellung der Wehe-Worte in der Verkündigung des Propheten Habakuk," *ZAW* 89 (1977): 73–107.

31. For different reasons, Schart and Wöhrle suggest that Habakkuk (and Nahum) entered the expanded corpus prior to Joel. Schart argues that Nahum and Habakkuk entered shortly after the Book of the Four was created (Schart, *Die Entstehung des Zwölfprophetenbuchs*, 234–51). Wöhrle offers a complex hypothesis that Nahum and Habakkuk entered the larger corpus separately, largely because he sees Nahum as originally containing words of judgment against Judah (Wöhrle, *Der Abschluss des Zwölfprophetenbuches*, 24–66, 289–334). Dietrich argues for a three-stage development of Habakkuk that begins in the seventh century. Dietrich argues Habakkuk was joined with Nahum to create a book of two prophets in his second stage, dealing with the two previous regional superpowers. Dietrich's third stage occurs later in the Persian period with additions to Hab 3 and Nah 1:2-8 (Dietrich, *Nahum, Habakkuk, Zephaniah*, 100–101).

32. For example, while a few authors such as Dietrich consider the oracle (1:5-11) an integral part of the earliest portion of Habakkuk, the stronger evidence lies with those who treat the oracle as an inserted source, even though the absolute date of its composition and its attachment to the complaint material remain debated. The plural imperatives that begin the oracle convey a strong sense of disjuncture as an original response to the individual prayer of 1:2-4,

12-14, especially in light of the singular imperative responses to the prayer that occur in 2:1-3.

33. Many note that the complaint bears similarities to Jeremiah, a seventh-century prophet who would be roughly contemporary with the literary setting conceptualized for Habakkuk. Prior to the addition of the oracle (1:5-11), the generic nature of the complaint about the wicked and righteous also has strong parallels in Persian-period literature, most notably, Job and theocratic psalms. See Schmid, *The Old Testament: A Literary History*, 154–55 (Job) and 152–54 (theocratic psalms).

34. See Nogalski, *Micah–Malachi*, 689.

35. These positions are not unanimously held. Very few in recent decades argue Joel is preexilic. Kapelrud dated Joel to the latter half of the eighth century, but his arguments have been repeatedly refuted (Arvid S. Kapelrud, *Joel Studies*, Uppsala Universitets Arsskrift [Uppsala: Lundequistska, 1948]). Rudolph argues for an early sixth-century date (Rudolph, *Joel–Obadja–Jona*, KAT 13, pt. 2 [Gütersloh: Gütersloher Verlagshaus, 1971], 24–29). A few scholars date at least chapters 1–2 to the late sixth or early fifth century BCE. Most view Joel as a composite text with sources that stem from different times in the Persian period.

36. The allusive character of the material suggests Joel borrows from (or shows awareness of) Genesis, Exodus, Amos, Micah (or Isaiah), Zephaniah, Ezekiel, Obadiah, and Malachi. It hardly seems possible to account for Joel's use of this wide a range of texts prior to the end of the fifth or the beginning of the fourth century BCE.

37. See the summary of these arguments in Hans Walter Wolff, *Joel and Amos*, trans. Waldemar Janzen et al., Hermeneia (Philadelphia: Fortress, 1977), 4–6, 77–78.

38. See Nogalski, "Presumptions of Covenant in Joel," 211–28. This rhetoric derives from a covenant reasoning that posits the current setting results from the curse which YHWH has sent because of the people's disobedience. Joel's language is highly charged. The barbed edge with which the prophet challenges the people (e.g., calling them drunkards in 1:5) and the priests (whom he challenges to lament and wail in 1:13) presumes that the prophet sees a danger in the current state of the land that others do not. Yet, the prophet does not specify what Judah has done wrong.

39. See Siegfried Bergler, *Joel als Schriftinterpret*, BEATAJ 16 (Frankfurt: Lang, 1988); Nogalski, "Joel as Literary Anchor," 91–109; and idem, "Recurring Themes in the Book of the Twelve," 125–36.

40. How many preexisting sources have been utilized and how they came together remains a debated question. For some, the fractures merely reflect the points at which the prophet's own speeches have been joined together, while others doubt these materials come from a single hand. A third group discusses the book's development as the product of a lengthy transmission process. For the third group, see Jeremias, *Joel, Obadja, Jona, Micha*, 3–5; Wöhrle, *Die frühen Sammlungen des Zwölfprophetenbuches*, 391–435.

41. Siegfried Bergler astutely explains this collage of images as an expansion of a preexisting poem concerning a drought combined with curse language from Deut 27–28 and plague imagery from Exod 10 (Siegfried Bergler, *Joel als Schriftinterpret*, 247–94, 335–47; see also Nogalski, "Presumptions of Covenant in Joel," 211–28).

42. Nogalski, *Redactional Processes*, 23–26, 275–78. Rather than Bergler's model of a compilation of sources, some scholars suggest Joel 1 has been expanded over time. Most notably, the work of Jakob Wöhrle has taken this position (Jakob Wöhrle, *Die frühen Sammlungen des Zwölfprophetenbuches*, 391–435). Wöhrle sees only a very small foundational layer as the core of Joel (1:1-3, 5, 8-20; 2:1, 2*, 3, 6, 10, 11b, 15-17, 21-24, 26a) composed well into the Persian period, followed by a series of four redactional layers that last into the Hellenistic period.

43. Much ink has been spilled regarding whether the terms used for the locusts represent developmental stages or whether they represent different species. Unfortunately, much of this discussion erroneously treats the attacks (plural) as a single plague. Joel 1:4 warns of multiple attacks, with each devouring what the others left behind.

44. Some interpret the "nation" in 1:6 as a metaphor for the locust in 1:4, but this move hardly resolves the difficulty since it assumes the statement metaphorically portrays a real locust attack (singular) as an attacking army, which is then portrayed metaphorically as a lioness that literally attacks trees. Such imagery seems quite convoluted.

45. See Nogalski, "Presumptions of Covenant in Joel," 211–28.

46. Note especially the call for the priests to put on sackcloth and ashes, actions reserved for funerals and penitence. Joel, however, does not specify precisely

what the people or the priests have done wrong. At this point, context becomes telling. If one assumes that Joel represents the speech of a prophet designed to be read on its own, then it does so with a peculiar theology in which the prophet calls the entire population to approach an angry YHWH with the assumption that they have done wrong but without acknowledging precisely how they have erred. Given the extent that Joel's knowledge of other biblical texts has been documented, the citations and intertextual conceptualizations suggest that Joel was created from existing sources specifically to fit between Hosea and Amos. In other words, Joel (like Obad and Zech 9–14) should be understood as a literary product designed for its current location.

47. The phrase itself appears frequently in the Book of the Twelve, but that is only part of the story. Other phrases allude to the concept. Joel 2:1 represents the first instance of the phrase "day of YHWH," but the phrase "day of punishment" against Ephraim in Hos 5:9 draws upon similar tradition-historical concepts. See Rolf Rendtorff, "Alas for the Day! The Day of the Lord in the Book of the Twelve," in *God in the Fray: A Tribute to Walter Brueggemann*, ed. Tod Linafelt and Timothy K. Beal (Minneapolis: Fortress, 1998), 186–92, and James D. Nogalski, "The Day(s) of YHWH in the Book of the Twelve," 192–213.

48. This day has a particular target (foreign nations or YHWH's own people) in history (past, imminent future, or distant future). All these variables must be evaluated when the concept appears in prophetic literature. To wit, Joel exhibits a dialectic that plays with three variations of the day of YHWH: one directed against Judah in the imminent future (1:15; 2:1, 11), one anticipating deliverance for those who call on the name of YHWH (2:31-32 [Heb. 3:4-5]), and one that focuses upon the punishment of the nations (3:1-21 [Heb. 4:1-21]).

49. Nogalski, *Hosea–Jonah*, 229–33. Some scholars read this poem in light of Joel 1:4 as a description of the attacking locusts, but in so doing, they lessen the impact of the passage, essentially implying that it describes a natural calamity. Attentive readers, by contrast, note that 2:1 and 11 explicitly mention the day of YHWH.

50. Robert Alter makes this case by focusing upon several aspects of the parallelism in Joel 2:1-11 (Robert Alter, *The Art of Biblical Poetry* [New York: Basic Books, 1985], 40–43). He highlights how the parallelism intensifies the action using parallel actions through time, symmetrical repetition, and overlapping action through incremental repetition. Equally important, the descriptions of the enemy become increasingly threatening. Three times the poem describes the attacking enemy in frightening terms (2:3, 4-5, 7-9) and three times something

responds: the land burns (2:3), all humans cower in fear (2:6), and the cosmos trembles and grows dark (2:10). Spatially, the army begins on the distant mountaintops (2:5), then scales the wall (2:7), then leaps on top of the city walls (2:9), and then enters the houses through the windows (2:9). Finally, the reader learns that YHWH himself leads the massive army (2:11), which emphasizes that no one stood a chance against the power of YHWH's host.

51. The beginning and end of the poem describe the day of YHWH with phrases that will reappear across the Book of the Twelve. In 2:1, "the day of YHWH is near" appears as in Obad 15 (describing a day of judgment against all nations) and in Zeph 1:7 (directed against Jerusalem and Judah). Joel 2:11 foreshadows Mal 3:2, emphasizing that none can endure the great and terrible day of YHWH (cf. Mal 3:2b-3). Relatedly, the language of the sun, the moon, and the stars growing dark appears in all three portraits of the day of YHWH in Joel 2:10, 31; 3:15 (Heb. 2:10; 3:4; 4:15). The first of these (2:10) describes the reaction of the cosmos to YHWH's army as it threatens Judah. The second (3:4) refers back to 2:11 as the day of YHWH that cannot be endured, but provides an exception for those who call on the name of YHWH. The third instance (3:15) describes the day of YHWH against the nations where YHWH will sit as judge in the Valley of Jehoshaphat. Hence, both within Joel and across the Book of the Twelve, Joel's day of YHWH citations foreshadow variations of the day of YHWH: an imminent threat to Judah and Jerusalem and the nations, and a hope to be among the remnant in Zion.

52. It mentions gathering the people, sanctifying the congregation, and assembling the elderly, the newborns, and the newly married (2:15-16). The priests are admonished to solicit this repentance at the temple (2:17).

53. Exod 34:6-7 appears as part of YHWH's response to the making of the golden calf. This foundational self-description emphasizes YHWH's compassion, grace, and fidelity that show he is slow to anger (34:6-7a) and concludes by affirming that YHWH will punish the guilty even to the third and fourth generation (34:7b).

54. The language of Exod 34:6-7 reappears at the end of Joel (3:19-21 [Heb. 4:19-21]), at the end of Micah (7:18-20) and the beginning of Nahum (1:2-3), and (quite differently) in the book of Jonah. Rhetorically, both Joel passages and the combination of Mic 7/Nah 1 use a rather sophisticated thematic pairing in alluding to Exod 34:6 and 34:7. Mic 7:18-20 draws primarily on Exod 34:6 to pronounce YHWH's compassion upon YHWH's people, while Nah 1:2-3 relates thematically to Exod 34:7b (though it uses some terms from 34:6).

55. The change of themes between the two citations of Exod 34:6-7 in Joel also relates to the contexts in which the two citations appear. When drawing upon Exod 34:6, Joel 2 cites YHWH's compassion because the day of YHWH threatens Judah and Jerusalem. By contrast, the day of YHWH in Joel 3 focuses upon YHWH's judgment of the nations, resulting in the language of Exod 34:7, used to affirm that YHWH will punish the guilty nations who have sought to destroy Jerusalem (specifically, Egypt and Edom).

56. Nothing states how the people and the priests responded to the call in 2:12-17. Some interpreters argue that the promises in 2:18-27 *assume* that the people repented and YHWH responded favorably. They translate the verbs in 2:18-19 in past tense (cf. NRSV, CEB). Another group interprets 2:18-27 as a contingent promise that continues the call to repent in 2:12-17. This group translates the verbs in Joel 2:18-19 as future (cf. KJV, NAS, NIV). Both translations are syntactically possible, but the case for translating 2:18-19 as future is stronger contextually. First, agricultural fertility will be restored, and Judah will no longer be mocked among the nations (2:19; cf. 2:24); second, YHWH promises to remove the northern army that has invaded the land (2:20); and third, YHWH specifically promises restitution will come (see 2:25) for the locust plagues mentioned in 1:4. All these promises relate to future events. Moreover, the commands in 2:21-23 ("do not fear," "rejoice," and "be glad") exhort responses because the promises have not yet been fulfilled.

57. Since the nineteenth century, scholars have argued that Joel does not represent a unified composition. Some see the entire second half of the book as representative of later ideas. Some argue that 2:28-32 represents the latest and least cohesive block added to Joel. See the description of the history of these arguments in John Barton, *Joel and Obadiah*, OTL (Louisville: Westminster John Knox, 2001), 6–7. Wolff argues against this position (Wolff, *Joel and Amos*, 60). Still others recognize Joel as essentially the work of a single author/compiler who combines independent sources to cause his readers to reflect. See Barton, *Joel and Obadiah*, 7–10. Barton argues for both. He thinks chapters 1–2 reflect a single composition but sees 2:28–3:21 (Heb. 3:1–4:21) as a collection of sayings that are only loosely related. Barton makes an astute observation when he distinguishes between the organic and the imposed unity in Joel (Barton, *Joel and Obadiah*, 8–14). For him, Joel 1–2 represents a more sustained argument that is intended to be read together, while no real rhetorical logic connects the blocks in 2:28–3:21 (Heb. 3:1–4:21). Yet, Barton misses the fact that a chronological sequence has been imposed upon the material in these chapters ("afterwards"

278

in 2:28; "in those days and at that time" in 3:1). This signal alerts the reader to chronological expectations.

58. These verses are cited by Peter in Acts 2:16-21 as evidence that the Pentecost events were foretold by Joel, and the inclusiveness of the promise served the agenda of the author of Acts quite well.

59. See also Wolff, *Joel and Amos*, 83. Joel 3:18 announces that sweet wine will drip from the mountains, undoing the devastation of the sweet wine in 1:5. The wadis of Judah in 3:18 will overflow with water, whereas in 1:20 they were completely dry. Even when Joel 3:18 quotes (but alters) Amos 9:13, the change involves the hills flowing with milk, which reverses the distress affecting the cattle in 1:18. The expectation of a fountain flowing from the temple all the way to the Wadi Shittim in 3:18 defies reality, but symbolizes the temple as a source of water in terms associated with paradise, in contrast to the anemic state of the temple in 1:13-14. Specific threats against Egypt and Edom in 3:19 (especially in light of the previous mention of the Phoenician and Philistine regions along the coast in 3:4-8) reverse the threat of the enemy attack facing Judah (see especially 1:6-7). The final two verses reiterate the theme of Judah's restoration by alluding to Exod 34:7 (which pairs with the allusion to Exod 34:6-7 in 2:13-14). In short, 3:18-21 reverses the threats from Joel 1–2.

60. Joel 3:10 functions within the call to judgment upon the nations in 3:9-17 by reversing the utopian image of universal peace that appears in Mic 4:3 and Isa 2:4. Joel 3:10 calls upon the nations to beat their agricultural implements into weapons of war, a war against YHWH that they are bound to lose. In the end, then, Judah will have peace when the nations are judged in the symbolic valley of Jehoshaphat (see B, B´). Relatedly, Joel 3:16, 18 draw upon the beginning (1:2) and end (9:13) of Amos (the next book in the MT order of the Twelve).

61. So, for example, see Jeremias, *Joel, Obadja, Jona, Micha*, 41.

62. Joel 3:4-8 functions as a concrete example of the slavery motif of 3:3. Wolff and others have suggested that the political situation assumed in 3:4-8 likely reflects the latter part of the Persian period (between 400–350 BCE) when slave trade among the Greeks, Phoenicians, and Philistines would have been explainable (Wolff, *Joel and Amos*, 77–78). The content of 3:4-8 represents a judgment oracle against the coastal regions (Tyre, Sidon, and Philistia) for selling Judean slaves to the northwest across the Mediterranean Sea to serve as slaves to the Greeks. The judgment articulated in these verses offers a vision of poetic justice in which this prophetic text announces that the population of these coastal

regions will be sent in exactly the opposite direction to the southeast and across the desert.

63. Joel 3:14b reiterates the nearness of the day of Yahweh (cf. 1:15; 2:1) and describes that day as a day of darkness when the sun, moon, and stars will all go out as with the depiction of Yahweh's army threatening Jerusalem (3:15; cf. 2:10). While both of these quotes refer back to Joel 1–2, Joel 3:16, 18 draws upon Amos 1:2 and 9:13, citing the beginning and end of Amos, the next book in the Twelve.

64. James D. Nogalski, "Joel as the Literary Anchor," 91–109; Bergler, *Joel als Schriftinterpet*, 15–32.

65. Joel 1:1 imitates Hos 1:1. Joel 1:8 refers to Hosea's phrase "the Baal of her youth," albeit with a twist (cf. Joel 1:8 with Hos 2:14-17 [Heb. 2:16-19]). The agricultural products, particularly the promise of vine, wine, grain, and oil in Hos 2: 21-23 (Heb. 2:23-25) and 14:7 (Heb. 14:8), reappear as withered and cut off in Joel 1. Relatedly, the threat of the insufficiency of the threshing floor in Hos 9:2 serves as part of the promise of restoration in Joel 2:24.

66. Schart, *Die Entstehung des Zwölfprophetenbuchs*, 263–65.

67. Amos 4:6-12 recounts a litany of unsuccessful attempts to get Israel to change course; according to YHWH, five times they failed to respond: "Yet you did not return to me" (4:6, 8, 9, 10, 11). These punishments in Amos 4:6-12 align closely with the threats of Joel 1–2 including famine, drought, blight, mildew, and locusts. The day-of-YHWH theme plays a defining role in Amos 5:18-24, a text that challenges the assumption that YHWH will not judge his own people. Amos 5:18-24 uses imagery of the day of YHWH as darkness (5:18, 20) like the day of YHWH in Joel (cf. 2:2). YHWH rejects the cultic acts of Israel (Amos 5:21-23) because justice is missing from the land. When read after the open-ended calls to repentance to Israel in Hos 14 and to Judah in Joel 1–2, Amos 4:6-11 challenges the idea that a reader of the Twelve should assume that the people actually did repent in Hosea or Joel.

68. See Nogalski, *Hosea–Jonah*, 11–13, 212–13, 219.

69. Locust imagery appears in Amos 4:9 as part of YHWH's unsuccessful attempts to force Israel to return. Nation-locust imagery, however, appears to have been deliberately adapted in Nah 3:15-17 to enhance the picture of one locust devouring another, and in that context one locust refers to Assyria and the other to Babylon. Hab 1:9 does not use the language of Joel but does portray Babylon moving forward in an unstoppable mass, not unlike the description of YHWH's

punishing army in Joel 2:6-7. Likewise, Mal 3:11 uses the language of "devourer" to refer to "locusts" who have destroyed the fertility of the land.

70. From Hos 2 to Mal 3, this triad appears prominently. Hosea, Joel, and Haggai utilize the triad in the same order to establish the motif of the "grain, wine, and oil" whose presence or absence denotes YHWH's favor or punishment bestowed on the land as a sign of the people's commitment to YHWH. This phrase reflects Deuteronomic images of covenant blessing and curse. In the Torah and the Nevi'im, this phrase appears only in the Twelve, in Deuteronomy, and once in Jeremiah (a scroll known to interact with Deuteronomy): Deut 7:13; 11:14; 12:17; 14:23; 18:4; 28:51; Jer 31:12; Hos 2:8, 22 (Heb. 2:10, 24); Joel 1:10; 2:19, 24; and Hag 1:11. Among the Writings, Nehemiah and Chronicles use this phrase (2 Chr 31:5; 32:28; Neh 5:11; 10:39; 13:5, 12), which could suggest that the popularity of this triad was well established in Levitical circles of the fourth century BCE.

71. Odil Hannes Steck, *The Prophetic Books and the Theological Witness*, trans. James D. Nogalski (St. Louis: Chalice, 2000), 49–52, 118–20, 162–72. Steck builds upon the work of Klaus Koch and defines metahistory as "thematic 'history' led by tradition that is seen, experienced, viewed, and desired *sub specie dei* (from the perspective of God)." It is a perspective that "specifically includes the experience of a lengthy time span by selection, concentration, depth of meaning, and order of meaning, as these elements correspond to the perspective, plan, and activity of God" (49).

72. The omission of a ruling monarch is not surprising given that scholars widely presuppose the composition of the book occurred after the last king of Judah was removed from the throne in 587 BCE. No real significance can be attributed to the lack of a monarch in the Persian period, since the books of Haggai and Zechariah refer to the Persian king Darius, though Malachi—like Obadiah—mentions no ruler either.

73. See the discussion in Leslie C. Allen, *The Books of Joel, Obadiah, Jonah, and Micah*, NICOT (Grand Rapids: Eerdmans, 1976), 136; Marvin A. Sweeney, *The Twelve Prophets*, Berit Olam (Collegeville: Liturgical Press, 2000), 280, 286.

74. Barton, *Joel and Obadiah*, 133; Ehud Ben Zvi, *A Historical-Critical Study of the Book of Obadiah*, BZAW 242 (Berlin: de Gruyter, 1996), 14–19.

75. For one thing, the Edomites benefitted more than Judah from the stability of the Assyrian Empire, even though they were also required to pay heavy

tribute. This increased economic stability came, in part, from the control of trade routes in the southern Levant. Evidence now exists of increasing Edomite presence in formerly Judean territory by the end of the seventh century BCE. The upshot of recent investigations is that Edom, like most of the Transjordan, evidences relatively stable cultural continuity, though outside forces in the forms of attacks from desert tribes and the last Babylonian king Nabonidus (555–539 BCE) created pressures for Edomite migration. Ironically (when compared to Obadiah and Malachi), the Edomites eventually settled in southern Judah and by the Roman period were known as Idumeans. This migration suggests that they were not so powerful politically during the time of Persian dominance, and furthermore, that the Edomites (like the Moabites) were not given the status of their own satrapy in the Persian period. See the up-to-date summary in Joel S. Burnett, "Transjordan: The Ammonites, Moabites, and Edomites," in *The World Around the Old Testament: The People and Places of the Ancient Near East*, 333–39.

76. In fact, Jeremias sees the entire book of Obadiah as a commentary upon Jer 49:7-22 (Jeremias, *Joel, Obadja, Jona, Micha*, 57–59).

77. For example, see Hans Walter Wolff, *Obadiah and Jonah*, trans. Margaret Kohl (Minneapolis: Augsburg, 1986), 22; Barton, *Joel and Obadiah*, 157.

78. James D. Nogalski, "Not Just Another Nation: Obadiah's Placement in the Book of the Twelve," in *Perspectives on the Formation of the Book of the Twelve*, 102.

79. Such knowledge is presumed from not only Jer 49:7-22 but also Ezek 25:12-14; 35:1-15. The final note about Edom in the Twelve appears in Mal 1:2-5, which presumes Edom's punishment has begun. Hence, in the prophetic corpus, YHWH warns Edom not do to (Obad 11-14) what it did (Jeremiah and Ezekiel), for which it was judged (Mal 1:2-5). Obadiah's Persian-period date confuses its literary function within the Twelve. The former assumes knowledge of 587, while the latter anticipates the judgment of both Judah and Edom.

80. See the visual depiction of this repossession in Nogalski, *Hosea–Jonah*, 391.

81. Obad 18 anticipates a reunified northern and southern force would "repossess the remnant of Edom and all the nations over whom my name is called" (Amos 9:11-12). Verses 19-20 offer hope to Judah that it will one day have its territory restored to the full extent of the ideal kingdom. In either case, the final verse functions well for both Obad 18 and 19-20, but the most explicit connec-

tion (Zion will rule over Esau because the kingdom belongs to YHWH) links v. 21 more directly to v. 18, further suggesting 19-20 expanded 16-18 + 21.

82. Jeremias, *Joel, Obadja, Jona, Micha*, 57.

83. See the Hebrew texts side by side in Wolff, *Obadiah and Jonah*, 39.

84. Jeremias (*Joel, Obadja, Jona, Micha*, 64–65) summarizes the arguments for Obadiah as the borrower with eight lines of evidence: (1) the differences between the two texts look more like expansions in Obad 3-5; (2) Obad 5 and 6 twice use the word *'yk* ("alas"), which does not appear in the parallel text but conveys a sense of mourning over a past event; (3) Jer 49:7-22 contains many more traditional themes from oracles against the nations that are not present in Obadiah; (4) the report in Jer 49:14 is received by the prophet ("I have heard") while Obad 1 refers to the entire nation ("we have heard") as the recipient; (5) in at least five instances, Obadiah changes examples of *parallelismus memborum* by actualizing them for the present; (6) the phrase "utterance of YHWH" functions well as the end of a unit in Jer 49:16, but not in Obad 4; (7) the beginning of Jer 49:7 makes good sense as the superscription of the collection, but is literarily awkward in Obad 1; (8) the parallels to Jer 49 continue beyond Obad 1-5.

85. Allen, *Joel, Obadiah, Jonah, and Micah*, 131–32; Jeremias, *Joel, Obadja, Jona, Micha*, 59, 64–65; Barton, *Joel and Obadiah*, 125–26; Nogalski, "Not Just Another Nation: Obadiah's Placement in the Book of the Twelve," 89–107.

86. Jeremias, *Joel, Obadja, Jona, Micha*, 59.

87. Jeremias does not note this connection, but see Nogalski, "Not Just Another Nation," 94.

88. The first section (1-7) recounts Edom's defeat in the prophet's own time as a fulfillment of Jer 49:7-16; the second section (8-14) interprets the ultimate destruction of Edom as caused by its treatment of Judah; and the third section (15-21) presupposes that Edom's downfall signals the beginning of the day of YHWH against the nations.

89. Umberto Cassuto, "The Sequence and Arrangement of the Biblical Sections," 5-6. Of course, other scholars dispute the degree to which these reflect deliberate points of connection. See Ehud Ben Zvi, "Twelve Prophetic Books or 'The Twelve': A Few Preliminary Considerations," in *Forming Prophetic Literature*, 125–56.

90. The diversity of the first group can be illustrated by the work of Ehud Ben Zvi, who dismisses the possibility of reconstructing earlier versions and interprets Obadiah as a Persian-period product to be read and reread (Ehud Ben Zvi, *Obadiah*, 7–9, 247–48). Leslie Allen's commentary falls into this camp as well, but he argues historically (Leslie Allen, *Joel, Obadiah, Jonah, and Micah*, 129–33). Allen focuses upon the fact that Nabatean and Arabic tribal forces are already forcing Edomite migration into southern Judah by the end of the sixth century. Allen rejects the idea that vv. 19-21 reflect a late perspective and argues that the idea of resettlement of the territory could just as readily come from the end of the sixth century. Jakob Wöhrle, a redaction critic who is not averse to reducing the foundational layer of prophetic books in the Twelve to a very small kernel, also argues that Obadiah (with the exception of v. 17a) represents the work of a single author who draws together a collage of anti-Edom sayings to create the book (Wöhrle, *Der Abschluss des Zwölfprophetenbuches*, 192–218). Wöhrle differs from Ben Zvi in that Wöhrle considers that the omission of Babylon in Obad 11-14 means the destruction by a foreign nation refers to the capture of Jerusalem by Ptolemy I in 302 BCE. This suggestion creates more problems than it solves.

91. John Barton represents the second group. Barton confesses that the thematic, syntactical, and theological changes from 1-15 and 16-21 are so dramatic that it is hard to envision that they come from one author writing a single composition (Barton, *Joel and Obadiah*, 118–19). He admits that the two halves of the hinge verse (15) between these two parts actually fit better if reversed, a theory that has continued to have supporters since it was first introduced by Wellhausen at the end of the nineteenth century (Julius Wellhausen, *Die kleinen Propheten übersetzt und erklärt*, 3rd ed. [Berlin: Georg Reimer, 1898], 213). Barton is less clear about vv. 19-21. He admits to reading it as a piece of 15-21, all of which could have arisen later than 1-14 in the late Persian or Hellenistic period (Barton, *Joel and Obadiah*, 123). He does not, however, speculate as to who added it or why, though he does suggest that Obadiah's placement in the Twelve could have factored into this process for Obad 19-20 (Barton, *Joel and Obadiah*, 157).

92. Jörg Jeremias differs from the majority of scholars who see a two-part division to the body of Obadiah. For Jeremias, Obadiah contains a three-part structure that runs through Obad 1-17, followed by two expansions (18, 19-20; Jeremias, *Joel, Obadja, Jona, Micha*, 57–59). Jeremias downplays the change of theme and addressee that appear with v. 15a-16 and focuses instead upon the claim that scholars have overlooked the extent to which Obad 1-17 represents an exegetical treatise focused on Jer 49:7-22. Note, for example, that Allen only recognizes the connections to Jer 49:7-22 in Obad 1-9, while Jeremias sees the

parallels extending to v. 17 (Allen, *Joel, Obadiah, Jonah, and Micah*, 131–32). By contrast, Ben Zvi only recognizes these parallels in 1-7 rather than v. 9 or v. 17 (Ben Zvi, *Obadiah*, 99–114). In so doing, Jeremias considers Obadiah to be one of the earliest exemplars of scribal prophecy, and he argues that scholars have erred when they have attempted to date the book of Obadiah too closely to Jerusalem's destruction in 587 BCE. His confident assertions belie the fact that Jeremias himself provides no framework for an absolute dating.

93. Hans Walter Wolff exemplifies the third group. He argues that 1-14 + 15b (and perhaps v. 21) represents a unified writing, but that 15a belongs with 16-18 as a separate (i.e., independent) literary unit that was joined to the preceding. Wolff argues that Obad 19-20 represents two late additions representing a late Persian-period theology aimed at reconstituting the kingdom. These texts were inserted in order to provide commentary to the existing units (Hans Walter Wolff, *Obadiah and Jonah*, 21–22). Wolff also recognizes v. 21 as a literary problem and suggests that, while the verse could represent a late addition to highlight YHWH's kingship, it is better understood as the original conclusion to 1-14 + 15b because of its close association with the theme of Edomite punishment.

94. One could note a fourth pattern which sees a gradual accretion of redactional material as the key to explaining the diversity. Peter Weimar, for example, argues seven redactional layers are needed to account for the material in this small book, but very few have been willing to walk this path with him. See Peter Weimar, "Obadja: Eine redaktionskritische Analyse," *BN* 27 (1985): 35–99.

95. Linguistically, the high number of Aramaisms suggest a time when Aramaic was replacing Hebrew as the spoken language. In terms of the intellectual streams in which Jonah operates, its openness to foreigners has generally been interpreted as a late development in Hebrew thought. Some aspect of this idea appears in other texts in Isaiah and the Twelve, but they are generally considered late compositions: Isa 2:2-4 (= Mic 4:1-4); 56:1-7; 66:18-21; Zech 8:20-23; Mal 1:11-14. Scholars have put forward numerous theories about the genre of Jonah, but satire and novella are probably the two most commonly found. Its artistic plot line and humor put it in line with other writings like Ruth and Esther, both considered narratives from the Persian period that struggle with the question of the relationship to foreigners in various ways. Jonah draws on motifs of sea tales in chapter 1, and such tales are more common in the Hellenistic period (Wolff, *Obadiah and Jonah*, 78).

96. Jonah refers to Nineveh as though it were the chief city of the country, but it was not yet Assyria's capital in the time of Jeroboam. Also, Jonah 3

describes Nineveh as a massive city that would take three days to walk through (3:3), yet modern excavations of ancient Nineveh reveal that the circumference of its city wall extended only about seven miles, a big city by ancient standards, but a distance that could be covered in a single morning.

97. Daniel is later than Jonah and appears among the Prophets in the Christian canon, but among the Writings in the Jewish canon. In all likelihood, Daniel was composed at the beginning of the second century BCE, by which time the book of Sirach already presupposes the existence of the Twelve Prophets as a scroll.

98. Jonathon Magonet, *Form and Meaning: Studies in Literary Techniques in the Book of Jonah*, BBET 2 (Bern: Herbert Lang, 1976), 56–57. Magonet's predecessors who made similar observations include Norbert Lohfink, "Jona ging zur Stadt hinaus (Jona 4,5)," *BZ* 5 (1961): 193–96, 200–201; and Rudolph Pesch, "Zur konzentrischen Struktur von Jona 1," *Biblica* 47 (1966): 577-81.

99. See Nogalski, *Redactional Processes*, 251–52 n.4.

100. A few have postulated that chapters 3–4 could have existed in oral or written form as a story of Jonah's encounter with Nineveh before having the sea voyage added to heighten the obduracy of Jonah. See the works of Kraeling and Schmidt for theories regarding how this development happened (for a summary of their arguments, see Nogalski, *Redactional Processes*, 255–60). Kraeling argues that the early form starts in the Persian period and was later influenced by Greek sea-faring stories, but he does not lay out a systematic development of the book (Emil G. Kraeling, "The Evolution of the Story of Jonah," in *Hommages à André Dupont-Sommer*, ed. André Dupont-Sommer [Paris: Librairie d'Amrique et d'Orient Adrien Maisonneuve, 1971], 305–18). Schmidt argues that the beginning of Jonah in chapters 3–4 (along with 1:2) was a written composition in the form of a didactic narrative, written to expand Deuteronomistic repentance theology into the international arena on the basis of Jer 18:7-8 (Ludwig Schmidt, *'De Deo': Studien zur Literarkritik und Theologie des Buches Jona, des Gesprächs zwischen Abraham und Jahwe in Gen 18:22ff. und von Hi 1*, BZAW 143 [Berlin: de Gruyter, 1976], 43–47, 124–26).

101. See the discussions in Wolff, *Obadiah and Jonah*, 128–31, and Nogalski, *Redactional Processes*, 250–52. Wolff argues that only the psalm shows Jonah in a pious light. Jeremias argues that the chapter's addition means one must interpret Jonah in two ways, the earlier version without the psalm and the later version with the psalm (Jörg Jeremias, *Joel, Obadja, Jona, Micha*, 78).

102. James S. Ackerman, "Satire and Symbolism in the Song of Jonah," in *Traditions in Transformation: Turning Points in Biblical Faith*, ed. Baruch Halpern and Jon D. Levenson (Winona Lake, IN: Eisenbrauns, 1981), 213–46; Kenneth M. Craig, "Jonah and the Reading Process," *JSOT* 47 (1990): 103–14.

103. Wolff, *Obadiah and Jonah*, 130.

104. Phyllis Tribble, *Rhetorical Criticism: Context, Method, and the Book of Jonah* (Minneapolis: Fortress, 1994), 162–73. Tribble interprets the psalm's function in terms of three kinds of dissonance: disruption, delay, and irony (162). This dissonance grows the more one reads the "Jonah" of the psalm knowing the Jonah of the narrative, thus accentuating the satire and highlighting Jonah's arrogance toward foreigners and God (171–72).

105. In fact, no substantive variants of 4:5 exist in the ancient texts including Mur XII, 4QXIIg, 8ḥev gr, and the Old Greek, even though some of these contain only fragments of 4:5. This evidence suggests that 4:5 was fully ensconced in the text by the second century BCE.

106. Jeremias credits the change to Lohfink's article in 1961 and the further evidence compiled by Wolff. Lohfink reads the scene as a flashback and treats the verbs as pluperfects (Jeremias, *Joel, Obadja, Jona, Micha*, 108; Lohfink, "Jona," 185–203; Hans Walter Wolff, *Studien zum Jonabuch: Mit einem Anhang von J. Jeremias: Das Jonabuch in der Forschung seit Hans Walter Wolff* [Neukirchen-Vluyn: Neukirchener Verlag, 2003], 40–48).

107. See the works of Weimar and Wöhrle (Peter Weimar, "Literarische Kritik und Literarkritik: Unzeitgemässe Beobachtungen zu Jon 1:4-16," in *Künder des Wortes: Beiträge zur Theologie der Propheten, Festschrift für Josef Schreiner*, ed. L. Ruppert et al. [Würzburg: Echter, 1982], 217–35; idem, "Jon 4,5: Beobachtungen zur Entstehung der Jonaerzählung," *BN* 18 [1982]: 86–109; idem, "Jonapsalm und Jonaerzählung," *BN* 28 [1984]: 43–68; and Wöhrle, *Der Abschluss des Zwölfprophetenbuches*, 365–99). In his articles, Peter Weimar describes a three-stage development of the book. His foundational narrative includes: 1:1 + 2, 3a*, 3b*, 4abb, 5a, 7, 11a, 12a, 15a; 2:1, 11; 3:3a, 4b, 5, 10b; 4:5a, 6aa, 6b*, 7, 8*, 11a, 11ba. His first redactional adaptation includes: 1:4aa, 5a*, 5b, 6, 8a, 10, 11b, 13, 14a, 16; 2:2 + 3aa*, 3b, 4a*, 7b; 3:1f, 3b, 6-10a; 4:1-2a, 3f, 5b, 6ab, b*, 8aa, 9f, 11bb. A second redactional adaptation added the remainder: 1:8b + 9, 14ab, b; 2:3ab, 4b-7a, 8-10; 4:2b. Wöhrle argues for two layers, a foundational layer (1:1-5a, 7, 8aab, 9, 11-13, 15; 2:1, 11; 3:1-5; 4:5, 6*, 7-9), to which an editor added material highlighting YHWH's grace (1:5b, 6, 8aβ, 10a, bα, 14,

16; 2:2-10; 3:6-10; 4:1-4, 6*, 10-11). While Weimar and Wöhrle do not agree precisely upon what was contained in the foundational narrative in Jonah 4, both of them observe that 4:5 (or at least 4:5a for Weimar) existed as part of the foundational narrative.

108. The order of the adjectives *gracious* and *merciful* correlates in Joel and Jonah, and the motif of relenting from punishment also appears in Joel and Jonah but not in Exodus.

109. See Thomas B. Dozeman, "Inner-Biblical Interpretation of Yahweh's Gracious and Compassionate Character," *JBL* 105 (1989): 227–33; see a more extensive interaction with Dozeman in Nogalski, *Hosea–Jonah*, 446.

110. See Beate Ego, "The Repentance of Nineveh in the Story of Jonah and Nahum's Prophecy of the City's Destruction: Aggadic Solutions for an Exegetical Problem in the Book of the Twelve," in *Society of Biblical Literature Seminar Papers* 39 (Atlanta: SBL Press, 2000), 243–53. Ego shows that long before the modern critical era, the two books were read in tandem, resulting in the need for a theological interpretation in rabbinic literature that sought to harmonize the message of the two prophets.